King James Games

Study Puzzles Crafted for the Learning and Memorization of God's Word

Elder Timothy E. Parker

Foreword by Bishop T. D. Jakes

Andrews McMeel Publishing, LLC
Kansas City

King James Games: Volume 1

 For information, write Andrews McMeel Publishing, LLC, an Andrews McMeel Universal company, 1130 Walnut Street, Kansas City, Missouri 64106.

10 11 WKT 10 9 8 7 6 5 4 3

ISBN-13: 978-0-7407-6501-8
ISBN-10: 0-7407-6501-9

www.andrewsmcmeel.com

The Word of God tells us to "Study to show thyself approved unto God, a workman that needeth not to be ashamed, rightly dividing the word of truth." 2 Timothy 2:15

It is God's desire that every Christian would come to know Him intimately through the discipline of study. There are many books on the market that will help us do just that, but you will find that *King James Games* takes a different approach. *King James Games* contains hundreds of entertaining and challenging word games and puzzles, all based on the Lord's Word. These games will inspire you to dig deeper into the Word of God, ultimately causing you to memorize scripture. These truly wonderful word games can be solved during quiet time, or the entire family can join in on the fun. What a great idea for family fun night! All of the content comes directly from the King James Version of the Holy Bible, which was the inspiration for the author, Elder Timothy E. Parker, Guinness World Records' "Most Syndicated Puzzle Compiler," editor of the *USA Today* line of crossword puzzles, and a servant of God. I am excited to add *King James Games* to my library, and I encourage you to do the same. You won't be disappointed.

Bishop T. D. Jakes

INTRODUCTION

In 1996, I was attending Bible study and church on a very regular basis. I was becoming closer and closer to a man from Haiti, Elder Petersem Burke, who seemed to speak to my soul with his messages. He was a frequent guest speaker at our church, and I was startled by something he said to me at a Bible study: "You are operating at 10 percent of what God has for you." *Ten percent*, I thought. *Is that all?*

I began to seek the Lord more diligently. After all, 90 percent of untapped anything is far too much to leave on the table. I was working in corporate America, managing automotive service centers, and serving on a board that determined store policy for hundreds of other service centers. I knew this was not what God had called me to do with my life. I was unfulfilled. I was bored. I needed more. I wanted to give more so I sought Him. I wanted a closer walk with Him, and I wanted to know what path He had chosen for my life.Then it happened, suddenly and without warning.

I attended a Friday night service where the presence of the Lord was so thick and palpable that all the children at the service began to weep. Just the children! It was miraculous. Even my son, Timothy, fell to the floor, sobbing uncontrollably. Elder Petersem Burke, the speaker of the night, was so caught up in the presence of God that he could not deliver a message. No message was delivered that entire service. For the first time in my life, I could actually feel the Lord gently pulling me to the altar. I had always been too shy to go to the altar before, but this was different. I was not the one in control. I stood at the altar, and I could hear God telling me to bow down! I could *hear* Him! I obeyed His word, and I was slain in the spirit in front of the entire assembly, unable to move my arms and legs. My face hit the carpet. All I could do was say over and over, "Thank you, Jesus . . . thank you, Jesus." I had witnessed my first true miracle. I had felt it. I was a part of it. I knew my time was coming. I knew God was going to do something miraculous in my life. A few days later, He did.

Puzzles. That's the word I heard from God. I had just attended a service that Sunday morning and was driving with my wife to a furniture store. Elder Petersem Burke had once again been the guest speaker, and during his message I had an overwhelming feeling that something was about to change in my life.

I said it out loud: *puzzles.* My wonderful wife, Giselle, said she felt a spiritual electricity run through her body when I uttered that one strange word. I had no idea what it meant at the time, but I knew I had heard it from God. I had always loved puzzles and logic games, but what was the significance of that word now?

By faith, I created a fun, challenging interactive crossword, and it was discovered by the good people at Universal Press Syndicate. I then developed trivia games, word searches, cryptograms, and other intelligent family word games. Within a few years I became the "World's Most Syndicated Puzzle Compiler," according to Guinness World Records. My puzzle, *Universal Crossword*, became a tremendous success worldwide. In May 2003, I was chosen to become the new crossword editor of *USA Today*.

Elder Petersem Burke went on to become the pastor of the Tabernacle of Deliverance Christian Center in Baltimore, Maryland, and I became his assistant pastor and an elder of the church. My wife is now Evangelist Giselle Parker at the church.

That God would do these things for me, a simple, flawed individual, is testimony to His grace and love. I thank you, Jesus, for everything you've done for me. I offer you, my Lord and my Savior, your book, *King James Games*. May this book help others to learn and enjoy your magnificent Word.

Elder Timothy E. Parker

How to Solve *King James Games* Puzzles

These select puzzles are designed to teach as well as entertain. They are to be solved slowly, sipped rather than gulped. They are to be savored rather than wolfed down. Some puzzles may take only a few minutes, while others may take more than one sitting. Take your time, carefully following the instructions for each puzzle. By concentrating on solving the puzzles, you will absorb God's Word into your memory and learn as you are entertained.

As you learn, be not merely a hearer of the Word, but glorify God by being a doer of the Word.

But be ye doers of the word, and not hearers only, deceiving your own selves. For if any be a hearer of the word, and not a doer, he is like unto a man beholding his natural face in a glass: For he beholdeth himself, and goeth his way, and straightway forgetteth what manner of man he was.

James 1:22–24

How to Solve *King James Games* Puzzles

"LETTER SQUARES" Puzzles

These puzzles reveal vital scriptures and should be done slowly. By patiently solving the puzzle, you will be better able to memorize it.

T H E	H E	D T	H E	N I N	I N	C R E	B E
A N	D T	A T E	E A R	G I N	T H .	H E A	V E N
G G	O D						

Arrange the tiles to form a verse from the Holy Bible. The letters inside the squares stay exactly the same. Only the squares are rearranged.

The squares in this example can be arranged to reveal the correct answer:

IN THE BEGINNING GOD CREATED THE HEAVEN AND THE EARTH.

"VERSE DECODER" Puzzles

A Verse Decoder is a coded verse from the Holy Bible. Each letter in the puzzle actually represents a different letter. If a coded word was spelled "G A C E C" in the puzzle, you must substitute letters, through trial and error, until the word makes sense.

In the above example "G A C E C" equals "J E S U S." The "G" is actually a "J" in the puzzle, and the "C" is actually an "S." How would you figure that out? The best way to solve these types of puzzles is to first figure out the small words in the puzzle. Helpful hints to get you started are also provided.

Let's give it a try:

BC GKD RDFBCCBCF FYI XWDJGD GKD KDJLDC JCI GKD DJWGK.

By examining the coded letters, you see three different cases of the three-letter word "GKD." This word is probably "THE" or "AND." By substituting letters, you'd find that "G-K-D" is actually "T-H-E." You may now substitute any "G" in the puzzle for "T" and change every "K" into an "H" and every "D" into an "E." You're now well on your way to solving the puzzle, which is:

IN THE BEGINNING GOD CREATED THE HEAVEN AND THE EARTH.

"COLUMN PHRASE" Puzzles

The puzzle to the right has 23 columns going across, filled with squares. Each black square is a space in the verse you are trying to piece together. The letters listed below the puzzle go in the spaces in the column directly above the letters. **Letters only go in blank spaces in the column directly above them. However, they need to be placed in the correct squares to reveal the verse and solve the puzzle. The letters *always* stay in the same column, but their order may need to be shuffled. Study the sample, and then review the answer.**

ANSWER:
IN THE BEGINNING GOD CREATED THE HEAVEN AND THE EARTH. AND THE EARTH WAS WITHOUT FORM, AND VOID;

"SCRAMBLED VERSE" Puzzles

To solve these puzzles, simply unscramble each word in the list and then use them to fill in the blanks until the verse makes perfect sense. For example:

In the ____ God ____ the heaven and the ____. And the earth was without ____, and void;

GGINBNIEN **DATRECE** **RAHET** **ORFM**

Using the words from the list, the correct verse is:

In the **beginning** God **created** the heaven and the **earth**. And the earth was without **form**, and void;

How to Solve *King James Games* Puzzles

"WORD SEARCH" Puzzles

Word search puzzles are fun to do and easy to play. Simply find each listed word hidden in the grid below. The words may be up, down, forward, backward, or diagonal. They can also overlap, meaning that a single letter can be part of two or more words.

JESUS

CHRIST

LORD

SAVIOR

SECOND

COMING

SHEPHERD

B	M	D	R	E	H	P	E	H	S
N	M	X	Q	K	S	C	N	T	N
L	O	R	D	V	U	Q	C	V	K
V	K	S	Z	L	S	G	X	K	K
R	L	X	A	Q	E	M	T	C	S
R	P	C	R	V	J	S	O	F	E
F	R	G	L	R	I	M	J	V	C
J	M	R	K	R	I	O	D	R	O
R	V	K	H	N	J	C	R	C	N
H	C	C	G	R	L	H	J	T	D

SINNER'S PRAYER

Heavenly Father,
I believe that Jesus Christ
was punished, crucified, and died
for all my sins.
I believe that he was resurrected from the dead
and he is alive forevermore.
Jesus, come into my heart
and be Lord of my life.

God, You said,
"That if thou shalt confess with thy mouth
the Lord Jesus,
and shalt believe in thine heart
that God hath raised him from the dead,
thou shalt be saved."

Thank you, Father,
for forgiving my sins
and cleansing me
with the precious blood of Jesus Christ.

In the name of Jesus Christ,
my Lord and my Savior,
I have prayed this prayer,
Amen.

CHAPTER 1

BOOKS OF THE BIBLE

CROSSWORD: **Biblical Passsages**

By Barbara A. Marques

ACROSS

1 European mountains
5 NYC transport
8 Health-store offering
12 "... but they that __ truly are his delight" (Prov. 12:22)
13 He gives a hoot
14 Major musical composition
15 Calendar part
16 "__, temperance: against such there is no law" (Gal. 5:23)
18 Certain Muslim
20 "... but one __ destroyeth much good" (Eccl. 9:18)
21 Kind of trip taken by one person
22 "Be still, ye inhabitants of the __" (Isa. 23:2)
23 They judged Jesus
26 Be nosy
29 *Sesame Street* lesson
30 Period of many years
31 Manitoba Indian
32 "__ unto you that laugh now! for ye shall mourn and weep" (Luke 6:25)
33 Risky
35 "Which are a shadow of things to come; but the __ is of Christ" (Col. 2:17)
36 Total
37 Disinherit
40 "... but the way of the wicked he turneth __ down" (Ps. 146:9)
43 "... worship the Lord in the beauty of __" (1 Chron. 16:29)
45 Where most humans reside
46 Elevator inventor
47 "And __ if there be any wicked way in me" (Ps. 139:24)
48 "Then the beasts go into __, and remain in their places" (Job 37:8)
49 Cross a shallow creek
50 "... when ye fast, be not, as the hypocrites, of a __ countenance" (Matt. 6:16)
51 "If the iron be blunt, and he do not whet the __" (Eccl. 10:10)

DOWN

1 Puts two and two together
2 Rachel's sister
3 "... let us run with __ the race that is set before us" (Heb. 12:1)
4 Snow vehicles
5 "... for ye know not what hour your Lord doth __" (Matt. 24:42)
6 "... let all the inhabitants of the world stand in __ of him" (Ps. 33:8)
7 "... there shall be showers of __" (Ezek. 34:26)
8 1,000 kilograms
9 "Thou shalt __ thine hand wide unto thy brother"(Deut. 15:11)
10 Merge
11 Former communist country
17 Firing oven
19 Part of the foot
22 Biting wit
23 "And God __ everything that he had made" (Gen. 1:31)
24 Native Australian
25 "... neither yet the __ of Sarah's womb" (Romans 4:19)
26 "Which he had __ afore by his prophets in the holy scriptures" (Romans 1:2)
27 Peleg's son (Gen. 11:18)
28 "And she answered and said unto him, __, Lord" (Mark 7:28)
31 Holy war
33 "I will both lay me __ in peace, and sleep" (Ps. 4:8)
34 Sixth sense
35 Idaho capital
37 Lateen-rigged sailboat
38 Very small amount
39 Beat the tag, perhaps
40 "... with their tongues they have __ deceit" (Romans 3:13)
41 "__-dong!" (doorbell sound)
42 "His soul shall dwell at __" (Ps. 25:13)
44 "So they took up Jonah, and cast him forth into the __" (Jonah 1:15)

LETTER SQUARES: **Bible Passages**

1 Genesis 4:9

?	S A	I D	U N T	S A	A I N	T H	H E R
T H	E I	E L	Y B	, W	H E R	B E L	O C
O R D	A N D	R O T					

2 Exodus 2:1

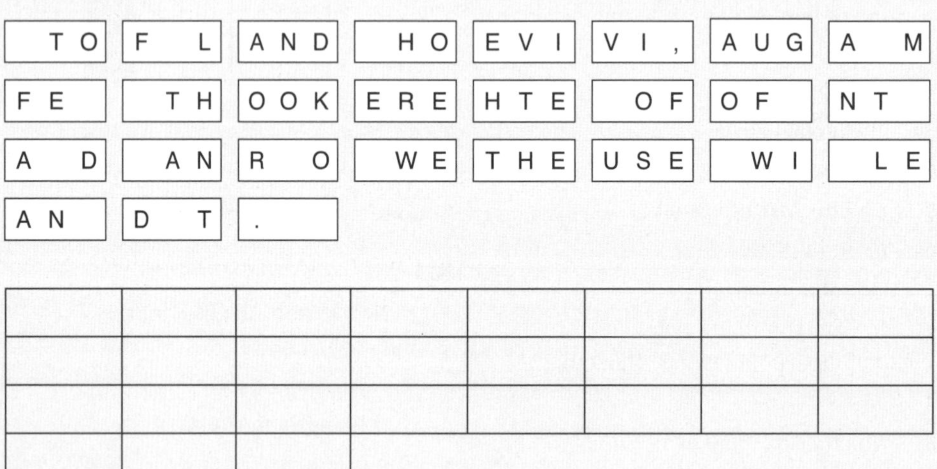

T O	F L	A N D	H O	E V I	V I ,	A U G	A M
F E	T H	O O K	E R E	H T E	O F	O F	N T
A D	A N	R O	W E	T H E	U S E	W I	L E
A N	D T	.					

3 Leviticus 3:7

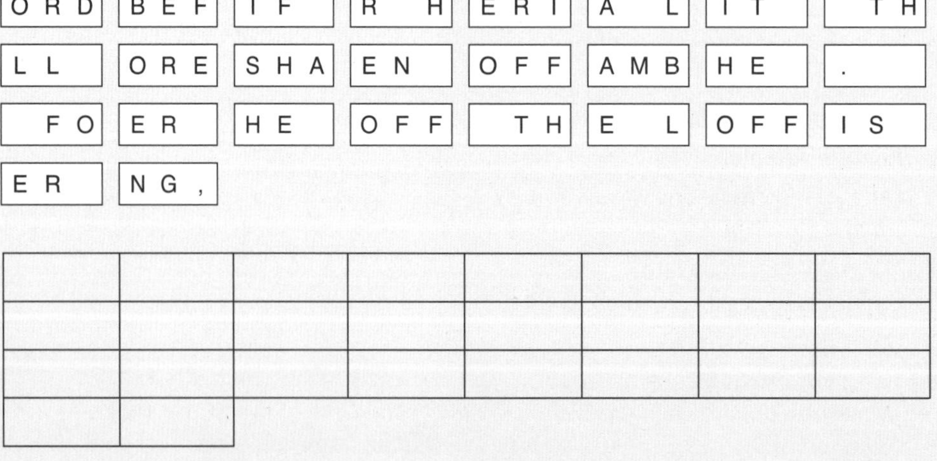

O R D	B E F	I F	R H	E R I	A L	I T	T H
L L	O R E	S H A	E N	O F F	A M B	H E	.
F O	E R	H E	O F F	T H	E L	O F F	I S
E R	N G ,						

VERSE DECODER: **Bible Passages**

1 Genesis 24:12
HINT: In the puzzle below, "D" is actually an "O."

MAS TZ CMQS D KDWS UDS DE HO HMCPZW MBWMTMH, Q

VWMO PTZZ, CZAS HZ UDDS CVZZS PTQC SMO, MAS CTZL FQASAZCC

NAPD HO HMCPZW MBWMTMH.

2 Psalms 28:7
HINT: In the puzzle below, the letter "A" is actually an "E."

LHA QNBF IO VU OLBAXGLH CXF VU OHIAQF; VU HACBL LBKOLAF IX

HIV, CXF I CV HAQZAF; LHABADNBA VU HACBL GBACLQU BATNIWALH; CXF

RILH VU ONXG RIQQ I ZBCIOA HIV.

MULTIPLE CHOICE: **Books of the Bible**

1 Who spoke to Abram while he was in a deep sleep, according to Genesis 15:12?

A. Sarai
B. An angel
C. Moses
D. God

2 In John's Gospel, what was Jesus' second miracle?

A. Raising of Lazarus
B. Walking on the sea
C. Healing the man born blind
D. Healing an official's son in Cana

MULTIPLE CHOICE: **Books of the Bible**

1 What is the punishment for committing adultery, according to Leviticus 20:10?

A. Crucifixion
B. Scourging
C. Death
D. Exile

2 What book mentions a hard-working woman who plants her own vineyard?

A. Matthew
B. Proverbs
C. Galatians
D. Ecclesiastes

3 What book states that witchcraft is an abomination unto the Lord?

A. Genesis
B. Proverbs
C. Psalms
D. Deuteronomy

4 What book states, "Thou shalt not suffer a witch to live"?

A. Genesis
B. Mark
C. Exodus
D. Proverbs

5 Which Epistle urges believers to be alert, not asleep?

A. Genesis
B. Judges
C. Mark
D. 1 Thessalonians

***King James Games* Facts:**

The shortest verse of the Bible is John 11:35, "Jesus wept."

LETTER SQUARES: **Bible Passages**

1 Numbers 9:2

E L	F I	A L S	N O	S E	A P P	N .	T H
O K	O I N	O V E	I S	E C	A S S	T H	A S O
E E P	T E D	L E T	H I L	E P	R A	S R A	D R E
T H							

MULTIPLE CHOICE: **Books of the Bible**

1 Which book speaks of the "sons of God" taking the "daughters of men" as wives?

A. Genesis
B. Numbers
C. Leviticus
D. Exodus

2 Which book mentions a dark Shulamite woman singing to her loved one?

A. Ruth
B. Esther
C. Song of Solomon
D. Proverbs

3 Who was Ruth's first husband?

A. Chilion
B. Mahlon
C. Hezron
D. Elimelech

4 In Romans 16, who did Paul refer to as apostles?

A. Aquila and Priscilla
B. Titus and Timothy
C. Andronicus and Junia
D. Silas and Barnabas

LETTER SQUARES: **Bible Passages**

1 Deuteronomy 26:6

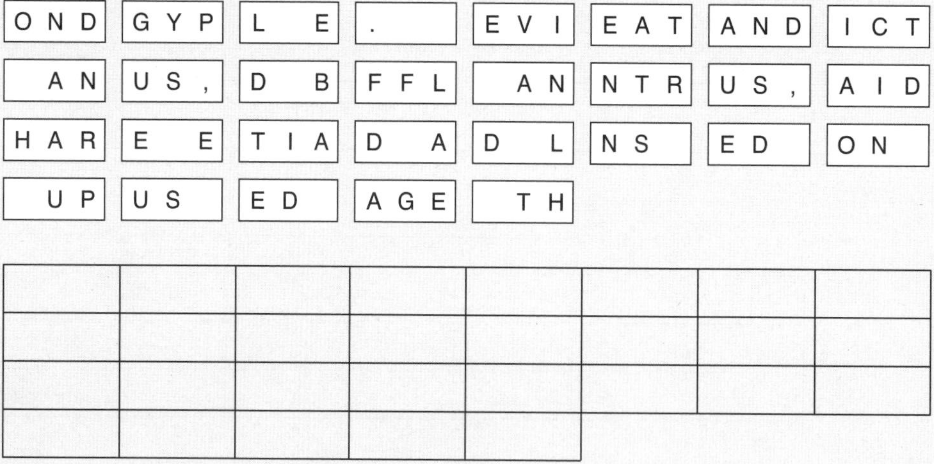

2 Judges 1:2

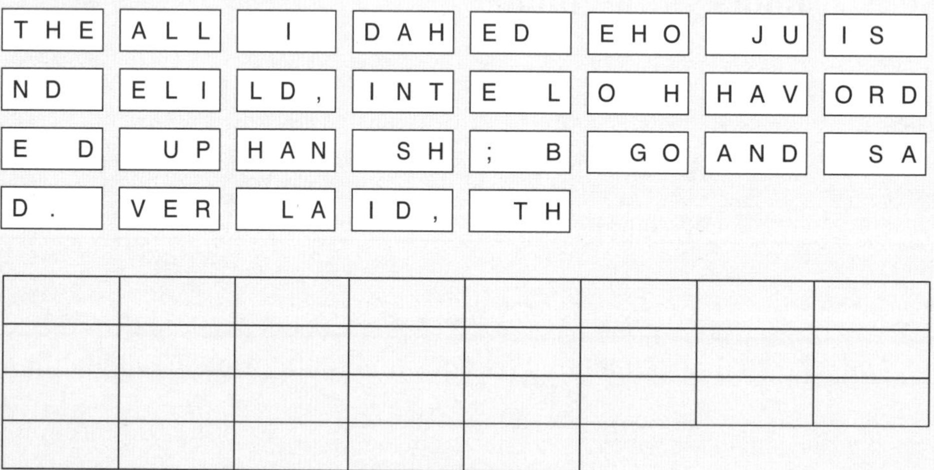

MULTIPLE CHOICE: **Books of the Bible**

1 Who was Timothy's grandmother?

A. Lois
B. Leah
C. Milcah
D. Kezia

2 Ecclesiastes states what is better than being a dead lion?

A. A live dog
B. An orphan
C. A beggar
D. A widow

CROSSWORD: **Bible Stories**

By Timothy Parker

ACROSS

1 "And thou shalt make __ of shittim wood" (Ex. 26:26)

5 Submissions to mags.

8 "And he said, Take now thy son, thine __ son Isaac" (Gen. 22:2)

12 Nastase of tennis

13 Pie __ mode

14 Gravy base

15 Computer info

16 Retired servicemen's grp.

17 Splashy party

18 A whale __ Jonah

21 *Ben* __

22 Jesus, in the Trinity

23 Uses a shovel

25 Beaver's construction

28 "Go to the __, thou sluggard" (Proverbs 6:6)

30 Prince William's mother

33 Commedia dell' __

35 "And these __ they by the way side" (Mark 4:15)

37 Wilma Flintstone's husband

38 Male duck

40 Swellhead's trouble

42 Mauna __, Hawaii

43 "Turn from him, that he may __" (Job 14:6)

45 Wildebeest

47 Brewed drink

49 Moses parted __ (3 words)

54 Boater's blades

56 "Much __ About Nothing"

57 "If I have __ iniquity, I will do no more." (Job 34:32)

58 The "G" in GTO

59 Zilch

60 Turkish official

61 Section of the choir

62 Nickelodeon's "Kenan & __"

63 Give a makeover

DOWN

1 Auction actions

2 "There ought to be __" (2 words)

3 Actress Moreno

4 The seven of Revelation

5 The Virgin Mary

6 Cole __ (picnic dish)

7 "Who hath __ us, and called us with an holy calling" (2 Timothy 1:9)

8 Assoc.

9 Boat in a flood (2 words)

10 Humdinger

11 "And it came to pass in the fortieth __"(Deuteronomy 1:3)

19 Hawaii's Mauna ___

20 "And he __ that which was evil in the sight of the Lord" (2 Kings 24:19)

24 Web pic file

25 Mom's partner

26 Opposite of "Dep" on a flight board

27 Landing place for 9-Down (2 words)

29 Uno and Due

31 Formerly, on the society pages

32 Dentists' org.

34 Barely get by (with "out")

36 Chinese menu item (2 words)

39 Best guess, for short

41 "He said, I am the voice of __ crying in the wilderness"(John 1:23)

44 "Father, I __ thee that thou hast heard me" (John 11:41)

46 Cow's milk provider

47 Roman costume

48 Spouse of a countess

50 Actress Adams

51 "But there are __ of you that believe not" (John 6:64)

52 *National Velvet* author Bagnold

53 Dynamic opener?

55 ___-cone (county fair concoction)

VERSE DECODER: **Bible Passages**

1 Psalms 1:3

HINT: In the puzzle below, the letter "W" is actually an "E."

KQB CW ECKAA GW AFTW K UNWW DAKQUWB GM UCW NFRWNE SI ZKUWN,

UCKU GNFQVWUC ISNUC CFE INYFU FQ CFE EWKESQ; CFE AWKI KAES

ECKAA QSU ZFUCWN; KQB ZCKUESWRWN CW BSWUC ECKAA DNSEDWN.

2 Nehemiah 9:1

HINT: In the puzzle below, the letter "E" is actually an "I."

BTM EB HZQ HMQBHS GBD PTIKHZ DGS TP HZEF OTBHZ HZQ JZEYDKQB

TP EFKGQY MQKQ GFFQOAYQD MEHZ PGFHEBU, GBD MEHZ FGJLJYTHZQF,

GBD QGKHZ INTB HZQO.

MULTIPLE CHOICE: **Books of the Bible**

1 Which book has a man asking his loved one to come down from the place where lions dwell?

A. Exodus
B. Deuteronomy
C. Psalms
D. Song of Solomon

2 According to 1 Peter, what person is like a ravenous lion?

A. Satan
B. Judas
C. Herod
D. Elymas

3 In Exodus 30:23-33, what Hebrew officials were anointed with holy oil perfumed with aromatic spices?

A. Israel's judges
B. Israel's prophets
C. Israel's priests
D. Israel's kings

LETTER SQUARES: **Bible Passages**

1 Ruth 1:10

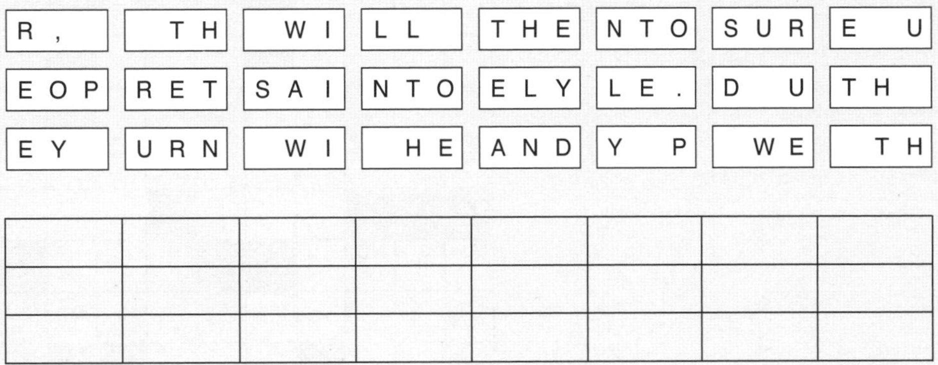

2 Ezra 4:4

E H	W E	A K E	T H E	D A H	J U	S O	O F
P E O	E L	A N D	H E	P E O	F T	P L E	O F
T H	N E D	T H	N T	A N D	P L E	H E	.

MULTIPLE CHOICE: **Books of the Bible**

1 What do ointment and perfume do, according to Proverbs 27:9?

A. Make a cheerful countenance
B. Rejoice the heart
C. Bring glory to God
D. Turn away wrath

2 What woman of Proverbs 7 perfumed her bed with myrrh, aloes, and cinnamon?

A. The virtuous woman
B. Jezebel
C. The adulteress
D. The woman at the well

CROSSWORD: **Biblical Vessels**

By Rowan Millson

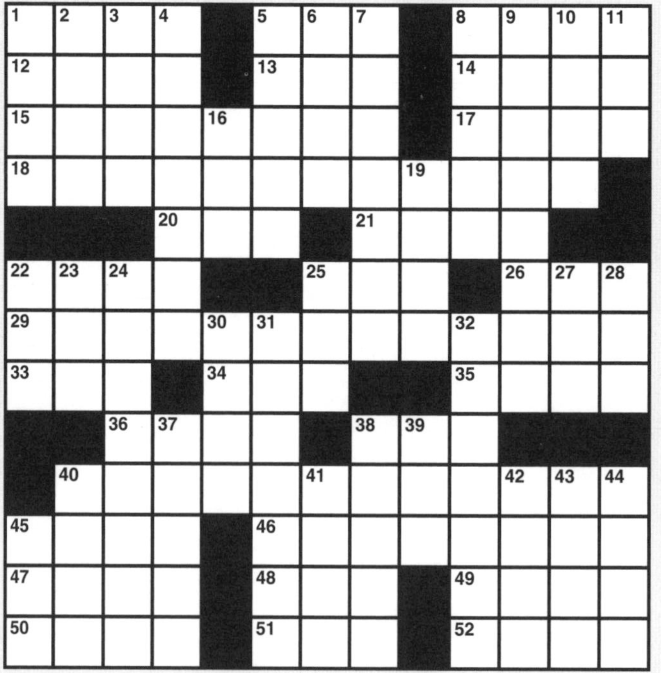

ACROSS

1 Norwegian king
5 Group of wise guys
8 "... and ye shall __ no longer" (Ex. 9:28)
12 "Even as __ obeyed Abraham" (1 Peter 3:6)
13 Brian of Roxy Music
14 Opera solo
15 Communicator
17 Cot
18 "Thy navel is like __" (Song of Sol. 7:2) (3 words)
20 They can get personal
21 A sworded affair
22 "... and if any __ hath cleaved to mine hands" (Job 31:7)
25 "... and I will __ evil beasts out of the land" (Lev. 26:6)
26 Sound of surprise
29 "You anoint my head with oil; __" (Ps. 23:5) (shortened) (3 words)
33 "They are __ with the showers of the mountains" (Job 24:8)
34 Charged atom
35 Word of action
36 Lhasa __
38 "Out of whose womb came the __?" (Job 38:29)
40 "For now we see through __" (1 Cor. 13:12) (3 words)
45 Plant mixed with myrrh in John 19:39
46 Ta-ta
47 Singer Horne
48 Allen-wrench shape
49 7-Down's Prince
50 For fear that
51 Thing, on deeds
52 Italian princely family

DOWN

1 Mountain in Thessaly
2 Animal shelter
3 Jason's ship
4 New Hebrides, today
5 Pinochle combos
6 NASA pressure unit
7 "Polovtsian Dances" composer
8 Luxurious fur
9 Sweetheart (2 words)
10 "__ Misbehavin'"
11 Talk like an ox?
16 So-so connection
19 "... and brought forth __" (Num. 17:8)
22 Mercedes rival
23 Soap component
24 Stop-sign shapes
25 "... many shall __ to and fro" (Dan. 12:4)
27 "... consider __ ways, and be wise" (Prov. 6:6)
28 Symbol of royal power
30 Leaning Tower locale
31 Barnyard strutter
32 Rest upon
37 Dress feature
38 "Turn ye not unto __" (Lev. 19:4)
39 Heel
40 Away from a weather
41 One and only
42 Casks
43 Plunder
44 Yesteryear
45 The whole enchilada

VERSE DECODER: **Bible Passages**

1 **Nahum 1:2**
HINT: In the puzzle below, the letter "I" is actually an "O."

EIU QB KRWHIAB, WSU VCR HINU NRGRSERVC; VCR HINU NRGRSERVC, WSU QB PANQIAB; VCR HINU OQHH VWXR GRSERWSJR IS CQB WUGRNBWNQRB, WSU CR NRBRNGRVC ONWVC PIN CQB RSRMQRB.

2 **Leviticus 1:2**
HINT: In the puzzle below, "I" is actually an "E."

SAIQW EMYH YOI XOBNVFIM HL BSFQIN, QMV SQR EMYH YOIT, BL QMR TQM HL RHE PFBMG QM HLLIFBMG EMYH YOI NHFV, RI SOQNN PFBMG RHEF HLLIFBMG HL YOI XQYYNI, IZIM HL YOI OIFV, QMV HL YOI LNHXW.

3 **Judges 1:1**
HINT: In the puzzle below, the letter "D" is actually an "A."

JAU DVQYN QEY LYDQE AV PAKEHD ZQ XDSY QA RDKK, QEDQ QEY XEZCLNYJ AV ZKNDYC DKOYL QEY CANL, KDTZJG, UEA KEDCC GA HR VAN HK DGDZJKQ QEY XDJDDJZQYK VZNKQ, QA VZGEQ DGDZJKQ QEYS?

MULTIPLE CHOICE: **Books of the Bible**

1 What book mentions a woman using such perfumes as myrrh, spikenard, saffron, cinnamon, and many others?

A. Song of Solomon
B. Genesis
C. Revelation
D. Ruth

LETTER SQUARES: **Bible Passages**

1 1 Kings 3:10

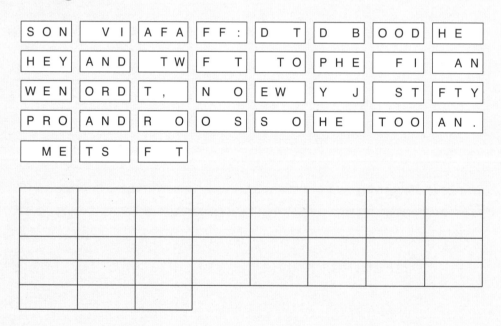

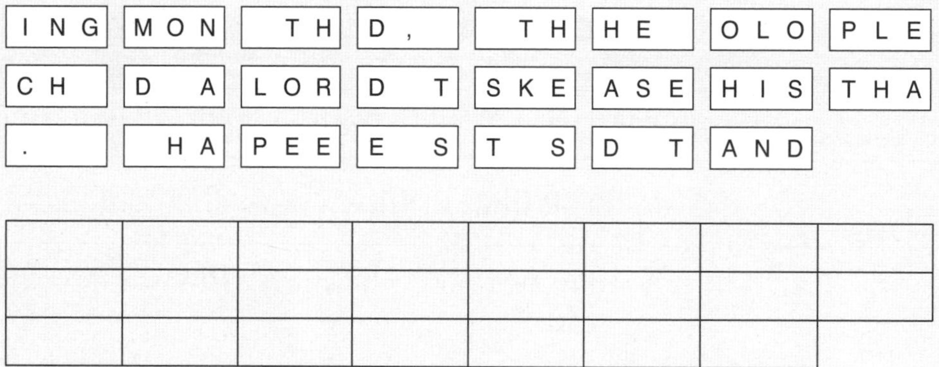

2 2 Kings 2:7

SON	VI	AFA	FF:	D T	D B	OOD	HE
HEY	AND	TW	F T	TO	PHE	FI	AN
WEN	ORD	T,	N O	EW	Y J	ST	FTY
PRO	AND	R O	O S	S O	HE	TOO	AN.
ME	TS	F T					

VERSE DECODER:

1 Jude 1:1

HINT: In the puzzle below, the letter "C" is actually a "T."

VALU, CJU PUIDEHC RZ VUPAP GJISPC, EHL TIRCJUI RZ VEQUP,

CR GJUQ CJEC EIU PEHGCSZSUL TF MRL CJU ZECJUI, EHL OIUPUIDUL SH

VUPAP GJISPC, EHL GENNUL.

CROSSWORD: **Books of the Bible**

By Thomas W. Schier

1	2	3	■	4	5	6	■	7	8	9	10	11
12			■	13			■	14				
15			16				■	17				
18							19					■
■	■	20				■	21			■	■	■
22	23			■	■	24			■	25	26	27
28				29	30				31			
32			■	33			■	■	34			
■	■	■	35			■	36	37			■	■
■	38	39				40					41	42
43					■	44						
45					■	46			■	47		
48					■	49			■	50		

ACROSS

1 Abraham found one in the bush
4 Gospel music lover's buys
7 __ of Cyrene
12 Matador's motivation
13 Reine's counterpart
14 Do a Sunday school blackboard chore
15 Last king of Macedon
17 Comaneci the gymnast
18 TWENTY-FIRST BOOK
20 "Shall I __ from Abraham that thing which I do" (Genesis)
21 "And if any man will __ thee at the law" (Matthew)
22 Greenspan or Alda
24 "One Day __ Time" (2 words)
25 Poem of devotion
28 TWENTY-SECOND BOOK (3 words)
32 "... and when the sun waxed __, it melted." (Exodus)
33 Do followers on a music scale
34 "... and they __ unto him with their tongues." (Psalms)
35 "... beast of the earth, and to every fowl of the __" (Genesis)
36 Foamy lather
38 FOURTEENTH BOOK
43 "... she __ be called Woman" (Genesis)
44 Disobeying the Ten Commandments
45 Snicker
46 One __ kind (2 words)
47 Get a lode of this?
48 "And the earth brought forth __" (Genesis)
49 Type of Christmas tree
50 U.S. basketball tournament

DOWN

1 You can skip it?
2 Actor Baldwin
3 "He is a __, the balances of deceit are in his hand"
4 The Apostle's __
5 Pour water on
6 Spanish ayes?
7 Carnal
8 Hopping mad
9 "And God __ the firmament" (Genesis)
10 Psych suffix
11 Cultural funding grp.
16 David's weapon
19 Two words meaning "regarding"
22 Lenten Wednesday
23 Old card game
24 Palm Sunday mount
25 Sin of __ (negligence)
26 Mate for Bambi
27 "... God maketh from the beginning to the __" (Ecclesiastes)
29 Baltimore nine
30 Garden of Eden plant, perhaps
31 Ancient
35 Van Gogh painted here
36 Futuristic literature
37 Opposite of radial
38 One-named singer/actress
39 Punch line reaction
40 "Time __ the essence" (2 words)
41 Crucifix inscription
42 "This is the thanks __?" (2 words)
43 Abbreviation on some silver

MULTIPLE CHOICE: **Books of the Bible**

1 In Malachi, what were the people of Judah stealing from God?

A. Grace **C**. Tithes

B. Taxes **D**. Land

2 How many sons did Naomi have?

A. Three **C**. Two

B. Seven **D**. Nine

LETTER SQUARES: **Bible Passages**

1 **1 Chronicles 1:34**

R A H	I S A	B E G	E L .	A B	T H	A M	A A C
A N	O N S	E S	O F	A C .	D I	; E	A N D
S A U	A T	S R A	I S				

2 **2 Chronicles 9:28**

B R O	E Y	O N	T ,	O U	A N D	S O	L A N
T H	O U	T O	F E	S E S	A N D	H O R	L L
U G H	N T O	D S .	F A	L O M	T O	T U	G Y P

VERSE DECODER: **Bible Passages**

1 Jeremiah 1:5
HINT: In the puzzle below, the letter "J" is actually an "E."

QJGYBJ E GYBMJC XRJJ EH XRJ QJUUK E LHJS XRJJ; PHC QJGYBJ XRYN WPMJTX GYBXR YNX YG XRJ SYMQ E TPHWXEGEJC XRJJ, PHC E YBCPEHJC XRJJ P ZBYZRJX NHXY XRJ HPXEYHT.

2 Genesis 44:1
HINT: In the puzzle below, the letter "Y" is actually an "E."

FTD LY GEZZFTDYD RLY VRYKFXD ES LMV LEAVY, VFCMTU, SMOO RLY ZYT'V VFGNV KMRL SEED, FV ZAGL FV RLYC GFT GFXXC, FTD JAR YWYXC ZFT'V ZETYC MT LMV VFGN'V ZEARL.

MULTIPLE CHOICE: **Books of the Bible**

1 Which book mentions a virtuous woman more valuable than rubies?

A. Psalms
B. Job
C. Numbers
D. Proverbs

2 What is the second oldest book of the Bible?

A. Job
B. Leviticus
C. Exodus
D. Proverbs

CROSSWORD: **Biblical Beasts**

By Rowan Millson

ACROSS

1 Elliptical

5 Aaron's fishing pole?

8 Kind of test

12 Saharan watercourse

13 ET's craft

14 "And thou saidst, I shall be a __ for ever" (Isa. 47:7)

15 "... and the __ shall melt with fervent heat!" (2 Peter 3:12)

17 "Be still, ye inhabitants of the __" (Isa. 23:2)

18 Mister, in Mexico

19 "... and touched the __ of his garment" (Matt. 9:20)

21 Kennedy or Koppel

22 Siouan language

24 "Why make ye this __" (Mark 5:39)

26 TV signal

28 Type of bread

32 Method

34 Four quarters

35 Sicilian erupter

36 Lasting three seasons or more

39 Bomb of a bomb

40 Ginger drink

41 "For this is an heinous __" (Job 31:11)

43 Droop

45 Court

47 Strauss' jeans?

50 Better to strike while it is hot

52 Spoiled

54 "Jesus saith unto them, Come and __" (John 21:12)

55 It had no room for Mary and Joseph

56 Hodgepodge

57 "The land of Nod, on the __ of Eden"

58 NYC's time zone

59 __ buco

DOWN

1 Is outstanding, in a way

2 "In the __ of Siddim, which is the salt sea" (Gen. 14:3)

3 "And I will make Jerusalem heaps, and __" (Jer. 9:11) (4 words)

4 Opening-night stretches

5 "Shall horses __ upon the rock?" (Amos 6:12)

6 "... heard me from the horns __" (Ps. 22:21) (3 words)

7 Prescription amount

8 Cassius Clay, familiarly

9 "Go ye, and tell that fox, Behold, I __" (Luke 13:32) (3 words)

10 "Why stand ye here all the day __?" (Matt. 20:6)

11 "And the covering of rams' skins __ red" (Ex. 39:34)

16 Pitchers' stats

20 "And they said unto her, Thou art __" (Acts 12:15)

23 Hooligan

25 Buck's mate

26 Sport judge, shortly

27 Tilling tool

29 "... neither __ you up a standing image" (Lev. 26:1)

30 African antelope

31 Ate or owned

33 Moray

37 Testament adjective

38 Happy tune

42 Cousin of "I agree" (2 words)

43 Entrée accompaniment

44 Puccini song

46 New York stage award

48 Mythical goddess of fertility

49 "Am-scray!"

51 "For he is cast into a __ by his own feet" (Job 18:8)

53 Insect in one's pants?

MULTIPLE CHOICE: **Books of the Bible**

1 How many times is God mentioned in the book of Esther?

A. None
B. Three
C. Seven
D. Ten

2 What is the shortest chapter in the Bible?

A. Jude 1
B. Psalms 23
C. Amos 1
D. Psalms 117

VERSE DECODER: **Bible Passages**

1 Acts 1:2
HINT: In the puzzle below, the letter "U" is actually a "T."

LKUEX UIY WOF EK TIEGI IY TOP UOSYK LB, OCUYZ UIOU IY UIZQLDI UIY IQXF DIQPU IOW DEAYK GQVVOKWVYKUP LKUQ UIY OBQPUXYP TIQV IY IOW GIQPYK:

2 2 John 1:3
HINT: In the puzzle below, the letter "G" is actually an "A."

TFGBQ ZQ XCSO WID, VQFBW, GNJ UQGBQ, LFIV TIJ SOQ LGSOQF, GNJ LFIV SOQ EIFJ KQYDY BOFCYS, SOQ YIN IL SOQ LGSOQF, CN SFDSO GNJ EIMQ.

WORD SEARCH: **Animals in the Bible**

K Y L E O P A R D F N R N G P Q G
M X J M P P M N F K X H E P N P V
Z D P G W B E A R K E M P X Q O D
M G A Z E L L E W I W L O J V R C
N O F A P C M P F N A C L J W C G
R L N F R R K E R K K K E Z C U R
N B Z K E B R O C W Z T T T N P E
Y R F G E Y O A K T R H N T V I Y
F A D X C Y J C M R D J A T T N H
H A N N O E L E M A H C N V X E O
B M L E E S R O H K R A L B Y R U
T K R C Y N K Q W K H C B M E X N
M L P A D H X M W P A K K R K X D
P W D M Y T G F E T B L Q G N A L
K N M E N G K L T C N O M X O R W
D N R L M F E L T T M X A K D Y R
R B D Y T N E D J G Z H K R B H W

ANTELOPE **COBRA** **HORSE**
BADGER **DONKEY** **HYENA**
BEAR **ELEPHANT** **HYRAX**
BOAR **GAZELLE** **JACKAL**
CAMEL **GECKO** **LEOPARD**
CATTLE **GREYHOUND** **MONKEY**
CHAMELEON **HEIFER** **PORCUPINE**

WORD SEARCH: **The Burning Bush**

M	J	Q	N	N	W	G	T	T	L	S	I	N	A	I
D	E	C	V	O	A	F	N	P	E	V	F	W	P	X
N	T	B	D	I	L	D	K	O	Y	J	B	R	M	F
U	H	U	F	T	N	P	H	W	M	G	M	R	E	B
O	R	S	L	C	I	S	T	H	O	N	E	Y	R	D
R	O	H	W	I	R	H	S	E	S	O	M	I	I	W
G	T	T	R	L	E	A	N	G	E	L	N	A	F	I
Y	B	K	J	F	H	W	S	Q	M	G	R	R	F	L
L	B	U	B	F	T	T	R	T	F	F	T	Q	O	D
O	V	B	R	A	A	X	N	O	A	K	M	Z	E	E
H	H	K	X	N	F	M	R	U	C	F	F	H	M	R
Q	L	O	Q	L	I	T	J	O	O	R	F	K	A	N
T	K	F	R	L	H	N	L	L	C	M	N	H	L	E
T	R	Y	K	E	K	F	G	R	Z	N	N	K	F	S
Q	H	Y	N	N	B	L	R	E	V	I	L	E	D	S

AFFLICTION
AFRAID
ANGEL
BRING FORTH
BURNING
BUSH
DELIVER
EGYPT
FATHER IN LAW
FLAME OF FIRE
FLOCK
HOLY GROUND
HONEY
HOREB
JETHRO
MILK
MOSES
MOUNT
SHOES
SINAI
STAFF
WILDERNESS

WORD SEARCH: **Cain and Abel**

R	N	K	H	L	N	D	E	L	L	I	K	D	O	B
C	K	W	X	M	H	D	M	L	K	H	S	L	F	N
R	R	R	D	E	P	Y	P	E	B	G	E	O	F	K
S	Y	Y	A	L	R	Q	E	R	N	K	C	F	E	T
A	R	S	I	G	E	P	B	I	R	R	N	N	R	N
C	T	E	N	N	E	I	L	T	E	M	A	E	I	E
R	G	A	L	R	G	T	F	R	J	N	N	V	N	M
I	R	F	L	L	S	L	E	M	Q	K	E	E	G	H
F	O	V	U	R	I	D	N	R	X	B	T	S	C	S
I	U	H	I	G	N	T	N	R	T	C	N	M	U	I
C	N	F	R	A	I	B	L	O	O	D	U	A	R	N
E	D	V	W	N	N	T	R	F	K	L	O	D	S	U
T	K	Q	T	F	R	U	I	T	R	W	C	A	E	P
D	Z	Q	B	M	L	T	L	V	N	E	D	E	D	Y
L	A	N	D	O	F	N	O	D	E	K	G	B	K	N

ADAM
ANGRY
BLOOD
COUNTENANCE
CRYING
CURSED
EAST
EDEN
FIELD
FIRSTLINGS
FRUIT
FUGITIVE
GROUND
KEEPER
KILLED
LAND OF NOD
OFFERING
PUNISHMENT
SACRIFICE
SEVENFOLD
TILLER
WANDERER

MULTIPLE CHOICE: **Birds in the Bible**

1 According to James, what cannot be tamed even though all birds can be tamed?

A. The mind
B. The tongue
C. The heart
D. The soul

2 What form did the Holy Spirit assume at Jesus' baptism?

A. Raven
B. Pigeon
C. Dove
D. Eagle

3 How old was Abraham when he departed out of Haran?

A. 80
B. 90
C. 70
D. 75

4 Who had a vision of a woman with eagle's wings flying to the desert?

A. John
B. Paul
C. James
D. Peter

5 What bird in great droves fed the Israelites in the wilderness?

A. Eagles
B. Quails
C. Doves
D. Ravens

6 In what parable of Jesus do greedy birds play a major role?

A. The Tares
B. The Growing Seed
C. The Sower
D. The Great Supper

MULTIPLE CHOICE: **Birds in the Bible**

1 What king instructed people in bird lore?

A. David
B. Solomon
C. Jeroboam I
D. Nadab

2 What Babylonian king had a dream of a tree where every bird found shelter?

A. Belshazzar
B. Darius
C. Ahaziah
D. Nebuchadnezzar

3 What prophet said that Ephraim was as easily deceived as a foolish dove?

A. Hosea
B. Nahum
C. Jacob
D. Elisha

4 What nation would, according to Obadiah, be brought down by God even though it had soared like an eagle?

A. Israel
B. Syria
C. Edom
D. Greece

5 What prophet warned of a destruction in which all birds would be swept from the earth?

A. Zedekiah
B. Hezekiah
C. Zephaniah
D. Tehu

6 What prophet warned that he would wail like an owl and walk about barefoot and naked?

A. Enoch
B. Joshua
C. Micah
D. Isaiah

WORD SEARCH: **Disasters**

N	B	F	B	E	S	T	N	E	P	R	E	S	C	X	Z
L	U	C	F	O	G	R	Q	L	T	H	U	N	D	E	R
K	L	K	L	F	I	E	E	N	X	Q	F	L	G	N	P
G	C	F	O	T	J	L	I	T	T	J	F	K	B	R	P
D	E	D	O	V	T	K	S	S	S	D	H	T	A	E	D
X	R	C	D	M	M	N	S	G	A	A	J	K	M	K	F
F	S	X	I	T	I	D	F	R	H	R	S	L	K	A	V
H	I	C	W	A	O	X	K	S	C	C	F	I	L	U	S
L	E	R	L	R	V	N	R	H	L	A	Z	J	D	Q	E
P	R	B	E	H	E	O	L	I	B	P	C	N	L	H	R
M	J	M	N	S	M	V	T	P	T	T	R	V	T	T	O
G	E	F	S	U	L	M	S	W	K	I	V	M	Z	R	S
M	F	N	T	W	Q	F	A	R	Z	V	B	L	B	A	L
B	L	O	O	D	B	J	E	E	H	I	P	N	X	E	M
B	Z	G	W	R	K	B	B	C	Y	T	T	H	L	Z	L
F	A	M	I	N	E	N	B	K	K	Y	T	J	L	Y	H

BEAST
BLAINS
BLOOD
BOILS
CAPTIVITY
DARKNESS
DEATH
DISASTERS
EARTHQUAKE
EMERODS
FAMINE
FIRE
FLOOD
MICE
SERPENTS
SHIPWRECK
SIEGE
SORES
THUNDER
TUMORS
ULCERS

S	H	S	N	O	I	S	I	C	E	R	P	T	L	V	K
C	S	G	S	L	X	T	H	T	P	E	F	E	M	A	P
M	E	E	N	E	G	H	H	M	X	G	P	N	K	L	K
Q	I	R	N	M	N	T	G	A	R	S	H	E	X	I	L
M	L	N	T	L	P	E	C	K	O	T	C	N	M	D	T
J	N	M	F	A	A	T	U	G	U	K	O	I	Y	I	R
R	O	R	T	A	I	U	T	R	M	D	R	U	C	T	L
I	I	W	R	L	L	N	T	A	T	L	R	N	A	Y	E
G	T	K	U	X	H	L	X	C	A	V	E	E	R	K	G
H	C	W	I	Y	X	I	I	U	A	D	C	G	U	J	I
T	E	K	S	B	M	W	T	B	R	F	T	T	C	W	T
N	F	C	M	P	M	C	N	Q	L	F	N	R	C	K	I
E	R	V	E	R	A	C	I	T	Y	E	E	P	A	D	M
S	E	L	M	Q	M	T	C	A	F	K	S	T	T	K	A
S	P	X	T	M	N	R	T	H	R	F	S	R	R	W	C
H	O	N	E	S	T	A	U	T	H	E	N	T	I	C	Y

ACCURACY
ACTUAL
AUTHENTIC
CERTAIN
CORRECTNESS
EXACT
FACT
FACTUALNESS
GENUINE
GOSPEL
HONEST
INFALLIBLE
LEGITIMACY
MAXIM
PERFECTION
PRECISION
RIGHTNESS
TRUENESS
TRUISM
TRUTH
VALIDITY
VERACITY

WORD SEARCH: **Trust**

E T M L K C Q N F L Y Z B B X L E
B G F K R R O B J D E L I V E R T
M F R P T H X N H N W H C R T Y A
T R X A O L A R F V O O N L R M G
C C V P H L J S T I N K K Q U X E
E O E V H C D O S S D R C P T A L
T N Q F B L L B I U E E L E H U E
A F Z F H L A G Y T R N J N R T R
C I K A A N N L A K N A G Y P H E
O D D I K N E G H J D U N X D O C
L E N T J R E T M Y Q E O C H R N
L N E H D L I G N L L M P C E I E
A C M Z E M Y T N I A T R E C Z D
D E M D M K S U R E N E S S N E E
C D O O B T S E V N I Q R N G D R
W B C M Q N O I T C I V N O C N C
W G V C O N F E R Z L A S S I G N

ALLOCATE
ALLOT
ASSIGN
ASSURANCE
AUTHORIZE
BANK
CERTAINTY
CHARGE
COMMEND
COMMIT

CONFER
CONFIDE
CONFIDENCE
CONSIGN
CONVICTION
COUNT
CREDENCE
DELEGATE
DELIVER
DEPEND

FAITH
HOPE
INVEST
RECKON
RELEGATE
RELY
SURENESS
TRUTH

MULTIPLE CHOICE: **Biblical Trivia**

1 The Ten Commandments can be found in which book of the Bible?

A. Genesis
B. Exodus
C. Leviticus
D. Numbers

2 What man was stoned to death for preaching the gospel of Jesus Christ?

A. Paul
B. Peter
C. Stephen
D. Matthew

3 Which two spied the land of Canaan and gave a good report?

A. Joshua and Caleb
B. Moses and Aaron
C. Elisha and Elijah
D. Jacob and Esau

4 The land of Canaan flowed with what?

A. Wheat and barley
B. Streams and rivers
C. Milk and honey
D. Apples and figs

5 How many hours did Jesus hang on the cross?

A. Four
B. Five
C. Six
D. Ten

6 God changed which man's name to Israel?

A. Abraham
B. Lot
C. Moses
D. Jacob

MULTIPLE CHOICE: **Biblical Trivia**

1 Who became angry when his preaching caused a whole city to repent?

A. Job
B. Jonah
C. Joseph
D. Jeremiah

2 Sea creatures and fowl were created on what day?

A. The first day
B. The second day
C. The fourth day
D. The fifth day

3 What sorcerer was struck blind by the apostle Paul?

A. Elymas
B. Mathias
C. Silas
D. Eliud

4 What island did Paul swim to when he was shipwrecked?

A. Patmos
B. Melita
C. Achaia
D. Macedonia

5 Who was the wife of Lapidoth?

A. Sarah
B. Hannah
C. Deborah
D. Mary

6 Who slept in the land called Nod?

A. Cain
B. Abel
C. Adam
D. Abram

N	P	L	T	H	M	G	F	X	T	E	A	C	H	E	R
K	N	R	B	X	N	Y	M	A	S	T	E	R	T	X	H
V	R	F	O	O	N	K	T	L	L	R	F	Q	C	E	Y
I	X	B	S	V	Z	D	H	J	E	P	D	M	I	Z	R
C	T	N	D	P	I	M	T	L	W	N	L	S	R	M	E
T	Q	M	A	L	L	D	K	M	F	B	E	M	Q	Y	D
O	F	R	E	L	T	C	E	L	Q	K	I	L	L	P	E
R	R	G	R	D	U	R	E	R	R	W	H	Z	R	G	E
Y	I	D	B	B	E	V	G	T	M	E	S	T	N	Y	M
P	E	L	R	F	D	B	D	G	O	P	P	I	C	K	E
D	N	Y	U	E	F	Y	U	M	R	W	K	L	L	P	R
V	D	G	G	K	H	A	J	K	X	Q	E	N	E	Y	R
M	E	J	T	M	T	P	T	W	K	P	B	R	B	H	P
D	V	Q	K	R	N	L	E	H	R	E	L	A	E	H	L
K	C	O	R	H	R	K	T	H	E	M	V	L	N	R	C
D	E	L	I	V	E	R	E	R	S	R	H	C	Y	M	K

BREAD
BUCKLER
DELIVERER
FATHER
FRIEND
HEALER
HE IS
HELPER
JUDGE
KING
MASTER
PROVIDER
REDEEMER
REFUGE
ROCK
SHEPHERD
SHIELD
SONG
TEACHER
TOWER
VICTORY

WORD SEARCH: **Levite Cities**

W	T	H	K	A	N	A	T	H	O	T	H	G	X
M	I	A	N	A	H	A	M	X	P	F	F	J	T
Q	Z	Z	M	D	R	G	S	H	E	C	H	E	M
H	R	H	N	P	K	T	H	X	M	R	W	X	R
T	E	A	B	G	N	L	A	R	R	Y	F	F	M
E	L	J	R	E	P	O	I	N	O	R	B	E	H
M	T	G	L	M	E	T	B	G	N	B	L	K	D
E	E	T	T	A	T	S	O	H	L	M	N	E	P
L	K	T	Y	A	L	L	H	I	S	O	K	D	N
A	E	K	J	R	A	A	B	T	M	E	N	E	O
V	H	Y	O	N	M	N	H	L	E	R	H	S	M
X	K	B	C	M	A	J	A	A	Z	R	Y	H	M
G	A	B	T	H	N	J	O	K	N	E	A	M	I
T	H	Y	F	G	L	A	H	S	A	M	T	H	R

ALEMETH
ALMON
ANATHOTH
BEESHTERAH
ELTEKEH
GOLAN
HEBRON
HESHBON
JAHZAH
JATTIR
JOKNEAM
KARTAN
KEDESH
LIBNAH
MAHANAIM
MASHAL
NAHALAL
RIMMON
SHECHEM
TABOR

MULTIPLE CHOICE: **Laughter in the Bible**

1 Who was snickered at for claiming that a dead girl was only asleep?

A. Paul
B. Jesus
C. Peter
D. Jairus

2 What old man laughed at God's promise that he would father a child in his old age?

A. Noah
B. Methuselah
C. Abraham
D. Saul

3 Who danced with all his might when the Ark of the Covenant was brought to Jerusalem?

A. David
B. Solomon
C. Obed
D. Uzziah

4 Who laughed when she heard she would bear a son in her old age?

A. Rebekah
B. Anna
C. Leah
D. Sarah

5 Whom did Jesus speak of as dancing in the streets?

A. The Pharisees
B. The priests
C. The children
D. The disciples

6 What graven image did the Israelites dance in front of?

A. The golden calf
B. Baal
C. The Massekah molten image
D. The Semel carved image

MULTIPLE CHOICE: **Laughter in the Bible**

1 What old woman said, "God hath made me to laugh so that all who hear will laugh with me"?

A. Eve
B. Rebekah
C. Leah
D. Sarah

2 In the Beatitudes, who does Jesus promise laughter to?

A. Those who mourn
B. Those who are sad
C. Those who weep
D. Those who hunger

3 What Old Testament character's name means "laughter"?

A. Moses
B. Isaac
C. Abel
D. Naomi

4 Whose ill-fated daughter came out dancing after his victory over the Ammonites?

A. Jacob's
B. Job's
C. Nebuchadnezzar's
D. Jephthah's

5 What group of people were busy dancing and partying when David caught up with them?

A. The Moabites
B. The Canaanites
C. The Amalekites
D. The Philistines

6 Who laughed at Nehemiah's plans to rebuild Jerusalem?

A. Sanballat
B. Eliashib
C. Shallum
D. Benaiah

C	R	J	Y	W	V	S	E	S	R	U	N	R	G	B
M	W	T	F	Q	T	D	Y	L	D	O	G	C	Q	D
L	K	L	N	T	F	E	J	W	Z	M	H	N	X	P
M	T	B	H	Y	R	E	M	O	O	W	E	J	F	N
A	L	U	L	B	H	R	S	N	C	D	T	E	R	V
I	K	L	C	A	Z	O	T	T	D	H	T	B	Y	P
D	C	R	H	B	H	H	A	I	A	C	E	Q	N	R
F	F	U	Y	D	S	J	H	R	H	F	M	B	W	F
J	L	S	B	T	O	W	N	L	A	T	F	R	E	F
X	K	H	J	I	T	O	T	L	E	H	E	K	R	D
N	T	E	W	N	T	N	G	K	P	V	P	Y	B	T
W	T	S	A	H	O	U	S	E	I	C	W	L	E	N
L	J	T	G	Z	G	A	M	R	Z	H	Q	N	H	T
G	G	R	E	Q	B	R	F	E	Y	B	A	T	H	E
C	C	D	S	I	S	T	E	R	N	Y	J	C	B	N

BABY
BASKET
BATHE
BITUMEN
BULRUSHES
FETCH
GODLY
GOOD
HEBREW
HIDDEN
HOUSE
JOCHEBED
MAID
MONTHS
NURSE
PHARAOH
REEDS
RIVER
SISTER
STAFF
WAGES

WORD SEARCH: **New Testament Books**

```
T B N P E M A R K H K L V N P
S M R N R P Q S E W D J X E H
N T A J O D H B U Y R P R W I
A H T T B I R E H T E X K T L
M E G G T E T T S T I M P E I
O S A F W H O A E I K T S S P
R S L S Q M E R L G A N T T P
Z A A G I R L W D E A N C A I
L L T T H X J E J I V Y S M A
E O I N F C K Y S S G E C E N
D N A M H U T S N T X G R N S
U I N J L O O F T C L R K T T
J A S F W L J K L A S E M A J
F N M N O M E L I H P P F W C
N S Q C C O R I N T H I A N S
```

ACTS
COLOSSIANS
CORINTHIANS
EPHESIANS
GALATIANS
HEBREWS
JAMES
JOHN
JUDE
LUKE
MARK
MATTHEW
NEW TESTAMENT
PETER
PHILEMON
PHILIPPIANS
REVELATION
ROMANS
THESSALONIANS
TIMOTHY
TITUS

```
A T Y M O N O R E T U E D R X
D U Q C N T N H L R R N N K L
K N H X R U M E K L K D E K E
H P K S M G N I Z M K H H N V
T Z Y B O S N S C R B A E G I
U N E D E J F E M A A I M E T
R R G G J R L L C V H M I N I
S C D O E E P C Q P P E A E C
N U N H U X K I S R P R H S U
J A T M T T V N R M F E W I S
H S A B J W K O L L L J C S T
E S B R E V O R P P R A M T N
E X O D U S C H H J N L S Z H
N R T R N T F C K I N G S P T
H C T N E M A T S E T D L O B
```

CHRONICLES	**JONAH**	**NUMBERS**
DEUTERONOMY	**JOSHUA**	**OLD TESTAMENT**
ESTHER	**JUDGES**	**PROVERBS**
EXODUS	**KINGS**	**PSALMS**
EZRA	**LEVITICUS**	**RUTH**
GENESIS	**MICAH**	**SAMUEL**
JEREMIAH	**NEHEMIAH**	

MULTIPLE CHOICE: **Seek First the Kingdom of God**

1 Who had King Zedekiah of Judah blinded?

A. Belshazzar
B. Baruch
C. Nebuchadnezzar
D. Naphtali

2 Whose servant did Jesus heal without being near the man?

A. The ruler's
B. The centurion's
C. Annas'
D. Pilate's

3 What apostle healed the man in Lystra who had been crippled since birth?

A. Thomas
B. Judas
C. Andrew
D. Paul

4 Once a disciple of John the Baptist, who was thought to have been crucified on an X-shaped cross?

A. Andrew
B. Thaddaeu
C. Bartholomew
D. Alphaeus

5 The enemies of Jesus met to plot against him in which priest's home?

A. Zacharias'
B. Annas'
C. Caiaphas'
D. Pilate's

6 What military commander sent Paul from Jerusalem to Caesarea?

A. Cornelius
B. Claudius
C. Appolosr
D. Agabus

MULTIPLE CHOICE: **Seek First the Kingdom of God**

1 According to the Law, how much tax did all adult Israelites have to pay for the census?

A. A half-shekel each
B. One shekel each
C. Two shekels each
D. Five shekels each

2 What prophet's wife was a harlot before marriage and an adulteress afterward?

A. Iddo's
B. Jehu's
C. Joel's
D. Hosea's

3 Who was eight years old when he became king of Judah?

A. Gallio
B. Dariu
C. Josiah
D. Ahimoth

4 What Roman official told a centurion to allow Paul freedom to see whomever he wishes?

A. Felix
B. Cyrus
C. Gamaliel
D. Agrippa

5 Who agreed that Paul deserved no punishment after hearing he defend himself in Caesarea?

A. Caesar
B. Festus
C. Tiberius
D. Caiaphas

6 What woman accused Elijah of murdering her son, whom Elijah then raised from the dead?

A. The Shulamite woman
B. The widow with two mites
C. The wench of En Rogel
D. The widow of Zarephath

WORD SEARCH: **Sovereign One**

Z	S	V	D	R	O	L	W	R	Z	W	K	B	G	P	W
H	K	S	H	O	P	E	E	N	O	I	Y	R	T	F	S
L	F	R	E	P	Y	R	X	N	N	L	S	I	B	O	U
P	K	G	R	N	E	Z	D	D	O	K	E	G	D	R	O
V	P	R	G	V	D	E	K	H	B	J	S	H	G	T	I
M	W	O	I	T	R	O	L	L	Y	Q	S	T	J	R	C
Y	F	L	W	F	P	T	O	T	F	G	E	E	U	E	A
Y	E	O	U	E	Z	N	H	G	L	T	L	O	S	S	R
D	T	L	R	J	R	G	K	O	J	R	B	U	T	S	G
N	Y	S	J	G	I	F	R	Q	Y	U	T	S	I	T	P
P	R	Z	E	M	I	I	U	C	Y	G	D	W	C	K	C
Y	H	K	D	J	O	V	W	L	L	J	M	G	E	X	P
C	P	C	G	U	A	T	I	H	F	E	A	R	E	D	K
R	Z	P	S	K	L	M	F	N	M	W	C	R	V	M	V
E	G	D	E	L	W	O	N	K	G	L	W	P	F	L	Q
M	W	L	B	D	Q	V	W	P	E	R	F	E	C	T	D

BLESSES
DELIVERER
FEARED
FORGIVING
FORTRESS
GLORIOUS
GOODNESS
GRACIOUS
HOLY
HOPE
JUDGE
JUSTICE
KIND
KNOWLEDGE
LORD
MAJESTY
MERCY
MIGHTY
PERFECT
POWERFUL
RIGHTEOUS
WONDERFUL

MULTIPLE CHOICE: **The Word is Life**

1 Who was the first murderer?

A. Adam
B. Abel
C. Enoch
D. Cain

2 Where did shepherds receive angels as late visitors?

A. Near Nazareth
B. Near Egypt
C. Near Bethlehem
D. Near Jerusalem

3 What son of David led a revolt against his father?

A. Absalom
B. Jesse
C. Nathan
D. Jonathan

4 What widowed prophetess was eighty-four years old when she saw the young Jesus in the temple?

A. Elizabeth
B. Priscilla
C. Sapphira
D. Anna

5 What was Sarai's name changed to?

A. Salah
B. Zillah
C. Sarah
D. Mother of all living

6 Who had to shave their whole bodies as part of the ceremony of consecrating themselves to the Lord?

A. The Amorites
B. The Levites
C. The Philistines
D. The Gibeonites

MULTIPLE CHOICE: **The Word is Life**

1 What did Joseph accuse his brothers of stealing?

A. His silver cup
B. His coat
C. His sack of gold
D. His birthright

2 How many times is Adam mentioned in the Bible?

A. Only 20
B. Only 25
C. Only 30
D. Only 35

3 One of Gideon's soldiers dreamed of a Midianite tent being overturned by what object?

A. A storm
B. A quail from heaven
C. A battle
D. A cake of barley bread

4 What king of Gerar took Sarah away from Abraham?

A. Abimelech
B. Saul
C. Baasha
D. Pekah

5 According to Job, whose children dance about and make music?

A. The children of God
B. The children of the wicked
C. Job's children
D. The children of the righteous

6 In Romans 16, who did Paul refer to as apostles?

A. Aquilla and Priscilla
B. Titus and Timothy
C. Andronicus and Junias
D. Silas and Barnabas

WORD SEARCH: **This is Only a Test**

M	V	C	N	V	B	J	B	Q	B	L	E	S	S	Z	V
D	N	K	D	R	R	K	R	E	R	H	Y	L	O	V	E
N	M	G	Y	E	C	T	F	V	K	S	N	M	W	S	K
N	U	A	K	B	S	I	E	Y	T	N	G	K	E	S	H
L	L	G	Z	H	N	C	Q	S	M	R	Q	H	N	E	C
S	T	P	Z	K	J	M	E	M	T	O	Z	J	E	S	Z
N	I	Q	P	T	N	A	R	N	M	H	K	M	M	S	Q
T	P	N	X	Y	Y	H	B	E	D	N	M	J	I	O	Z
M	L	D	Q	Q	W	A	Q	M	F	A	L	K	E	P	L
T	Y	N	N	Q	T	R	Q	T	O	F	N	G	S	N	K
H	N	N	X	A	F	B	X	L	Z	U	O	T	A	K	M
I	V	B	V	T	H	A	E	H	K	C	N	T	S	F	N
C	R	C	E	T	A	G	B	K	N	K	I	T	I	P	M
K	J	R	L	Y	N	X	C	B	K	O	J	R	A	F	Y
E	H	F	M	A	X	L	B	M	N	Y	E	B	H	I	R
T	D	E	Y	E	B	O	Y	S	W	O	R	N	M	D	N

ABRAHAM
ANGEL
BLESS
DESCENDANTS
ENEMIES
FIRE
GATE
HAND
HORNS
KNIFE
LOVE
MOUNTAIN
MULTIPLY
NATIONS
OBEYED
OFFER
POSSESS
SLAY
SWORN
TEST
THICKET

WORD SEARCH: **Timber**

D	E	T	J	R	L	B	T	E	R	E	B	I	N	T	H
D	P	N	J	K	A	J	L	E	Y	G	R	H	D	D	N
T	F	K	I	D	I	L	T	P	A	L	M	N	K	Z	L
Z	R	T	H	M	C	S	Q	T	X	K	O	J	T	H	Q
D	H	E	X	C	A	M	X	T	D	M	R	W	M	P	X
R	Y	C	E	E	C	C	B	M	L	R	E	H	N	L	N
B	J	Y	L	S	A	V	Y	A	F	Z	P	T	C	A	E
D	M	O	Z	M	M	C	P	S	W	B	I	F	H	N	R
Y	N	O	B	E	Y	L	E	I	L	R	N	Y	E	E	O
F	K	R	R	P	I	Z	O	D	N	V	U	M	S	W	M
N	Q	R	R	E	V	X	H	H	A	E	J	H	T	I	A
L	T	E	T	N	R	M	W	L	L	R	I	N	N	L	C
W	S	X	B	T	L	N	K	N	T	T	H	Y	U	L	Y
S	Y	R	R	E	B	L	U	M	T	N	Z	Y	T	O	S
W	H	K	J	J	T	L	M	A	C	K	W	F	R	W	H
V	Z	Q	R	N	V	X	H	H	B	A	L	S	A	M	Y

ACACIA **HOLM** **SHITTAH**
ALMOND **JUNIPER** **SYCAMINE**
BALSAM **MULBERRY** **SYCAMORE**
CEDAR **OLEASTER** **TEIL**
CHESTNUT **PALM** **TEREBINTH**
CYPRESS **PINE** **TREES**
EBONY **PLANE** **WILLOW**

SOLUTIONS

Page 3

CROSSWORD: Biblical Passages

1 A	2 L	3 P	4 S	■	5 C	6 A	7 B	■	8 T	9 O	10 F	11 U
12 D	E	A	L	■	13 O	W	L	■	14 O	P	U	S
15 D	A	T	E	■	16 M	E	E	17 K	N	E	S	S
18 S	H	I	I	19 T	E	■	20 S	I	N	N	E	R
■	■	21 E	G	O	■	22 I	S	L	E	■	■	■
23 S	24 A	N	H	E	25 D	R	I	N	■	26 P	27 R	28 Y
29 A	B	C	S	■	30 E	O	N	■	31 C	R	E	E
32 W	O	E	■	33 D	A	N	G	34 E	R	O	U	S
■	■	■	35 B	O	D	Y	■	36 S	U	M	■	■
37 D	38 I	39 S	O	W	N	■	40 U	P	S	I	41 D	42 E
43 H	O	L	I	N	E	44 S	S	■	45 A	S	I	A
46 O	T	I	S	■	47 S	E	E	■	48 D	E	N	S
49 W	A	D	E	■	50 S	A	D	■	51 E	D	G	E

Page 4

LETTER SQUARES: Bible Passages

1 solution:

And the LORD said unto Cain, Where is Abel thy brother?
Genesis 4:9

2 solution:

And there went a man of the house of Levi, and took to wife a daughter of Levi.
Exodus 2:1

3 solution:

If he offer a lamb for his offering, then shall he offer it before the LORD.
Leviticus 3:7

Page 5

VERSE DECODER: Bible Passages

1 solution:

And he said O LORD God of my master Abraham, I pray thee, send me good speed this day, and shew kindness unto my master Abraham.
Genesis 24:12

2 solution:

The LORD is my strength and my shield; my heart trusted in him, and I am helped; Therefore my heart greatly rejoiceth; and with my song will I praise him.
Psalms 28:7

MULTIPLE CHOICE: Books of the Bible

1 solution: **D**; 2 solution: **D**.

Page 6

MULTIPLE CHOICE: Books of the Bible

1 solution: **C**; 2 solution: **B**; 3 solution: **D**;
4 solution: **C**; 5 solution: **D**.

Page 7

LETTER SQUARES: Bible Passages

1 solution:

Let the children of Israel also keep the passover at his appointed season.
Numbers 9:2

MULTIPLE CHOICE: Books of the Bible

1 solution: **A**; 2 solution: **C**; 3 solution: **B**;
4 solution: **C**.

SOLUTIONS

Page 8

LETTER SQUARES: Bible Passages

1 solution:

And the Egyptians evil entreated us, and afflicted us, and laid upon us hard bondage.
Deuteronomy 26:6

2 solution:

And the LORD said, Judah shall go up; behold, I have delivered the land into his hand.
Judges 1:2

MULTIPLE CHOICE: Books of the Bible

1 solution: **A**; 2 solution: **A.**

Page 9

CROSSWORD: Bible Stories

1 B	2 A	3 R	4 S		5 M	6 S	7 S		8 O	9 N	10 L	11 Y
12 I	L	I	E		13 A	L	A		14 R	O	U	X
15 D	A	T	A		16 D	A	V		17 G	A	L	A
18 S	W	A	L	19 L	O	W	E	20 D		21 H	U	R
			22 S	O	N		23 D	I	24 G	S		
25 D	26 A	27 M		28 A	N	29 T		30 D	I	A	31 N	32 A
33 A	R	T	34 E		35 A	R	36 E		37 F	R	E	D
38 D	R	A	K	39 E		40 E	G	41 O		42 K	E	A
		43 R	E	S	44 T		45 G	N	46 U			
47 T	48 E	A		49 T	H	50 E	R	E	D	51 S	52 E	53 A
54 O	A	R	55 S		56 A	D	O		57 D	O	N	E
58 G	R	A	N		59 N	I	L		60 E	M	I	R
61 A	L	T	O		62 K	E	L		63 R	E	D	O

Page 10

VERSE DECODER: Bible Passages

1 solution:

And He shall be like a tree planted by the rivers of water, that bringeth forth his fruit in his season; His leaf also shall not wither; and whatsoever he doeth shall prosper.
Psalms 1:3

2 solution:

Now in the twenty and fourth day of this month the children of Israel were assembled with fasting, and with sackclothes, and earth upon them.
Nehemiah 9:1

MULTIPLE CHOICE: Books of the Bible

1 solution: **D**; 2 solution: **A**; 3 solution: **C.**

Page 11

LETTER SQUARES: Bible Passages

1 solution:

And they said unto her, Surely we will return with thee unto thy people.
Ruth 1:10

2 solution:

Then the people of the land weakened the hands of the people of Judah.
Ezra 4:4

MULTIPLE CHOICE: Books of the Bible

1 solution: **B**; 2 solution: **C.**

SOLUTIONS

Page 12

CROSSWORD: Biblical Vessels

[1] O	[2] L	[3] A	[4] V		[5] M	[6] O	[7] B		[8] S	[9] T	[10] A	[11] Y
[12] S	A	R	A		[13] E	N	O		[14] A	R	I	A
[15] S	I	G	N	[16] A	L	E	R		[17] B	U	N	K
[18] A	R	O	U	N	D	G	O	[19] B	L	E	T	
			[20] A	D	S		[21] D	U	E	L		
[22] B	[23] L	[24] O	T			[25] R	I	D		[26] O	[27] H	[28] O
[29] M	Y	C	U	[30] P	[31] R	U	N	S	[32] O	V	E	R
[33] W	E	T		[34] I	O	N			[35] V	E	R	B
		[36] A	[37] P	S	O		[38] I	[39] C	E			
	[40] A	G	L	A	S	[41] S	D	A	R	[42] K	[43] L	[44] Y
[45] A	L	O	E		[46] T	O	O	D	L	E	O	O
[47] L	E	N	A		[48] E	L	L		[49] I	G	O	R
[50] L	E	S	T		[51] R	E	S		[52] E	S	T	E

Page 13

VERSE DECODER: Bible Passages

1 solution:

God is jealous, and the LORD revengeth; the LORD revengeth, and is furious; the LORD will take vengeance on his adversaries, and he reserveth wrath for his enemies.
Nahum 1:2

2 solution:

Speak unto the children of Israel, and say unto them, if any man of you bring an offering unto the LORD, ye shall bring your offering of the cattle, even of the herd, and of the flock.
Leviticus 1:2

Page 13, con't

VERSE DECODER: Bible Passages

3 solution:

Now after the death of Joshua it came to pass, that the children of Israel asked the LORD, saying, who shall go up for us against the Canaanites first, to fight against them?
Judges 1:1

MULTIPLE CHOICE: Books of the Bible

1 solution: **A.**

Page 14

LETTER SQUARES: Bible Passages

1 solution:

And the speech pleased the LORD, that Solomon had asked this thing.
1 Kings 3:10

2 solution:

And fifty men of the sons of the prophets went, and stood to view afar off: and they two stood by Jordan.
2 Kings 2:7

VERSE DECODER:

1 solution:

Jude, the servant of Jesus Christ, and brother of James, to them that are sanctified by God the Father, and preserved in Jesus Christ, and called.
Jude 1:1

SOLUTIONS

Page 15

CROSSWORD: Books of the Bible

R	A	M		C	D	S		S	I	M	O	N
O	L	E		R	O	I		E	R	A	S	E
P	E	R	S	E	U	S		N	A	D	I	A
E	C	C	L	E	S	I	A	S	T	E	S	
		H	I	D	E		S	U	E			
A	L	A	N			A	T	A		O	D	E
S	O	N	G	O	F	S	O	L	O	M	O	N
H	O	T		R	E	S			L	I	E	D
			A	I	R		S	U	D	S		
	C	H	R	O	N	I	C	L	E	S	I	I
S	H	A	L	L		S	I	N	N	I	N	G
T	E	H	E	E		O	F	A		O	R	E
G	R	A	S	S		F	I	R		N	I	T

Page 16

MULTIPLE CHOICE: Books of the Bible

1 solution: **C**; 2 solution: **C.**

LETTER SQUARES: Bible Passages

1 solution:

And Abraham begat Isaac. The sons of Isaac; Esau and Israel.
1 Chronicles 1:34

2 solution:

And they brought unto Solomon horses out of Egypt, and out of all lands.
2 Chronicles 9:28

Page 17

VERSE DECODER: Bible Passages

1 solution:

Before I formed thee in the belly I knew thee; and before thou camest forth out of the womb I sanctified thee, and I ordained thee a prophet unto the nations.
Jeremiah 1:5

2 solution:

And he commanded the steward of his house, saying, fill the men's sacks with food, as much as they can carry, and put every man's money in his sack's mouth.
Genesis 44:1

MULTIPLE CHOICE: Books of the Bible

1 solution: **D**; 2 solution: **A.**

SOLUTIONS

Page 18

CROSSWORD: Biblical Beasts

1 O	2 V	3 A	4 L	■	5 R	6 O	7 D	■	8 A	9 C	10 I	11 D
12 W	A	D	I	■	13 U	F	O	■	14 L	A	D	Y
15 E	L	E	M	16 E	N	T	S	■	17 I	S	L	E
18 S	E	N	O	R	■	19 H	E	20 M	■	21 T	E	D
■	■	22 O	S	A	23 G	E	■	24 A	25 D	O	■	■
26 U	27 H	F	■	28 S	O	U	29 R	D	O	U	30 G	31 H
32 M	O	D	33 E	■	34 O	N	E	■	35 E	T	N	A
36 P	E	R	E	37 N	N	I	A	38 L	■	39 D	U	D
■	■	40 A	L	E	■	41 C	R	I	42 M	E	■	■
43 S	44 A	G	■	45 W	46 O	O	■	47 L	E	V	48 I	49 S
50 I	R	O	51 N	■	52 B	R	53 A	T	T	I	S	H
54 D	I	N	E	■	55 I	N	N	■	56 O	L	I	O
57 E	A	S	T	■	58 E	S	T	■	59 O	S	S	O

Page 19

MULTIPLE CHOICE: Books of the Bible

1 solution: **A**; 2 solution: **D**.

VERSE DECODER: Bible Passages

1 solution:

Until the day in which he was taken up, after that he through the Holy Ghost had given commandments unto the apostles whom he had chosen:
Acts 1:2

2 solution:

Grace be with you, mercy, and peace, from God the Father, and from the LORD Jesus Christ, the Son of the Father, in truth and love.
2 John 1:3

Page 20

WORD SEARCH: Animals in the Bible

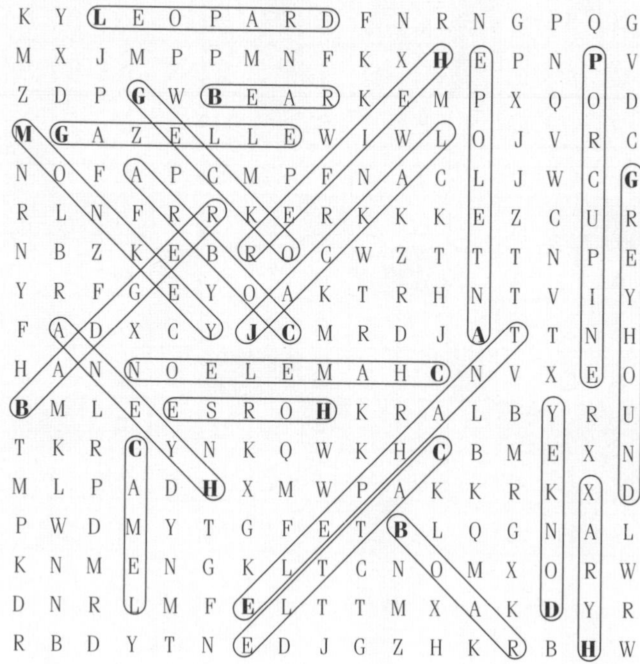

Page 21

WORD SEARCH: The Burning Bush

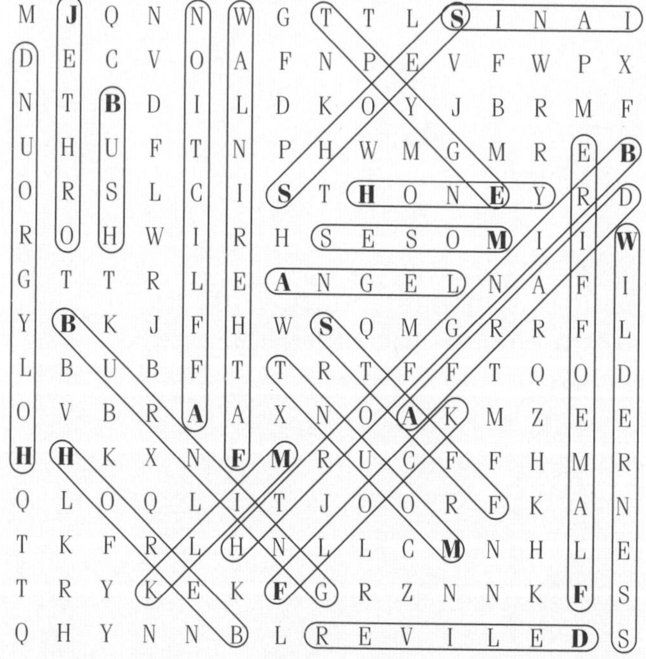

SOLUTIONS

Page 22

WORD SEARCH: Cain and Abel

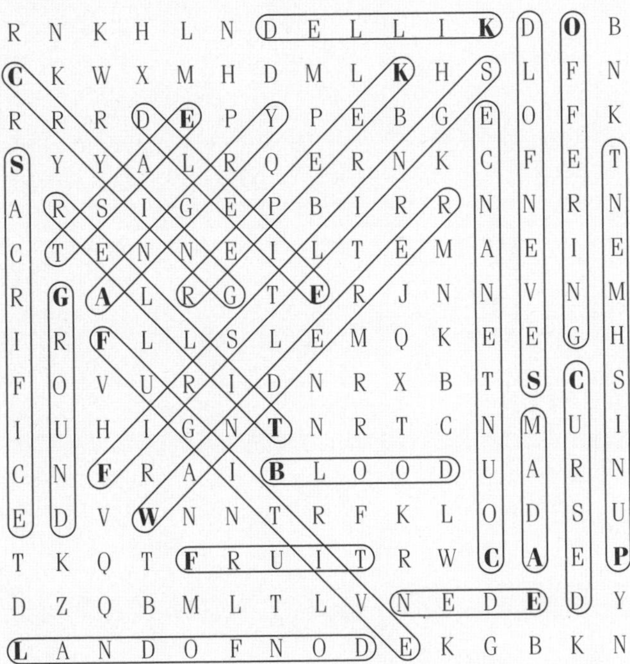

Page 23

MULTIPLE CHOICE: Birds in the Bible

1 solution: **B**; 2 solution: **C**; 3 solution: **D**;
4 solution: **A**; 5 solution: **B**; 6 solution: **C.**

Page 24

MULTIPLE CHOICE: Birds in the Bible

1 solution: **B**; 2 solution: **D**; 3 solution: **A**;
4 solution: **C**; 5 solution: **C**; 6 solution: **C.**

Page 25

WORD SEARCH: Disasters

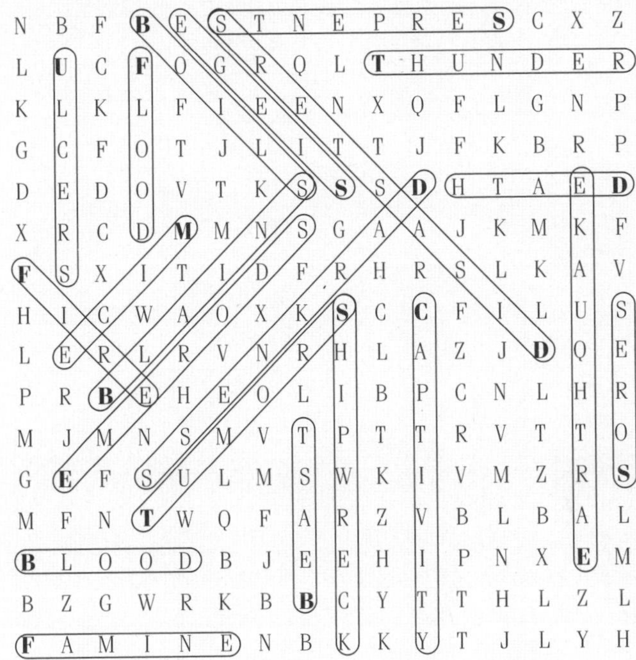

Page 26

WORD SEARCH: Truth Be Told

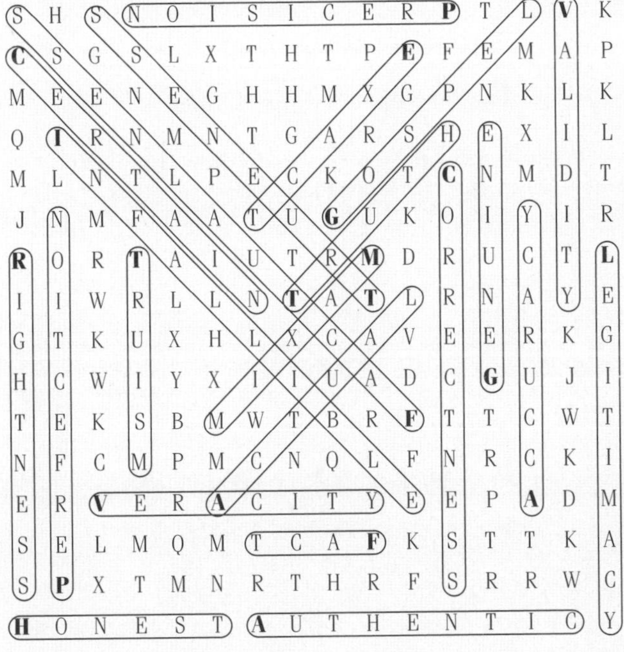

SOLUTIONS

Page 27

WORD SEARCH: Trust

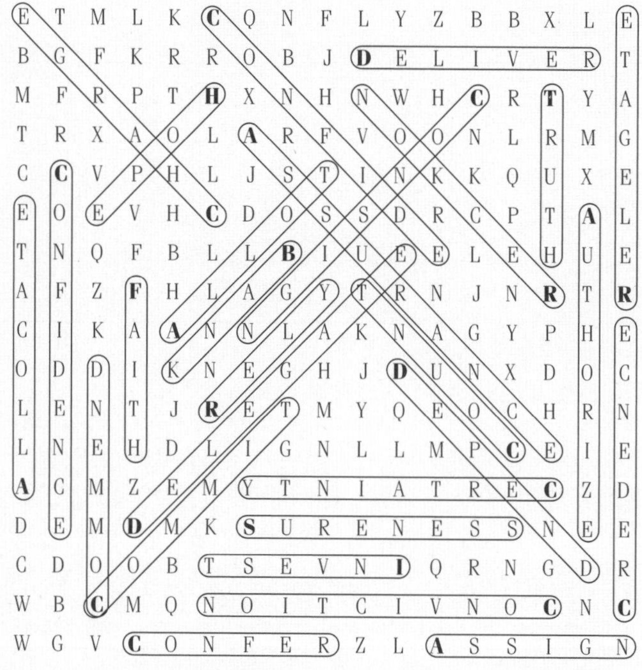

Page 28

MULTIPLE CHOICE: Biblical Trivia

1 solution: **B**; 2 solution: **C**; 3 solution: **A**;
4 solution: **C**; 5 solution: **C**; 6 solution: **D**.

SOLUTIONS for Page 29

MULTIPLE CHOICE: Biblical Trivia

1 solution: **B**; 2 solution: **D**; 3 solution: **A**;
4 solution: **B**; 5 solution: **C**; 6 solution: **A**.

Page 30

WORD SEARCH: He Is

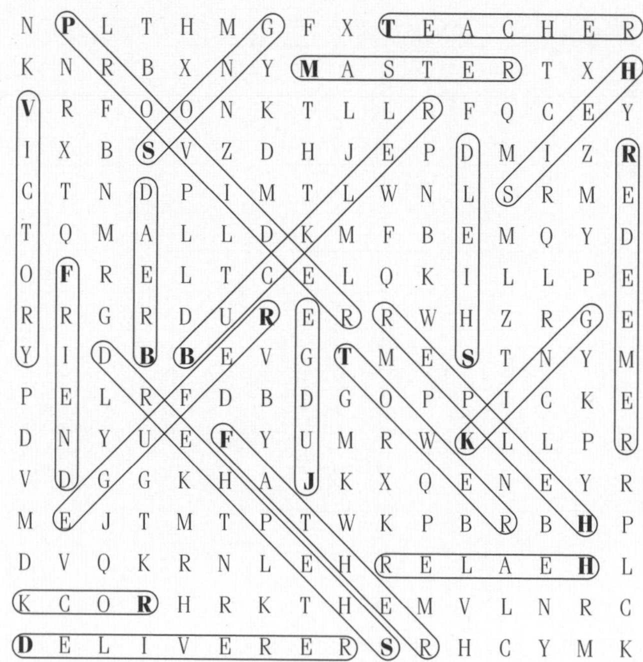

Page 31

WORD SEARCH: Levite Cities

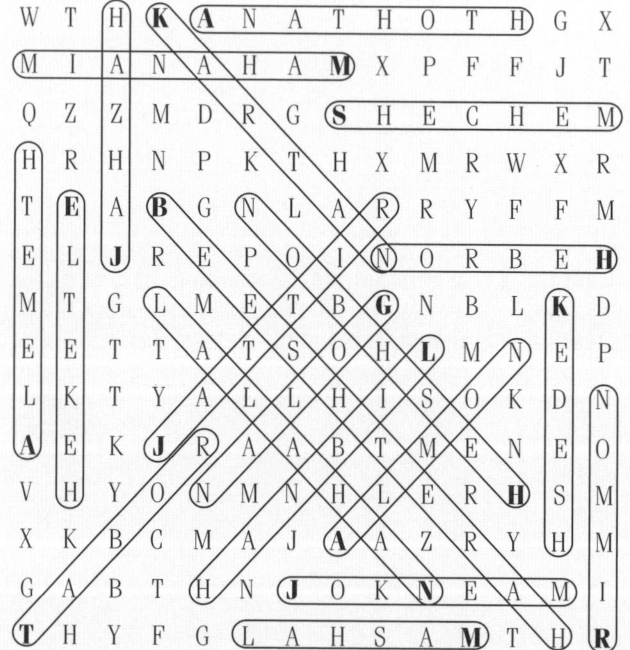

SOLUTIONS

Page 32

MULTIPLE CHOICE: Laughter in the Bible

1 solution: **B**; 2 solution: **C**; 3 solution: **A**;

4 solution: **D**; 5 solution: **C**; 6 solution: **A.**

Page 33

MULTIPLE CHOICE: Laughter in the Bible

1 solution: **D**; 2 solution: **C**; 3 solution: **B**;

4 solution: **D**; 5 solution: **C**; 6 solution: **A.**

Page 34

WORD SEARCH: Moses

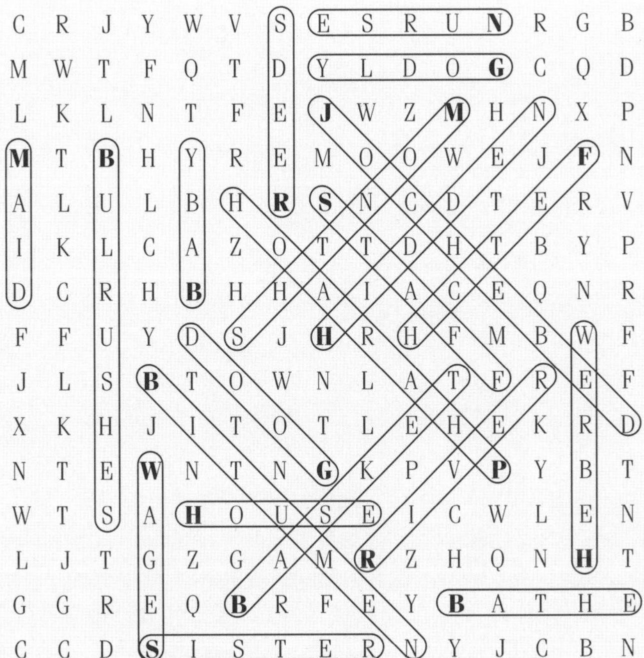

Page 35

WORD SEARCH: New Testament Books

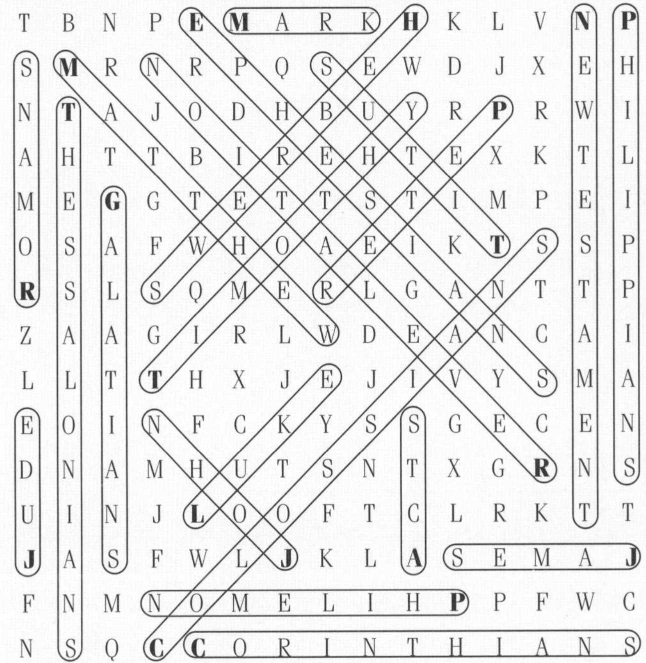

Page 36

WORD SEARCH: Old Testament Books

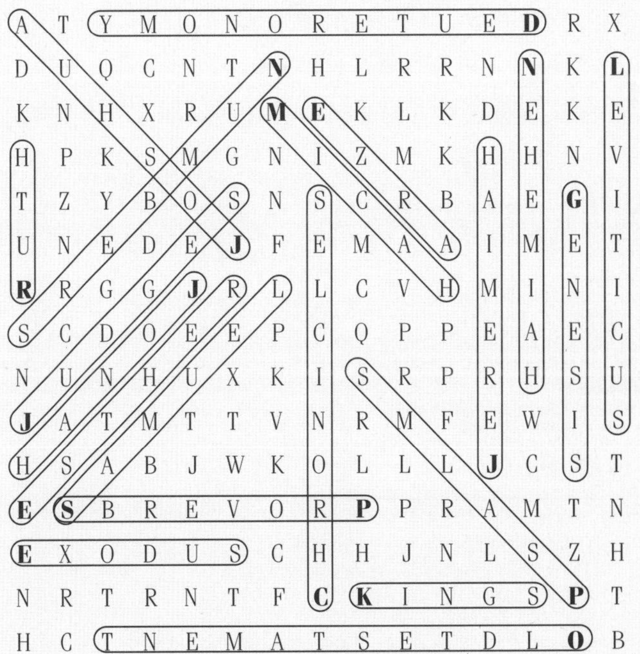

SOLUTIONS

Page 37

MULTIPLE CHOICE: Seek First the Kingdom of God

1 solution: **C**; 2 solution: **B**; 3 solution: **D**;

4 solution: **A**; 5 solution: **C**; 6 solution: **B.**

Page 38

MULTIPLE CHOICE: Seek First the Kingdom of God

1 solution: **A**; 2 solution: **D**; 3 solution: **C**;

4 solution: **A**; 5 solution: **B**; 6 solution: **D.**

Page 39

WORD SEARCH: Sovereign One

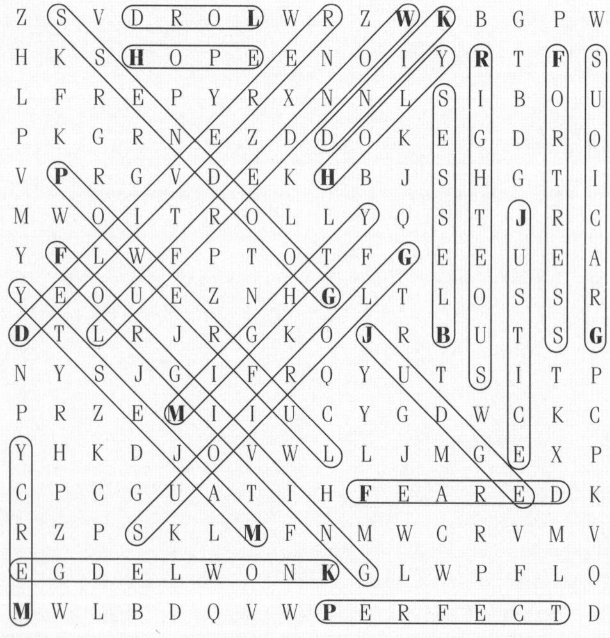

Page 40

MULTIPLE CHOICE: The Word is Life

1 solution: **D**; 2 solution: **C**; 3 solution: **A**;

4 solution: **D**; 5 solution: **C**; 6 solution: **B.**

Page 41

MULTIPLE CHOICE: The Word is Life

1 solution: **A**; 2 solution: **C**; 3 solution: **D**;

4 solution: **A**; 5 solution: **B**; 6 solution: **C.**

Page 42

WORD SEARCH: This is Only a Test

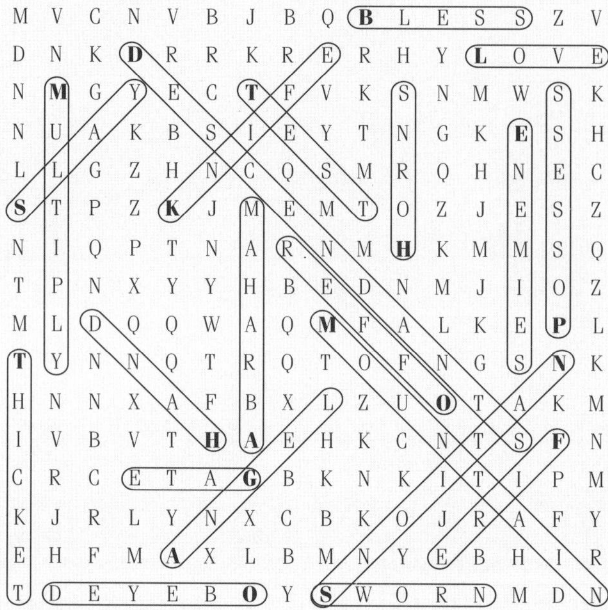

Page 43

WORD SEARCH: Timber

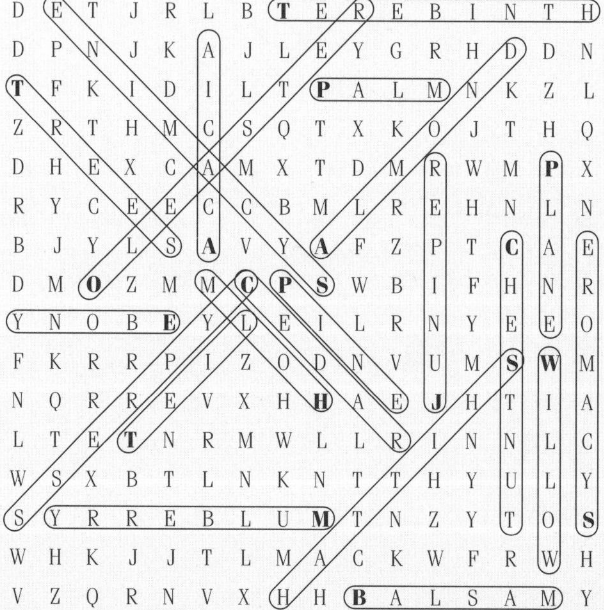

CHAPTER 2

CROSSWORD: **Biblical Rulers**

By Rowan Millson

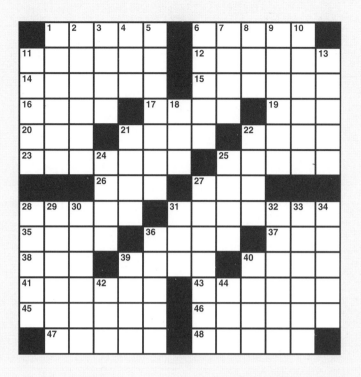

ACROSS

1 "Great" king of Judea

6 King who was "the sweet psalmist of Israel"

11 Strip, as bark off trees

12 Compounds derived from ammonia

14 Wipes out

15 __ telepathy

16 Diamonds and pearls

17 "Seeing __ that all these things shall be dissolved" (2 Peter 3:11)

19 History unit

20 Ended a fast

21 Raw materials

22 Handlebar feature

23 Biblical song king

25 Melodies

26 Get nosy

27 Moses parted the Red __

28 Very, musically speaking

31 Egyptian king

35 First king of Israel

36 Great pleasures

37 Health club feature

38 Long sandwich, for short

39 "God hath given thee all them that __ with thee" (Acts 27:24)

40 Kind of diver

41 "The Star-Spangled Banner" is one

43 Picnic, perhaps

45 Ill will

46 Stiff-necked birds?

47 Ninth mos.

48 Bible book appropriate to this puzzle

DOWN

1 Legalese for "pertaining to this" (2 words)

2 Glossy paint

3 Moscow's land (abbr.)

4 Poem to a nightingale

5 "Think not that I am come to __ the law" (Matt. 5:17)

6 Agatha Christie and Judi Dench

7 "So be it!"

8 Sportscaster Scully or hoopster Baker

9 Medical staff member

10 Term of affection

11 French painter of ballet dancers

13 Three Stooges actions

18 Farm layer

21 King of Israel, father of Ahab

22 Gum-producing plant

24 Another variety of 16-Across

25 Pekoe and Lipton

27 Moneylender in *The Merchant of Venice*

28 State of India

29 Finnish steam rooms

30 Not blatant

31 Hawaiian dish

32 Making inquiries

33 Speaks up

34 Puts up, as pictures

36 Kingly version of the Bible

39 Religious order

40 "The Man" Musical

42 "And he smote them __ and thigh" (Judges 15:8)

44 Spoon bender Geller

VERSE DECODER: **Bible Passages**

1 Genesis 18:6
HINT: In the puzzle below, the letter "N" is actually an "A."

NKC NUJNWNE WNRDSKSC FKDX DWS DSKD HKDX RNJNW, NKC RNFC,

ENZS JSNCM VHFLZTM DWJSS ESNRHJSR XP PFKS ESNT, ZKSNC

FD, NKC ENZS LNZSR HGXK DWS WSNJDW.

MULTIPLE CHOICE: **People: Saints and Sinners**

1 Who heard a voice telling of the fall of Babylon?

A. John
B. Barnabas
C. Ashpenaz
D. David

2 Which of Joseph's brothers did he keep bound until they brought back Benjamin?

A. Judah
B. Levi
C. Asher
D. Simeon

3 Pharaoh told Joseph that his father and brothers shall eat what?

A. Honeycombs
B. Fat of the land
C. Manna
D. Locusts

VERSE DECODER: **Bible Passages**

2 Exodus 32:2
HINT: In the puzzle below, the letter "P" is actually an "A."

PWH PPZMW UPLH IWCM CGFO YZFPN MJJ CGF TMQHFW FPZZLWTU

DGLVG PZF LW CGF FPZU MJ SMIZ DLBFU MJ SMIZ UMWU PWH MJ

SMIZ HPITGCFZU PWH YZLWT CGFO IWCM OF.

CROSSWORD: **Biblical Women**

By Rowan Millson

ACROSS

1 Constrictor
4 Mexican house
8 Many of them have big mouths
12 Sphere
13 Landed (variant)
14 Woodwind
15 "Welcome to Hawaii" gift
16 "And David comforted __ his wife" (2 Sam. 12:24)
18 Religious doctrines
20 Thespian Hal
21 Suffer somewhat
22 "Then the beasts go into __, and remain in their places" (Job 37:8)
23 "And after those days his wife __ conceived" (Luke 1:24)
26 Promos
29 Grain used in brewing
30 Ginger __
31 Singers' club
32 Fed Ex rival
33 Paul's helper; wife of Aquila
35 Units of electrical resistance
36 "And thine __ shall be clearer than the noonday" (Job 11:17)
37 "Ars __ artis"
40 Chastises
43 Manasseh's mother (2 Kings 21:1)
45 Internet address
46 "For thou desirest not sacrifice; __ would I give it" (Ps. 51:16)
47 January 2nd, for example
48 Three, to Nero
49 One who ogles
50 "That innocent blood be not __ in thy land" (Deut. 19:10)
51 Likely

DOWN

1 "... the righteous are __ as a lion" (Prov. 28:1)
2 White-centered cookie
3 Nabal's wife and David's sister
4 Secret science or doctrine
5 "__ for the day!" (Joel 1:15)
6 "Then said she, __ still, my daughter" (Ruth 3:18)
7 Olympians
8 Zebedee's son and Zacharias' son
9 "His cheeks are as __ of spices" (Song of Sol. 5:13) (2 words)
10 "And David was clothed with a __ of fine linen" (1 Chron. 15:27)
11 Actor Connery
17 Hyperbolic function
19 "But there went up a __ from the earth" (Gen. 2:6)
22 Sub shops
23 Outback bird
24 "The lot is cast into the __" (Prov. 16:33)
25 Tavern employees
26 "... voice of much people in heaven, saying, __" (Rev. 19:1)
27 Dover is its cap.
28 "And Moses stretched forth his hand over the __ still, my" (Ex. 14:27)
31 Common PC acronym
33 Dickens' illustrator's (H.K. Browne) nickname
34 Stashed
35 "For we write none __ still, my things unto you" (2 Cor. 1:13)
37 Clarified butter
38 Depend
39 Domed church area
40 To satisfy
41 Leaks sometimes do this
42 Cut
44 Often found with "humbug"

MULTIPLE CHOICE: **People: Saints and Sinners**

1 Who was awakened from a deep sleep by an earthquake so strong that it toppled a prison?

A. Crispus, the Gentile
B. Barnabas
C. The Philippian jailor
D. Mark

2 What priest is mentioned as having no mother or father?

A. Ananias
B. Melchizedek
C. Joshua
D. Ezekiel

3 Who was the father of David?

A. Jephunneh
B. Nabal
C. Jesse
D. Nemuel

4 Who is the only person mentioned in the Bible as having worn gloves?

A. Job
B. Isaiah
C. David
D. Jacob

5 What man and his daughters lived in a cave after the destruction of Sodom and Gomorrah?

A. Abraham
B. Caleb
C. Lot
D. Elisha

VERSE DECODER: **Bible Passages**

1 **2 Timothy 1:8**
HINT: In the puzzle below, the letter "L" is actually an "E."

TL UZH HGZD HGLALIZAL RKGRFLB ZI HGL HLKHEFZUS ZI ZDA JZAB,

UZA ZI FL GEK MAEKZULA: TDH TL HGZD MRAHRXLA ZI HGL

RIIJENHEZUK ZI HGL VZKMLJ RNNZABEUV HZ HGL MZQLA ZI VZB;

CROSSWORD: **Angelic Orders**

By Thomas W. Schier

Across

1 Title for God, in the New Testament
5 Ginger __ (soda choice)
8 Bloke
12 Papal name
13 Actor Mineo
14 David, after slaying Goliath
15 Order of angels
17 "... the Lord sendeth __ upon the earth" (1 Kings 17:14)
18 Fish-eating bird
19 __ Lingus
20 Evangelist Graham
21 Mean mutt
22 Owns
23 Like some Vatican bulls
26 Order of angels
30 "__ eagle stirreth up her nest" (Deut. 32:11) (2 words)
31 Palmer of baseball
32 "... he went his way __ his own land" (Ex. 18:27)
33 Order of angels
35 Song of praise
36 Macadamia, for one
37 It's mightier than the sword?
38 The Shroud of __
41 __ of Galilee
42 The king of Assyria brought men from here (2 Kings 17:24)
45 Like Homer's *Iliad*
46 Order of angels
48 Soul singer James
49 "... as a __ doth gather her brood" (Luke 13:34)
50 "Stand By Me" singer __ King (2 words)
51 "The First" yuletide song
52 Palm Sunday mount
53 Lands in the Seine

Down

1 Vaulted part of a church
2 Coffin support
3 Ruin the roast
4 Hard-rock link (2 words)
5 Jacob's second son by Zilpah
6 Animal shelter
7 Tree or street name
8 "Almost thou persuadest me to be a __" (Acts 26:28)
9 Restore to spiritual wholeness
10 Nutmeg covering
11 Word with tail or express
16 Apostle to the Gentiles
20 Prohibit
21 Authoritative
22 "And the Lord said unto __" (Gen. 4:15)
23 Game-show host Sajak
24 __ Wednesday
25 Golf standard
26 Word before and after "-a´-"
27 One, to Jeanne d'Arc
28 The 7th letter of the Greek alphabet
29 Trinity figure
31 Black shade
34 Sister
35 Bosc, for one
37 Hammer heads
38 Youth group participant
39 "And Joseph went __ bury his father" (Gen. 50:7) (2 words)
40 Baptism, for one
41 Mares and ewes
42 Seth's brother
43 "In my dream, behold, a __ was before me" (Gen. 40:9)
44 Iowa State city
46 A dance, when doubled
47 When, in Latin

MULTIPLE CHOICE: **People: Saints and Sinners**

1 David's oldest surviving son tried to make himself king of Israel. Who is he?

A. Abner **C.** Solomon
B. Adonijah **D.** Jesse

2 At more than 700 times, which leader is the third most mentioned in the Bible?

A. David **C.** Moses
B. Adam **D.** Paul

3 Who slept on a stone pillow at Bethel and dreamed of a stairway to heaven?

A. Elisha **C.** Jacob
B. Esther **D.** Pilate

***King James Games* Facts:**

After the advent of printing, verses were notated in 1551 by Robertus Stephanus.

---

4 Who did Paul say masquerades as an angel of light?

A. Michael **C.** Satan
B. Gabriel **D.** The Witch of Endor

5 In the time of Joshua, what people were cursed to be Israel's servants?

A. The Levites **C.** The Amorites
B. The Hittites **D.** The Hivites

6 Who constructed the first altar?

A. Adam **C.** Noah
B. Cain **D.** Abraham

CROSSWORD: **Heavenly Notes**

By Diane Epperson

ACROSS

1 __ of Solomon
5 Late-night Leno
8 "... and he that loseth his life for my __ shall find it" (Matt. 10:39)
12 __ about (approximately)(2 words)
13 "... man __ mouse?" (2 words)
14 Holy __ (Bible)
15 Attendants of God's throne
17 New Testament book
18 Moving vehicle?
19 "... he planteth an __, and the rain doth nourish it" (Isa. 44:14)
20 Heavenly servant of God
23 Heavenly guardian of Israel
27 Ten or pen suffix
28 Manner of doing
29 Where Kings play?
30 __-Jo (name from the Olympics)
31 Despotic King of Judea
32 Precious stone
33 "And Noah was five hundred years __" (Gen. 5:32)
34 Relative of etc. (2 words)
35 Belgrade resident
36 Heavenly messenger of God
38 Epsom and smelling
39 "And all that handle the __, The mariners" (Ezek. 27:29)
40 "... that when Isaac was old, and his eyes were __" (Gen. 27:1)
41 "And there shall come forth __ out of the stem of Jesse" (Isa.11:1) (2 words)
43 Guardians of the Tree of Life
48 H.H. Munro's pen name
49 River inlet
50 Architect Saarinen
51 Mexican monetary unit
52 Strange
53 Son of Jacob and Leah

DOWN

1 Marine mayday
2 "Behold, the man is become as __ of us" (Gen. 3:22)
3 "__ since thou hast spoken unto thy servant" (Ex. 4:10)
4 __ image (false god)
5 One of the Apostles
6 Jackie's second mate
7 Sweet potato, popularly
8 Letter flourish
9 23-or 36-Across, for example
10 Young fox
11 "Independence Day" invaders
16 Sidekick
19 Scored on a serve
20 The rain was as thick __ (2 words)
21 Nabisco's __ Wafers
22 Bibles, familiarly (2 words)
23 Conduct espoused in Proverbs
24 False god
25 Film critic Roger
26 Sacrificial objects
28 Measure out
31 Successor
35 Prophet who anointed Saul and David as kings
37 Pretelevision entertainment
38 "And I said unto him, __, thou knowest" (Rev. 7:14)
40 "And Abraham stood up from before his __" (Gen. 23:3)
41 Egyptian cobra
42 "Norma __" (Sally Field film)
43 __-Magnon (man)
44 "The five kings are found __ in a cave at Makkedah" (Josh. 10:17)
45 "... and for the __ that is in the land of Assyria" (Isa. 7:18)
46 Journalist Kupcinet
47 Miss Piggy's favorite pronoun

MULTIPLE CHOICE: **People: Saints and Sinners**

1 Who was with David when Bathsheba and Nathan pleaded with him to make Solomon his successor?

A. Joab
B. Abishag
C. Haggith
D. Abiathar

2 Who pretended to be a madman in order to escape from King Achish?

A. Samuel
B. Saul
C. David
D. Jonathan

3 Who had surgery performed on him as he slept?

A. Jesus
B. Adam
C. Paul
D. Abraham

4 Who heard God's voice coming out of a whirlwind?

A. Elisha
B. Nathan
C. Paul
D. Job

5 Who was the name of Elisha's servant?

A. Elijah
B. Gehazi
C. Nimrod
D. Naaman

VERSE DECODER: **Bible Passages**

1 **Daniel 1:5**

HINT: In the puzzle below, the letter "T" is actually an "A."

TLX FSG RPLY TQQWPLFGX FSGU T XTPDI QZWCPMPWL WO FSG RPLY'M

UGTF, TLX WO FSG BPLG BSPNS SG XZTLR: MW LWJZPMSPLY FSGU FSZGG

IGTZM, FSTF TF FSG GLX FSGZGWO FSGI UPYSF MFTLX AGOWZG FSG RPLY.

CROSSWORD: **Places in the Bible**

By Thomas W. Schier

ACROSS

1 Andy Capp's wife
4 Summer breeze sources
8 __ Ness monster
12 Minister, for short
13 Skin lotion ingredient
14 Southwest stewpot
15 "Thou believest that there is __ God" (James 2:19)
16 Water-to-wine town
17 He lived for awhile in 18-Across
18 First paradise (3 words)
21 Like July
22 __ Cruces, NM
23 Eat like a rodent
25 Christian, fashion designer
27 King of Judah (1 Kings 15:9)
30 Hill where Jesus rested and prayed (3 words)
33 Final amt.
34 Man-__ (race horse)
35 Neckline shapes
36 Word that modifies a noun (abbr.)
37 OT Book before Kgs.
38 Abram took Sarai and family to this place (Genesis) (3 words)
44 Join the choir
45 Saint Philip __ (Renaissance figure)
46 __ de Janeiro
47 Bowling surface
48 Thames school since 1440
49 Where Mary and Joseph sought refuge
50 Pitcher Hershiser
51 It precedes Oct.
52 Broke bread

DOWN

1 Type of edible legs
2 Musical Horne
3 Modernize
4 Gem surface
5 Astronaut Shepard
6 Banned act
7 The Israelites walked on this to flee the Egyptians
8 Prepares a cannon
9 Ye __ Shoppe
10 Scottish family line
11 Son of Noah
19 "A lioness: she lay __ among lions" (Eze. 19:2)
20 Rank below marquis
23 Greenwich time zone
24 "And mine eye shall __ spare thee" (Eze. 7:4)
25 Industrial average of Wall Street (2 words)
26 "And __ man smite his servant" (Ex. 21:20) (2 words)
27 Popular hymn (2 words)
28 "Come, __ a man" (John 4:29)
29 Balaam's beast
31 "Sweeney __"
32 Name of three czars
36 Messenger of God
37 Mark, for one
38 Ananias was one
39 Prince Charles' sister
40 Pay honor to
41 Corn or wheat, collectively
42 "__ Misbehavin'"
43 "__ of you shall approach" (Lev. 18:6)
44 __-mo replay

VERSE DECODER: **Bible Passages**

1 **Ruth 1:4**
HINT: In the puzzle below, the letter "C" is actually a "T."

WPS COTG CRRL COTV JBETU RY COT JRVTP RY VRWI; COT PWVT RY COT RPT JWU RHNWO, WPS COT PWVT RY COT RCOTH HDCO: WPS COTG SJTKKTS COTHT WIRDC CTP GTWHU.

MULTIPLE CHOICE: **People: Saints and Sinners**

1 Who told Jezebel's priests that Baal was sleeping on duty?

A. Elisha
B. Ahab
C. Elijah
D. Joshua

2 Who could not sleep while Daniel was in the lion's den?

A. Belshazzar
B. King Darius
C. Nebuchadnezzar
D. Arioch

3 Who does the Bible state invented the art of working with metal?

A. Abel
B. Tubalcain
C. Noah
D. Seth

4 Who was given a miraculous supply of food by the prophet Elijah?

A. Jezebel
B. The widow of Zarephath
C. The woman at the well
D. The Shulamite woman

5 Who used the first false name in the Bible?

A. Esther
B. Eve
C. Ruth
D. Deborah

***King James Games* Facts:**

A Bible translated into Latin was the first book Gutenberg printed on his newly invented printing press.

MULTIPLE CHOICE: **People: Saints and Sinners**

1 Which king is mentioned as one of the authors of Proverbs?

A. Saul
B. Joram
C. Solomon
D. Menahem

2 How many men did Joshua send out to spy the land of Jericho?

A. 3
B. 2
C. 6
D. 8

3 What son of David led a revolt against his father?

A. Absalom
B. Nathan
C. Jesse
D. Jonathan

4 What woman stricken with grief turned from her husband because of his breath?

A. Bathsheba
B. Abraham's wife
C. Delilah
D. Job's wife

5 Whose dance resulted in death for John the Baptist?

A. Herodias
B. Herod
C. Philip's wife
D. Salomé

6 Who was in exile for three years after killing his half-brother Amnon?

A. Achish
B. Absalom
C. Peter
D. Elijah

CROSSWORD: **Righteous Brothers**

By Joseph Mantell

1	2	3	4	■	5	6	7	■	8	9	10	11
12				■	13			■	14			
15				16				17				
18					■	19				■	■	■
■	■	■	20		21	■	■	22		23	24	25
26	27	28		■	29	30	31		■	32		
33				34					35			
36			■	37				■	38			
39			40		■	■	41	42		■	■	■
■	■	■	43		44	45	■	46		47	48	49
50	51	52					53					
54				■	55			■	56			
57				■	58			■	59			

ACROSS

1 Mondesi of the diamond
5 Chicken-king connection
8 Office in the White House
12 West Coast Bruins
13 Light brush stroke
14 Mentor in spiritual topics
15 "... neither he __ his brother" (1 John 3:10) (3 words)
18 From this time
19 Sheltered side
20 Companion of cry
22 Opposite of zenith
26 "... when thou wilt __ thyself abroad" (Deut. 23:13) (4 words)
29 Type of excuse or duck
32 Perry Mason's org.
33 "... his brother, and the stranger __" (Deut. 1:16) (4 words)
36 Swindle
37 "... all the inhabitants of Canaan shall __ away" (Ex. 15:15)
38 Antiquated old times
39 Monster slain by Hercules in myth
41 __ chi (meditative exercise)
43 Prayer ending
46 Unrefined
50 "Because his own __, and his brother's righteous" (1 John 3:12) (3 words)
54 __ vera
55 Epoch
56 Fly alone
57 The sun does it once a day
58 "And the second __ shall be an emerald..." (Ex. 28:18)
59 Quid pro quo (variant)

DOWN

1 Her book is in the Bible
2 Feel pain
3 __ Bator, capital of Mongolia (variant)
4 Shoestring
5 Fuss
6 Volcanic flow
7 Biblical victim
8 Hollywood's Milo
9 Cargo vehicle
10 In the past
11 "And God said, __ there be light" (Gen. 1:3)
16 Romanian money
17 Basic belief
21 "Give me children, or __ I die" (Gen. 30:1)
23 Arlene or Roald
24 Literally in the same place
25 Meadow animals
26 Engrave
27 Nautical attention grabber
28 Hourglass filler
30 Cobbler's tool
31 Baseball glove
34 Officiating priests at mosques
35 Female inheritor
40 Gathers leaves
42 Hole-in-one
44 Decorative pitcher
45 Rome burned during his reign
47 Swear
48 Fodder storage
49 Feed for hogs
50 "And John __ clothed with camel's hair" (Mark 1:6)
51 Bravo for a matador
52 Decay
53 Uncooked

MULTIPLE CHOICE: **People: Saints and Sinners**

1 Who held a big feast when his son returned?

A. Abraham
B. Joseph
C. The father of the prodigal son
D. Jacob

2 What smooth-skinned man had a hairy twin brother?

A. Jonathan
B. Esau
C. Joseph
D. Jacob

3 Who did the prophet Nathan confront about an adulterous affair?

A. Samson
B. David
C. Solomon
D. Joshua

4 What brave soldier in David's army killed a lion in a pit on a snowy day?

A. Benaiah
B. Uriah
C. Shimei
D. Joab

5 According to David, what father and son were stronger than lions?

A. Jacob and Joseph
B. Saul and Jonathan
C. Abraham and Isaac
D. Noah and Japheth

VERSE DECODER: **Bible Passages**

1 **Ezra 1:2**
HINT: In the puzzle below, the letter "Q" is actually an "T."

QXPV VDNQX HWUPV INCO LA KMUVND, QXM JLUE OLE LA XMDTMC XDQX

ONTMC ZM DJJ QXM INCOELZV LA QXM MDUQX; DCE XM XDQX HXDUOME

ZM QL FPNJE XNZ DC XLPVM DQ RMUPVDJMZ, BXNHX NV NC RPEDX.

VERSE DECODER: **Bible Passages**

1 Nehemiah 9:1

HINT: In the puzzle below, the letter "Q" is actually an "E."

BTM EB HZQ HMQBHS GBC PTIKHZ CGS TP HZEF OTBHZ HZQ

JZEYCKQB TP EFKGQY MQKQ GFFQOAYQC MEHZ

PGFHEBU, GBC MEHZ FGJLJYTHZQF, GBC QGKHZ INTB HZQO.

MULTIPLE CHOICE: **People: Saints and Sinners**

1 What gluttonous priest was selfish enough to keep sacrificial meat for himself?

A. Caiaphas
B. Aaron
C. Hophni
D. Ahimelech

2 Moses was taught to administer justice among the Hebrews by what priest of Midian?

A. Jethro
B. Eli
C. Eleazar
D. Aaron

3 Which priest scolded a distressed woman because he thought she had been drinking at the tabernacle?

A. Eli
B. Phinehas
C. Joshua
D. Abiathar

4 What priest was known as the "king of peace"?

A. Zacharias
B. Melchizedek
C. Ezra
D. Zadok

5 Which of the twelve disciples betrayed Jesus?

A. Andrew
B. John
C. Philip
D. Judas

CROSSWORD: **The Wicked**

By Joseph Mantell

1	2	3	4	■	5	6	7	■	8	9	10	11
12				■	13			■	14			
15				16				17				
18					■	19				■	■	■
■	■	■	20		21	■	■	22		23	24	25
26	27	28		■	29	30	31		■	32		
33				34					35			
36			■	37				■	38			
39			40		■	■	41	42		■	■	■
■	■	■	43		44	45	■	46		47	48	49
50	51	52					53					
54				■	55			■	56			
57				■	58			■	59			

ACROSS

1 "He is the __, his work is perfect" (Deu. 32:4)
5 Freud subject
8 "Surely the serpent will __" (Ecc. 10:11)
12 Citrus fruit
13 Former Dodgers great, __ Hodges
14 Particle
15 "... the perverseness of __ shall destroy them" (Prov. 11:3)
18 Bushes forming a fence
19 Graph points
20 Fond du __ (Wisconsin city)
22 Capital of Ghana
26 Ancient alphabetic symbol
29 German gent
32 Purpose
33 "A wholesome tongue __" (Prov. 15:4) (5 words)
36 Procure
37 Wise birds
38 "And all their wealth, and all their little __" (Gen. 34:29)
39 Decorate
41 "With him is an __ of flesh" (2 Chron. 32:8)
43 Notion
46 Put off
50 "__ discern perverse things?" (Job 6:30) (3 words)
54 Work by Chopin
55 Born as
56 Bring up
57 Heredity factor
58 "Go to the __, thou sluggard" (Prov. 6:6)
59 "None is so fierce that __ stir him up" (Job 41:10)

DOWN

1 Her book is in the Bible
2 Folklore fiend
3 Attired
4 Small, crested bird
5 Fabergé art object
6 Female child
7 Butter substitute
8 Kind of training
9 Skater Midori
10 Rocky hill
11 Swimming center?
16 Moses parted the Red one
17 Neck warmer
21 Get one's teeth into
23 First biblical felon
24 Excessively abundant
25 Singing brothers
26 Capital of Latvia
27 "The people of the land have __ oppression" (Eze. 22:29)
28 Organization created in 1949
30 Conger or moray
31 Bus-boycotting Parks
34 Last movement of a sonata
35 1930s actress Carole __
40 Washing machine cycle
42 It's sometimes studied in a lab
44 Volcano in Sicily
45 It's shouted on Sundays
47 Lost
48 "When they saw the __, they rejoiced" (Matt. 2:10)
49 "Behold, I stand __ by the well of water" (Gen. 24:13)
50 Tooth on a wheel
51 Mimic
52 Woman with a habit?
53 Nevertheless

MULTIPLE CHOICE: **People: Saints and Sinners**

1 Who designed the first city?

A. Abel
B. Cain
C. Adam
D. Noah

2 Who was the first farmer?

A. Abel
B. Adam
C. Cain
D. Noah

3 Who was the son of Nun?

A. Caleb
B. Joshua
C. Jethro
D. Aaron

4 Who was the father of Moses?

A. Amram
B. Aaron
C. Naaman
D. Ammiel

5 What did Lot's wife turn into?

A. A pillar of salt
B. A cloud
C. A bronze statue
D. A tree

VERSE DECODER: **Bible Passages**

1 **Nehemiah 11:1**
HINT: In the puzzle below, the letter "P" is actually an "A."

PTF NOU MDGUMI SY NOU HUSHGU FBUGN PN EUMDIPGUK: NOU MUIN SY NOU HUSHGU PGIS WPIN GSNI, NS AMCTJ STU SY NUT NS FBUGG CT EUMDIPGUK NOU OSGX WCNX, PTF TCTU HPMNI NS FBUGG CT SNOUM WCNCUI.

CROSSWORD: **What Kind of Fool?**

By Joseph Mantell

1	2	3	4	■	5	6	7	■	8	9	10	11
12				■	13			■	14			
15				16				■	17			
18								19				■
■	■	■	20			■	21			■	■	■
22	23	24		■	■	25			■	26	27	28
29				30	31				32			
33			■	34			■	■	35			
■	■	■	36			■	37	38		■	■	■
■	39	40				41				42	43	44
45				■	46							
47				■	48			■	49			
50				■	51			■	52			

ACROSS

1 Singer __ Domino
5 Number of gods in monotheism
8 Be angry
12 Speed skater Heiden
13 Woman with a habit?
14 Organic compound
15 Skilled tumblers
17 The Golden Calf, for one
18 "The fool hath said in his heart, __" (Ps. 14:1) (4 words)
20 For each
21 Barley beard
22 Delhi dress
25 Wrath
26 Public transportation
29 "Even a fool, when he holdeth his peace, __" (Prov. 17:28) (3 words)
33 Watering hole?
34 "Go ye, __ you straw where you can find it" (Ex. 5:11)
35 Mountain wild goat
36 "And Sisera gathered together __ his chariots" (Jud. 4:13)
37 Pablo or Jose lead-in
39 "The way of a fool is right __" (Prov. 12:15) (4 words)
45 "That was the __ Light" (John 1:9)
46 Respectful
47 Verdi opus
48 It's east of Eden
49 Biblical herb
50 Exploited
51 "... pure in heart: for they shall __ God"(Matt. 5:8)
52 Persistently annoying person

DOWN

1 Notable achievement
2 Curved structure
3 Run down
4 Sign of the zodiac
5 Broadcasting (2 words)
6 Party favorites
7 Catch in a trap
8 Represent falsely
9 Reverse an action
10 Frame of mind
11 Right-angled bend
16 Quilting or spelling
19 "... the one __ five hundred pence" (Luke 7:41)
22 Sib
23 Cleopatra's undoing
24 Record label
25 The Addams Family cousin
26 Napkin under the chin
27 "But when ye pray, __ not vain repetitions" (Matt. 6:7)
28 Gender
30 Citrus fruit
31 Ozzie and Harriet
32 Apple variety
36 In the lead
37 Scandinavian native
38 *Wheel of Fortune* selection
39 Author Murdoch
40 Like Adam and Eve in the garden, originally
41 Woodwind instrument
42 Home of the Elis
43 Grandson of Adam
44 Printing term
45 St. Anthony's cross

VERSE DECODER: **Bible Passages**

1 **Job 1:1**
HINT: In the puzzle below, the letter "N" is actually an "E."

KLNQN IRT R SRG OG KLN ARGB ZU XJ, ILZTN GRSN IRT PZW;

RGB KLRK SRG IRT ENQUNVK RGB XEQOCLK, RGB ZGN KLRK UNRQNB

CZB, RGB NTVLNINB NDOA.

MULTIPLE CHOICE: **People: Saints and Sinners**

1 What Hebrew leader, born in Egypt, predicted the coming of a prophet similar to himself?

A. Abraham
B. Noah
C. Moses
D. Daniel

2 How many stones did the Israelites take out of the river Jordan?

A. 24
B. 16
C. 12
D. 2

3 Who gave his son a coat of many colors?

A. Abraham
B. Noah
C. Jacob
D. Joseph

4 Whose daughter danced after his victory over the Ammonites?

A. Jochebed's
B. Job's
C. Jacob's
D. Jephthah's

5 The Israelites danced in front of what graven image?

A. Statue of a palm tree
B. Baal
C. The golden calf
D. A carved donkey

CROSSWORD: **Biblical Wives**

By Thomas W. Schier

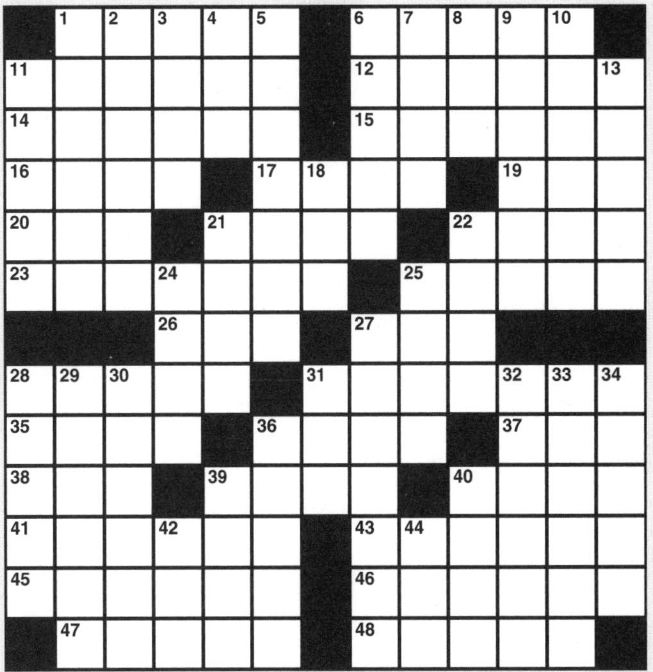

ACROSS

1 Trig. function
6 "__ man with seven wives" (3 words)
11 Jacob's wife
12 Dancing daughter of Herodias
14 __ plea of guilty or innocent (2 words)
15 Relating to families or clans
16 A bit of chemistry?
17 Like a storybook duckling
19 Neither Rep. nor Dem.
20 Type of dance
21 Entertainer/singer Adams
22 "And Joshua did unto them as the Lord __ him" (Josh. 11:9)
23 Nabal's wife
25 Composer of "The Merry Widow"
26 "... and, behold, it __ stiffnecked people" (Ex. 32:9) (2 words)
27 "And Esau __ to meet him, and embraced him" (Gen. 33:4)
28 "... for the bread is __ in our vessels" (1 Sam. 9:7)
31 Ahab's wife
35 Charlie Chan expression
36 "__ it" ("as you wish") (2 words)
37 Alter __
38 Pied Piper follower
39 Fit to __ (2 words)
40 Singer Vikki
41 "Ain't That __" (Fats Domino tune) (2 words)
43 "Am I my brother's __?" (Gen. 4:9)
45 One paying careful attention
46 Take to the sky
47 Cara of *Fame* fame
48 The __ of justice

DOWN

1 Harvard student, for short
2 Eight-armed creatures
3 Noah's firstborn
4 End of profit or auction
5 Pilate's wife
6 Rope-making fiber
7 Joseph's wife
8 A judge of Israel
9 Ammonite servant
10 Actresses Plummer or Blake
11 Gaucho's rope
13 Church official
18 Gerard, TV's Buck Rogers
12 The wise men came from this direction
22 "Stand By Me" singer __ King (2 words)
24 Football Hall-of-Famer Marchetti
25 Loll about
27 Isaac's wife
28 Abraham's wife
29 Start of a master plan
30 Ahasuerus' wife
31 Yankees manager Torre
32 "C'mon, __!" (help me out) (3 words)
33 White herons
34 *Casablanca* actor Peter
36 Guide
39 Prayer closer
40 Apply plaster
42 Fruity drink
44 Zsa Zsa's sister

MULTIPLE CHOICE: **People: Saints and Sinners**

1 Who had one of his soldiers killed in order to cover up his adulterous affair?

A. Boaz
B. Ahab
C. Herod
D. David

2 What was the name of the son born to Ruth and Boaz?

A. Obed
B. Asher
C. Shelumiel
D. Eliab

3 Who murdered Shallum and took his place on Israel's throne?

A. Jehoshaphat
B. Ahaziah
C. Baasha
D. Menahem

4 Who was imprisoned as a political enemy of the Philistines?

A. Samson
B. Jethro
C. Jehu
D. Zophar

5 Who tricked Samson into revealing the secret of his strength?

A. Bathsheba
B. Delilah
C. Haggith
D. Kezia

VERSE DECODER: **Bible Passages**

1 **Galatians 2:2**
HINT: In the puzzle below, the letter "S" is actually an "I."

DVG S NZVW RJ AO PZBZEDWSIV, DVG FICCRVSFDWZG RVWI WXZC

WXDW YIQJZE NXSFX S JPZDFX DCIVY WXZ YZVWSEZQ, ARW JPSBDWZEO

WI WXZM NXSFX NZPZ IT PZJRWDWSIV, EZQW AO DVO CZDVQ S

QXIREG PRV, IP XDG PRV, SV BDSV.

CROSSWORD: **Biblical Prophets**

By Rowan Millson

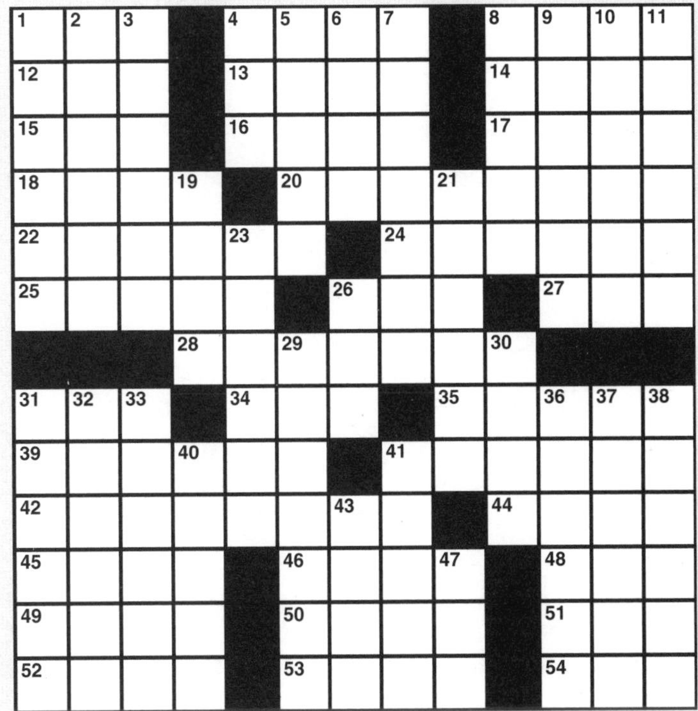

ACROSS

1 Pod occupant
4 What Peter wore in Rome, perhaps
8 Where Jesus was pierced with a spear
12 Ems followers
13 Egyptian canal
14 "__ Death" (Grieg composition)
15 "And I __ another sign in heaven" (Rev. 15:1)
16 __ colada
17 Soda jerk's offering
18 Long-distance runner Zatopek
20 Prophet whose book precedes Lamentations
22 Saintly Mother of Calcutta
24 Deranged
25 Islamic deity
26 "Why is thy countenance __" (Neh. 2:2)
27 "And they departed from Mount __" (Num. 33:41)
28 Flash flood
31 Org. with refunds
34 Suffix for sermon or motor
35 Prophet in Exodus 7:1
39 Rogaine alternative
41 Valuable weasel fur
42 Prophet whose book follows Nahum
44 "Now my days are swifter than a __" (Job 9:25)
45 Prophet whose book is between Joel and Obadiah
46 Spring bloom
48 Make lace
49 Official doc.
50 *Giant* author Ferber
51 Building extension
52 "Comus" composer Thomas
53 Totes
54 Poor grade

DOWN

1 Former currency in Spain
2 Kind of paint
3 Eddying
4 Recipe amt.
5 Board used in séances
6 Actor Wilder
7 Prophet in 2 Chronicles 15:1-8
8 Emma of *Dynasty*
9 Prophet whose book follows Song of Solomon
10 FDR's middle name
11 She prevented the massacre of the Persian Jews
19 "Wilt thou break a __ driven to and fro?" (Job 13:25)
21 Make beloved
23 Utter a shrill cry
26 Opposite of NNW
29 Prophet whose book precedes Daniel
30 Pack down
31 Locale of Cornell University
32 Nomad
33 Induce to commit a crime
36 Had a public outburst
37 Bargain-hunter's favorite words (2 words)
38 Bother
40 School glue
41 __ out an existence (scraping by)
43 Language of Pakistan
47 Airline to Stockholm (abbr.)

MULTIPLE CHOICE: **People: Saints and Sinners**

1 Who was the first apostle to be martyred?

A. Luke
B. Mark
C. James
D. Matthew

2 Who was a servant to the Persian king Artaxerxes?

A. Herod
B. Nehemiah
C. Belshazzar
D. Nimrod

3 Which of Pharaoh's servants was in prison with Joseph?

A. The chief butler
B. The interpreter
C. The cupbearer
D. The architect

4 Who ordered the killing of infant boys in Bethlehem?

A. Judas
B. Pilate
C. Caiaphas
D. Herod

5 Who heard a divine voice telling him to eat unclean animals?

A. John
B. Judas
C. Thaddaeus
D. Peter

VERSE DECODER: **Bible Passages**

1 **Titus 1:1**
HINT: In the puzzle below, the letter "B" is actually an "A."

ZBFR, B XQMJBTG HK WHU, BTU BT BZHXGRQ HK AQXFX YSMPXG,

BYYHMUPTW GH GSQ KBPGS HK WHU'X QRQYG, BTU GSQ BYCTHIRQUWPTW

HK GSQ GMFGS ISPYS PX BKGQM WHURPTQXX;

WORD SEARCH: **Assassins**

K	N	K	H	C	T	R	L	E	A	M	H	S	I	L
T	K	S	H	A	S	N	I	S	S	A	S	S	A	Y
A	T	B	H	A	I	A	G	N	J	H	G	T	B	H
L	E	Q	J	I	M	L	W	D	R	T	Y	K	O	X
E	R	D	M	A	M	A	A	D	A	K	L	S	Z	Z
X	E	A	S	R	S	I	N	H	H	N	H	I	M	M
A	S	A	D	A	D	B	R	C	T	E	B	M	Y	W
N	H	D	M	O	T	B	E	R	A	A	E	H	U	D
D	K	E	P	N	N	L	Z	R	I	W	M	H	A	A
E	D	M	L	Q	E	I	D	R	B	R	A	H	H	I
R	Q	N	K	M	K	N	J	T	A	K	Z	A	S	L
M	V	T	I	V	J	L	N	A	E	U	Y	Z	A	A
C	C	B	L	Q	W	T	W	P	H	M	H	A	A	Z
N	A	R	A	B	S	A	L	O	M	P	K	E	B	O
W	M	K	S	A	N	B	A	L	L	A	T	L	J	J

ABIATHAR
ABIMELECH
ABSALOM
ADONIJAH
ALEXANDER
AMASA
ASSASSINS
ATHALIAH
BAASHA
DEMAS
EHUD
HAMAN
HAZAEL
HOSHEA
ISHMAEL
JEHU
JOZALIAD
PEKAH
SANBALLAT
SHIMI
TERESH
ZIBA

```
T D Y Y D J H Y Y R H F H M L Z F M
B M Y T C E J T V F L A N K W K A T
M L Q C M Z M D L E I B I R V T T C
C N Q A X M Q V U R R N F M T J D T
M D N G L G M M A K Y C B H E L M V
V I T Y K T A H J F F H E L H H L K
K V M L M S C Y N M A W W C Z Z E N
M A A D H E H A K I Y F G L J Q L N
J D L K Z A H R M K A E S O H R M H
M H A R L T B E L Y X Q D N M X N A
H J C F E Z R A T P D K B N Y J Y I
A S H L R E L M K X S O L O M O N D
G E I L J N Q N L K H M J K K K K A
G M R M U H A N P E U A L P N K Z B
A A J O S H U A F N M K I G Y K X O
I J T L E Z E K I E L U Y A R J B H
H R N L D K H Z H R Y M E Y S J R N
J X C K C Q C X J R T P B L Y I J W
```

DAVID
ETHAN
EZEKIEL
HABAKKUK
HAGGAI
HEMAN
HOSEA
ISAIAH
JAMES
JEREMIAH
JOSHUA
LEMUEL
MALACHI
MATTHEW
NAHUM
NEHEMIAH
OBADIAH
SAMUEL
SOLOMON
ZECHARIAH

MULTIPLE CHOICE: **Royal Trivia**

1 Who asked her royal son to surrender his father's concubine to another son?

A. Manoah
B. Bathsheba
C. Deborah
D. Rahab

2 Who was brought down to Egypt and sold to a man named Potiphar?

A. Daniel
B. Samson
C. Joseph
D. Jacob

3 What woman from an idol-worshiping nation became an ancestor of Christ?

A. Ruth
B. Esther
C. Mary
D. Miriam

4 What king of Gezer opposed Joshua's army and was totally defeated, with no soldiers left alive?

A. Menahem
B. Horam
C. Joram
D. Pekah

5 Who was the son of Ner?

A. Abner
B. Ish-bosheth
C. Benjamin
D. Asahel

6 Who reigned in Jerusalem when the Babylonian king's forces first attacked Judah?

A. Jesaiah
B. Jehoiakim
C. Berechiah
D. Hilkiah

MULTIPLE CHOICE: **Royal Trivia**

1 Who healed the paralytic Aeneas?

A. John
B. Jesus
C. Stephen
D. Peter

2 What Jewish Christian woman lived in Rome, Corinth, and Ephesus?

A. Anna
B. Bernice
C. Priscilla
D. Lydia

3 Which of these women married her cousin, King Jehoboam?

A. Maachan
B. Joanna
C. Tamar
D. Michal

4 What king of Assyria had sent foreigners to settle in Israel after the Israelites had been taken away?

A. Elimelech
B. Togarmah
C. Esarhaddon
D. Rechab

5 What army did Elisha strike with blindness?

A. The Egyptians
B. The Syrians
C. The Midianites
D. The Philistines

6 What strong man killed himself along with a houseful of Philistines?

A. Samson
B. David
C. Saul
D. Judas

WORD SEARCH: **Captains of the Land**

N	J	X	M	H	V	Z	H	A	A	R	I	O	C	H
K	M	Q	R	A	F	X	R	C	S	R	R	H	Z	N
W	H	K	E	K	H	C	S	N	I	A	T	P	A	C
B	H	H	Z	E	G	A	G	N	R	T	H	B	L	N
V	L	A	E	P	M	M	R	E	T	K	R	E	Z	A
N	Q	C	I	P	Y	P	N	A	H	N	O	N	L	A
K	X	J	B	T	H	B	N	T	I	M	S	A	F	M
K	N	D	A	N	A	Z	T	H	R	I	R	I	P	A
H	E	L	E	Z	I	L	K	I	R	M	B	A	N	N
T	A	R	T	A	N	F	E	A	Z	I	D	H	L	I
M	C	G	T	W	A	I	S	P	D	I	T	K	A	R
F	Z	K	B	B	N	B	A	K	L	Y	M	D	R	F
M	N	B	D	K	A	K	A	D	B	R	L	R	M	C
N	C	W	C	R	H	R	W	Z	O	E	M	N	I	N
N	A	N	A	H	O	H	E	J	H	D	L	T	D	L

ABIEZER
ABNER
ARIOCH
ASAHEL
BENAIAH
BIDKAR
CAPTAINS
DODAI
HANANIAH
HELDAI
HELEZ
JEHOHANAN
MAHARAI
NAAMAN
OMRI
PEKAH
PELATIAH
RABSARIS
TARTAN
ZIMRI

WORD SEARCH: **Daniel and the Boys**

Y	D	C	T	Q	G	K	T	B	B	N	N	F	I	D	O	L	Q
N	E	M	R	U	O	F	D	B	O	W	P	W	V	N	L	V	N
G	D	T	J	N	C	N	P	L	T	R	C	Y	Z	K	D	F	P
R	E	J	M	H	H	M	Y	K	O	R	N	K	H	R	K	I	F
H	T	R	M	L	R	B	M	C	L	D	V	M	E	M	H	G	T
J	F	D	R	Z	A	F	L	H	X	A	T	A	L	S	N	D	K
M	I	G	W	B	K	A	X	T	K	N	M	I	R	I	R	N	L
E	G	D	R	I	M	C	D	G	T	I	T	O	K	O	B	A	K
G	C	T	D	A	N	R	H	S	N	E	W	O	G	G	T	T	I
T	B	A	T	O	Z	T	H	A	R	L	O	K	G	E	W	S	N
B	L	I	N	G	G	A	E	A	L	L	M	G	W	N	Z	R	G
H	O	L	J	R	D	F	T	R	D	D	C	L	T	D	V	E	D
N	X	N	R	R	U	U	O	O	P	H	E	T	M	E	B	D	O
R	N	X	A	N	R	F	O	N	V	R	Z	A	M	B	V	N	M
M	R	C	K	E	B	G	P	J	O	N	E	Z	N	A	V	U	B
L	H	H	C	W	N	N	R	R	L	S	N	T	P	S	N	Q	L
Y	N	Y	M	N	Z	B	E	L	T	E	S	H	A	Z	Z	A	R
N	K	H	C	A	H	S	E	M	F	D	F	V	H	N	Q	F	B

ABEDNEGO
BABYLON
BELTESHAZZAR
CHALDEANS
DANIEL
DREAM
FOUR MEN
FURNACE
GIFTED
GOOD LOOKING
IDOL
INTERPRET
KINGDOM
LITERATURE
MESHACH
PROCLAMATION
SHADRACH
SON OF GOD
UNDERSTAND
WORSHIP

WORD SEARCH: **Dreamers and Visionaries**

```
J N D R E A M E R S Z W R V C D
R B M Z M R Z C J T J E R U G H
K R H A N A N I A S T G P K T L
F X C C N J B P Z E R B L T Q K
S K E H L B T A P R E Y R A M W
A W L A J A P R L A R D Q D M R
I P E R M K T X R A N K K N M R
R D M I T E L E I N A D N A K J
A P I A Y R R O L K J M H W T E
H J B H B M B Z D O L A F G L R
C J A O M P T P H D R H J C U E
A N C M P U H N Q B I A F V A M
Z A Q Z E G H M A W K I T B P I
J N J H K S V A R C J A X Z M A
R C H R R Z M Z N Q M S T D K H
M V K Y S O L O M O N I V L N Y
```

ABIMELECH	**DREAMERS**	**MARY**
ABRAHAM	**IDDO**	**NAHUM**
ANANIAS	**ISAIAH**	**PAUL**
BAKER	**JACOB**	**PETER**
BALAAM	**JAMES**	**SOLOMON**
CUPBEARER	**JEREMIAH**	**ZACHARIAH**
DANIEL	**JOHN**	**ZACHARIAS**

MULTIPLE CHOICE: **Men Divinely Commissioned**

1 What apostle was a tax collector from Capernaum?

A. Paul
B. Matthew
C. John
D. Bartholomew

2 What hard-working companion of Paul was called an apostle?

A. Peter
B. Titus
C. Barnabas
D. John

3 Who was not one of the original twelve, though he probably labored harder for the gospel than anyone else?

A. Paul
B. Timothy
C. Titus
D. Matthias

4 Who doubted the resurrected Jesus?

A. Judas
B. Barnabas
C. Silas
D. Thomas

5 What is the fourteenth book of the New Testament?

A. 1 Timothy
B. Titus
C. Hebrews
D. 1 Thessalonians

6 According to tradition, which apostle was a missionary to India?

A. Paul
B. Matthew
C. James, the son of Zebedee
D. Thomas

MULTIPLE CHOICE: **Men Divinely Commissioned**

1 In which gospel is John not named?

A. Matthew
B. Mark
C. Luke
D. John

2 Who brought Peter to Jesus?

A. Matthew
B. Andrew
C. John
D. Philip

3 Who was the father of John the Baptist?

A. Bartholomew
B. Elioenai
C. Zacharias
D. Hakkatan

4 Who is thought to have been pushed from the summit of the temple, then beaten to death?

A. Paul
B. James the Lesser
C. Judas Iscariot
D. Peter

5 Who asked Jesus to show the disciples the Father?

A. Philip
B. Thomas
C. Peter
D. John

6 Who is supposed to have been flayed to death?

A. Alphaeus
B. Simon
C. Bartholomew
D. Philip

WORD SEARCH: **Sinners and Victims**

B	A	H	A	R	M	M	C	V	S	J	G	C	T	V	W
B	B	F	B	R	O	O	K	M	J	E	Z	E	B	E	L
V	Y	T	T	D	Z	T	I	M	S	G	R	B	N	R	P
R	J	M	O	B	N	T	N	A	H	A	N	I	D	N	Q
K	X	S	I	O	C	B	I	E	N	W	B	N	L	Y	L
K	Q	W	N	I	Q	D	A	M	B	D	Z	K	V	D	L
P	J	M	V	N	O	D	T	T	O	U	L	T	K	K	P
E	A	R	T	R	T	L	M	L	H	A	E	F	L	H	J
R	D	T	E	R	F	T	O	R	R	S	B	R	I	R	D
G	D	H	C	M	T	M	L	Z	N	L	H	N	X	Q	O
A	N	T	O	J	O	L	A	C	K	M	E	E	K	L	R
M	O	M	R	M	C	G	S	P	T	A	N	K	B	N	E
O	S	K	I	N	R	M	B	X	S	L	M	Q	D	A	H
S	M	J	N	M	Y	T	A	B	A	L	A	A	M	X	Q
F	A	K	T	G	Q	N	H	R	M	T	A	M	A	R	Y
T	S	F	H	L	R	Q	H	L	Q	L	N	F	V	M	M

ABSALOM
AMNON
BALAAM
BATHSHEBA
CORINTH
COZBI
DINAH
GOMER
HEROD
HERODIAS
JEZEBEL
MOAB
PERGAMOS
PHINEAS
RAHAB
REUBEN
SAMSON
SODOM
TAMAR
VICTIMS

WORD SEARCH: **Giants and Enemies**

M	R	H	I	T	T	I	T	E	S	L	R	N	Q	H	J
M	S	I	D	O	N	Y	N	A	I	D	I	M	P	A	E
M	T	R	V	F	R	I	Z	X	S	K	C	A	Q	I	B
M	O	D	E	F	K	M	S	E	K	A	S	C	Y	T	U
W	T	R	P	T	J	A	T	H	N	F	G	C	F	S	S
D	T	B	T	Q	R	I	D	A	B	A	N	A	K	I	I
K	X	A	A	B	R	L	A	M	H	I	W	T	R	L	T
E	D	Z	R	O	B	N	H	T	O	Q	B	R	B	I	E
N	B	T	M	B	M	J	A	D	B	N	T	E	Y	H	S
I	A	A	H	R	A	I	N	K	K	L	I	P	N	P	H
Z	B	H	M	F	L	S	N	K	A	S	N	T	Y	O	C
Z	Y	M	Z	O	Y	R	O	H	M	T	F	N	E	G	B
I	L	V	G	R	Q	X	M	X	N	N	F	J	B	S	E
T	O	Y	I	T	C	I	M	K	Z	A	M	K	Y	X	W
E	N	A	M	F	M	N	A	N	B	I	K	H	N	Z	K
S	K	T	X	Y	L	L	W	B	B	G	K	J	W	R	W

AMMON
AMORITES
ANAK
ARBA
BABYLON
CANAAN
EDOM
EGYPT
GIANTS
GOLIATH
HITTITES
ISHBIBENOB
JEBUSITES
KADMONITES
KENIZZITES
LAHMI
MIDIAN
MOAB
PHILISTIA
SAPH
SIDON
SYRIA

WORD SEARCH: **God Asked**

M	M	D	F	P	R	N	R	V	V	H	L	L	V	L	Q	M	D
A	Q	L	I	P	I	Y	L	S	E	E	S	I	R	A	H	P	R
N	J	T	T	S	B	L	Q	X	Q	V	B	G	W	R	G	Y	B
O	Z	Q	R	Y	C	N	I	J	Z	H	A	I	A	S	I	K	L
A	T	R	X	K	M	I	R	H	O	R	J	O	N	A	H	J	R
H	J	Q	N	N	T	C	P	N	P	H	D	A	V	I	D	L	K
N	E	O	N	G	P	F	D	L	W	F	N	Z	N	T	E	S	C
Z	Z	M	S	Y	N	N	R	P	E	P	N	H	B	U	U	V	M
B	E	A	R	H	N	T	W	K	J	S	E	Z	M	E	R	A	N
S	K	H	K	R	U	D	Q	H	T	R	H	A	A	N	R	Z	V
E	I	A	F	S	D	A	M	D	O	A	S	M	J	T	M	Y	G
E	E	R	R	E	D	Y	P	D	I	J	I	H	H	B	L	R	N
C	L	B	T	M	J	G	I	M	L	T	T	A	B	P	A	U	L
U	L	A	K	A	P	A	E	D	R	P	Z	C	F	O	Z	H	L
D	M	M	M	J	N	R	N	A	R	T	N	L	D	F	C	Q	H
A	Y	H	T	S	E	R	B	L	D	L	L	Q	H	M	H	A	R
S	L	T	T	J	M	T	H	T	K	R	D	W	Y	J	V	M	J
M	J	X	K	Q	R	R	G	C	Q	L	T	K	L	N	Z	F	K

ABRAHAM
BARTIMAEUS
DAVID
DISCIPLES
EZEKIEL
HERODIANS
ISAIAH
JACOB
JAMES
JEREMIAH
JOHN
JONAH
JOSHUA
MANOAH
MARTHA
PAUL
PHARISEES
PHILIP
SADUCEES
SAMUEL

MULTIPLE CHOICE: **Wisdom is Better Than Strength**

1 What is the greatest number of lepers Jesus healed at any one time?

A. Three
B. Five
C. Ten
D. Twelve

2 Who was the first person to practice wine-making?

A. Noah
B. Adam
C. John the Baptist
D. Solomon

3 What righteous man started the practice of herding sheep?

A. Cain
B. David
C. Abel
D. Job

4 Who committed the first murder?

A. Adam
B. Abel
C. Enoch
D. Cain

5 How many years were the Israelites in Egypt?

A. 12 years
B. 40 years
C. 120 years
D. 430 years

6 Who was imprisoned for prophesying the destruction of the kingdom of Judah?

A. Jeremiah
B. Jonah
C. Nathan
D. David

MULTIPLE CHOICE: **Wisdom is Better Than Strength**

1 What prophet was commanded to make a model of Jerusalem and set battering rams against it?

A. Isaiah
B. Amos
C. Micah
D. Ezekiel

2 Who was the man after God's own heart?

A. Saul
B. David
C. Herod
D. Pharaoh

3 What Christian witness was killed by the people of Pergamos?

A. Cornelius
B. Ahasuerus
C. Antipas
D. Barnabas

4 What king of Assyria was murdered at worship by his two sons?

A. Joram
B. Pekahiah
C. Hoshea
D. Sennacherib

5 What Israelite sinned in the wilderness by taking a harlot, a Midianite woman?

A. Zimri
B. Ahab
C. Jehu
D. Shallum

6 What Assyrian field commander tried to intimidate King Hezekiah by speaking to the people of Jerusalem?

A. Caleb
B. Rabshakeh
C. Naaman
D. Amasa

WORD SEARCH: **Her Children Call Her Blessed**

B	N	B	Q	C	G	L	G	V	A	H	M	N	V	R	W	Q	R
T	C	A	P	P	H	I	A	J	I	Z	A	K	B	J	M	F	G
K	Y	C	L	K	M	Z	D	J	A	A	Y	C	D	R	A	C	F
M	P	H	Q	K	Z	V	C	Q	M	I	Y	F	A	H	L	Z	L
J	K	L	F	H	Q	H	J	L	V	D	R	R	T	A	M	T	L
W	C	O	N	N	K	Z	H	T	R	U	R	R	U	V	M	T	T
Y	X	E	Q	M	I	R	I	A	M	E	A	D	X	T	T	T	D
K	J	D	B	T	F	Q	W	T	H	M	I	M	L	C	W	Q	Q
D	A	X	N	L	R	T	G	M	A	A	F	C	Y	F	H	B	L
C	E	H	A	L	I	L	E	D	L	D	E	B	E	H	C	O	J
T	L	Y	S	K	R	B	D	Y	O	Q	G	Y	P	K	F	G	G
D	M	B	N	A	G	N	S	X	H	F	B	V	M	R	N	J	T
N	P	Y	W	T	L	M	C	A	A	U	G	I	M	P	O	F	K
C	G	Y	H	M	P	O	R	Z	C	B	L	D	T	A	T	Z	P
R	M	H	G	A	D	E	M	Z	N	R	N	D	N	H	P	C	L
M	Q	M	N	Z	M	D	B	E	J	N	O	N	A	L	I	R	R
M	Z	N	V	O	C	J	K	N	G	Q	A	D	Z	H	L	A	Y
L	A	L	G	R	X	Z	H	A	N	N	A	H	Q	R	K	R	H

AHOLAH
ANNA
APPHIA
BITHIAH
CHLOE
CLAUDIA
DELILAH
DORCAS
EUDIA
GOMER
HANNAH
HULDAH
JAEL
JOANNA
JOCHEBED
MAACAH
MAIA
MARTHA
MIRIAM
SALOME

P	H	O	E	B	E	N	S	L	L	T	J	Z	L	D	K
M	F	T	R	Y	H	A	R	O	B	E	D	L	D	R	X
F	B	W	R	T	C	L	K	R	R	C	S	T	R	U	N
B	K	A	L	R	Z	I	H	T	M	A	M	H	H	T	R
I	M	N	O	W	G	A	D	A	R	R	W	A	H	H	H
B	P	D	K	M	V	G	N	A	L	R	G	G	A	P	A
L	R	L	L	D	N	I	H	L	Z	I	Z	A	E	T	N
E	Y	R	T	X	M	B	X	R	N	H	L	R	L	X	I
W	B	E	L	I	Z	A	B	E	T	H	H	E	D	M	D
O	B	A	T	H	S	H	E	B	A	A	X	A	D	M	K
M	K	E	M	R	Z	B	T	W	N	H	M	N	A	J	X
E	H	B	S	L	A	L	I	N	H	A	T	O	B	K	T
N	H	K	X	T	T	C	A	L	R	N	N	I	Z	D	B
K	T	P	R	H	H	H	H	I	H	I	K	B	D	M	K
M	K	T	D	W	J	E	S	E	H	A	T	T	N	U	J
L	E	B	E	Z	E	J	R	A	L	N	H	P	Q	V	J

ABIGAIL
AHINOAM
BATHSHEBA
BIBLE WOMEN
BILHAH
DAMARIS
DEBORAH
DELILAH
DINAH
DORCAS
ELIZABETH
ESTHER
HAGAR
HANNAH
JEZEBEL
JUDITH
LEAH
MARY
PHOEBE
RACHEL
RUTH
SARAH

MULTIPLE CHOICE: **Women in the Bible**

1 Which of David's wives was described as "very beautiful to look upon"?

A. Michal
B. Abigail
C. Bathsheba
D. Anna

2 Who died giving birth to Benjamin?

A. Rachel
B. Rebekah
C. Rahab
D. Hannah

3 How much time did cousins Mary and Elizabeth spend together during their pregnancies?

A. 1 month
B. 2 months
C. 3 months
D. 4 months

4 Who criticized her brother for being married to an Ethiopian woman?

A. Rahab
B. Miriam
C. Deborah
D. Ruth

5 What woman was the wife of the king responsible for the death of John the Baptist?

A. Herodias
B. Haggith
C. Helah
D. Hodesh

6 What woman was the mother of two of Jesus' disciples?

A. Salome
B. Priscilla
C. Anna
D. Dorcas

MULTIPLE CHOICE: **Women in the Bible**

1 Who asked Jesus for special water that would quench her thirst forever?

A. The Samaritan woman

B. The Phoenician woman

C. Rhoda

D. Anna

2 Who tricked a strong man into revealing the source of his strength?

A. Dinah

B. Diane

C. Delilah

D. Deborah

3 What Old Testament woman is mentioned in the roll of the faithful in Hebrews 11?

A. Rahab

B. Rebekah

C. Rachel

D. Hannah

4 Who lay down at her future husband's feet and was blessed by him?

A. Hannah

B. Esther

C. Rahab

D. Ruth

5 Which wife of a sheepherder admitted that her husband was a complete fool?

A. Hannah

B. Esther

C. Abigail

D. Ruth

6 Who was the royal mother of Nathan, Shobab, and Shimea?

A. Bathsheba

B. Esther

C. Vashti

D. Michal

M	I	S	A	I	A	H	C	H	R	I	S	T	T	F
K	K	T	Y	C	R	J	D	N	P	K	P	T	Z	B
P	R	M	G	D	E	H	J	O	C	H	L	S	D	P
C	Y	L	M	S	A	N	E	E	M	N	P	A	A	W
C	T	N	U	I	S	F	R	D	T	Y	M	M	V	L
D	L	S	D	K	S	A	E	I	L	V	K	U	I	H
V	E	A	D	E	S	Y	M	G	J	K	D	E	D	A
N	B	Y	O	A	G	H	I	S	P	A	A	L	R	O
O	A	R	R	J	N	B	A	C	O	S	C	R	T	N
R	E	A	K	D	Z	I	H	C	O	N	V	O	Z	J
H	H	R	A	H	A	B	E	M	I	F	G	Z	B	E
L	E	O	J	L	M	N	A	L	B	M	N	Q	M	P
G	T	K	T	M	O	R	E	H	T	S	E	W	P	V
Z	K	K	X	C	G	Z	L	Q	J	M	Y	L	L	T
C	T	R	H	H	Y	X	X	Z	J	M	R	T	D	W

ABEL
AMOS
CHRIST
DANIEL
DAVID
ENOCH
ESTHER
EZRA
GIDEON
HEROES
ISAIAH
JACOB
JEREMIAH
JESUS
JOEL
MICAH
NOAH
OBADIAH
RAHAB
SAMSON
SAMUEL
SARAH

WORD SEARCH: **Holy Men**

A	B	I	S	H	U	A	R	L	D	Z	J	C	M	H
K	H	T	P	K	N	A	R	Z	E	D	R	T	H	A
J	J	A	O	M	M	Z	P	J	M	D	E	T	R	J
N	J	D	I	A	H	N	D	P	M	F	M	F	Y	I
H	A	O	H	K	N	Q	B	T	W	R	M	T	B	R
Z	A	T	S	A	L	A	Q	W	X	Z	I	N	R	U
P	I	I	D	H	U	I	H	K	T	E	G	O	C	K
L	B	A	A	H	U	L	H	I	L	P	D	R	J	P
R	B	V	I	R	J	A	V	I	J	H	K	A	L	H
Y	N	B	L	T	E	Z	A	A	T	A	N	A	M	I
W	A	V	T	X	X	S	M	N	M	N	H	Y	A	N
G	W	V	K	Z	H	Z	P	N	Z	I	T	Q	T	E
S	T	S	E	I	R	P	R	A	N	A	B	C	T	H
D	C	W	B	B	V	T	W	S	P	H	D	Z	A	A
J	N	D	J	E	H	O	I	A	D	A	K	H	N	S

AARON
ABIHU
ABISHUA
AHIJAH
ANNAS
ELIASHIB
EZRA
HILKIAH
IMMER
ITHAMAR
JEHOIADA
JOSHUA
MATTAN
NADAB
PHINEHAS
PRIESTS
SERAIAH
URIJAH
ZADOK
ZEPHANIAH

WORD SEARCH: **I Saw an Angel**

D	W	B	V	B	N	J	H	Y	N	K	M	H	N	F	K
A	K	D	R	N	R	A	E	S	E	R	A	P	H	I	M
N	B	B	G	V	I	G	M	S	L	E	I	R	B	A	G
I	B	A	L	A	A	M	S	R	U	L	B	T	K	D	J
E	R	B	S	C	T	X	R	U	E	S	Q	J	N	Y	L
L	Z	I	Z	D	O	F	T	A	R	Z	C	T	T	E	M
H	P	E	S	O	J	R	H	M	T	A	M	N	L	G	B
N	Z	Y	C	H	K	C	N	J	K	N	Z	I	G	Q	N
W	H	N	J	H	I	F	O	E	O	B	J	A	D	M	K
T	R	F	O	M	A	H	X	L	L	A	M	X	L	A	R
Q	G	R	X	E	N	R	L	J	H	I	N	P	H	H	A
L	D	R	Y	L	D	O	I	O	H	D	U	Z	A	A	G
D	H	C	L	K	P	I	K	A	R	X	C	S	O	R	A
M	R	V	N	A	P	N	G	N	S	T	R	L	N	B	H
T	J	A	C	O	B	L	R	N	D	L	Y	K	A	A	R
N	G	G	H	T	R	K	W	A	J	T	J	C	M	W	P

ABRAHAM
APOLLON
BALAAM
CORNELIUS
DANIEL
ELIJAH
GABRIEL
GIDEON
HAGAR
ISAIAH
JACOB
JESUS
JOANNA
JOHN
JOSEPH
LAZARUS
MANOAH
MICHAEL
SERAPHIM
ZECHARIAS

WORD SEARCH: **Jobs**

H N C Y Y Z T K Y L T S E I R P B V
J T M W J T M I M R K M R N L B N R
S C R I B E E N L E D F E N Q W L E
P T R F W T Y H C L S N R B H T X P
W V N I D H F L P H E S A R R J Y E
C N C S R H W A D O R R E B F C T E
F A M H E G K C R W R L B N S D Y K
P C I E H L R C L M I P R N G U X N
V I D R P Y Y N T A E B O M G E H N
N L W M E K T Z J L T R M K L E R I
N B I A H B R L K G M R R N R R V T
L U F N S L Q K G I C B A D E T M S
V P E C O M M A N D E R S G T K T N
L N Y C W R B I Z M N M N F F E M R
R E T N U H S Z M W A I N V W T E T
W Y P T R T L Z M N S F Q A G K V L
K Z N Y E L T K L M Q T R J A H R H
H B M R X X J U D G E D P B C V Y G

ARMOR BEARER
BAKER
COMMANDER
FARMER
FISHERMAN
HERDSMAN
HUNTER
HUSBANDRY
INNKEEPER
JAILER
JUDGE
MESSENGER
MIDWIFE
MINISTER
PRIEST
PROPHET
PUBLICAN
SCRIBE
SHEPHERD
SINGER
STEWARD
TILLER

WORD SEARCH: **Judah's Progeny**

M	I	M	V	Y	A	M	E	H	S	K	T	G
E	A	A	J	O	R	K	O	A	M	J	A	M
M	L	H	M	P	N	Q	R	R	R	Z	P	U
M	A	I	A	A	Y	A	U	P	E	H	P	L
A	T	O	S	R	S	Z	R	Z	H	Q	U	L
R	Z	C	N	H	H	I	H	A	N	P	A	A
E	R	X	R	T	A	D	S	A	H	I	H	H
S	G	W	E	D	A	M	T	L	W	A	N	S
H	T	B	H	B	B	H	A	H	L	T	O	E
A	X	A	A	K	A	G	H	J	X	T	R	P
H	J	Z	V	N	T	E	L	A	P	A	B	H
Q	E	L	E	A	S	A	H	B	C	B	E	A
M	R	K	G	M	E	H	S	E	G	R	H	H

ATTAI	**HARAN**	**PALET**
BETHZUR	**HEBRON**	**RAHAM**
ELEASAH	**JAHDAI**	**SHALLUM**
ELISHAMA	**JORKOAM**	**SHEMA**
EPHAH	**MAON**	**SISAMAI**
GAZEZ	**MARESHAH**	**TAPPUAH**
GESHEM	**NATHAN**	**ZABAD**

WORD SEARCH: **King Saul's Family**

K	J	A	R	A	H	R	R	E	P	H	A	I	A	H
M	L	L	A	A	B	H	S	E	G	M	T	K	G	G
L	L	H	H	A	I	D	A	B	O	O	K	M	V	X
R	P	C	A	J	C	E	R	A	K	I	N	K	G	K
K	Z	R	C	I	L	K	E	R	H	H	E	L	T	C
M	I	X	K	E	R	R	N	T	Z	A	N	Q	P	G
A	L	S	A	M	H	A	E	L	M	B	A	A	L	W
L	A	S	H	A	D	V	E	R	N	J	H	P	F	F
C	A	L	T	A	A	B	L	H	O	N	K	L	X	L
H	B	N	D	M	J	O	R	V	S	D	M	V	E	P
I	B	I	Z	Z	X	C	T	Y	Y	V	E	A	T	J
S	I	A	N	B	M	H	X	I	X	X	M	G	R	F
H	R	R	C	E	D	E	M	W	M	H	L	H	C	N
U	E	G	V	H	A	R	M	X	S	R	M	W	Y	R
A	M	N	V	R	C	U	X	I	L	Y	I	G	P	N

AHIO
AZMAVETH
BAAL
BINEA
BOCHERU
ELEASAH
ESHBAAL
GEDOR
HANEN
ISHMAEL
JARAH
KISH
MALCHISHUA
MERIBBAAL
NADAD
OBADIAH
REPHAIAH
SHEARIAH
TAHREA
TIMRI

WORD SEARCH: **Naomi and Ruth**

C O N C E P T I O N L F K K F J M Y
C L O H N M W T T R S A N D A L V C
M V L A E R I P V F E Y R X M W W K
N K H P H L C D J S A S C D I C W K
H L A R P H I K N R H V R L N M B G
H A M O L J M M A I M E X U E M N T
R P D N R O W M E W G R A G N I R Y
M Q D U R W Y T T L X H N V M J B R
T K M N J F G Z N F E Z T E E D H M
M K I J M W W M I K L C E N W S E L
R N Z M Q J R B O L G D H L X H T K
G K T T R N T D N M E L N B L K G L
M J H T R H K P A R V Q K E B L K K
L C F S U O I C A R G G H V E M Q D
Z W W F H Q Z G W R M T H A L O P L
H H M E A L T I M E E N N B X A L Y
K H K J Z B D F K B N E P N T B K C
Y J I M O A N R Y N D K C C V K X Y

ANOINT
BETHELHEM
CONCEPTION
ELIMELECH
FAMINE
GLEANED
GRACIOUS
JUDAH
MAHLON
MARA
MEALTIME
MIDNIGHT
MOAB
MORNING
NAOMI
NURSE
ORPAH
REDEEMING
SANDAL
SHEAVES

MULTIPLE CHOICE: **Women in the Bible**

1 Who was the mother of John the Baptist?

A. Elizabeth
B. Mary
C. Eunice
D. Priscilla

2 Who begged her sister for some mandrakes, hoping they would help her bear children?

A. Rebekah
B. Rachel
C. Rahab
D. Ruth

3 To what woman did Jesus declare, "I am the resurrection and the life"?

A. Mary
B. Martha
C. Mahlah
D. Matred

4 Who sat at Jesus' feet while her sister kept house?

A. Mary
B. Martha
C. Mahlah
D. Matred

5 What two women witnessed Jesus' tears over their dead brother?

A. Elizabeth and Mary
B. Eunice and Euodias
C. Mary and Martha
D. Rhoda and Mary

6 What disciple's mother-in-law was healed of a fever by Jesus?

A. Mark
B. Peter
C. Luke
D. Timothy

MULTIPLE CHOICE: **Women in the Bible**

1 Who offered to bear the guilt if her scheme to deceive her old husband was found out?

A. Rachel
B. Rahab
C. Rhoda
D. Rebekah

2 Which of Jacob's wives was the first to bear children?

A. Leah
B. Rachel
C. Rebekah
D. Rahab

3 What woman was called a prophetess by Luke?

A. Priscilla
B. Dorcas
C. Anna
D. Rhoda

4 Who called Jesus "Rabboni"?

A. Mary, mother of Jesus
B. Mary, mother of John
C. Mary Magdalene
D. Mary, Martha's sister

5 What wife, seeing her husband on the verge of death, circumcised their son?

A. Miriam
B. Zipporah
C. Rahab
D. Deborah

6 What woman gave needed courage to the fainthearted military man Barak?

A. Deborah
B. Hannah
C. Abigail
D. Rahab

WORD SEARCH: **Over 100 Years Old**

```
J R X T B N M T R Y S E S O M
G O K T V O L E A M H S I L Z
F P S T T R C Q L Q G H V L M
X Y M H T A T E R A H T P A T
W L G E U A J O S E P H H K Z
A D A M T A B H H Z Y A Q K B
G P F L L H T O I A R Y A Z M
E L C T P E U S C B O D N A H
N A Z A S B A S A A A N H C G
O M N D I A R R E I J A T D R
C E H M C N G L O L L T T E R
H C A R R K A H R A A R J R B
X H R Z X T E N L G N H Y A L
G P A T D J K E Q L P N T J Q
T L S N N L L L J L M Y L N R
```

AARON
ABRAHAM
ADAM
CAINAN
ENOCH
ISAAC
ISHMAEL

JACOB
JARED
JEHOIADA
JOSEPH
JOSHUA
LAMECH
MAHALALEL

METHUSELAH
MOSES
NOAH
SARAH
SETH
TERAH

WORD SEARCH: **Paul's Journey**

```
A X T R O A S S X T A I C Y L Q
I G T W D C A A S I A T B D A K
N E A P O L I S C W T X Y I K S
O C L P A K J R V L H X N R N U
D B L M A N R Y M S L O C V E S
E M I H N T C M D G L V Y N R R
C S C C V X A N Z O L N P T Y A
A H R O Q M V R P G T L R M G T
M K J I L P A P A E A E U R Q G
R Q H T M O A R N N C I S P A F
H Z J N L D S E T A R M R L Z P
O M C A D C L S R S K B A Y N J
D L J G T Y V H E P Y T L F S M
E M Q C T G T R Y X I L X D L V
S N T I D M L N H A B L Z M R X
L K M D T Q F X N C Z Y G F G J
```

ANTIOCH
APPOLONIA
ASIA
COLOSSE
CYPRUS
GALATIA
LYCIA
LYSTRA
MACEDONIA
MITYLENE
NEAPOLIS
PATARA
RHODES
SALAMIS
SMYRNA
SYRIA
TARSUS
THRACE
TROAS
TYRE

WORD SEARCH: **Prodigal Son**

```
M S H O E S F W R E H T A F P
Y H T R Y T R E V O P C D W H
T X P E V Z M N W M K Z I D N
M T P G T B R M H N Z N V E O
L M X N R K I S S E D R I R S
T L F A R Z K R P R P X D E L
G C C O M P A S S I O N E H A
K E Q D D P D R K C K R D T G
D X D N O E E A S M Z G Y A I
J P M O S H N G N I Z E Z G D
S O R U T D N R R C N J N F O
W D X O S I L X U R I N C P R
I S R Z R I C E U T M N E Y P
N B N Q K T C O I K E J G D J
E Q Q H R Y J M D F V R Z D R
```

ANGER
BROTHER
COMPASSION
DANCING
DIVIDED
EMBRACED
FATHER
FIELDS
GATHERED
JOURNEY
KISSED
MUSIC
PODS
POOR
POVERTY
PRODIGAL SON
RETURNED
RING
SHOES
SINNED
SWINE

WORD SEARCH: **Prophets**

C	G	L	A	S	H	E	M	A	I	A	H	Z	R	M
X	N	E	Z	R	M	J	N	K	Q	A	L	V	N	L
B	R	U	A	W	R	O	D	M	J	J	V	X	R	M
K	D	M	R	X	H	E	D	I	O	W	A	M	O	S
U	D	A	I	A	W	L	H	H	M	K	G	K	J	M
K	R	S	A	G	N	A	N	L	P	L	X	J	Z	K
K	P	X	H	T	K	N	T	I	S	A	I	A	H	L
A	H	F	C	M	M	Y	A	W	H	Q	S	W	A	N
B	H	A	R	O	B	E	D	Q	F	K	U	N	I	A
A	B	P	J	M	J	P	N	V	N	R	B	D	N	H
H	B	S	P	I	A	E	H	Q	Y	N	A	L	A	T
N	X	F	E	E	L	H	S	B	L	N	G	P	H	A
B	Q	R	S	S	F	E	R	U	I	G	A	W	P	N
C	T	O	R	H	O	N	B	E	S	N	P	Y	E	W
I	H	C	A	L	A	M	L	M	D	R	M	K	Z	M

AGABUS
AHIJAH
AMOS
ANNA
AZARIAH
DANIEL
DEBORAH
ELIJAH
HABAKKUK
HOSEA
ISAIAH
JESUS
JOEL
JOHN
MALACHI
MOSES
NATHAN
SAMUEL
SHEMAIAH
ZEPHANIAH

WORD SEARCH: **Royal Women**

F	K	T	A	T	H	A	L	I	A	H	M	K	C	D
D	H	E	P	H	Z	I	B	A	H	A	L	O	R	C
B	J	H	X	A	R	R	W	C	A	J	Z	X	M	A
A	A	D	A	M	T	C	H	C	L	B	R	R	K	N
H	J	T	R	S	B	H	H	E	I	K	L	W	Q	D
S	E	R	H	R	S	A	S	V	R	A	M	S	T	A
U	H	O	H	S	H	A	D	U	T	O	E	K	C	C
R	O	Y	T	K	H	M	D	U	H	N	D	H	J	E
E	A	A	I	G	X	E	M	A	E	E	T	I	R	Y
J	D	L	G	A	G	A	B	P	H	A	N	T	A	W
K	D	W	G	H	H	G	H	A	N	K	T	T	H	S
Q	A	O	A	S	P	A	R	E	H	T	S	E	H	K
D	N	M	H	I	T	D	S	G	J	K	N	M	X	F
J	N	E	W	B	R	A	Z	R	Z	J	H	Q	W	M
V	L	N	V	A	S	H	T	I	G	B	A	R	E	M

ABISHAG
ASENATH
ATHALIAH
BATHSHEBA
CANDACE
COZBI
ESTHER
HADASSAH
HAGGITH
HAMUTAL
HEPHZIBAH
HERODIAS
JEHOADDAN
JERUSHA
MAACHAH
MERAB
NEHUSHTA
ROYAL WOMEN
TAHPENES
VASHTI

SOLUTIONS

Page 55

CROSSWORD: Biblical Rulers

■	1 H	2 E	3 R	4 O	5 D	■	6 D	7 A	8 V	9 I	10 D	■
11 D	E	N	U	D	E	■	12 A	M	I	N	E	13 S
14 E	R	A	S	E	S	■	15 M	E	N	T	A	L
16 G	E	M	S	■	17 T	18 H	E	N	■	19 E	R	A
20 A	T	E	■	21 O	R	E	S	■	22 G	R	I	P
23 S	O	L	24 O	M	O	N	■	25 T	U	N	E	S
■	■	■	26 P	R	Y	■	27 S	E	A	■	■	■
28 A	29 S	30 S	A	I	■	31 P	H	A	R	32 A	33 O	34 H
35 S	A	U	L	■	36 J	O	Y	S	■	37 S	P	A
38 S	U	B	■	39 S	A	I	L	■	40 S	K	I	N
41 A	N	T	42 H	E	M	■	43 O	44 U	T	I	N	G
45 M	A	L	I	C	E	■	46 C	R	A	N	E	S
■	47 S	E	P	T	S	■	48 K	I	N	G	S	■

Page 56

VERSE DECODER: Bible Passages

1 solution:

And Abraham hastened into the tent unto Sarah, and said, make ready quickly three measures of fine meal, knead it, and make cakes upon the hearth.
Genesis 18:6

MULTIPLE CHOICE: People: Saints and Sinners

1 solution: **A**; 2 solution: **D**; 3 solution: **B**.

VERSE DECODER: Bible Passages

2 solution:

And Aaron said unto them break off the golden earrings which are in the ears of your wives of your sons and of your daughters and bring them unto me.
Exodus 32:2

Page 57

CROSSWORD: Biblical Women

1 B	2 O	3 A	■	4 C	5 A	6 S	7 A	■	8 J	9 A	10 R	11 S
12 O	R	B	■	13 A	L	I	T	■	14 O	B	O	E
15 L	E	I	■	16 B	A	T	H	17 S	H	E	B	A
18 D	O	G	19 M	A	S	■	20 L	I	N	D	E	N
■	■	21 A	I	L	■	22 D	E	N	S	■	■	■
23 E	24 L	I	S	A	25 B	E	T	H	■	26 A	27 D	28 S
29 M	A	L	T	■	30 A	L	E	■	31 G	L	E	E
32 U	P	S	■	33 P	R	I	S	34 C	I	L	L	A
■	■	■	35 O	H	M	S	■	36 A	G	E	■	■
37 G	38 R	39 A	T	I	A	■	40 S	C	O	L	41 D	42 S
43 H	E	P	H	Z	I	44 B	A	H	■	45 U	R	L
46 E	L	S	E	■	47 D	A	T	E	■	48 I	I	I
49 E	Y	E	R	■	50 S	H	E	D	■	51 A	P	T

Page 58

MULTIPLE CHOICE: People: Saints and Sinners

1 solution: **C**; 2 solution: **B**; 3 solution: **C**;
4 solution: **D**; 5 solution: **C**.

VERSE DECODER: Bible Passages

1 solution:

Be not thou therefore ashamed of the testimony of our LORD, nor of me his prisoner: but be thou partaker of the afflictions of the gospel according to the power of God;
2 Timothy 1:8

SOLUTIONS

Page 59

CROSSWORD: Angelic Orders

1 A	2 B	3 B	4 A	■	5 A	6 L	7 E	■	8 C	9 H	10 A	11 P
12 P	I	U	S	■	13 S	A	L	■	14 H	E	R	O
15 S	E	R	A	16 P	H	I	M	■	17 R	A	I	N
18 E	R	N	■	19 A	E	R	■	20 B	I	L	L	Y
■	■	■	21 C	U	R	■	22 H	A	S	■	■	■
23 P	24 A	25 P	A	L	■	26 V	I	R	T	27 U	28 E	29 S
30 A	S	A	N	■	31 J	I	M	■	32 I	N	T	O
33 T	H	R	34 O	N	E	S	■	35 P	A	E	A	N
■	■	■	36 N	U	T	■	37 P	E	N	■	■	■
38 T	39 U	40 R	I	N	■	41 S	E	A	■	42 A	43 V	44 A
45 E	P	I	C	■	46 C	H	E	R	47 U	B	I	M
48 E	T	T	A	■	49 H	E	N	■	50 B	E	N	E
51 N	O	E	L	■	52 A	S	S	■	53 I	L	E	S

Page 60

MULTIPLE CHOICE: People: Saints and Sinners

1 solution: **B**; 2 solution: **C**; 3 solution: **C**;
4 solution: **C**; 5 solution: **D**; 6 solution: **C**.

Page 61

CROSSWORD: Heavenly Notes

1 S	2 O	3 N	4 G	■	5 J	6 A	7 Y	■	8 S	9 A	10 K	11 E
12 O	N	O	R	■	13 O	R	A	■	14 W	R	I	T
15 S	E	R	A	16 P	H	I	M	■	17 A	C	T	S
■	■	■	18 V	A	N	■	■	19 A	S	H	■	■
20 A	21 N	22 G	E	L	■	23 M	24 I	C	H	A	25 E	26 L
27 S	I	O	N	■	28 M	O	D	E	■	29 N	B	A
30 F	L	O	■	31 H	E	R	O	D	■	32 G	E	M
33 O	L	D	■	34 E	T	A	L	■	35 S	E	R	B
36 G	A	B	37 R	I	E	L	■	38 S	A	L	T	S
■	■	39 O	A	R	■	■	40 D	I	M	■	■	■
41 A	42 R	O	D	■	43 C	44 H	E	R	U	45 B	46 I	47 M
48 S	A	K	I	■	49 R	I	A	■	50 E	E	R	O
51 P	E	S	O	■	52 O	D	D	■	53 L	E	V	I

Page 62

MULTIPLE CHOICE: People: Saints and Sinners

1 solution: **B**; 2 solution: **C**; 3 solution: **B**;
4 solution: **D**; 5 solution: **B**.

VERSE DECODER: Bible Passages

1 solution:

And the King appointed them a daily provision of the King's meat, and of the wine which he drank: so nourishing them three years, that at the end thereof they might stand before the King.
Daniel 1:5

SOLUTIONS

Page 63

CROSSWORD: Places in the Bible

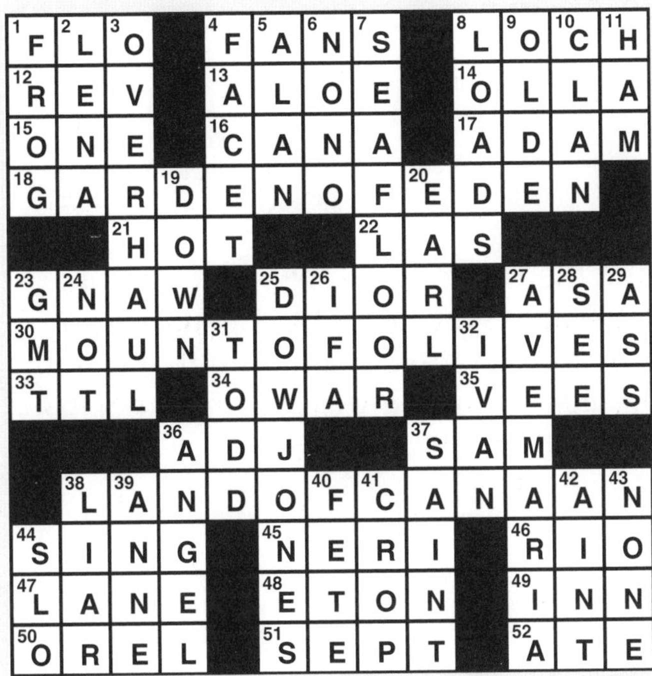

Page 64

VERSE DECODER: Bible Passages

1 solution:

And they took them wives of the women of Moab; the name of the one was Orpah, and the name of the other Ruth: And they dwelled there about ten years. Ruth 1:4

MULTIPLE CHOICE: People: Saints and Sinners

1 solution: **C**; 2 solution: **B**; 3 solution: **B**;

4 solution: **B**; 5 solution: **A**.

Page 65

MULTIPLE CHOICE: People: Saints and Sinners

1 solution: **C**; 2 solution: **B**; 3 solution: **A**;

4 solution: **D**; 5 solution: **D**; 6 solution: **B**.

Page 66

CROSSWORD: Righteous Brothers

1 R	2 A	3 U	4 L	■	5 A	6 L	7 A	■	8 O	9 V	10 A	11 L
12 U	C	L	A	■	13 D	A	B	■	14 S	A	G	E
15 T	H	A	T	16 L	O	V	E	17 T	H	N	O	T
18 H	E	N	C	E	■	19 A	L	E	E	■	■	■
■	■	■	20 H	U	21 E	■	■	22 N	A	23 D	24 I	25 R
26 E	27 A	28 S	E	■	29 L	30 A	31 M	E	■	32 A	B	A
33 T	H	A	T	34 I	S	W	I	T	35 H	H	I	M
36 C	O	N	■	37 M	E	L	T	■	38 E	L	D	S
39 H	Y	D	40 R	A	■	■	41 T	42 A	I	■	■	■
■	■	■	43 A	M	44 E	45 N	■	46 C	R	47 A	48 S	49 S
50 W	51 O	52 R	K	S	W	E	53 R	E	E	V	I	L
54 A	L	O	E	■	55 E	R	A	■	56 S	O	L	O
57 S	E	T	S	■	58 R	O	W	■	59 S	W	O	P

Page 67

MULTIPLE CHOICE: People: Saints and Sinners

1 solution: **C**; 2 solution: **D**; 3 solution: **B**;

4 solution: **A**; 5 solution: **B**.

VERSE DECODER: Bible Passages

1 solution:

Thus saith Cyrus King of Persia, the LORD God of heaven hath given me all the kingdoms of the earth; and he hath charged me to build him an house at Jerusalem, which is in Judah.
Ezra 1:2

SOLUTIONS

Page 68

VERSE DECODER: Bible Passages

1 solution:

Now in the twenty and fourth day of this month the children of Israel were assembled with fasting, and with sackclothes, and earth upon them.
Nehemiah 9:1

MULTIPLE CHOICE: People: Saints and Sinners

1 solution: **C**; 2 solution: **A**; 3 solution: **A**;

4 solution: **B**; 5 solution: **D**.

Page 69

CROSSWORD: The Wicked

1 R	2 O	3 C	4 K		5 E	6 G	7 O		8 B	9 I	10 T	11 E
12 U	G	L	I		13 G	I	L		14 A	T	O	M
15 T	R	A	N	16 S	G	R	E	17 S	S	O	R	S
18 H	E	D	G	E		19 L	O	C	I			
			20 L	A	21 C			22 A	C	23 C	24 R	25 A
26 R	27 U	28 N	E		29 H	30 E	31 R	R		32 A	I	M
33 I	S	A	T	34 R	E	E	O	F	35 L	I	F	E
36 G	E	T		37 O	W	L	S		38 O	N	E	S
39 A	D	O	40 R	N			41 A	42 R	M			
			43 I	D	44 E	45 A		46 A	B	47 A	48 S	49 H
50 C	51 A	52 N	N	O	T	M	53 Y	T	A	S	T	E
54 O	P	U	S		55 N	E	E		56 R	E	A	R
57 G	E	N	E		58 A	N	T		59 D	A	R	E

Page 70

MULTIPLE CHOICE: People: Saints and Sinners

1 solution: **B**; 2 solution: **C**; 3 solution: **B**;

4 solution: **A**; 5 solution: **A**.

VERSE DECODER: Bible Passages

1 solution:

And the rulers of the people dwelt at Jerusalem: the rest of the people also cast lots, to bring one of ten to dwell in Jerusalem the Holy City, and nine parts to dwell in other cities.
Nehemiah 11:1

Page 71

CROSSWORD: What Kind of Fool?

1 F	2 A	3 T	4 S		5 O	6 N	7 E		8 F	9 U	10 M	11 E
12 E	R	I	C		13 N	U	N		14 E	N	O	L
15 A	C	R	O	16 B	A	T	S		17 I	D	O	L
18 T	H	E	R	E	I	S	N	19 O	G	O	D	
			20 P	E	R		21 A	W	N			
22 S	23 A	24 R	I			25 I	R	E		26 B	27 U	28 S
29 I	S	C	O	30 U	31 N	T	E	D	32 W	I	S	E
33 S	P	A		34 G	E	T			35 I	B	E	X
			36 A	L	L		37 S	38 A	N			
	39 I	40 N	H	I	S	41 O	W	N	E	42 Y	43 E	44 S
45 T	R	U	E		46 O	B	E	I	S	A	N	T
47 A	I	D	A		48 N	O	D		49 A	L	O	E
50 U	S	E	D		51 S	E	E		52 P	E	S	T

SOLUTIONS

Page 72

VERSE DECODER: Bible Passages

1 solution:

There was a man in the land of Uz, whose name was Job; and that man was perfect and upright, and one that feared God, and eschewed evil.
Job 1:1

MULTIPLE CHOICE: People: Saints and Sinners

1 solution: **C**; 2 solution: **C**; 3 solution: **C**;

4 solution: **D**; 5 solution: **C**.

Page 73

CROSSWORD: Biblical Wives

■	1 C	2 O	3 S	4 E	5 C	■	6 I	7 M	8 E	9 T	10 A	■
11 R	A	C	H	E	L	■	12 S	A	L	O	M	13 E
14 E	N	T	E	R	A	■	15 T	R	I	B	A	L
16 A	T	O	M	■	17 U	18 G	L	Y	■	19 I	N	D
20 T	A	P	■	21 E	D	I	E	■	22 B	A	D	E
23 A	B	I	24 G	A	I	L	■	25 L	E	H	A	R
■	■	■	26 I	S	A	■	27 R	A	N	■	■	■
28 S	29 P	30 E	N	T	■	31 J	E	Z	E	32 B	33 E	34 L
35 A	H	S	O	■	36 S	O	B	E	■	37 E	G	O
38 R	A	T	■	39 A	T	E	E	■	40 C	A	R	R
41 A	S	H	42 A	M	E	■	43 K	44 E	E	P	E	R
45 H	E	E	D	E	R	■	46 A	V	I	A	T	E
■	47 I	R	E	N	E	■	48 H	A	L	L	S	■

Page 74

MULTIPLE CHOICE: People: Saints and Sinners

1 solution: **D**; 2 solution: **A**; 3 solution: **D**;

4 solution: **A**; 5 solution: **B**.

VERSE DECODER: Bible Passages

1 solution:

And I went up by revelation, and communicated unto them that gospel which I preach among the Gentiles, but privately to them which were of reputation, lest by any means I should run, or had run, in vain.
Galatians 2:2

Page 75

CROSSWORD: Biblical Prophets

1 P	2 E	3 A	■	4 T	5 O	6 G	7 A	■	8 S	9 I	10 D	11 E
12 E	N	S	■	13 S	U	E	Z	■	14 A	S	E	S
15 S	A	W	■	16 P	I	N	A	■	17 M	A	L	T
18 E	M	I	19 L	■	20 J	E	R	21 E	M	I	A	H
22 T	E	R	E	23 S	A	■	24 I	N	S	A	N	E
25 A	L	L	A	H	■	26 S	A	D	■	27 H	O	R
■	■	■	28 F	R	29 E	S	H	E	30 T	■	■	■
31 I	32 R	33 S	■	34 I	Z	E	■	35 A	A	36 R	37 O	38 N
39 T	O	U	40 P	E	E	■	41 E	R	M	I	N	E
42 H	A	B	A	K	K	43 U	K	■	44 P	O	S	T
45 A	M	O	S	■	46 I	R	I	47 S	■	48 T	A	T
49 C	E	R	T	■	50 E	D	N	A	■	51 E	L	L
52 A	R	N	E	■	53 L	U	G	S	■	54 D	E	E

SOLUTIONS

Page 76

MULTIPLE CHOICE: People: Saints and Sinners

1 solution: **C**; 2 solution: **B**; 3 solution: **A**;

4 solution: **D**; 5 solution: **D.**

VERSE DECODER: Bible Passages

1 solution:

Paul, a servant of God, and an apostle of Jesus Christ, according to the faith of God's elect, and the acknowledging of the truth which is after godliness;
Titus 1:1

Page 77

WORD SEARCH: Assassins

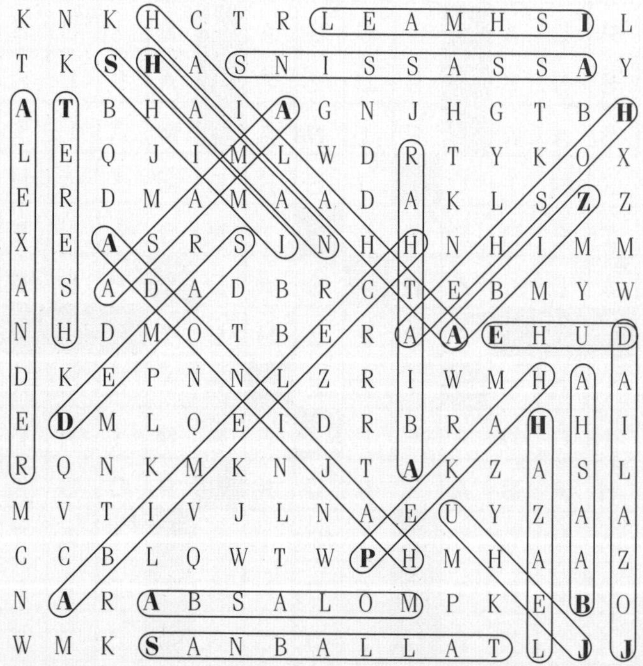

Page 78

WORD SEARCH: Biblical Names

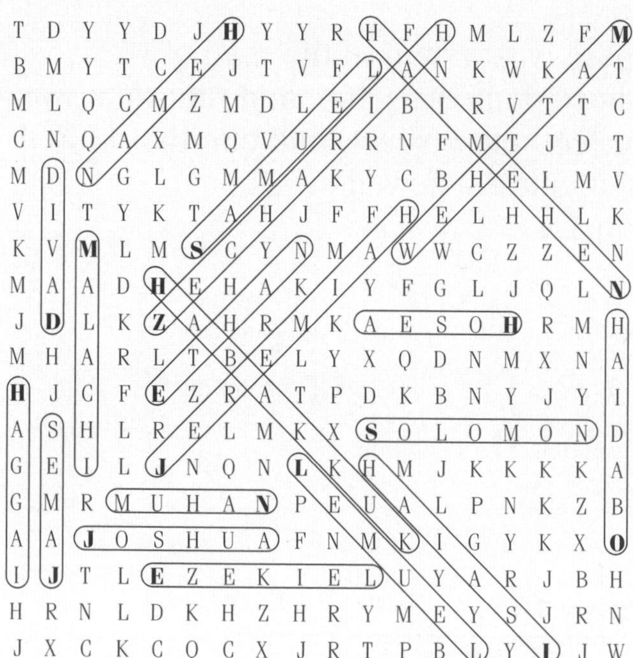

Page 79

MULTIPLE CHOICE: Royal Trivia

1 solution: **B**; 2 solution: **C**; 3 solution: **A**;

4 solution: **B**; 5 solution: **A**; 6 solution: **B.**

Page 80

MULTIPLE CHOICE: Royal Trivia

1 solution: **D**; 2 solution: **C**; 3 solution: **A**;

4 solution: **C**; 5 solution: **B**; 6 solution: **A.**

SOLUTIONS

Page 81

WORD SEARCH: Captains of the Land

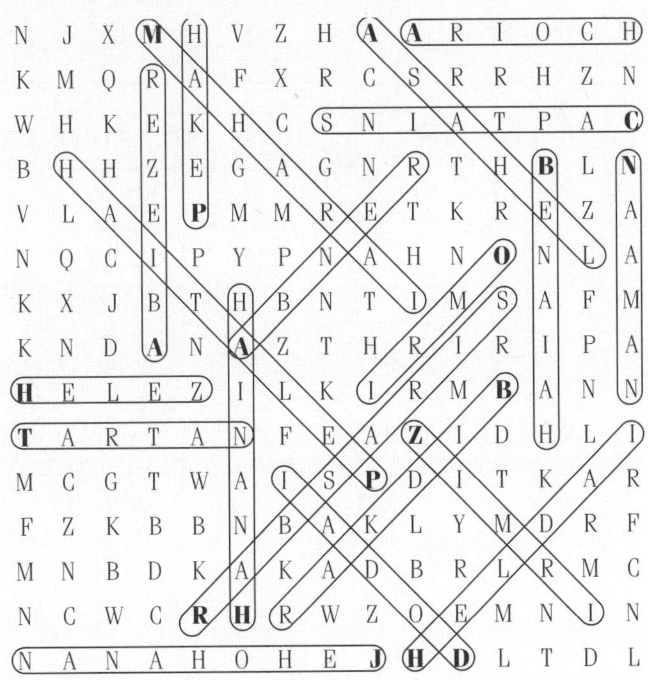

Page 82

WORD SEARCH: Daniel and the Boys

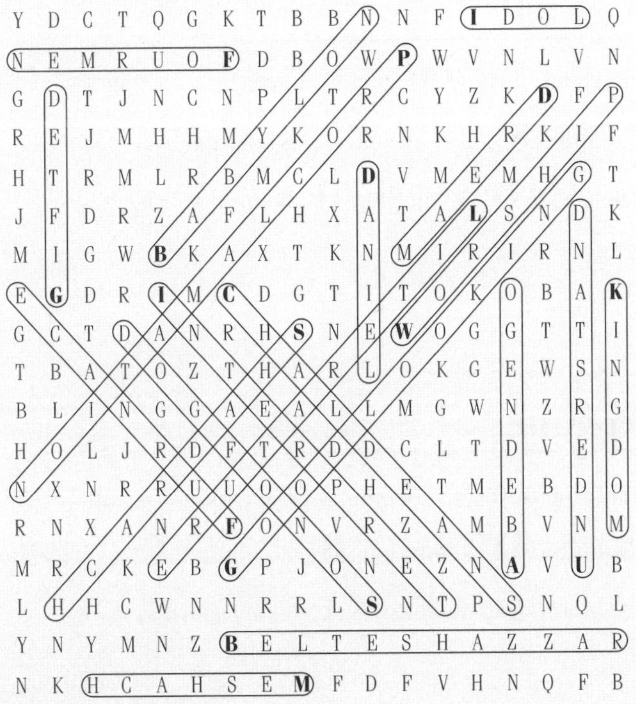

Page 83

WORD SEARCH: Dreamers and Visionaries

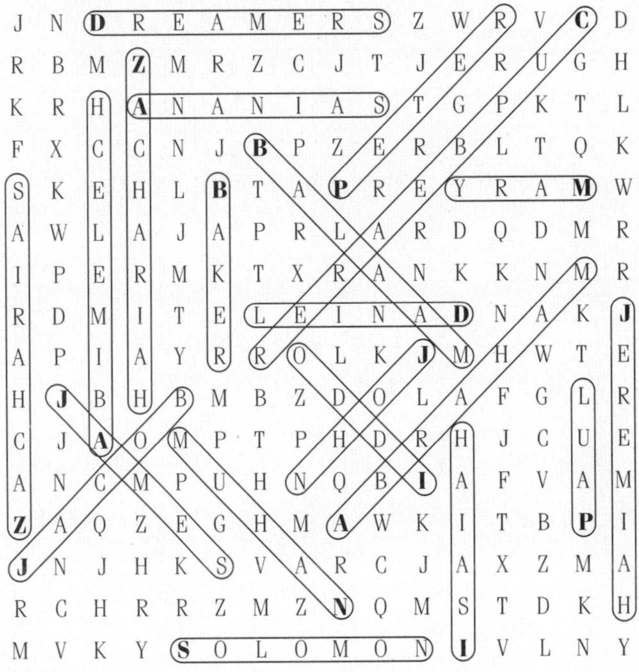

Page 84

MULTIPLE CHOICE: Men Divinely Commissioned

1 solution: **B**; 2 solution: **C**; 3 solution: **A**;

4 solution: **D**; 5 solution: **D**; 6 solution: **D.**

Page 85

MULTIPLE CHOICE: Men Divinely Commissioned

1 solution: **D**; 2 solution: **B**; 3 solution: **C**;

4 solution: **B**; 5 solution: **A**; 6 solution: **C.**

SOLUTIONS

Page 86

WORD SEARCH: Sinners and Victims

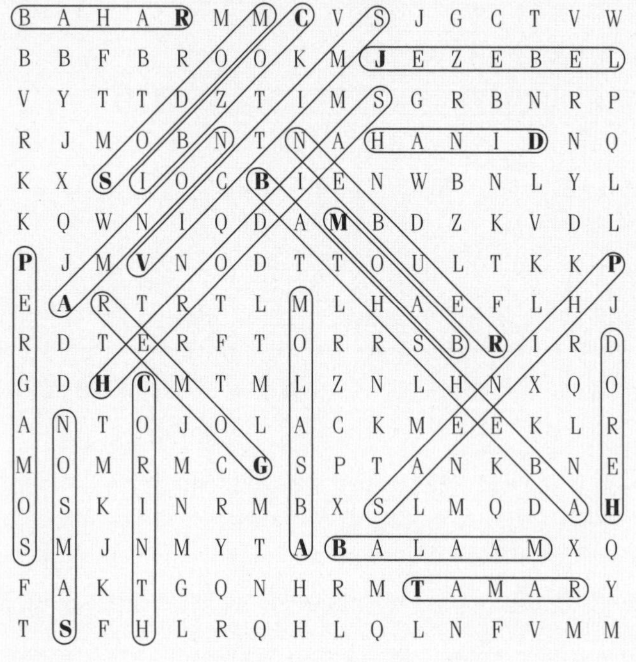

Page 87

WORD SEARCH: Giants and Enemies

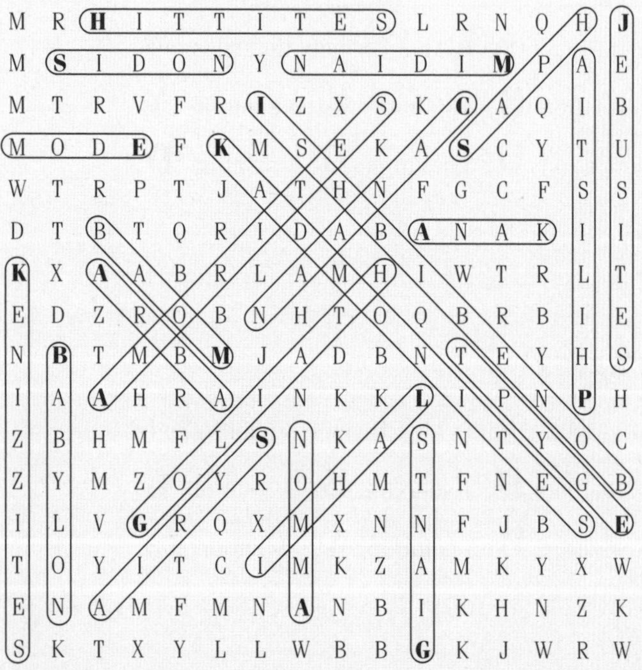

Page 88

WORD SEARCH: God Asked

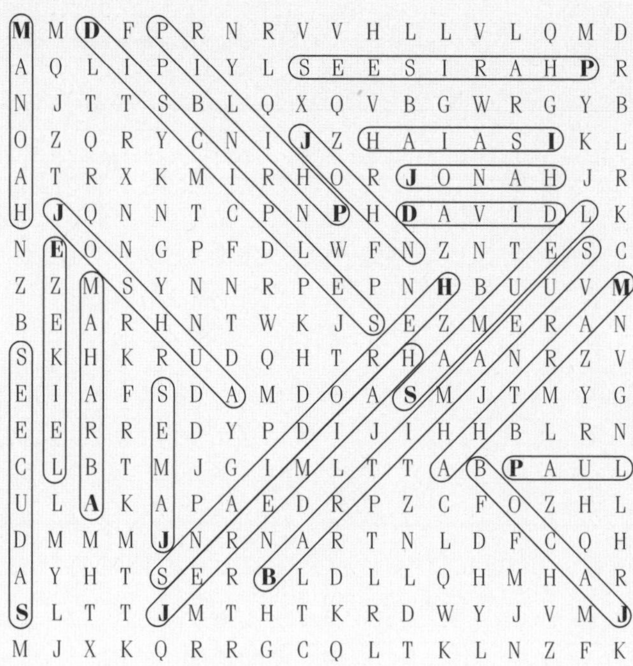

Page 89

MULTIPLE CHOICE: Wisdom is Better than Strength

1 solution: **C**; 2 solution: **A**; 3 solution: **C**;

4 solution: **D**; 5 solution: **D**; 6 solution: **A.**

Page 90

MULTIPLE CHOICE: Wisdom is Better than Strength

1 solution: **D**; 2 solution: **B**; 3 solution: **C**;

4 solution: **D**; 5 solution: **A**; 6 solution: **B.**

SOLUTIONS

Page 91

WORD SEARCH: Her Children Call Her Blessed

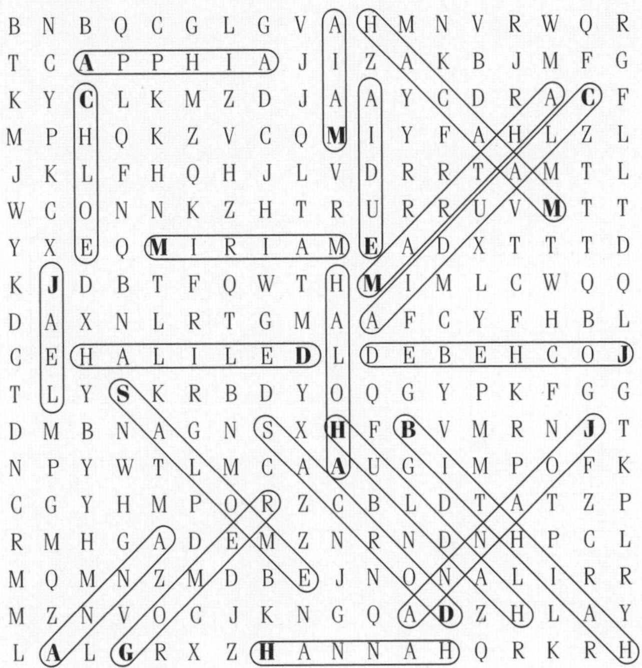

Page 92

WORD SEARCH: Holy Women

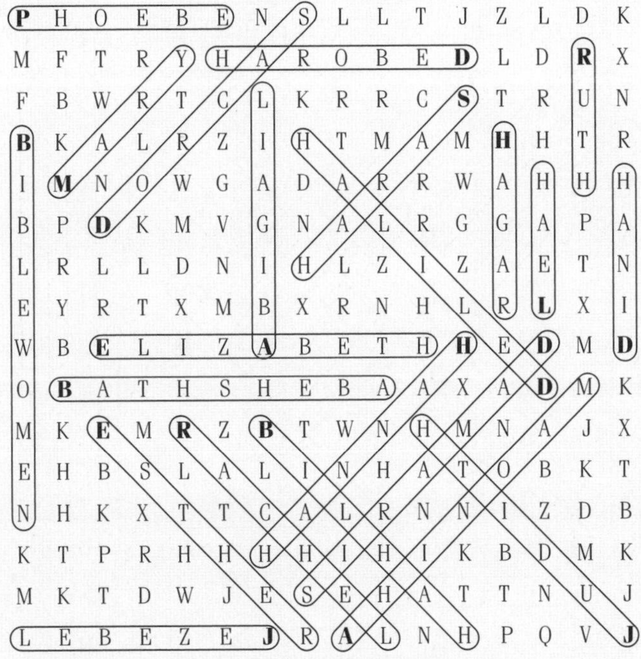

Page 93

MULTIPLE CHOICE: Women in the Bible

1 solution: **C**; 2 solution: **A**; 3 solution: **C**;
4 solution: **B**; 5 solution: **A**; 6 solution: **A.**

Page 94

MULTIPLE CHOICE: Women in the Bible

1 solution: **A**; 2 solution: **C**; 3 solution: **A**;
4 solution: **D**; 5 solution: **C**; 6 solution: **A.**

Page 95

WORD SEARCH: Heroes

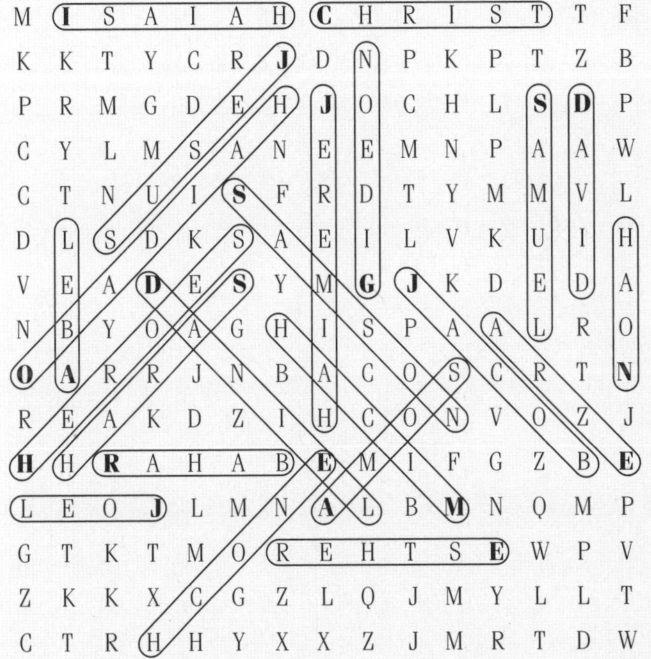

SOLUTIONS

Page 96

WORD SEARCH: Holy Men

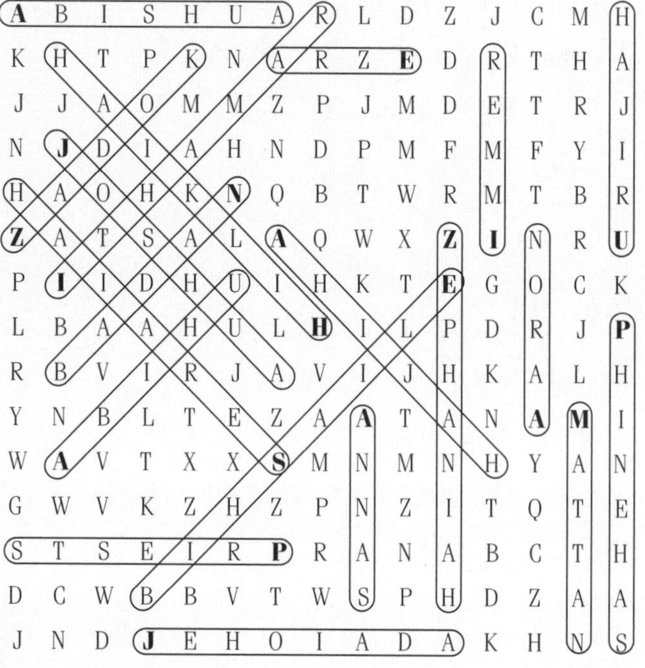

Page 97

WORD SEARCH: I Saw an Angel

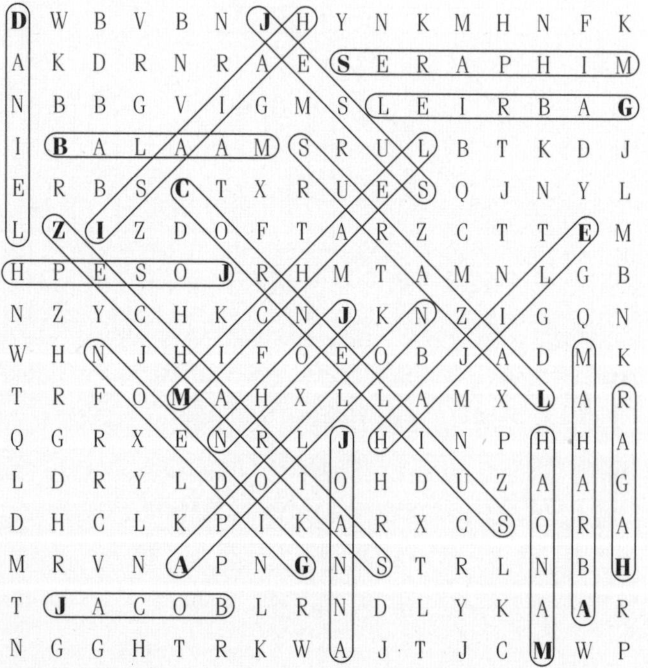

Page 98

WORD SEARCH: Jobs

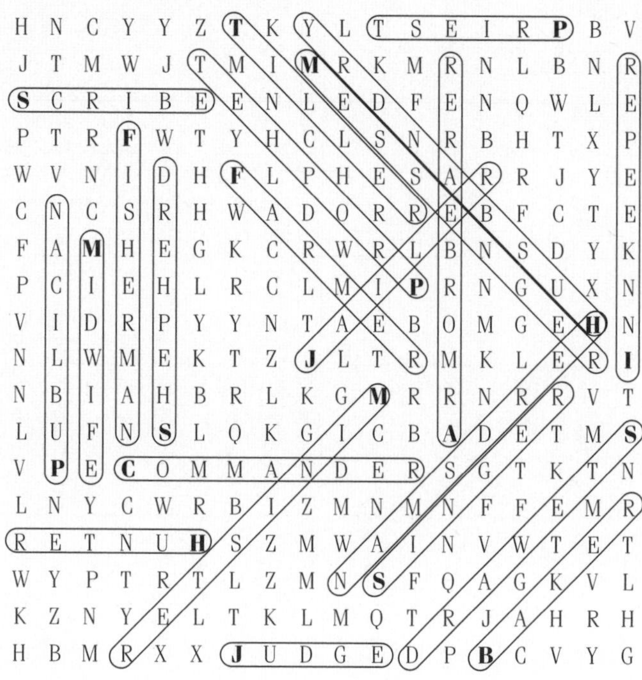

Page 99

WORD SEARCH: Judah's Progeny

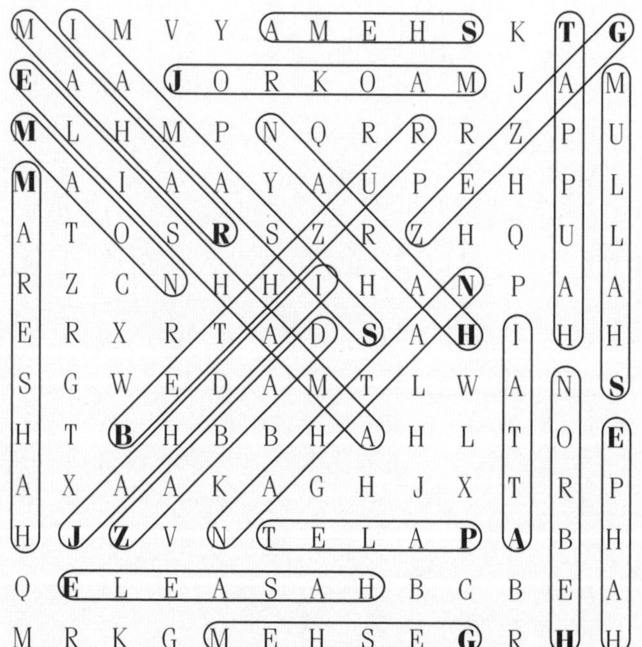

SOLUTIONS

Page 100

WORD SEARCH: King Saul's Family

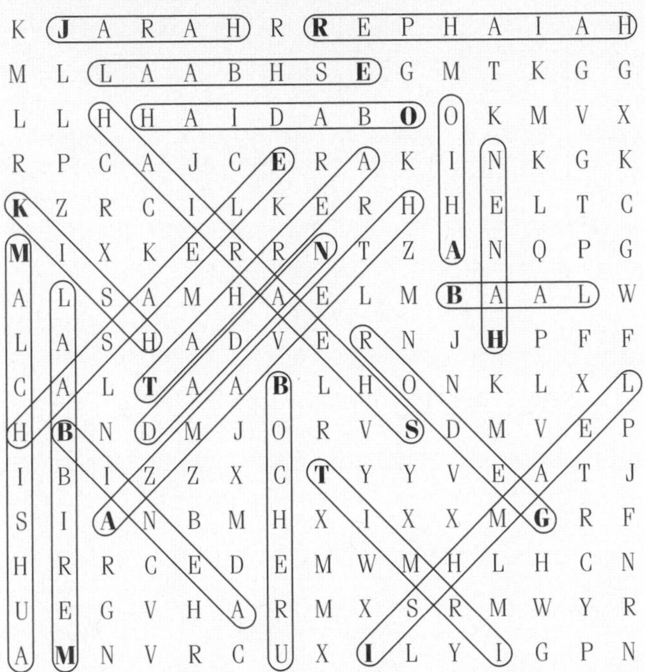

Page 102

MULTIPLE CHOICE: Women in the Bible

1 solution: **A**; 2 solution: **B**; 3 solution: **B**;
4 solution: **A**; 5 solution: **C**; 6 solution: **B.**

Page 103

MULTIPLE CHOICE: Women in the Bible

1 solution: **D**; 2 solution: **A**; 3 solution: **C**;
4 solution: **C**; 5 solution: **B**; 6 solution: **A.**

Page 101

WORD SEARCH: Naomi and Ruth

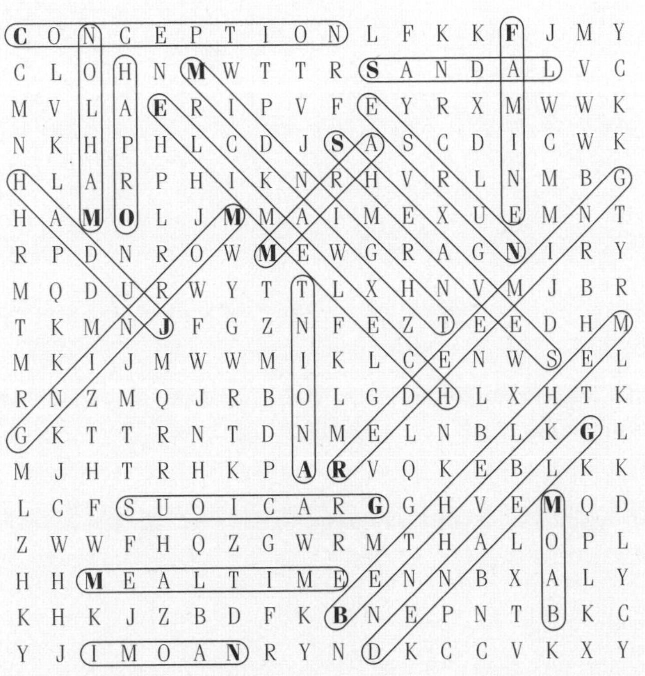

Page 104

WORD SEARCH: Over 100 Years Old

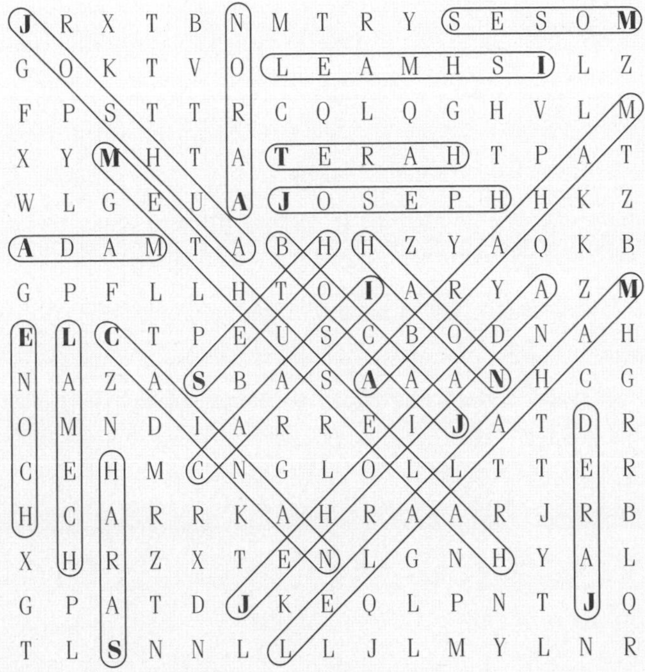

SOLUTIONS

Page 105

WORD SEARCH: Paul's Journey

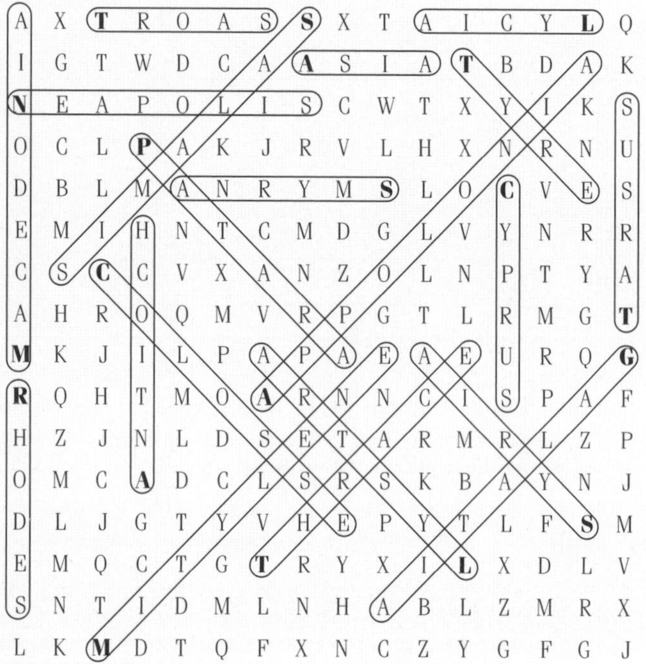

Page 106

WORD SEARCH: Prodigal Son

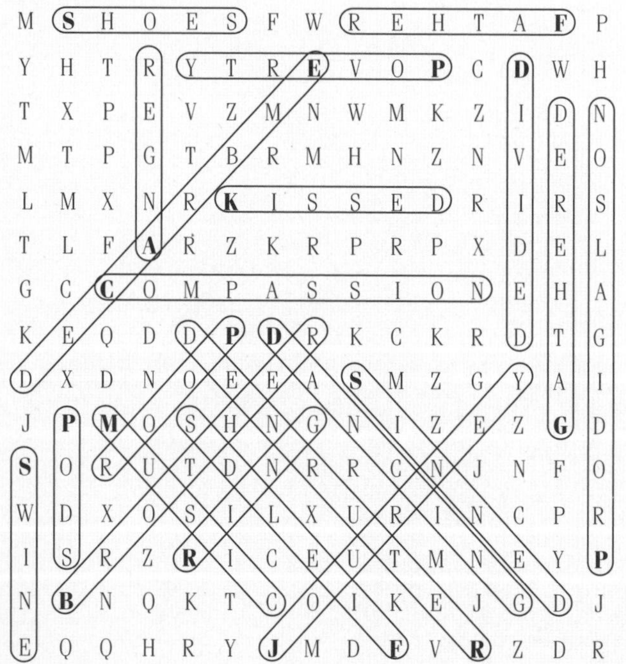

Page 107

WORD SEARCH: Prophets

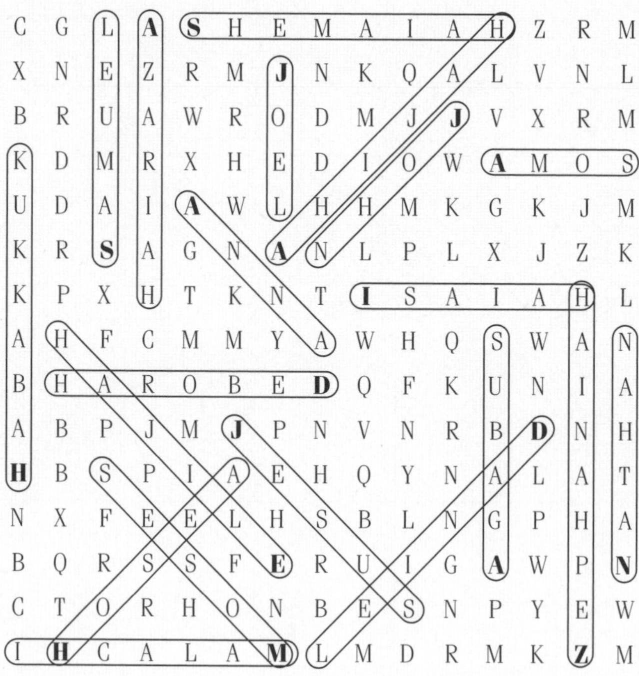

Page 108

WORD SEARCH: Royal Women

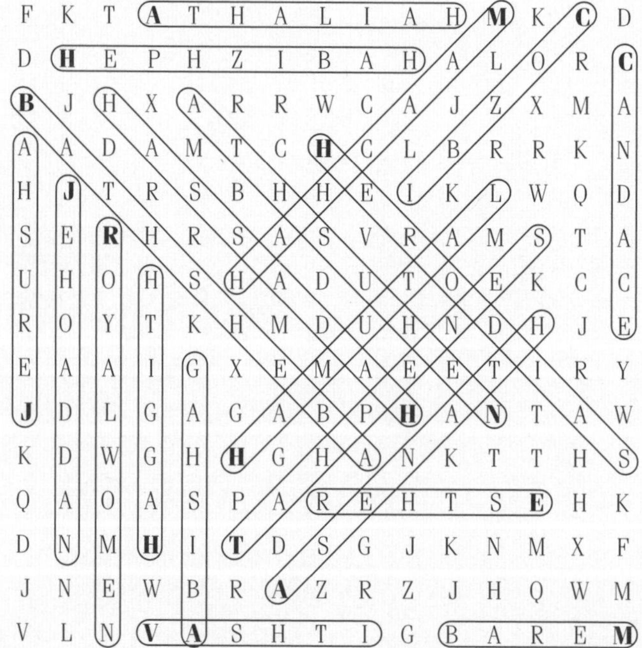

CHAPTER 3

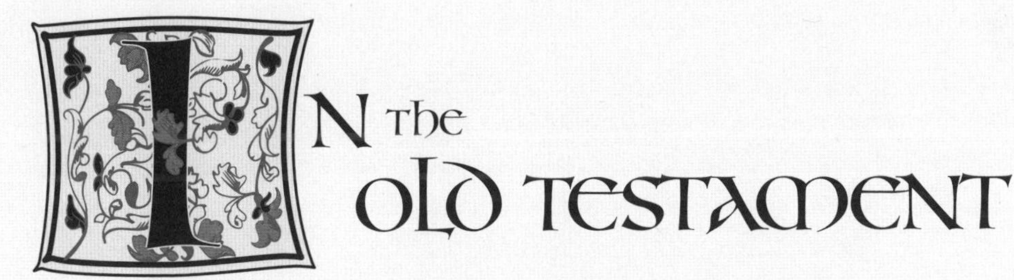

MULTIPLE CHOICE: **In the Old Testament**

1 How many years did Noah live?

A. 950 years
B. 750 years
C. 890 years
D. 670 years

2 When Moses left Egypt for the promised land, whose bones did he take along?

A. Jacob's
B. Joseph's
C. Noah's
D. Abraham's

3 Who built an altar and called it Jehovahnissi, or "The Lord is my banner"?

A. Abraham
B. Noah
C. Moses
D. Aaron

4 While being pursued by his enemies, whose hair became caught in an oak tree?

A. Absalom
B. Jonathan
C. Solomon
D. Adonijah

LETTER SQUARES:

1 **Deuteronomy 1:32**

NO	DID	ELI	NG	EVE	THI	ORD	GOD
T B	UR	TH	YE	E L	IS	TH	YET
YO	IN	,					

CROSSWORD: **Vanity**

By Joseph Mantell

1	2	3	4	■	5	6	7	■	8	9	10	11
12				■	13			■	14			
15				16				17				
18					■	19				■	■	■
■	■	■	20		21	■	■	22		23	24	25
26	27	28		■	29	30	31		■	32		
33				34					35			
36			■	37				■	38			
39			40		■	■	41	42		■	■	■
■	■	■	43		44	45	■	46		47	48	49
50	51	52					53					
54				■	55			■	56			
57				■	58			■	59			

ACROSS

1 Site of a ship's controls
5 Astern
8 Maryland cake ingredient
12 Operatic melody
13 Auto-grille protector
14 "And it is a __ thing that the king requireth" (Dan. 2:11)
15 "... for vanity shall be __" (Job 15:31) (2 words)
18 "As a __ which melteth" (Ps. 58:8)
19 Fermented honey drink
20 Prefix with life or wife
22 Heavenly body
26 Arrogant person
29 "And the men __ up from thence" (Gen. 18:16)
32 Santa __, California
33 "... __ saith the Lord God" (Ezek. 13:8) (4 words)
36 "Who __ to judge?" (2 words)
37 Jamaican citrus fruit
38 "Pharaoh's chariots and his __ hath he cast into the sea" (Ex. 15:4)
39 Gold or silver, e.g.
41 Golf course standard
43 "And saw two ships standing by the __" (Luke 5:2)
46 Initiates a phone call
50 "The Lord knoweth the __" (Ps. 94:11) (3 words)
54 "What time they wax __" (Job 6:17)
55 "Go to the __, thou sluggard" (Prov. 6:6)
56 Dorothy's companion to Oz
57 City in Iowa
58 Negative vote
59 Apply spin

DOWN

1 Exclamations of surprise
2 Ireland, romantically
3 Da Vinci's Mona
4 Xylophone-like instrument
5 Grade-school song start
6 "Cease ye __ man" (Isa. 2:22)
7 Make the wild mild
8 System of beliefs
9 Was on the ballot
10 Circle portion
11 Stinging pest
16 Priest of Israel who looked after Samuel
17 Walks back and forth
21 Air resistance
23 Deli spread (abbr.)
24 Grandson of Adam
25 Without any slack
26 Thailand, once
27 "The __ of the first is Pison" (Gen. 2:11)
28 Leave out
30 "__ for the light" (Ex. 25:6)
31 Salon sound
34 Russian prison camp
35 Penny-pinchings
40 Grads
42 "Much __ About Nothing"
44 Genghis or Kubla
45 Volcano in Sicily
47 Berserk
48 "Even of __ my people is risen up ..." (Micah 2:8)
49 "If I wash myself with __ water" (Job 9:30)
50 Former U.S. airline
51 Son of Noah
52 Lode product
53 Pig's digs

MULTIPLE CHOICE: **In the Old Testament**

1 Who lied to Ahab about the result of a battle?

A. Iddo **B.** Micaiah **C.** Micah **D.** Azariah

2 Whose brothers were imprisoned after being falsely accused of being spies in Egypt?

A. Job's **B.** Jacob's **C.** Joseph's **D.** Joshua's

3 What judge built an altar and called it Jehovahshalom, or "The Lord is peace"?

A. Othniel **B.** Gideon **C.** Moses **D.** Aaron

4 Whose lips were touched by a coal from the altar in the temple?

A. Aaron **B.** Isaiah **C.** Jeremiah **D.** Elijah

5 Who went mad as a result of a prideful heart?

A. Nehum **B.** Pedaiah **C.** Nebuchadnezzar **D.** Jeroham

6 When God said, "Before I formed thee in the belly I knew thee." Who was He speaking to?

A. Jeremiah **B.** John **C.** Jehoshaphat **D.** Joshua

VERSE DECODER:

1 **Amos 1:6**

HINT: In the puzzle below, the letter "K" is actually a "T."

KADY YHLKA KAO MWFZ; UWF KAFOO KFHTYEFOYYLWTY WU EHXH, HTZ

UWF UWDF, L JLMM TWK KDFT HJHQ KAO IDTLYAVOTK KAOFOWU;

GOBHDYO KAOQ BHFFLOZ HJHQ BHIKLRO KAO JAWMO BHIKLRLKQ,

KW ZOMLROF KAOV DI KW OZWV:

CROSSWORD: **Old Testament Books**

By Thomas W. Schier

1	2	3	4	■	5	6	7	8	■	9	10	11
12				■	13				■	14		
15				16					17			
■	■	■	18				■	■	19			
20	21	22					23	24				
25				■	■	26			■	■	■	■
27				28	29	■	30		31	32	33	34
■	■	■	■	35		36	■	■	37			
38	39	40	41				42	43				
44				■	■	45				■	■	■
46				47	48					49	50	51
52			■	53				■	54			
55			■	56				■	57			

ACROSS

1 Water-to-wine town
5 "..., and it shall be thy __" (Ex. 29:26)
9 Noah's son
12 Sensory stimulant
13 Together, in music
14 Honest president?
15 Two OT books (3 words)
18 "And God __ the firmament" (Gen. 1:7)
19 "As an eagle stirreth up her __" (Deut. 32:11)
20 Two OT books (3 words)
25 Jai __
26 Drop of gel
27 Señor on the Sullivan show
30 Perfumed ointment
35 Spanish aunt
37 *Night* author Wiesel
38 Two OT books (3 words)
44 This, señora
45 Mythical queen of Carthage
46 Two OT books (3 words)
52 Actress Zadora
53 *Green Mansions* girl
54 OT book
55 French possessive
56 Slangy snack
57 Lyricist Lorenz

DOWN

1 Runner Sebastian
2 Wood-dressing tool (variant)
3 "... will not fail thee, __ forsake thee" (Josh. 1:5)
4 Biblical language
5 National zoo animal
6 Number next to a plus sign
7 Wish one could take back
8 ___-Mex food
9 Mythical hell
10 Mistreatment
11 River of Thrace or hostess Perle
16 Checkup sound
17 Yoko __
20 "... with the __ of an ass ..." (Judg. 15:16)
21 Grand __ Opry
22 One of the Bobbsey twins
23 Skip, as a stone on water
24 Cable station
28 LAX guesstimate
29 Go against God's commandments
31 Hanukkah centerpiece
32 1996 Olympic torch lighter
33 "Ye shall not surely __" (Gen. 3:4)
34 Serpentine swimmer
36 Uncle Fester or Morticia
38 WWII vehicles
39 Actor Davis
40 Kett and James
41 ___-di-dah
42 Leah's daughter
43 Say a bit more
47 Flying fish-eater
48 Brazilian city, for short
49 Actress Thurman
50 Rocky pinnacle
51 FDR's successor

LETTER SQUARES: **In the Old Testament**

1 Deuteronomy 6:4

E L	R D :	T H	O R D	E L :	S R A	I S	R G
R ,	O D	H E A	O U	L O	O I	O N E	

MULTIPLE CHOICE:

1 Who slept at Bethel and dreamed about angels?

A. Esau **B.** Eli **C.** Joseph **D.** Jacob

2 What boy was awakened out of his sleep by the voice of God?

A. Samuel **B.** Aaron **C.** David **D.** Josiah

3 Who was the first man to have more than one wife?

A. Adam **B.** Abel **C.** Cain **D.** Lamech

4 Which book of the Bible begins, "How doth the city sit solitary, that was full of people!"

A. Isaiah **B.** Lamentations **C.** Daniel **D.** Ezekiel

VERSE DECODER:

1 Ezra 10:8
HINT: In the puzzle below, the letter "Q" is actually a "T."

SEL QUSQ NUIKIYZYV NIDCL EIQ TIOY NMQUME QUVYY LSWK, STTIVLMER

QI QUY TIDEKYC IP QUY FVMETYK SEL QUY YCLYVK, SCC UMK KDGKQSETY

KUIDCL GY PIVPYMQYL, SEL UMOKYCP KYFSVSQYL PVIO QUY TIERVYRSQMIE

IP QUIKY QUSQ USL GYYE TSVVMYL SNSW.

CROSSWORD: **Praises**

By Rowan Millson

ACROSS

1 Windbag?
5 "... of wines on the __ well refined" (Isa. 25:6)
9 "Because thou saidst, __, against my sanctuary" (Eze. 25:3)
12 Balm ingredient, perhaps
13 First gardener?
14 Brooklyn Dodger sobriquet
15 "And the __ man shall be brought down" (Isa. 5:15)
16 Org. for Senator Glenn
17 Ginger __ (soda choice)
18 "Get thee __" (Matt. 16:23) (3 words)
21 Tree with tough, useful wood
22 "Ten-__!"
23 __ chi (martial art)
26 Direction of Nod from Eden
29 Part of the mezzanine
32 "Get wisdom, get __" (Prov. 4:5)
35 Ill-mannered type
36 "... and his commandments are __" (Ps. 111:7)
37 Floor cover
38 Pastureland
40 Boston party drink
42 "And I will get them __ ..." (Zeph. 3:19) (3 words)
49 Gone for the day
50 "... and they could not __ him" (Matt. 17:16)
51 "... thou shalt not lift up any iron __ upon them" (Deut. 27:5)
52 "I am the voice of __ crying in the wilderness" (John 1:23)
53 Food morsels
54 He lived for 905 years
55 For every
56 Yo-yos and pogo sticks
57 Descartes or Russo

DOWN

1 "Behold the __ of God" (John 1:29)
2 "Golden" role for Peter Fonda
3 Father of Japheth, Ham and Shem
4 Three wishes giver of myth
5 Asia, for one
6 Mild cheese
7 Comfort
8 Good kind of hit
9 Slaughterhouse
10 Hawaiian dance
11 End of The Lord's Prayer
19 NY Met, e.g.
20 "__ Lang Syne"
23 Place for a soak?
24 *Wheel of Fortune* selection
25 Golden calf adorer, for one
27 R-V connection?
28 Sourness
30 Bearded antelope
31 "... is there any taste in the white of an __?" (Job 6:6)
33 "Able was I __ saw Elba" (2 words)
34 "For ye have __ of patience" (Heb. 10:36)
39 Broad necktie
41 "And it came to pass __ seven days" (Gen. 7:10)
42 Certain ship deck
43 Ancient alphabetic symbol
44 Continental currency
45 Pretentious, in a way
46 Tip-top
47 "Praise ye him, sun and __" (Ps. 148:3)
48 "Give me children, or __ I die" (Gen. 30:1)

LETTER SQUARES: **In the Old Testament**

1 **Exodus 12:47**

A T I	E P	O F	A L L	E C	T H	O N	A E L
I S R	I T .	S H	O N G	R E G	A L L	K E	

MULTIPLE CHOICE:

1 Who was married to Jezebel?

A. Agag
B. Agee
C. Ader
D. Ahab

2 What prophet refused to use anointing oils during a mourning period of three weeks?

A. Nathan
B. Joel
C. Daniel
D. Isaiah

3 To avoid the wrath of Saul, who hid in caves?

A. David
B. Jonathan
C. Solomon
D. Samuel

LETTER SQUARES:

2 **Jonah 1:15**

N A H	:	U P	O O K	F O R	T H	Y T	H E
T H	S E A	O T	S O	C A S	T H E	J O	, A
N D	I M	I N T					

LETTER SQUARES: **In the Old Testament**

1 **Jonah 4:4**

O R D	O E S	H O U	L L	T T	, D	A I D	T H E
E L	B E	W E	R Y ?	T H	A N G	T O	N S

MULTIPLE CHOICE:

1 The men of Israel laughed at whose decree for a Passover celebration?

A. Isaiah **B.** Hezekiah **C.** Saul **D.** David

2 Othniel was the first judge of Israel. Who followed him as the second?

A. Samuel **B.** Jehu **C.** Deborah **D.** Ehud

3 Which father of twelve sons had a father who became blind in his old age?

A. Jacob **B.** Abraham **C.** Isaac **D.** Job

4 Visitors to which city struck sinful men with blindness?

A. Ephesus **B.** Dan **C.** Sodom **D.** Gomorrah

VERSE DECODER:

1 **Exodus 6:1**

HINT: In the puzzle below, the letter "P" is actually an "E."

YWPX YWP KABM OVJM TXYA IAOPO, XAN OWVKY YWAT OPP NWVY J NJKK MA

YA RWVBVAW: SAB NJYW V OYBAXD WVXM OWVKK WP KPY YWPI DA, VXM

NJYW V OYBAXD WVXM OWVKK WP MBJGP YWPI ATY AS WJO KVXM.

CROSSWORD: **Honor**

By Joseph Mantell

1	2	3	4		5	6	7		8	9	10	11
12					13				14			
15				16				17				
18						19						
			20		21			22		23	24	25
26	27	28			29	30	31			32		
33				34					35			
36				37					38			
39			40				41	42				
			43		44	45		46		47	48	49
50	51	52					53					
54					55				56			
57					58				59			

ACROSS

1 In baseball, it's grand
5 Health resort
8 Son of Noah
12 Verdi opera
13 Be unwell
14 "Then the king arose, and __ his garments" (2 Sam. 13:31)
15 "A __ retaineth honour: and strong men retain riches" (Prov. 11:16) (2 words)
18 Brazilian dance
19 Head for the heavens
20 "And it came to pass at the __ of forty days" (Gen. 8:6)
22 "The __ saith, 'It is not in me'" (Job 28:14)
26 "At the __ it biteth like a serpent" (Prov. 23:32)
29 Seep
32 Baseball manager Piniella
33 "I will speak __ honour of thy majesty" (Ps. 145:5) (3 words)
36 Woman's garment
37 Make over
38 Commonly held false notion
39 Dolphin detector
41 Janitor's implement
43 Bag style
46 Called one's bluff
50 "__ honour come of thee" (1 Chron. 29:12) (3 words)
54 Muffin spread
55 Fraternity letter
56 Greek portico
57 Desires
58 Apply bread to gravy
59 "For my yoke is __, and my burden is light" (Matt. 11:30)

DOWN

1 Droops
2 Former Italian currency
3 Garden of Eden tender
4 Shakespeare character
5 __ Paulo (Brazilian city)
6 Name of 12 popes
7 Likewise
8 "Blessed shall be thy basket and thy __" (Deut. 28:5)
9 Brother of Japheth
10 Notable time period
11 "Young __ likewise exhort to be sober minded" (Titus 2:6)
16 Author Fleming
17 Long-legged bird
21 Chief official of Venice or Genoa
23 Tactical maneuver
24 Show off
25 Fall silent
26 High-arced tennis returns
27 Hair style
28 Hall-of-famer Musial
30 Like Methuselah
31 Certain lens
34 Misplay
35 Negotiation situation
40 One of the Three Musketeers
42 Keats' forte
44 Waiter's mainstay
45 Sound return
47 Pro __ (proportionately)
48 He lived for 905 years
49 June 6, 1944
50 Man-to-be
51 Matador's encouragement
52 Countdown starter
53 Body joint

King James Games Facts:

The verse (Psalms 118:8), "It is better to trust in the Lord than to put confidence in man," is between the shortest and longest chapters of the Bible.

LETTER SQUARES: **In the Old Testament**

1 Malachi 2:1

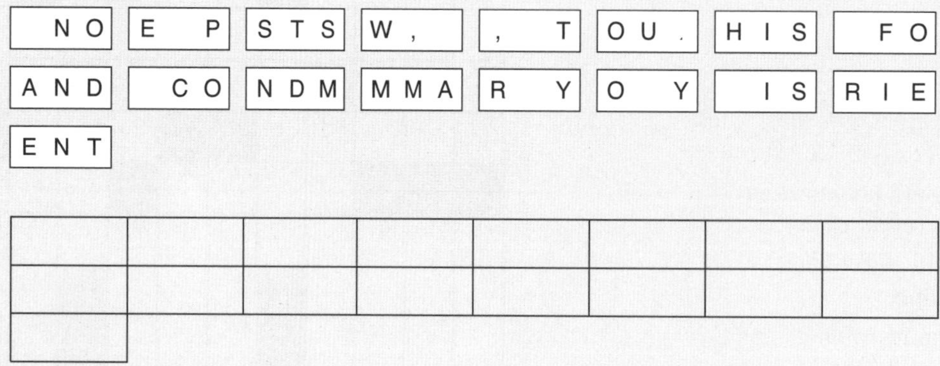

MULTIPLE CHOICE:

1 Which two tribes of Israel were descended from an Egyptian woman?

A. Reuben and Simeon
B. Manasseh and Ephraim
C. Dan and Naphtali
D. Benjamin and Judah

2 Who impressed the Queen of Sheba with his wisdom when she visited him?

A. Daniel
B. Solomon
C. King Saul
D. Job

3 Jemima was whose daughter?

A. Hosea
B. Moses
C. Job
D. Noah

4 Who rebuked David for committing murder and having an adulterous affair with Bathsheba?

A. Samuel
B. Saul
C. Uriah
D. Nathan

LETTER SQUARES: **In the Old Testament**

1 Malachi 3:6

A M	N O	T ;	I	N G E	R D ,	T H E	C H A
F O R	I	L O					

MULTIPLE CHOICE:

1 How long did it take Abraham to travel to the place where he would offer Isaac as a sacrifice?

A. Three days
B. Three weeks
C. One month
D. One year

2 Who ran away from Queen Jezebel and heard God's voice?

A. Elisha
B. Elijah
C. David
D. Gomer

3 What did the Lord rain down upon Sodom and Gomorrah?

A. Frogs
B. Locusts
C. Fire and brimstone
D. Thunder and lightning

VERSE DECODER:

1 Genesis 43:2

HINT: In the puzzle below, the letter "Y" is actually an "E."

FUC BM WFEY ML JFHH, QZYU MZYK ZFC YFMYU GJ MZY WLDU QZBWZ

MZYK ZFC VDLGXZM LGM LR YXKJM, MZYBD RFMZYD HFBC GUML MZYE,

XL FXFBU, VGK GH F NBMMNY RLLC.

CROSSWORD: **Knowledge**

By Joseph Mantell

1	2	3	4	■	5	6	7	■	8	9	10	11
12				■	13			■	14			
15				16				17				
18					■	19				■	■	■
■	■	■	20		21	■	■	22		23	24	25
26	27	28		■	29	30	31		■	32		
33				34					35			
36			■	37				■	38			
39			40		■	■	41	42		■	■	■
■	■	■	43		44	45	■	46		47	48	49
50	51	52					53					
54				■	55			■	56			
57				■	58			■	59			

ACROSS

1 Mild punishment, when applied to the wrist
5 Author Fleming
8 Church recess
12 Source of Samson's strength
13 __ Jo (Olympic athlete)
14 Horse coloring
15 "Take you wise men, and __" (Deut. 1:13)
18 Finger-lickin' good
19 Buckeye State
20 End of a British alphabet
22 Boardroom easel display
26 Adolescent's bane
29 Informal agreement
32 Grazing land
33 "__ God knowledge?" (Job 21:22) (3 words)
36 Small fruit seed
37 Scandinavian saga
38 Inquires
39 "... they cast four anchors out of the __" (Acts 27:29)
41 "Whereas thou __ been forsaken and hated" (Isa. 60:15)
43 Above
46 Supreme Ross
50 "But of the tree of the knowledge __" (Gen 2:17) (4 words)
54 Stead
55 Egg cells
56 "And Jacob said, __ me this day thy birthright" (Gen. 25:31) (4 words)
57 Farmer's place, in song
58 Confederate soldier, for short
59 A low card

DOWN

1 "And Miriam was __ out from the camp" (Num. 12:15)
2 Turner of films
3 Helps out
4 Knotted snack
5 No __, ands or buts
6 Certain choir member
7 Father of Japheth, Ham and Shem
8 Intense feeling of love
9 Maui finger food
10 Start for Diego or Francisco
11 MIT grad, perhaps
16 Type of bread
17 "... and the darkness he called __" (Gen. 1:5)
21 Couple
23 "__, poor Yorick"
24 Legendary actor Gregory
25 Exclamations of surprise
26 Egyptian cobras
27 Bill in a restaurant
28 Back of the neck
30 "The __ of all flesh is come before me" (Gen. 6:13)
31 Indian nurse
34 Slow, in music
35 Most effortless
40 French artist Dufy
42 "The Lord shall __ to me another son" (Gen. 30:24)
44 Offensive smell
45 Surface
47 Declare as true
48 World's longest river
49 Colleague
50 "And Noah was five hundred years __" (Gen. 5:32)
51 Exclamation of disgust
52 Mousse alternative
53 Get the bad guy

LETTER SQUARES: **In the Old Testament**

1 Joel 1:15

F O R	H A N	Y !	E D	L O	D .	D A	S F
O F	A T	T H E	I S	A L A	T H E	T H	O R
A Y	R D						

MULTIPLE CHOICE:

1 Jacob had twelve sons. In order, what number was Joseph?

A. 11th **B.** 9th **C.** 4th **D.** 12th

2 Which of these men followed in their father's footsteps by calling their wife their sister?

A. Adam **B.** Isaac **C.** Abel **D.** Moses

3 Out of these four sons of Jacob, who was the only one born in Canaan?

A. Judah **B.** Benjamin **C.** Joseph **D.** Levi

4 Who as a child fought and defeated the giant Goliath?

A. Samuel **B.** Jesse **C.** David **D.** Saul

5 Which of these prophets had two sons named Shear-jashub and Maher-shalal-hash-baz?

A. Jeremiah **B.** Ezekiel **C.** Isaiah **D.** Habakkuk

6 Whose mother died while giving birth to him?

A. Judah **B.** Benjamin **C.** Levi **D.** Reuben

***King James Games* Facts:**

Several verses in the King James Version of the Bible contain all the letters of the alphabet except one.

- Ezra 7:21 contains all the letters except J.
- Joshua 7:24, 1 Kings 1:9, 1 Chronicles 12:40, 2 Chronicles 36:10, Ezekiel 28:13, Daniel 4:37, and Haggai 1:1 contain all the letters except Q.
- 2 Kings 16:15 and 1 Chronicles 4:10 contain all the letters except X.
- Galatians 1:14 contains all the letters except K.

MULTIPLE CHOICE: **In the Old Testament**

1 Whose father was the wicked king Ahaz?

A. Nahum **B.** Hezekiah **C.** Malachi **D.** Zechariah

2 Joseph allowed his father and brothers to dwell in which land?

A. Moab **B.** Goshen **C.** Beulah **D.** Canaan

3 Which prophet declared that the people robbed God in their tithes and offerings?

A. Zephaniah **B.** Malachi **C.** Micah **D.** Hosea

4 Who was the brother of Rebekah and father of Rachel and Leah?

A. Laadan **B.** Kohath **C.** Laban **D.** Lamech

VERSE DECODER:

1 Genesis 28:12

HINT: In the puzzle below, the letter "H" is actually an "A."

HSC GQ CWQHJQC, HSC RQGNBC H BHCCQW OQX DT NS XGQ QHWXG,

HSC XGQ XNT NM LX WQHEGQC XN GQHYQS: HSC RQGNBC XGQ HSAQBO

NM ANC HOEQSCLSA HSC CQOEQSCLSA NS LX.

CROSSWORD: **Numbers**

By Rowan Millson

1	2	3	4	■	5	6	7	■	8	9	10	11
12				■	13			■	14			
15				16				■	17			
18								19				
■	■	■	20			■	21				■	■
22	23	24		■	■	25			■	26	27	28
29				30	31				32			
33			■	34			■	■	35			
■	■	36	37			■	38	39		■	■	■
40	41					42				43	44	45
46				■	47							
48				■	49			■	50			
51				■	52			■	53			

ACROSS

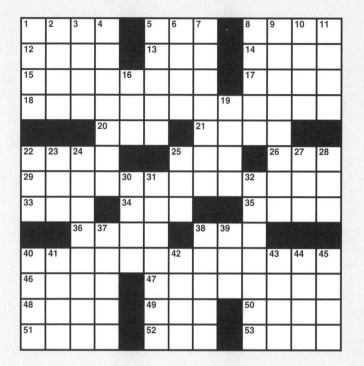

1 "... now the coat was without __" (John 19:23)
5 __ Aviv
8 Catch fly balls
12 Yen
13 Food label info
14 *The Ghost and Mrs.* __
15 Transfer
17 Letters meaning "King of the Jews"
18 Jesus (Heb. 1:6) (2 words)
20 Ill temper
21 Employs
22 Southwestern desert feature
25 Feel ill
26 Gaping hole
29 Jesus (Rev. 1:8) (3 words)
33 Tire pressure unit
34 Frigid
35 Grandson of Eve
36 Mock fanfare
38 Charged-up atom
40 Jesus (1 Cor.15:45, 47) (3 words)
46 Clods
47 Doubt-ridden
48 "We are __ men" (Gen. 42:31)
49 Hotshot
50 Pianist Gilels or actor Jannings
51 River deposit
52 "I do __ my bow in the cloud" (Gen. 9:13)
53 Quarrel

DOWN

1 Ride the waves
2 "I kiss'd thee __ kill'd thee" (*Othello*) (2 words)
3 "For this __ is mount Sinai in Arabia" (Gal. 4:25)
4 Savior of the world
5 One of twelve of Israel
6 "And Israel smote him with the __ of the sword" (Num. 21:24)
7 Lethargic
8 Strike forcefully
9 Esau and Nimrod
10 Suffix with million
11 Toothy look
16 Viola or cello (Abbr.)
19 Norwegian city
22 Atlas feature
23 Cid and Greco
24 Mean
25 Whatever
27 Sixth word of the Gettysburg Address
28 "For he __ numbered with us" (Acts 1:17)
30 Military assistant
31 These yield gum arabic
32 Threatens
37 Balance sheet entry
38 Graphic within 22-Down
39 Lyric poem
40 Toys for __
41 Mata __
42 "God hath spoken __; twice have I heard this" (Ps. 62:11)
43 Landfill site
44 Soprano's solo, perhaps
45 "... and every man's heart shall __" (Isa. 13:7)

LETTER SQUARES: **In the Old Testament**

1 **Esther 7:1**

I T H	H E	Q U E	T O	R T	Q U E	A N D	E N .
S O	N G	T W	T H E	C A	H A	K I	M E
M A N	B A N	T H E	E S				

MULTIPLE CHOICE:

1 Samuel anointed what shepherd boy, the youngest of eight sons, in front of his brothers?

A. Josiah **B.** David **C.** Joseph **D.** Solomon

2 What man of the military conquered 31 kings?

A. Samson **B.** David **C.** Joshua **D.** Nimrod

3 Who does the Bible say carried a staff that was as big as a weaver's beam?

A. Moses **B.** Goliath **C.** David **D.** Joseph

LETTER SQUARES:

2 **Psalms 1:6**

F T	Y O	S H .	H E	E L	O D L	H T E	Y S
R I G	F O R	H E	U T	K N	H A L	O W E	: B
L P	F T	O U S	W A	T H E	W A	O R D	T H E
U N G	E R I	T H	Y O	T H			

CROSSWORD: **Biblical Tribes**

By Thomas W. Schier

1	2	3	■	4	5	6	7	■	8	9	10	11
12			■	13				■	14			
15			■	16				17				
18			19				■	20				
■	■	21				■	22			■	■	■
23	24			■	■	25				26	27	28
29			■	30	31				■	32		
33			34				■	■	35			
■	■	■	36			■	37	38			■	■
39	40	41			■	42					43	44
45					46				■	47		
48				■	49				■	50		
51				■	52				■	53		

ACROSS

1 Priest's garb
4 Rude look
8 "... they have made them a molten __" (Ex. 32:8)
12 Coffee, slangily
13 Kind of fall
14 "Dies __" (Latin hymn)
15 Advice columnist Landers
16 Tribe member in Matthew 10:4
18 "__, O ye nations, with his people" (Deut. 32:43)
20 Tribe in Acts 2:9
21 Comic Johnson
22 "And the Lord said unto __" (Gen. 4:15)
23 "Behold the __ of God" (John 1:29)
25 Punishes again, Singapore-style
29 "Who __ to judge?" (2 words)
30 Communion service item
32 Actress Gardner
33 "I will not __ his parts" (Job 41:12)
35 Hotfooted it
36 Giant Giant
37 1979 exiled Iranian
39 Open-jawed
42 Sovereign's staff
45 Tribe member in 2 Kings 17:29
47 Santa __, CA
48 "... and his voice will we __" (Josh. 24:24)
49 Fix a sock
50 Actor Chaney
51 Swampy bogs
52 Length x width, for a rectangle
53 Believer's suffix

DOWN

1 Open a bit
2 Solitary
3 Tribe in Numbers 13:9
4 Bibliography abbr.
5 "... the __ of God was upon him" (Luke 2:40)
6 Primrose path, literally
7 H, to Homer
8 Movie theater
9 Moistureless
10 "Even of __ my people is risen up" (Micah 2:8)
11 Professional charges
17 Oblong priestly vestment
19 Sphere
22 __ up (plenty perturbed)
23 Varnish ingredient
24 Latin 101 word
25 "Too-Ra-Loo-Ra-Loo-___"
26 Tribe in Numbers 1:43
27 Mother of Cain
28 "Why is thy spirit so __" (1 Kgs. 21:5)
30 He was originally called Simon
31 Back muscle, familiarly
34 Some health insurers' requirements
35 Tree trickling
37 Frighten
38 Salon shade
39 Dating from (2 words)
40 Actor Kaplan
41 Sermon finale
42 Magi's directional guide
43 Genesis son
44 Bombastic language
46 Wyo. neighbor

LETTER SQUARES: **In the Old Testament**

1 Psalms 6:4

R D ,	T H Y	R E T	E S '	S A	, 0	O H	S A V
L I V	K E .	D E	O R	U R N	L :	M E	R C I
E M	E R	S O U	M Y	L O	E F		

MULTIPLE CHOICE:

1 What the penalty in Israel for disobeying a priest was?

A. Imprisonment for one year
B. Daily confessions for one year
C. Death
D. Daily sacrifices for one year

2 What was engraved on the twelve stones on the breastplate of the high priest?

A. The kings of Israel
B. The names of the tribes of Israel
C. Parables
D. The Ten Commandments

3 Who upset his brothers by telling them of his dreams?

A. Jacob
B. Joseph
C. Daniel
D. Jesus

VERSE DECODER:

1 Isaiah 1:4

HINT: In the puzzle below, the letter "V" is actually an "A."

VZ NSECIF EVPSXE, V GTXGFT FVOTE JSPZ SESRISPU, V NTTO XC TYSFOXTBN,

LZSFOBTE PZVP VBT LXBBIGPTBN: PZTU ZVYT CXBNVWTE

PZT FXBO, PZTU ZVYT GBXYXWTO PZT ZXFU XET XC SNBVTF IEPX VEKTB,

PZTU VBT KXET VJVU DVLWJVBO.

King James Games Facts:

The Old Testament was first separated into verses in 1448.

LETTER SQUARES: **In the Old Testament**

1 Psalms 7:1

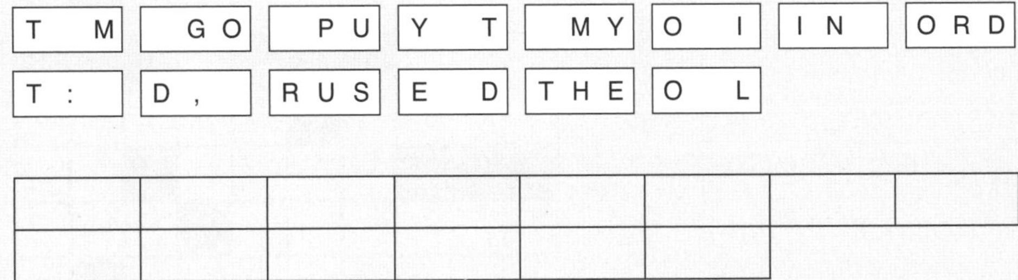

T M	G O	P U	Y T	M Y	O I	I N	O R D
T :	D ,	R U S	E D	T H E	O L		

MULTIPLE CHOICE:

1 Who did God tell to name his son Mahershalalhashbaz?

A. Hosea **B.** Jeremiah **C.** Isaiah **D.** Iddo

2 Who had an unusual vision of one angel running to meet another?

A. Isaiah **B.** Balaam **C.** Zechariah **D.** Seraiah

3 The ephod is an apron-like garment worn by whom?

A. The scapegoat **B.** The high priest **C.** Abraham **D.** The cherubim

4 Who told Job that God would fill a righteous man with laughter?

A. Elihu **B.** Zophar **C.** Bildad **D.** Eliphaz

5 All the priests come from what tribe of Israel?

A. Judah **B.** Benjamin **C.** Levi **D.** Joseph

CROSSWORD: **Biblical Browsing**

By Barbara A. Marques

ACROSS

1 "__ not the earth, neither the sea" (Rev. 7:3)

5 Dad's day gift?

8 "... dove found no rest for the __ of her foot" (Gen. 8:9)

12 A duke of the Horites (Gen. 36:21)

13 Noah's overacting son?

14 "O Lord is against them that do __" (Ps. 34:16)

15 "And they tied unto it a __ of blue" (Ex. 39:31)

16 "God with us" (Matt. 1:23)

18 He ordered Christ's crucifixion

20 Grads

21 Commotion

22 Insect life stage

23 Letters of the Apostles

25 "Pass through the __, and command the people" (Josh. 1:11)

29 Goal

30 Sister

31 Small job to do

33 "... man should be alone; I will make him an __ for him" (Gen. 2:18)

36 Founder of the Hebrew race

38 __ in rooster

39 "I __ unto Caesar" (Acts 25:11)

42 Feeble-minded

45 Jesus anointed his eyes with clay (John 9:6)

47 U.S. Treasury Agent (abbr.)

48 "For all have sinned, and __ short of the glory of God" (Rom. 3:23)

49 Alter __

50 "... earth, where moth and __ doth corrupt" (Matt. 6:19)

51 "... there shall come a __ out of Jacob" (Num. 24:17)

52 "And the strong shall be as __" (Isa. 1:31)

53 Regarding (2 words)

DOWN

1 Make oneself useful

2 Father of Palal (Neh. 3:25)

3 Takes back

4 Tramples

5 "... thou art my God; early will I seek __" (Ps. 63:1)

6 "... Israel, __ hath sent me unto you" (Ex. 3:14) (2 words)

7 Disciples talked with Jesus on the road to __

8 Father of Judah (Neh. 11:9)

9 Reproductive cell

10 "... and see where thou hast not been __ with" (Jer. 3:2)

11 Norse deity who defeated Thor

17 Swiss mountain

19 Young child

22 Originally called Simon

23 "... hungry, give him bread to __" (Prov. 25:21)

24 Daughter of Ingrid Bergman

26 Philemon's slave

27 "And if any man will __ thee at the law" (Matt. 5:40)

28 Explosive

32 Sharper

33 "... take the __ of salvation, and the sword of the Spirit" (Eph. 6:17)

34 Coming before

35 Sacred meditation

37 Not good

39 Alphabet to a preschooler

40 Secret plan

41 Southern Arizona Indian

42 "... they shall be as white as __" (Isa. 1:18)

43 Persevere

44 Prefix meaning "within"

46 "Hast thou not heard long __ how I have done it" (2 Kings 19:25)

LETTER SQUARES: **In the Old Testament**

1 Psalms 104:32

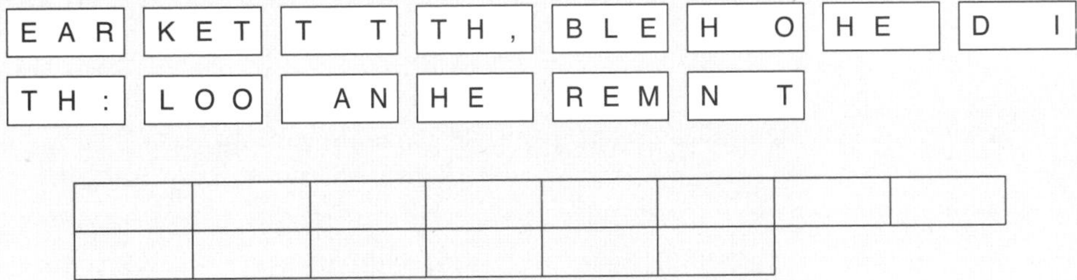

MULTIPLE CHOICE:

1 Who was the third son of Adam and Eve?

A. Seth **B.** Jared **C.** Methuselah **D.** Lamech

2 Who constructed the first temple in Jerusalem?

A. Joshua and Caleb
B. Rehoboam and Jeroboam
C. Solomon
D. Zerubbabel and Joshua

3 Who led in the construction of the second temple?

A. Joshua and Caleb
B. Zerubbabel and Joshua
C. Asa and Abijam
D. Rehoboam and Jeroboam

4 Who was Jacob's father-in-law?

A. Samuel **B.** Moses **C.** Eleazar **D.** Laban

5 God said that what city's cry was great and its sin very grievous?

A. Sodom **B.** Rome **C.** Egypt **D.** Enoch

6 What third king of Judah was also the great-grandson of Solomon?

A. Asa **B.** Jehoiada **C.** Josiah **D.** Ahab

MULTIPLE CHOICE: **In the Old Testament**

1 Which man was said to be an excellent speaker?

A. Aaron **B.** Phinehas **C.** Abiathar **D.** Ahimelech

2 What priest dedicated the newly rebuilt walls of Jerusalem during Nehemiah's ministry?

A. Pashur **B.** Eleazar **C.** Zadok **D.** Eliashib

VERSE DECODER:

1 **Joshua 1:2**

HINT: In the puzzle below, the letter "J" is actually an "E."

EYSJS EL SJXCRKH GS FJRF; KYI HTJXJUYXJ RXGSJ, VY YCJX HTGS

MYXFRK, HTYN, RKF RDD HTGS WJYWDJ, NKHY HTJ DRKF ITGQT G

FY VGCJ HY HTJE, JCJK HY HTJ QTGDFXJK YU GSXRJD.

***King James Games* Facts:**

The longest chapter in the Bible is Psalm 119.

LETTER SQUARES:

1 **1 Kings 1:33**

T O	T H E	O S	M ,	I T H	U T	A I D	Y O
E W	S E R	T S	T A K	T H E	U N	A L S	O F
O R D	V A N	N G	H E	R L	K I	Y O U	,

CROSSWORD: **Beasts of Prey**

By Rowan Millson

ACROSS

1 Norman of golf

5 "And after the __ Satan entered into him" (John 13:27)

8 "Be still, ye inhabitants of the __"(Isa. 23:2)

12 Not far

13 Flightless bird down under

14 "And the Lord spake unto Gad, David's __" (1 Chron. 21:9)

15 Sea between Italy and Albania

17 Healing mark

18 "... and the __ them, and scattereth the sheep" (John 10:12) (2 words)

20 "__ fi fo fum"

21 Three, on a sundial

22 Word with trust or social

25 __ and outs

26 What Joseph was cast into

29 "The old __ for lack of prey" (Job 4:11) (2 words)

33 Tree with tough, useful wood

34 Santa __, CA

35 "Take, thine __, eat, drink and be merry" (Luke 12:19)

36 "... he planteth an __" (Isa. 44:14)

37 Jetted bath

39 "And the beast which I saw was like __" (Rev. 13:2) (3 words)

45 Gemstone

46 Slight sleepwear

47 __ cloud in the sky (2 words)

48 Pigeon sound

49 Sisters

50 A book in *The Book of Mormon*

51 They're between ems and ohs

52 Chicken man, in the circus

DOWN

1 "... they __ not the bones till the morrow" (Zeph. 3:3)

2 Perform again

3 Viscount's superior

4 Merv of TV fame

5 Stiff bristles

6 Overlook

7 "Turandot" composer

8 First-generation Japanese immigrant

9 Split-off group

10 Rachel's sister

11 "It is a people that do __ in their heart" (Ps. 95:10)

16 Good serve

19 "... and shall __ at all the plagues thereof" (Jer. 49:17)

22 Ginger __ (soft drink)

23 Zip

24 Double this for a drum

25 One of David's captains

26 Small vegetable

27 __ *a Wonderful Life*

28 Popular title starter

30 El __, Texas

31 Add some pizzazz to

32 A __ spoonful

36 Map book

37 Lily varieties

38 Warsaw is its cap.

39 "Take my yoke __ you" (Matt. 11:29)

40 Org. celebrating 50 years in 1999

41 Juan Ponce de __

42 Feverish condition

43 Actress Russo

44 Schoolroom fixture

45 "And the whole earth was of __ language" (Gen. 11:1)

MULTIPLE CHOICE: **In the Old Testament**

1 The angel of the LORD appeared to what man and called him a mighty man of valor?

A. Gera **B.** Gideoni **C.** Gideon **D.** Giddalti

2 Which of these men pulled down the Temple of Dagon?

A. Solomon **B.** Salmon **C.** Samson **D.** Sargon

3 The prince of the eunuchs gave what man the name Shadrach?

A. Daniel **B.** Mishael **C.** Hananiah **D.** Azariah

4 Which man's strength departed from him when his head was shaved?

A. Nathan **B.** Bani **C.** Samson **D.** Daniel

5 Jacob built an altar to God in what city?

A. Damascus **B.** Nazareth **C.** Bethel **D.** Tyre

6 Which patriarch of the Old Testament was revealed as a prophet to King Abimelech?

A. Isaac **B.** Noah **C.** Abraham **D.** Jacob

LETTER SQUARES:

1 Isaiah 1:8

TH	AS	R O	E D	IS	ION	A	RD,
HTE	OTT	F Z	IN	AUG	LE	FT	VIN
AGE	EYA	A C	AND				

VERSE DECODER: **In the Old Testament**

1 Micah 1:4

HINT: In the puzzle below, the letter "G" is actually a "T."

TKZ GCU RDYKGTPKO OCTBB WU RDBGUK YKZUL CPR, TKZ GCU ATBBUXO OCTBB WU SBUVG, TO ITN WUVDLU GCU VPLU, TKZ TO GCU ITGULO GCTG TLU EDYLUZ ZDIK T OGUUE EBTSU.

MULTIPLE CHOICE:

1 Who was taken to Babylon and trained for the king's service?

A. Haggai
B. Amos
C. Jeremiah
D. Daniel

2 A ram in the bush once took which man's place?

A. Ishmael
B. Joseph
C. Isaac
D. Zebulun

3 Which man went from a pit to a palace?

A. Jacob
B. Elijah
C. Benjamin
D. Manasseh

LETTER SQUARES:

1 Isaiah 4:2

OUS	BR	ORI	H O	TIF	AY	AND	LOR
THE	T D	GL	HE	EAU	THA	E B	D B
SHA	ANC	F T	UL	LL	IN	,	

LETTER SQUARES: **In the Old Testament**

1 Amos 3:3

T O	T W	P T	O W	H E R	E D ?	C A N	G E T
G R E	, E	T H E	Y B	E A	X C E	A L K	

MULTIPLE CHOICE:

1 Whose amazing coat caused tremendous envy among his brothers?

A. Joseph's **B.** Daniel's **C.** Aaron's **D.** Jacob's

2 Joseph said, "... the man in whose hand the cup was found, he shall be my" what?"

A. King **B.** Brother **C.** Servant **D.** Betrayer

3 God made the first covenant with Noah. With whom did he make the second covenant?

A. Adam **B.** Abraham **C.** Cain **D.** David

VERSE DECODER:

1 Psalms 101:1

HINT: In the puzzle below, the letter "I" is actually an "A."

I RYIVGY EP UBG IPPXSFUGH, ABGD BG SQ EZGYABGXOGH, IDH

RECYGUB ECU BSQ FEORXISDU MGPEYG UBG XEYH. BGIY OV

RYIVGY, E XEYH, IDH XGU OV FYV FEOG CDUE UBGG.

CROSSWORD: **Biblical Armory**

Edited By Timothy E. Parker

ACROSS

1 Jason's fictional ship
5 Go wrong
8 One of seven in the Book of Revelation
12 "... is there __ in thy father's house" (Gen. 24:23)
13 Golly!
14 Length x breadth
15 "... her end is bitter as wormwood,sharp as a __" (Prov. 5:4) (3 words)
18 Marsh plant
19 "Wilt thou break a leaf driven to and __?" (Job 13:25)
20 Tofu source
21 "Therefore I will __ and howl" (Micah 1:8)
23 "These all continued with __ accord in prayer" (Acts 1:14)
25 "The Greatest" boxer
27 Guitarist's gadget
29 North Sea feeder
33 "And he had an __ upon his head" (1 Samuel 17:5) (3 words)
36 Fly alone
37 Wedding cake layer
38 Snooze
39 "__ to thee, Moab!" (Num. 21:29)
41 "And all flesh __ that moved upon the earth" (Gen. 7:21)
43 Hole-punching tool
46 Sardonic
48 Ant
51 "Above all, taking the __" (Eph. 6:16) (3 words)
54 Peachy __
55 "__ they not all ministering spirits" (Heb. 1:14)
56 "For we which have believed do enter __ rest" (Heb. 4:3)
57 Two-by-four
58 Coniferous evergreen
59 Suggestive look

DOWN

1 They can be fine or graphic
2 Poet laureate Nicholas
3 "With __ doing service, as to the Lord" (Eph. 6:7)
4 "... am Alpha and __" (Rev. 1:8)
5 Breakfast staple
6 Coral structure
7 Like some popular inns? (2 words)
8 "And I __ when the Lamb opened one of the seals" (Rev. 6:1)
9 Greek god of love
10 Word with dynamic or space
11 Tramp's spaghetti-dinner date
16 Clear a frozen windshield
17 Trinity member
22 The Church of Jesus Christ of __ Saints
24 Always, poetically
25 Contented sighs
26 __ the lion
28 Luau side dish
30 Hidden explosive
31 Scouting org.
32 Psychic's claim, for short
34 Use a scythe
35 Legal document
40 "There shall the great __ make her nest" (Isa. 34:15)
42 Electronic communication
43 Queries
44 "If he turn not, he will __ his sword" (Ps. 7:12)
45 Stead
47 Ancient times
49 Suffix with kitchen or luncheon
50 Comic book superhero
52 "... came to pass at the __ of forty days" (Gen. 8:6)
53 "And ye shall be left __ in number" (Deut. 28:62)

WORD SEARCH: **Abraham's Progeny**

L	H	Z	D	Z	T	M	H	G	J	F	N	N	H	H	F	J	K
M	D	B	G	L	I	T	M	I	D	I	A	N	A	R	W	R	K
M	I	H	N	C	Z	M	D	E	D	A	N	N	N	K	N	A	X
L	N	Z	D	R	J	P	R	L	P	L	E	N	O	N	L	D	P
Z	A	R	Z	V	Y	R	N	A	P	M	N	P	C	T	N	E	X
G	H	L	E	A	M	H	S	I	N	I	Z	A	H	J	D	K	R
J	A	P	M	L	H	L	X	C	J	R	F	B	H	R	Q	L	Q
F	T	L	Q	T	H	Y	J	X	L	U	G	T	V	S	A	L	K
L	H	L	F	K	P	L	Z	Q	N	H	H	K	N	M	K	I	D
M	Q	X	G	G	C	F	M	H	I	S	J	G	X	L	V	O	M
L	K	G	W	Z	Z	I	N	M	H	S	H	U	A	H	L	H	J
V	Y	M	D	X	M	E	R	N	X	A	Y	M	D	Y	E	Z	D
Y	G	G	C	M	B	A	M	H	G	R	M	K	Z	Z	X	B	P
B	L	B	U	A	C	Y	A	A	C	G	M	M	R	K	Z	T	M
R	L	E	J	L	C	L	T	B	K	F	L	O	A	H	D	W	R
T	L	O	B	W	E	V	D	E	X	R	N	C	R	H	F	F	G
R	T	J	R	H	P	T	N	H	T	W	T	D	L	Q	S	L	D
H	N	G	S	D	Q	N	M	S	Q	L	D	Z	E	R	E	P	W

ASSHURIM
CARMI
DEDAN
EPHRAIM
HANOCH
HEZRON
ISHMAEL
JOKSHAN
KEDAR
LEUMMIM
MIDIAN
MIZZAH
NAHATH
NEBAJOTH
PEREZ
SHAMMAH
SHEBA
SHELAH
SHUAH
ZIMRAN

WORD SEARCH: **Altar Sites**

K	P	Y	K	F	G	M	R	E	P	H	I	D	I	M	P	W
M	H	V	F	H	I	N	T	J	S	U	C	S	A	M	A	D
B	G	M	A	Z	F	T	L	N	T	N	C	T	R	F	M	W
M	H	M	P	M	Q	L	X	C	K	N	Q	A	C	X	M	N
B	A	E	N	V	C	V	X	R	O	N	Z	R	A	W	Q	R
R	H	B	E	E	R	S	H	E	B	A	D	A	N	J	G	H
N	H	E	R	O	M	H	B	L	X	J	N	R	A	L	Y	A
S	K	L	C	C	T	I	Y	V	V	B	W	A	A	Z	K	R
H	Z	H	J	Z	G	N	C	C	K	K	M	K	N	J	Y	H
E	S	H	E	T	P	A	T	X	W	S	C	R	P	D	M	P
C	M	A	W	B	R	B	R	M	N	Y	F	V	J	L	J	O
H	A	F	M	M	R	J	E	E	J	H	K	H	N	E	R	W
E	M	G	E	A	M	O	H	T	V	L	A	L	T	I	J	M
M	R	L	V	C	R	T	N	V	H	F	A	I	X	F	W	M
H	E	M	M	N	A	I	H	K	H	E	Q	B	R	Q	R	T
V	R	J	Q	J	F	X	A	X	F	Y	L	N	E	O	V	N
M	B	V	H	T	M	B	H	G	H	E	A	V	E	N	M	L

ARARAT
ATHENS
BEERSHEBA
BETHEL
CANAAN
CARMEL
DAMASCUS
EBAL
FIELD
GIBEON
HEAVEN
HEBRON
MAMRE
MIZPEH
MOREH
MORIAH
OPHRAH
RAMAH
REPHIDIM
SAMARIA
SHECHEM

MULTIPLE CHOICE: **Biblical Rulers**

1 According to Psalms, what trees are broken by the power of God's voice?

A. The sycamore trees
B. The cedars of Lebanon
C. The lilies of the field
D. The palm trees

2 Who heard God speaking out of a whirlwind?

A. Elisha
B. Nathan
C. Ahab
D. Job

3 What Hebrew captive interpreted the dreams of the Egyptian Pharaoh?

A. Jacob
B. Moses
C. Joseph
D. Reuben

4 What wise king made an alliance with Egypt when he married the pharaoh's daughter?

A. Jeroboam II
B. Solomon
C. Menahem
D. Saul

5 What book mentions a woman who plants a vineyard with her own hands?

A. Genesis
B. Proverbs
C. Joshua
D. Ecclesiastes

6 What king of Moab sent the prophet Balaam to curse Israel?

A. Balak
B. Ahaziah
C. Pharaoh
D. Saul

WORD SEARCH: **Israel's Enemies**

F	W	N	S	E	T	I	H	S	A	G	R	I	G	H
D	R	N	K	A	D	M	O	N	I	T	E	S	G	I
X	A	A	B	N	O	L	Y	B	A	B	A	E	W	T
F	S	M	N	G	B	F	M	K	F	H	N	T	T	T
B	E	I	O	Q	O	B	L	M	O	L	A	I	M	I
O	T	H	M	R	D	L	F	R	T	G	K	S	L	T
N	I	A	O	N	I	P	I	G	E	S	H	U	R	E
E	Z	Z	D	B	K	T	H	A	T	K	Q	B	R	S
B	Z	Y	E	M	E	K	E	C	T	Q	G	E	T	A
I	I	N	F	S	E	N	T	S	T	H	T	J	V	G
B	N	Y	A	L	L	P	A	M	M	O	N	V	H	N
H	E	Z	A	I	Y	X	X	A	T	R	I	K	M	Q
S	K	M	T	G	D	M	G	N	N	T	M	T	M	Z
I	A	Q	E	Z	F	I	M	C	E	A	H	K	F	D
B	R	L	N	G	M	M	M	S	C	L	C	G	C	R

AHIMAN
AMALEK
AMMON
AMORITES
ANAK
AVVITES
BABYLON
CANAAN
EDOM
EGYPT
GESHUR
GIRGASHITES
GOLIATH
HITTITES
HORITES
ISHBIBENOB
JEBUSITES
KADMONITES
KENIZZITES
MIDIAN

WORD SEARCH: **David's Men**

T	K	N	Q	T	Y	J	B	M	H	Z	R	N	R	Y	R	Z
A	Q	K	T	K	V	Q	M	L	A	K	A	N	Y	R	Q	C
J	M	U	Z	Z	I	A	E	C	K	H	C	L	L	F	B	M
I	J	A	S	I	E	L	D	L	A	Q	A	M	M	D	M	E
A	C	Z	H	B	L	M	D	R	H	L	F	R	L	O	C	B
C	D	X	D	S	L	Q	I	J	T	A	E	T	A	F	N	U
E	N	M	T	N	A	T	M	R	N	L	N	G	M	I	R	N
B	E	N	T	K	G	A	K	K	I	X	T	A	L	C	G	N
B	L	W	V	R	I	R	P	P	L	F	G	L	N	K	F	A
I	I	I	Z	H	T	Y	H	K	K	Z	N	E	V	D	R	I
S	A	T	A	K	K	E	L	H	Q	V	K	I	K	T	L	I
G	H	W	M	D	L	Z	A	L	M	R	G	B	V	T	A	Y
G	B	Z	G	E	D	I	N	A	N	A	H	A	K	T	N	T
R	A	R	T	H	R	I	R	L	F	K	K	N	T	F	D	J
D	V	G	L	U	V	N	H	W	W	D	Z	I	M	T	M	T
M	X	K	J	W	X	B	E	N	A	I	A	H	K	M	K	N
G	L	D	E	B	O	T	B	R	P	Y	P	L	N	J	Q	F

ABIEL
AHIAM
BENAIAH
ELHANAN
ELIAHBA
ELIPHELET
HANAN
HIDDAI
IGAL
ITTAI
JASIEL
MAHARAI
MEBUNNAI
NAHARI
OBED
SHAMA
SIBBECAI
URIAH
UZZIA
ZALMON

H Y W N M O L A D A H T Y M K Q X M
B M X F V T J E R U S A L E M G K E
J B R F S T D N X Q D C V G F T L L
N M M H M I H L I H S Y K J X G Q E
M L E Q M R C G R D A L O T L E H T
T M B O T C Q N X Z N N L N G V A L
A A N B R Y F H D M B T R A H J D E
K A N N M K K M B T I R L O F C A B
H B T N V J E B B N Z K D Q Z V D A
N W E B A J P D J L I J C L D A A O
W R R A M M R M E Z O D L W G N H T
C D Z N L B D L L S T R N B R Y C H
Y R R I G O F A J R H V R W M M N V
M R X N P K T Q M Y I F J W Q R O C
W G N T V H M H L V A N V M U K R G
M P K W K A Z X G B H N P G Y L B R
C G B P M K B A A L A H A N P K E L
T T N A T P D B T B N J B M F M H X

ADADAH
AMAM
BAALAH
BEALOTH
BIZIOTHIAH
DIMONAH
ELTOLAD
HAZOR
HEBRON
JAGUR
JERUSALEM
KEDESH
LEBAOTH
MADMANNA
MOLADAH
SHEMA
SHILHIM
TELEM
ZIKLAG
ZIPH

MULTIPLE CHOICE: **For the Equipping of the Saints**

1 Which of these men made his dwelling place in Uz?

A. Job
B. Peter
C. Moses
D. John

2 Who was Elisha's servant?

A. Elijah
B. Gehazi
C. Caleb
D. Naaman

3 Which man hid himself from God because he was naked?

A. Adam
B. Abraham
C. John
D. Jesus

4 Who was crippled when a servant woman dropped him as a baby?

A. Balaam
B. Saul's Brother
C. Mephibosheth
D. Jonathan's grandson

5 Which man pursued the life of David because of jealousy?

A. David
B. Zimri
C. Saul
D. Pekah

6 Who was so disgraced when Absalom did not follow his counsel that he hanged himself?

A. Ahitophel
B. Amnon
C. Hushi
D. Joab

WORD SEARCH: **Jewish Kings**

P	T	R	G	H	R	Z	H	M	A	H	A	Z	I	A	H	W
P	W	D	I	G	H	A	A	R	E	Z	J	X	G	M	T	T
G	J	R	P	G	A	H	B	E	G	H	R	V	R	P	P	R
N	M	W	Z	K	J	A	C	T	H	X	N	J	G	C	F	L
O	Q	V	T	Y	I	O	K	N	R	S	O	E	G	P	F	Z
J	J	J	B	D	B	H	K	X	C	T	O	V	M	T	B	W
H	O	N	E	V	A	E	Q	B	H	M	D	H	R	P	W	M
A	R	M	Y	H	B	J	T	A	H	A	I	K	E	Z	E	H
I	A	L	C	A	U	T	M	P	E	K	A	H	I	A	H	M
K	M	N	H	J	J	G	R	T	G	C	B	N	X	D	I	L
E	R	A	B	G	H	L	V	M	W	Y	B	A	M	K	V	P
D	X	D	T	J	E	H	O	S	H	A	P	H	A	T	P	Y
E	B	A	D	H	E	S	S	A	N	A	M	I	T	S	R	Y
Z	A	V	H	G	R	G	P	N	E	R	O	Y	K	K	H	J
Q	D	I	J	Y	V	M	R	L	D	H	N	M	J	C	B	A
P	A	D	Z	T	B	N	A	P	E	R	L	T	X	P	B	M
N	N	Z	J	V	C	H	C	J	Z	K	Q	M	N	D	T	V

ABIJAH
AHAB
AHAZIAH
BAASHA
DAVID
ELAH
HEZEKIAH
HOSHEA
JEHOAHAZ
JEHOIAKIM
JEHOSHAPHAT
JEHU
JORAM
JOTHAM
MANASSEH
MENHEM
NADAB
OMRI
PEKAHIAH
ZEDEKIAH

WORD SEARCH: **John the Baptist**

```
W V F R E P E N T T F L E A R S I
L Z B F D M P R E A C H I N G G F
F S T K X L T H Q B A P T I S M M
Q S G M K E B X E F W K Z C M M Z
T E W K N G T H B R R A R N C R Z
B N D W N N T K T S O L T A X S E
H E X G L A J P E E T D M E T T C
E V H E C N A D L T B E I N R S H
R I M E X F U Y T R L A L A R U A
O G G M A T N E L H E T Z T S C R
D R P X I D U C A R N H R I R O I
N O Q T J Q E I Y E W B T Z L L A
Z F L R N Y R D M H L I L A Y E H
G U R A M J N R O J R R M C E N K
M G B R T L A N K D X T Q L H L K
L R W K R G E X X R N H R M H G G
M M K P P Y Q K G I R D L E M X F
```

ANGEL
BANQUET
BAPTISM
BEHEADED
BIRTH
CAMEL HAIR
DANCE
ELIZABETH
FORGIVENESS
GARMENT
GIRDLE
HEROD
HERODIAS
HONEY
ISRAEL
LEATHER
LOCUSTS
MULTITUDES
PREACHING
REPENT
WATER
ZECHARIAH

WORD SEARCH: **Job's Sorrow**

N	Z	O	P	H	A	R	S	T	N	A	V	R	E	S
L	N	Q	H	B	B	L	A	M	E	L	E	S	S	D
R	N	J	X	S	H	T	S	B	D	N	V	M	A	M
S	Z	R	A	R	T	N	A	F	M	K	N	D	T	N
T	E	T	A	L	D	E	B	D	K	R	L	H	M	C
P	A	N	X	M	G	M	E	Z	P	I	G	K	A	W
N	E	T	U	R	S	T	A	A	B	I	X	M	J	O
K	L	E	W	T	R	N	N	H	R	B	E	L	L	R
C	R	R	H	N	R	I	S	P	L	L	D	L	M	S
N	W	F	X	S	V	O	U	I	S	O	X	E	N	H
N	E	G	B	Y	Q	P	F	L	M	B	D	J	B	I
R	L	N	E	Z	H	P	V	E	R	C	O	N	U	P
H	S	N	R	F	L	A	W	T	L	J	M	I	L	E
K	O	S	N	A	E	D	L	A	H	C	K	L	L	D
M	S	U	F	F	E	R	I	N	G	C	K	M	S	S

APPOINTMENT
BILDAD
BLAMELESS
BOILS
BULLS
CAMELS
CHALDEANS
ELIPHAZ
FORTUNES
MONEY
OXEN
RAMS
SABEANS
SATAN
SERVANTS
SHEEP
SLEW
SUFFERING
UPRIGHT
WORSHIPED
ZOPHAR

MULTIPLE CHOICE: **Go Therefore and Make Disciples**

1 Who built a city called Enoch east of Eden?

A. Cain
B. Adam
C. Noah
D. Abram

2 Who persuaded the clever woman of Tekoah to pretend to be a widow in order to play on King David's sympathy?

A. Joab
B. Uzzie
C. Tobiah
D. Hemam

3 Which of these men was killed with a stone?

A. Goliath
B. Samson
C. David
D. Methuselah

4 Where did Lot make his home?

A. Enoch
B. Rome
C. Corinth
D. Sodom

5 Who made numerous attempts to swindle Jacob, and ultimately prospered?

A. Joseph
B. Laban
C. Reuben
D. Mizpah

6 Where did the prostitute Rahab live?

A. Medes
B. Persia
C. Jericho
D. Sodom

WORD SEARCH: **Jonah and the Whale**

```
T R C A P T A I N M L K J M V M B
H H P H C C M T C R R D E Y A R P
R Y J D T A R S H I S H R T W Y Q
O D N W R F S P V Y Y G M O N L E
W X L E T O A T Y Y R J L T R M C
N G N K C I L L L E K L T P D H I
D V T G D N L L A O A F D N R N F
D P H F T E E T N W T X R I A T I
W W A X B N F S S H X S Y N O H R
N R N X N I P M E K X F L E B R C
E R O D S Y E T A R T M A V R E A
V L J H L R E F E R P T N E E E S
R T F X A M L L Q M I Z D H V D T
N J R P Q M S L T J P N B T O A N
Y K P L M Q A R J V K E E L Z Y Q
T O C D N I W T A E R G S R L S F
J M A D E V O W S V M N F T S D B
```

ASLEEP
BELLY
CAPTAIN
CAST LOTS
DRY LAND
GREAT FISH
GREAT WIND
JONAH
JOPPA
LORD
MADE VOWS
MARINERS
NINEVEH
OVERBOARD
PAID FARE
PRAYED
PRESENCE
SACRIFICE
SWALLOW
TARSHISH
TEMPEST
THREE DAYS
THROWN

WORD SEARCH: **Making the Tabernacle**

M	T	A	E	S	Y	C	R	E	M	J	M	Z	L	S
N	M	S	R	E	T	I	P	A	H	C	T	L	A	T
Y	K	M	F	R	F	T	M	H	S	N	E	T	M	E
L	K	X	A	V	L	C	R	B	D	N	L	F	P	K
X	C	T	K	I	Q	T	R	U	N	T	R	Q	S	C
Y	L	W	N	X	T	A	R	F	O	N	A	C	T	O
A	R	E	J	C	N	I	M	T	M	C	C	L	A	S
V	N	D	Q	C	A	I	M	L	L	K	S	H	N	H
B	G	T	H	H	T	L	S	Y	A	P	H	F	D	K
N	O	E	T	T	R	D	B	R	V	V	L	D	J	Q
T	S	A	I	T	L	L	O	Y	A	T	E	M	B	E
T	O	H	R	H	Y	Q	W	M	R	L	K	R	H	T
G	S	Y	M	D	T	N	L	D	G	O	L	D	P	A
Q	D	N	T	J	S	Z	S	Q	H	L	Z	I	T	G
B	L	U	E	T	B	S	I	L	V	E	R	H	P	C

ALMONDS
ALTAR
BLUE
BOARDS
BOWLS
BRANCHES
CHAPITERS
COURT
GATE
GOAT HAIR
GOLD
LAMPSTAND
LAVER
LINEN
MERCYSEAT
PILLARS
SCARLET
SHITTIM
SILVER
SOCKETS

MULTIPLE CHOICE: **I am Joseph**

1 How many of Joseph's brothers went to Egypt to buy grain?

A. 12
B. 10
C. 11
D. 6

2 Who was the youngest son of Jacob?

A. Reuben
B. Benjamin
C. Levi
D. Judah

3 How many days was Jonah in the belly of the great fish?

A. 3
B. 14
C. 20
D. 1

4 Who was the second son of Jacob?

A. Reuben
B. Manasseh
C. Levi
D. Simeon

5 What is the root of all evil?

A. Money
B. Fear
C. Temptation
D. Jealousy

6 Hannah was the first wife of Elkanah. Who was the second?

A. Hagar
B. Peninnah
C. Bithiah
D. Ahinoam

MULTIPLE CHOICE: **I am Joseph**

1 How many children were born to Hosea and Gomer?

A. Five
B. Seven
C. Three
D. Four

2 Where did the children of Israel dwell before their exodus out of Egypt?

A. Hushim
B. Goshen
C. Beulah
D. Moab

3 Which woman was known for her dressmaking?

A. Lydda
B. Dorcas
C. Elizabeth
D. Priscilla

4 How old was Joseph when he died?

A. 99
B. 100
C. 110
D. 120

5 Which of these men was half Hebrew and half Egyptian?

A. Jacob
B. Ephraim
C. Benjamin
D. Manasseh

6 Who was the daughter of Jacob and Leah?

A. Eglah
B. Iscah
C. Dinah
D. Jael

WORD SEARCH: **Men Found in the Old Testament**

```
F Y L N H Y K V B M M Z Q Q T L A
T J C A I H C A L A M V F K Y E H
Q M N N K D D N J H B A G Y R O S
V O J W Y A I E X A H N H K D J I
J H B N N S R T S R K Q M T M Q L
T M X I A E F O J B R H R B A B E
D L E A M K L R K A J P A T F O C
J L C I B O W A N T F L V J B A J
U N A J M W B K Z A R A M H I Z T
D H B O O S F H K O P G R O N L B
A D N J K S E L A C R X K S L L E
S J R Q K Q H S H G T K N E N Q J
D I V A D K F U O C G D Z A G N L
H L E A M H S I A M U A W N F X M
B H Z X J L T J A I B J I R N T Z
N O M L A S J D L G R J O S E P H
W Q N H T T A E M N E Z E K I E L
```

ABRAHAM	**ELIUD**	**JONAH**
ADAM	**EZEKIEL**	**JOSEPH**
ARAM	**HAGGAI**	**JOSHUA**
AZOR	**HOSEA**	**JUDAS**
BOAZ	**ISAAC**	**MALACHI**
DANIEL	**ISHMAEL**	**MOSES**
DAVID	**JEREMIAH**	**SALMON**
ELIJAH	**JOATHAM**	**SOLOMON**
ELISHA	**JOEL**	

WORD SEARCH: **Noah's Ark**

N	R	W	V	Y	Z	H	X	K	W	N	X	R	H	C
N	L	B	N	T	E	W	R	R	M	I	Y	D	V	R
L	K	T	C	L	K	A	A	S	G	E	N	C	Q	K
W	R	B	T	Q	S	V	B	F	L	J	H	D	D	N
Y	N	T	M	H	E	R	L	J	R	W	L	S	O	H
L	A	G	A	N	B	O	R	E	S	K	O	B	V	W
C	R	O	P	N	O	F	T	V	E	R	G	F	E	R
Z	N	M	D	D	R	A	Y	N	D	A	P	N	M	F
N	N	N	N	T	W	T	M	X	I	T	H	R	J	K
P	I	T	C	H	D	O	O	F	S	L	T	A	X	L
B	C	O	V	E	N	A	N	T	L	A	E	I	D	R
K	M	J	M	W	D	C	R	M	R	R	H	N	K	P
L	R	L	B	Q	L	O	W	A	K	C	P	B	T	R
B	V	K	W	I	F	E	O	W	I	N	A	O	R	H
T	H	W	S	M	O	O	R	R	K	N	J	W	R	R

ALTAR
CATTLE
COVENANT
DOOR
DOVE
FLOOD
FOOD
FOWLS
JAPHETH
NOAH'S ARK
PITCH
RAIN
RAINBOW
RAVEN
ROOMS
SHEM
SIDES
WATER
WIFE
WINDOW

MULTIPLE CHOICE: **Labor of Love**

1 Which of these men has a mark put on him by God?

A. Adam
B. Abel
C. Seth
D. Cain

2 Who was a just man and perfect in his generations, and walked with God?

A. Adam
B. Lamech
C. Noah
D. Abraham

3 Which wilderness man was taken to heaven in a chariot?

A. Jesus
B. Elijah
C. Noah
D. David

4 What son of Gera cursed King David and threw stones at him and all of his servants?

A. Shimei
B. Ziba
C. Zeruiah
D. Hushai

5 Which two men went down in a well to hide themselves from the servants of Absalom?

A. Ahithophel and Hushai
B. Jonathan and Ahimaaz
C. Zodak and Abiathar
D. Shobi and Barzillai

6 Who was the only daughter of Jacob?

A. Tamar
B. Deborah
C. Rahab
D. Dinah

MULTIPLE CHOICE: **Labor of Love**

1 What prophet was exiled in Egypt with other people from Judah?

A. Jeremiah
B. Jehu
C. Isaiah
D. Iddo

2 Who posed as her husband's sister while in Egypt?

A. Lot's wife
B. Abraham's wife
C. Jochebed
D. Joseph's sister

3 What book states, "Thou shalt not suffer a witch to live"?

A. Genesis
B. Matthew
C. Exodus
D. Revelation

4 What king of Bashan was famous for having an enormous iron bed?

A. Og
B. Goliath
C. Baasha
D. Shallum

5 What people were, in the time of Joshua, cursed to be Israel's servants?

A. The Amorites
B. The Hittites
C. The Levites
D. The Hivites

6 Which king was sixteen when he ascended to the throne?

A. Omri
B. Uzziah
C. Menahem
D. Amaziah

WORD SEARCH: **Plagues of Egypt**

S	H	Z	D	Q	N	R	E	V	O	S	S	A	P	L
K	E	L	Y	A	S	L	A	V	E	R	Y	C	K	I
M	B	I	I	S	R	A	E	L	I	T	E	S	L	C
L	D	M	L	X	L	K	X	L	M	H	G	I	F	E
P	I	B	T	F	R	M	N	N	S	D	V	D	K	R
D	S	R	Q	L	T	Y	K	E	F	E	V	E	N	E
B	E	V	B	O	I	L	S	H	S	D	S	W	H	V
N	A	X	X	V	V	V	L	T	O	S	D	O	J	I
N	S	V	N	R	K	I	O	O	R	O	A	L	M	R
J	E	R	N	T	A	C	R	K	O	R	G	L	S	E
T	X	D	H	H	K	P	V	L	A	R	P	A	G	L
S	T	S	U	C	O	L	B	H	L	P	X	N	O	I
N	M	Y	C	S	M	P	P	D	V	A	Z	X	R	N
C	X	M	T	F	G	K	B	C	M	Z	M	J	F	R
K	K	M	N	R	O	B	T	S	R	I	F	B	N	N

ALLOWED
BLOOD
BOILS
DARKNESS
DISEASE
DOORPOST
FIRSTBORN
FLIES
FROGS
HAIL
ISRAELITES
LAMB
LICE
LIVESTOCK
LOCUSTS
MOSES
NILE RIVER
PASSOVER
PHARAOH
SLAVERY

WORD SEARCH: **Queen Esther**

L	P	C	S	H	A	A	S	H	G	A	Z	T	N	J	M
H	L	O	Z	G	Q	R	H	R	E	H	T	S	E	T	M
V	O	N	T	Q	N	I	G	R	I	V	M	S	L	S	P
C	I	C	C	R	D	I	D	Q	C	Q	T	Y	E	A	C
M	N	U	D	X	L	G	N	N	N	F	N	C	L	R	J
B	T	B	B	M	K	S	R	E	I	T	I	A	O	R	S
J	M	I	K	E	O	J	E	G	V	P	C	W	J	U	Q
Z	E	N	G	D	A	R	L	C	S	E	N	H	R	R	J
S	N	E	M	E	Y	U	N	L	N	R	G	E	N	Z	B
T	T	S	Z	T	W	P	T	I	V	I	U	Q	G	M	G
N	S	Q	L	P	D	M	R	Y	N	S	R	C	T	D	M
A	V	N	Q	O	R	P	W	R	A	G	M	P	Z	Z	Q
V	L	B	L	D	O	F	X	H	Y	D	F	Y	Q	R	M
R	H	W	M	A	V	R	A	H	A	D	A	S	S	A	H
E	W	N	Z	X	A	D	B	A	N	Q	U	E	T	T	M
S	R	J	R	K	F	Q	D	D	E	S	A	E	L	P	Q

ADOPTED
AHASUERUS
BANQUET
BEAUTY
CONCUBINES
CROWN
ESTHER
EVENING
FAVOR
GIFTS
HADASSAH
MORNING
OINTMENTS
PALACE
PLEASED
PRINCES
SERVANTS
SHAASHGAZ
SPICES
VIRGIN

WORD SEARCH: **Rebekah and Isaac**

```
M D G W G R E T A W F O L L E W N
L R T L W B E T H U E L N M B V E
T T A K E A W I F E E T L R K Y D
P X Y D R I N K M Z E G O Y L Z I
H D W M K B Q W J S F T D H K D A
P G K A Y B K G O T H M E O E S M
M Q H H D O L R B E T L N T L L G
G M L A E R A R R L O D R R V E O
B T W R R N K F K V E A H M K M L
P R R B E J T H E L P S R P K A D
Z D B A V C M D F E T J S N V C R
Y R K W O T H G D N F R Z E L R I
F L J W C E C A A S I O M K D E N
K R T K R M N V K L G N O Z N T G
K K T S Z R R N K P H M M D T A T
N H J R O E R T L M Z R N Z M W G
N J R C S C D Z E C I O H C V N X
```

ABRAHAM
AROSE
BETHUEL
BLESSED
BORN
BROTHER
CHOICE
COSTLY
COVERED
DEPARTED
DRINK
FOOD
GOLD RING
HE LOVED HER
ISAAC
LODGE
MAIDEN
SERVANT
TAKE A WIFE
WATER CAMELS
WELL OF WATER

MULTIPLE CHOICE: **Looking Good, Smelling Good**

1 When God said, "The fear and dread of you shall be on every beast of the earth" who was He speaking to?

A. Noah
B. Abraham
C. Jacob
D. Isaiah

2 What book mentions a woman using such perfumes as spikenard, saffron, cinnamon, myrrh, and many others?

A. Ruth
B. Genesis
C. Revelation
D. The Song of Solomon

3 Which Old Testament book ends with these words: "But thou hast utterly rejected us; thou art very wroth against us"?

A. Daniel
B. Jonah
C. Lamentations
D. Zachariah

4 What man uses myrrh, frankincense, and other spices as perfumes?

A. David
B. The lover in the Song of Solomon
C. Samson
D. The lover in the book of Ruth

5 What woman, portrayed in Proverbs 7, perfumed her bed with myrrh, aloes, and cinnamon?

A. The virtuous woman
B. Jezebel
C. The adultress
D. Rahab

6 According to Proverbs 27:9, what do ointment and perfume do?

A. "Turn away wrath"
B. "Make a cheerful countenance"
C. "Bring glory to God"
D. "Rejoice the heart"

MULTIPLE CHOICE: **Looking Good, Smelling Good**

1 Which man thought Job was a hypocrite?

A. Bilgah
B. Bildad
C. Bilhan
D. Bilshan

2 What prophet speaks critically of women putting on eye makeup?

A. Isaiah
B. Jeremiah
C. Solomon
D. Hosea

3 Who was Sarah's maid?

A. Hagar
B. Gomer
C. Miriam
D. Milach

4 Which Hebrew officials were anointed with holy oil perfumed with aromatic spices?

A. Israel's kings
B. Israel's prophets
C. Israel's priests
D. Israel's judges

5 What evil queen "painted her face" before meeting with the rebel king Jehu?

A. Bathsheba
B. Potifar's wife
C. Esther
D. Jezebel

6 Who had a harem with women that were "purified" with perfumes?

A. King Saul
B. King David
C. King Ahasuerus
D. King Ahab

WORD SEARCH: **The First Couple**

F	Y	B	N	S	E	R	P	E	N	T	L	E	Y	C	D
F	F	D	E	S	R	U	C	J	R	P	V	K	T	G	D
T	T	R	L	B	E	G	U	I	L	E	D	V	I	W	X
P	R	N	U	M	P	Y	V	H	D	C	R	R	R	Z	N
P	L	E	F	I	Y	B	E	N	N	N	A	Y	U	F	Y
N	N	N	E	T	T	M	A	B	L	F	O	I	P	C	X
R	K	M	I	S	X	M	C	D	O	M	H	H	N	Y	H
H	C	M	H	K	A	D	H	P	D	S	B	Z	S	H	T
Y	N	C	W	D	B	X	E	X	Z	P	I	X	I	I	J
E	K	G	A	Z	L	P	R	X	G	L	V	D	G	L	P
T	M	I	N	N	E	L	U	C	M	P	D	L	S	C	T
N	L	H	C	M	B	Q	B	Y	N	E	H	R	L	Q	S
J	N	O	T	T	A	Y	I	T	K	B	E	A	N	Q	A
Q	Q	N	K	F	G	Y	M	E	N	V	Y	N	H	P	E
L	A	R	U	T	A	N	L	Y	I	R	D	G	D	F	K
T	N	T	R	E	U	P	H	R	A	T	E	S	D	W	X

ABEL
ADAM AND EVE
BEGUILED
CAIN
CHERUBIM
CLAY
CURSED
DISOBEY
EAST
ENMITY
EUPHRATES
FRUIT
GIHON
HIDDEKEL
NATURAL
PISHON
PURITY
RIVERS
SERPENT
TREES

WORD SEARCH: **The Spirit vs. The Flesh**

P	Y	F	R	W	O	R	S	H	I	P	K	Y	R	G	L
X	T	T	K	E	T	T	M	C	X	L	P	F	K	X	R
Y	I	S	L	W	M	F	X	T	G	Q	E	M	V	F	L
P	N	U	P	T	D	A	N	G	M	Q	A	N	B	X	B
P	A	R	C	D	V	E	H	T	B	M	C	X	J	V	D
A	V	T	E	K	L	Q	C	S	F	S	E	T	T	L	E
H	J	T	H	L	W	O	E	E	S	N	F	H	N	M	S
H	O	P	E	P	I	T	V	E	I	F	U	F	O	T	I
W	L	M	R	B	A	U	N	E	T	T	L	T	C	N	R
H	M	I	B	H	R	R	G	L	V	H	I	B	P	L	E
Y	D	R	L	L	E	X	T	K	T	O	F	N	R	K	L
E	Y	C	W	T	G	N	P	A	N	L	F	V	K	Y	W
G	D	N	T	Q	N	W	R	S	C	O	U	R	A	G	E
M	L	I	F	M	A	W	M	G	K	F	E	I	R	G	L
L	B	G	N	I	C	I	O	J	E	R	D	T	B	X	K
Q	S	U	F	F	E	R	I	N	G	B	B	Q	W	X	Y

ANGER
BITTERNESS
COURAGE
DECEIT
DESIRE
EMOTIONS
GRIEF
GUILE
HAPPY
HATE
HOPE
LOVE
PEACEFUL
PRIDE
REJOICING
SHAME
SUFFERING
TRUST
VANITY
WORSHIP
WRATH

MULTIPLE CHOICE: **My Name Means "O"**

1 Adam means what?

A. Blue sky
B. Messenger
C. Red earth
D. Light-giving

2 Gideon means what?

A. One with a burden
B. Compassionate
C. Help
D. Great warrior

3 Solomon means what?

A. Successor
B. Peace
C. Builder
D. Praise

4 Hannah means what?

A. Gracious
B. Completion
C. Conquering well
D. A star

5 Joshua means what?

A. Increaser
B. Dove
C. The Lord is salvation
D. Yahweh has judged

6 Daniel means what?

A. God is judge
B. Yahweh is bounteous
C. God sees
D. Yahweh strengthens

MULTIPLE CHOICE: **My Name Means "O"**

1 Ezekiel means what?

A. Abundance
B. God has healed
C. Vigilant
D. God is strong

2 Jonah means what?

A. Called
B. Tower of God
C. Dove
D. Peacemaker

3 Ruth means what?

A. Loyal
B. Something worth seeing
C. Favor
D. Kinsman-redeemer

4 Eglah means what?

A. Misfit
B. Chariot
C. Caged
D. Barren

5 Bithiah means what?

A. Fragrant
B. Blessed by God
C. Righteousness
D. A daughter of Jehovah

6 Aaron means what?

A. Burning
B. Intercessor
C. Enlightened
D. Humbled by Yahweh

R	H	Z	R	H	E	Y	T	M	K	V	V	K	N	N
D	A	N	M	R	N	I	S	R	A	E	L	I	L	M
O	O	C	M	X	H	D	R	A	G	O	N	N	L	N
R	T	J	X	T	A	J	B	C	D	N	T	G	A	Q
A	H	G	W	G	K	N	Z	B	K	K	O	S	H	J
H	P	D	H	M	K	N	O	E	B	I	G	H	A	K
N	E	D	F	T	O	L	W	L	M	W	B	M	I	T
A	N	H	L	R	R	C	K	A	T	A	R	P	R	G
I	N	G	B	J	E	N	D	W	Y	W	O	P	O	K
R	Y	E	L	G	A	S	M	S	R	K	M	L	I	M
A	H	V	Q	E	E	C	R	T	E	F	M	Z	I	L
M	N	N	S	H	W	E	O	L	E	W	M	X	O	S
A	B	E	T	L	W	L	L	B	B	K	L	W	V	C
S	K	E	P	O	K	B	M	I	S	M	E	D	H	V
Z	B	N	T	H	A	R	A	M	M	R	V	N	H	T

BEER **GIHON** **LOWER**
BETHESDA **HAROD** **MARAH**
DRAGON **HEBRON** **NEPHTOAH**
ELIM **ISRAEL** **SAMARIA**
ENHAKKORE **JACOBS** **SILOAM**
ESEK **KINGS** **TOWERS**
GIBEON **LAHAIROI**

WORD SEARCH: **Women of the Old Testament**

H	Z	H	N	O	A	D	A	I	H	D	V	M
P	A	B	A	H	A	R	O	H	A	G	A	R
E	Q	P	T	P	H	E	L	R	K	R	N	H
N	D	B	Z	T	N	H	M	J	P	K	B	A
I	M	H	U	I	F	T	W	N	N	A	K	K
N	A	R	A	Q	R	S	J	G	J	R	H	E
N	I	H	L	C	K	E	R	U	A	D	I	B
A	R	A	M	D	L	E	D	C	Y	M	P	E
H	I	N	L	Q	M	I	H	H	O	R	T	R
K	M	N	Z	O	T	E	M	A	P	L	G	C
W	G	A	G	H	L	P	N	K	G	N	B	R
K	P	H	A	R	U	T	E	K	Z	A	N	B
M	S	A	R	A	H	F	N	Y	B	K	R	J

ESTHER	**MILCAH**	**RACHEL**
GOMER	**MIRIAM**	**RAHAB**
HAGAR	**NAOMI**	**REBEKAH**
HANNAH	**NOADAIH**	**RIZPAH**
JUDITH	**ORPAH**	**RUTH**
KETURAH	**PENINNAH**	**SARAH**

SOLUTIONS

Page 123

MULTIPLE CHOICE: In the Old Testament

1 solution: **A**; 2 solution: **B**; 3 solution: **C**;

4 solution: **A**.

LETTER SQUARES:

1 solution:

Yet in this thing ye did not believe the LORD your God,
Deuteronomy 1:32

Page 124

CROSSWORD: Vanity

1 H	2 E	3 L	4 M		5 A	6 F	7 T		8 C	9 R	10 A	11 B
12 A	R	I	A		13 B	R	A		14 R	A	R	E
15 H	I	S	R	16 E	C	O	M	17 P	E	N	C	E
18 S	N	A	I	L		19 M	E	A	D			
			20 M	I	21 D			22 C	O	23 M	24 E	25 T
26 S	27 N	28 O	B		29 R	30 O	31 S	E		32 A	N	A
33 I	A	M	A	34 G	A	I	N	S	35 T	Y	O	U
36 A	M	I		37 U	G	L	I		38 H	O	S	T
39 M	E	T	40 A	L			41 P	42 A	R			
			43 L	A	44 K	45 E		46 D	I	47 A	48 L	49 S
50 T	51 H	52 O	U	G	H	T	53 S	O	F	M	A	N
54 W	A	R	M		55 A	N	T		56 T	O	T	O
57 A	M	E	S		58 N	A	Y		59 S	K	E	W

Page 125

MULTIPLE CHOICE: In the Old Testament

1 solution: **B**; 2 solution: **C**; 3 solution: **B**;

4 solution: **B**; 5 solution: **C**; 6 solution: **A**.

VERSE DECODER:

1 solution:

Thus saith the LORD; For three transgressions of Gaza, and for four, I will not turn away the punishment thereof; because they carried away captive the whole captivity, to deliver them up to Edom:
Amos 1:6

Page 126

CROSSWORD: Old Testament Books

1 C	2 A	3 N	4 A		5 P	6 A	7 R	8 T		9 H	10 A	11 M
12 O	D	O	R		13 A	D	U	E		14 A	B	E
15 E	Z	R	A	16 A	N	D	E	X	17 O	D	U	S
			18 M	A	D	E			19 N	E	S	T
20 J	21 O	22 N	A	H	A	N	23 D	24 H	O	S	E	A
25 A	L	A	I			26 D	A	B				
27 W	E	N	C	28 E	29 S		30 P	O	31 M	32 A	33 D	34 E
				35 T	I	36 A			37 E	L	I	E
38 J	39 O	40 E	41 L	A	N	D	42 D	43 A	N	I	E	L
44 E	S	T	A			45 D	I	D	O			
46 E	S	T	H	47 E	48 R	A	N	D	R	49 U	50 T	51 H
52 P	I	A		53 R	I	M	A		54 A	M	O	S
55 S	E	S		56 N	O	S	H		57 H	A	R	T

Page 127

LETTER SQUARES: In the Old Testament

1 solution:

Hear, O Israel: The LORD our God is one LORD:
Deuteronomy 6:4

MULTIPLE CHOICE:

1 solution: **D**; 2 solution: **A**; 3 solution: **D**;
4 solution: **B**.

VERSE DECODER:

1 solution:

And that whosoever would not come within three days, according to the counsel of the princes and the elders, all his substance should be forfeited, and himself separated from the congregation of those that had been carried away.
Ezra 10:8

Page 128

CROSSWORD: Praises

1 L	2 U	3 N	4 G	■	5 L	6 E	7 E	8 S	■	9 A	10 H	11 A
12 A	L	O	E	■	13 A	D	A	M	■	14 B	U	M
15 M	E	A	N	■	16 N	A	S	A	■	17 A	L	E
18 B	E	H	I	19 N	D	M	E	S	20 A	T	A	N
■	■	■	21 E	L	M	■	■	22 H	U	T	■	■
23 T	24 A	25 I	■	26 E	A	27 S	28 T	■	29 L	O	30 G	31 E
32 U	N	D	33 E	R	S	T	A	34 N	D	I	N	G
35 B	O	O	R	■	36 S	U	R	E	■	37 R	U	G
■	■	38 L	E	39 A	■	■	40 T	E	41 A	■	■	■
42 P	43 R	A	I	S	44 E	45 A	N	D	F	46 A	47 M	48 E
49 O	U	T	■	50 C	U	R	E	■	51 T	O	O	L
52 O	N	E	■	53 O	R	T	S	■	54 E	N	O	S
55 P	E	R	■	56 T	O	Y	S	■	57 R	E	N	E

SOLUTIONS

Page 129

LETTER SQUARES: In the Old Testament

1 solution:

All the congregation of Israel shall keep it.
Exodus 12:47

MULTIPLE CHOICE:

1 solution: **D**; 2 solution: **C**; 3 solution: **A**.

LETTER SQUARES:

2 solution:

So they took up Jonah, and cast him forth into the sea:
Jonah 1:15

Page 130

LETTER SQUARES: In the Old Testament

1 solution:

Then said the LORD, Doest thou well to be angry?
Jonah 4:4

MULTIPLE CHOICE:

1 solution: **B**; 2 solution: **D**; 3 solution: **A**;
4 solution: **C**.

VERSE DECODER:

1 solution:

Then the LORD said unto Moses, now shalt thou see what I will do to Pharaoh: For with a strong hand shall he let them go, and with a strong hand shall he drive them out of his land.
Exodus 6:1

SOLUTIONS

Page 131

CROSSWORD: Honor

S	L	A	M		S	P	A		S	H	E	M
A	I	D	A		A	I	L		T	A	R	E
G	R	A	C	I	O	U	S	W	O	M	A	N
S	A	M	B	A		S	O	A	R			
			E	N	D			D	E	P	T	H
L	A	S	T		O	O	Z	E		L	O	U
O	F	T	H	E	G	L	O	R	I	O	U	S
B	R	A		R	E	D	O		M	Y	T	H
S	O	N	A	R			M	O	P			
			T	O	T	E		D	A	R	E	D
B	O	T	H	R	I	C	H	E	S	A	N	D
O	L	E	O		P	H	I		S	T	O	A
Y	E	N	S		S	O	P		E	A	S	Y

Page 132

LETTER SQUARES: In the Old Testament

1 solution:

And now, O ye priests, this commandment is for you. Malachi 2:1

MULTIPLE CHOICE:

1 solution: **B**; 2 solution: **B**; 3 solution: **C**;

4 solution: **D**.

Page 133

LETTER SQUARES: In the Old Testament

1 solution:

For I am the LORD, I change not; Malachi 3:6

MULTIPLE CHOICE:

1 solution: **A**; 2 solution: **B**; 3 solution: **C**.

VERSE DECODER:

1 solution:

And it came to pass, when they had eaten up the corn which they had brought out of Egypt, their Father said unto them, go again, buy us a little food. Genesis 43:2

Page 134

CROSSWORD: Knowledge

S	L	A	P		I	A	N		A	P	S	E
H	A	I	R		F	L	O		R	O	A	N
U	N	D	E	R	S	T	A	N	D	I	N	G
T	A	S	T	Y		O	H	I	O			
			Z	E	D			G	R	A	P	H
A	C	N	E		Y	E	A	H		L	E	A
S	H	A	L	L	A	N	Y	T	E	A	C	H
P	I	P		E	D	D	A		A	S	K	S
S	T	E	R	N			H	A	S			
			A	T	O	P		D	I	A	N	A
O	F	G	O	O	D	A	N	D	E	V	I	L
L	I	E	U		O	V	A		S	E	L	L
D	E	L	L		R	E	B		T	R	E	Y

SOLUTIONS

Page 135

LETTER SQUARES: In the Old Testament

1 solution:

Alas for the day! For the day of the Lord is at hand.
Joel 1:15

MULTIPLE CHOICE:

1 solution: **A**; 2 solution: **B**; 3 solution: **B**;
4 solution: **C**; 5 solution: **C**; 6 solution: **B**.

Page 136

MULTIPLE CHOICE: In the Old Testament

1 solution: **B**; 2 solution: **B**; 3 solution: **B**;
4 solution: **C**.

VERSE DECODER:

1 solution:

And he dreamed, and behold a ladder set up on the earth, and the top of it reached to heaven: And behold the angels of God ascending and descending on it.
Genesis 28:12

Page 137

CROSSWORD: Numbers

1 S	2 E	3 A	4 M	■	5 T	6 E	7 L	■	8 S	9 H	10 A	11 G
12 U	R	G	E	■	13 R	D	A	■	14 M	U	I	R
15 R	E	A	S	16 S	I	G	N	■	17 I	N	R	I
18 F	I	R	S	T	B	E	G	19 O	T	T	E	N
■	■	■	20 I	R	E	■	21 U	S	E	S	■	■
22 M	23 E	24 S	A	■	■	25 A	I	L	■	26 M	27 A	28 W
29 A	L	P	H	30 A	31 A	N	D	O	32 M	E	G	A
33 P	S	I	■	34 I	C	Y	■	■	35 E	N	O	S
■	■	36 T	37 A	D	A	■	38 I	39 O	N	■	■	■
40 T	41 H	E	S	E	C	42 O	N	D	A	43 D	44 A	45 M
46 O	A	F	S	■	47 I	N	S	E	C	U	R	E
48 T	R	U	E	■	49 A	C	E	■	50 E	M	I	L
51 S	I	L	T	■	52 S	E	T	■	53 S	P	A	T

Page 138

LETTER SQUARES: In the Old Testament

1 solution:

So the king and Haman came to banquet with Esther the queen.
Esther 7:1

MULTIPLE CHOICE:

1 solution: **B**; 2 solution: **C**; 3 solution: **B**.

LETTER SQUARES:

2 solution:

For the Lord knoweth the way of the righteous: but the way of the ungodly shall perish.
Psalms 1:6

SOLUTIONS

Page 139

CROSSWORD: Biblical Tribes

1 A	2 L	3 B	■	4 O	5 G	6 L	7 E	■	8 C	9 A	10 L	11 F
12 J	O	E	■	13 P	R	A	T	■	14 I	R	A	E
15 A	N	N	■	16 C	A	N	A	17 A	N	I	T	E
18 R	E	J	19 O	I	C	E	■	20 M	E	D	E	S
■	■	21 A	R	T	E	■	22 H	I	M	■	■	■
23 L	24 A	M	B	■	■	25 R	E	C	A	26 N	27 E	28 S
29 A	M	I	■	30 P	31 L	A	T	E	■	32 A	V	A
33 C	O	N	34 C	E	A	L	■	■	35 S	P	E	D
■	■	■	36 O	T	T	■	37 S	38 H	A	H	■	■
39 A	40 G	41 A	P	E	■	42 S	C	E	P	T	43 E	44 R
45 S	A	M	A	R	46 I	T	A	N	■	47 A	N	A
48 O	B	E	Y	■	49 D	A	R	N	■	50 L	O	N
51 F	E	N	S	■	52 A	R	E	A	■	53 I	S	T

Page 140

LETTER SQUARES: In the Old Testament

1 solution:

Return, O LORD, deliver my soul: oh save me for thy mercies' sake.
Psalms 6:4

MULTIPLE CHOICE:

1 solution: **C**; 2 solution: **B**; 3 solution: **B**.

VERSE DECODER:

1 solution:

Ah sinful nation, a people laden with iniquity, a seed of evildoers, children that are corrupters: They have foresaken the LORD, they have provoked the Holy One of Israel unto anger, they are gone away backward.
Isaiah 1:4

Page 141

LETTER SQUARES: In the Old Testament

1 solution:

O LORD my God, in thee do I put my trust:
Psalms 7:1

MULTIPLE CHOICE:

1 solution: **C**; 2 solution: **C**; 3 solution: **B**;
4 solution: **C**; 5 solution: **C**.

Page 142

CROSSWORD: Biblical Browsing

1 H	2 U	3 R	4 T	■	5 T	6 I	7 E	■	8 S	9 O	10 L	11 E
12 E	Z	E	R	■	13 H	A	M	■	14 E	V	I	L
15 L	A	C	E	■	16 E	M	M	17 A	N	U	E	L
18 P	I	L	A	19 T	E	■	20 A	L	U	M	N	I
■	■	21 A	D	O	■	22 P	U	P	A	■	■	■
23 E	24 P	I	S	T	L	E	S	■	25 H	26 O	27 S	28 T
29 A	I	M	■	■	■	T	■	■	■	30 N	U	N
31 T	A	S	32 K	■	33 H	E	L	34 P	35 M	E	E	T
■	■	■	36 E	37 B	E	R	■	38 R	A	S	■	■
39 A	40 P	41 P	E	A	L	■	42 S	E	N	I	43 L	44 E
45 B	L	I	N	D	M	46 A	N	■	47 T	M	A	N
48 C	O	M	E	■	49 E	G	O	■	50 R	U	S	T
51 S	T	A	R	■	52 T	O	W	■	53 A	S	T	O

Page 143

LETTER SQUARES: In the Old Testament

1 solution:

He looketh on the earth, and it trembleth:
Psalms 104:32

MULTIPLE CHOICE:

1 solution: **A**; 2 solution: **D**; 3 solution: **A**;
4 solution: **D**; 5 solution: **A**; 6 solution: **A**.

SOLUTIONS

Page 144

MULTIPLE CHOICE: In the Old Testament

1 solution: **A**; 2 solution: **D**.

VERSE DECODER:

1 solution:

Moses my servant is dead; now therefore arise, go over this Jordon, thou, and all this people, unto the land which I do give to them, even to the Children of Israel.
Joshua 1:2

LETTER SQUARES:

1 solution:

The king also said unto them, Take with you the servants of your lord,
1 Kings 1:33

Page 145

CROSSWORD: Beasts of Prey

1 G	2 R	3 E	4 G		5 S	6 O	7 P		8 I	9 S	10 L	11 E
12 N	E	A	R		13 E	M	U		14 S	E	E	R
15 A	D	R	I	16 A	T	I	C		17 S	C	A	R
18 W	O	L	F	C	A	T	C	19 H	E	T	H	
			20 F	E	E		21 I	I	I			
22 A	23 N	24 T	I			25 I	N	S		26 P	27 I	28 T
29 L	I	O	N	30 P	31 E	R	I	S	32 H	E	T	H
33 E	L	M		34 A	N	A			35 E	A	S	E
			36 A	S	H		37 S	38 P	A			
	39 U	40 N	T	O	A	41 L	E	O	P	42 A	43 R	44 D
45 O	P	A	L		46 N	E	G	L	I	G	E	E
47 N	O	T	A		48 C	O	O		49 N	U	N	S
50 E	N	O	S		51 E	N	S		52 G	E	E	K

Page 146

MULTIPLE CHOICE: In the Old Testament

1 solution: **C**; 2 solution: **C**; 3 solution: **C**;

4 solution: **C**; 5 solution: **C**; 6 solution: **C**.

LETTER SQUARES:

1 solution:

And the daughter of Zion is left as a cottage in a vineyard,...
Isaiah 1:8

Page 147

VERSE DECODER: In the Old Testament

1 solution:

And the mountains shall be molten under him, and the valleys shall be cleft, as wax before the fire, and as the waters that are poured down a steep place.
Micah 1:4

MULTIPLE CHOICE:

1 solution: **D**; 2 solution: **C**; 3 solution: **D**.

LETTER SQUARES:

1 solution:

In that day shall the branch of the LORD be beautiful and glorious
Isaiah 4:2

SOLUTIONS

Page 148

LETTER SQUARES: In the Old Testament

1 solution:

Can two walk together, except
they be agreed?
Amos 3:3

MULTIPLE CHOICE:

1 solution: **A**; 2 solution: **C**; 3 solution: **B**.

VERSE DECODER:

1 solution:

A prayer of the afflicted, when he
is overwhelmed, and poureth out his
compliant before the Lord. Hear
my prayer, O LORD, and let my cry
come unto thee.
Psalms 101:1

Page 149

CROSSWORD: Biblical Armory

1 A	2 R	3 G	4 O	■	5 E	6 R	7 R	■	8 S	9 E	10 A	11 L
12 R	O	O	M	■	13 G	E	E	■	14 A	R	E	A
15 T	W	O	E	16 D	G	E	D	17 S	W	O	R	D
18 S	E	D	G	E	■	19 F	R	O	■	20 S	O	Y
■	■	21 W	A	I	22 L	■	23 O	N	24 E	■	■	■
25 A	26 L	I	■	27 C	A	28 P	O	■	29 E	30 L	31 B	32 E
33 H	E	L	34 M	E	T	O	F	35 B	R	A	S	S
36 S	O	L	O	■	37 T	I	E	R	■	38 N	A	P
■	■	■	39 W	40 O	E	■	41 D	I	42 E	D	■	■
43 A	44 W	45 L	■	46 W	R	47 Y	■	48 E	M	M	49 E	50 T
51 S	H	I	52 E	L	D	O	53 F	F	A	I	T	H
54 K	E	E	N	■	55 A	R	E	■	56 I	N	T	O
57 S	T	U	D	■	58 Y	E	W	■	59 L	E	E	R

Page 150

WORD SEARCH: Abraham's Progeny

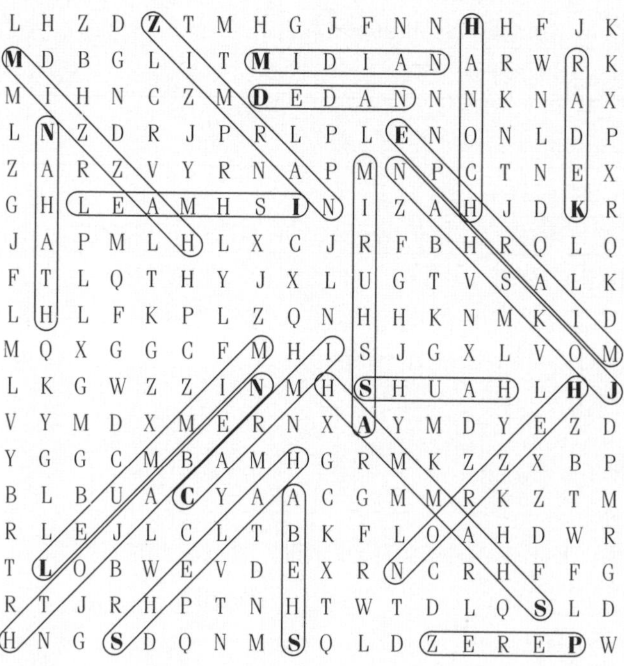

Page 151

WORD SEARCH: Altar Sites

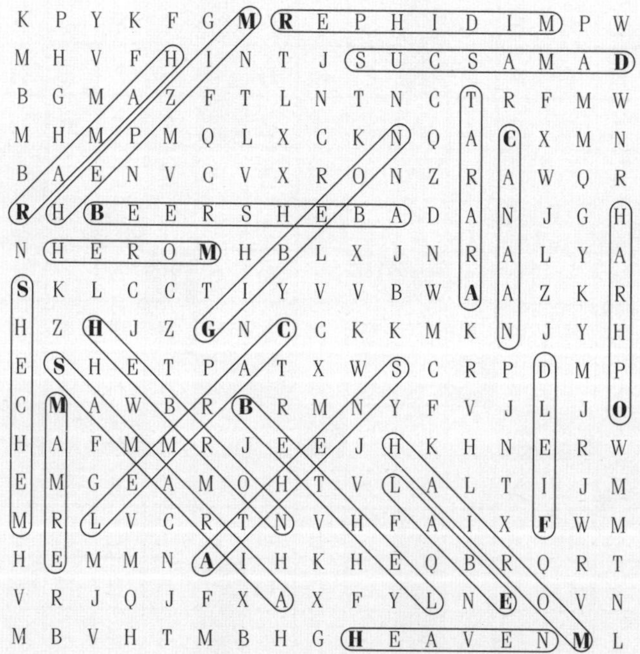

SOLUTIONS

Page 152

MULTIPLE CHOICE: Biblical Rulers

1 solution: **B**; 2 solution: **D**; 3 solution: **C**;

4 solution: **B**; 5 solution: **B**; 6 solution: **A.**

Page 153

WORD SEARCH: Israel's Enemies

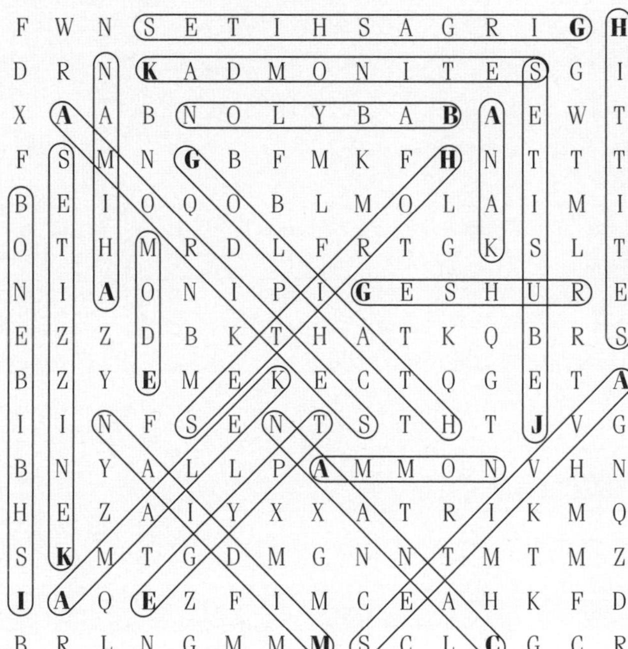

Page 154

WORD SEARCH: David's Men

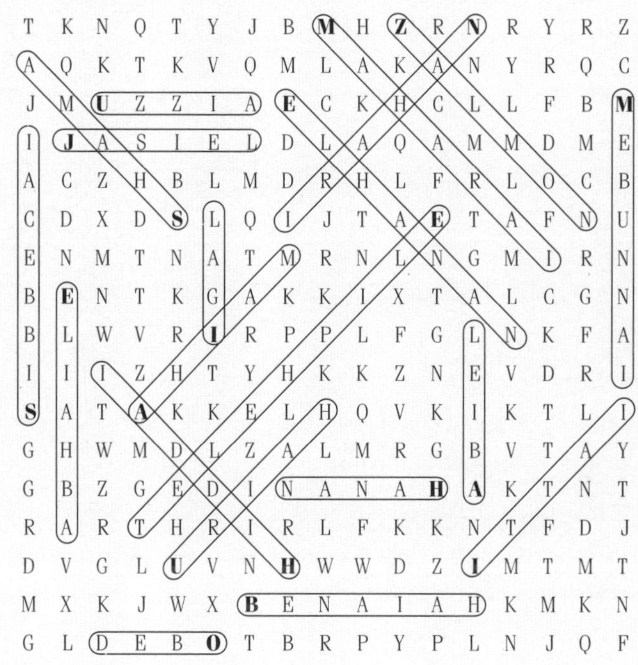

Page 155

WORD SEARCH: Cities of Judah

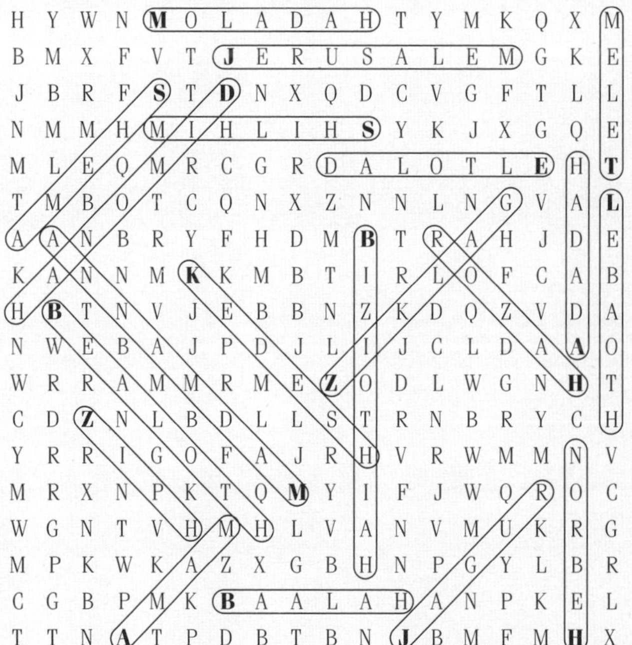

SOLUTIONS

Page 156

MULTIPLE CHOICE: For the Equipping of the Saints

1 solution: **A**; 2 solution: **B**; 3 solution: **A**;

4 solution: **C**; 5 solution: **C**; 6 solution: **A.**

Page 157

WORD SEARCH: Jewish Kings

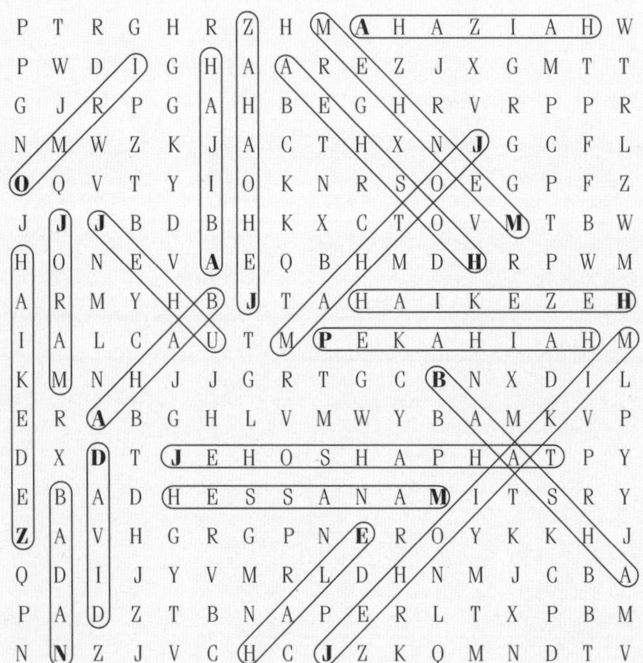

Page 158

WORD SEARCH: John the Baptist

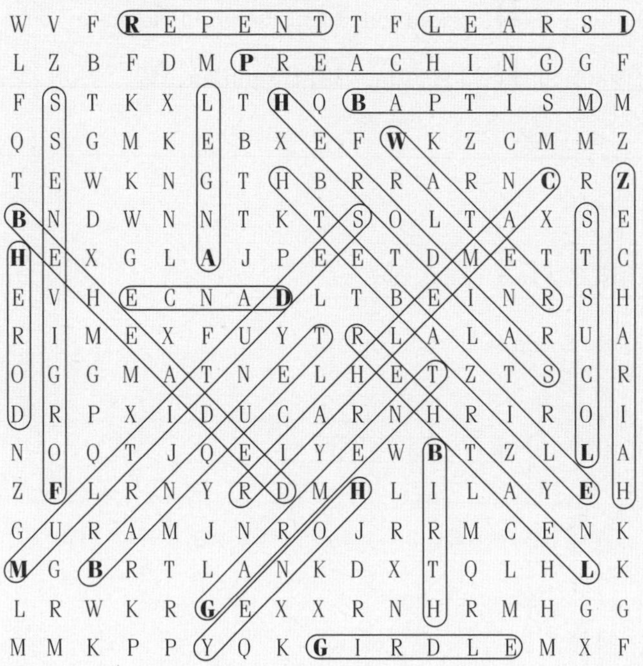

Page 159

WORD SEARCH: Job's Sorrow

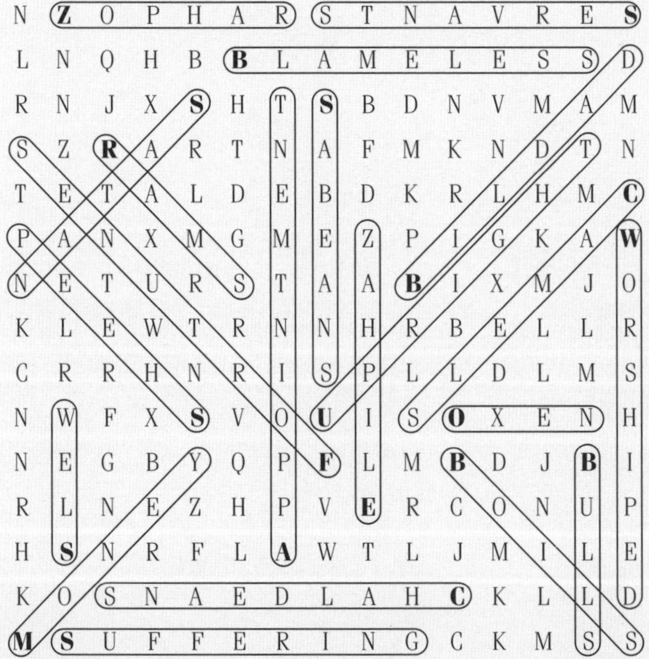

SOLUTIONS

Page 160

MULTIPLE CHOICE: Go Therefore and Make Disciples

1 solution: **A**; 2 solution: **A**; 3 solution: **A**;

4 solution: **D**; 5 solution: **B**; 6 solution: **C.**

Page 161

WORD SEARCH: Jonah and the Whale

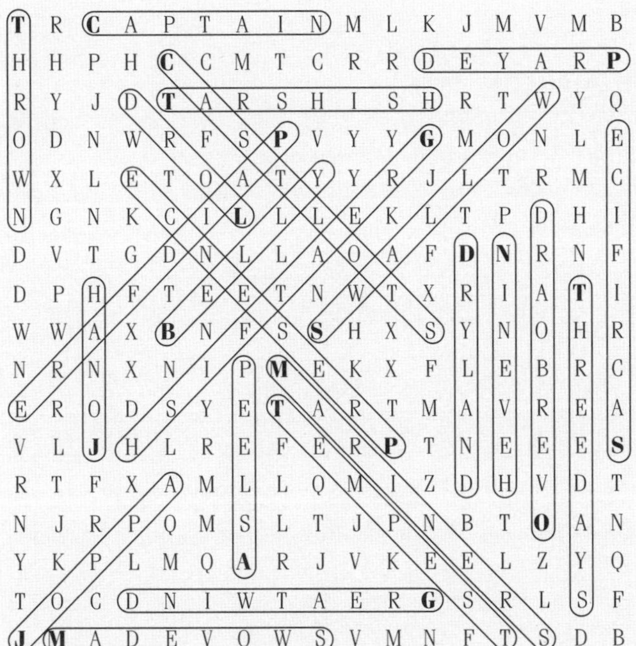

Page 162

WORD SEARCH: Making the Tabernacle

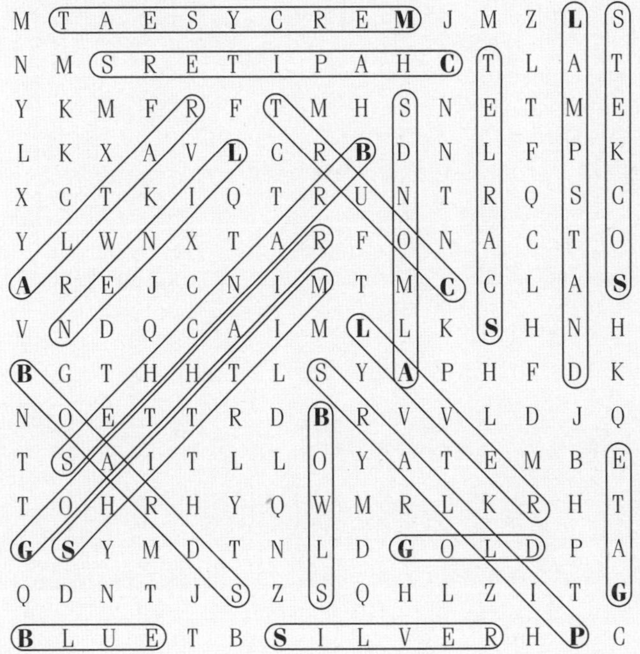

Page 163

MULTIPLE CHOICE: I am Joseph

1 solution: **B**; 2 solution: **B**; 3 solution: **A**;

4 solution: **D**; 5 solution: **A**; 6 solution: **B.**

Page 164

MULTIPLE CHOICE: I am Joseph

1 solution: **C**; 2 solution: **B**; 3 solution: **B**;

4 solution: **C**; 5 solution: **D**; 6 solution: **C.**

SOLUTIONS

Page 165

WORDSEARCH: Men Found in the Old Testament

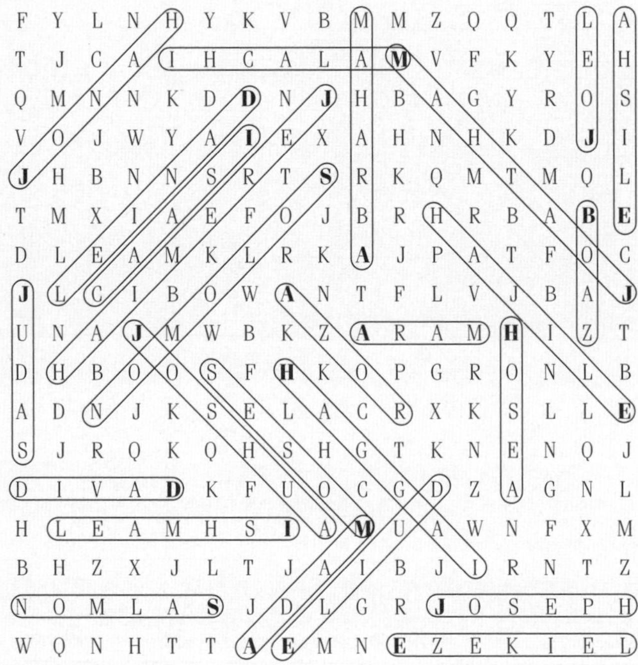

Page 166

WORD SEARCH: Noah's Ark

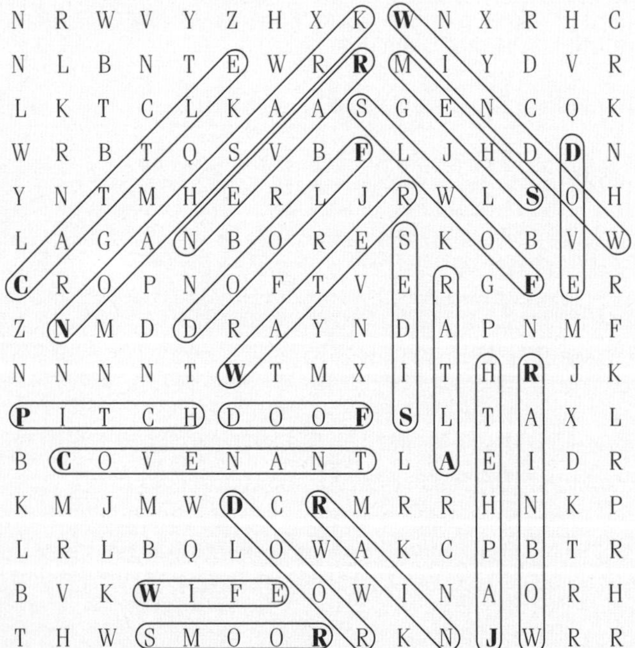

Page 167

MULTIPLE CHOICE: Labor of Love

1 solution: **D**; 2 solution: **C**; 3 solution: **B**;
4 solution: **A**; 5 solution: **B**; 6 solution: **D.**

Page 168

MULTIPLE CHOICE: Labor of Love

1 solution: **A**; 2 solution: **B**; 3 solution: **C**;
4 solution: **A**; 5 solution: **D**; 6 solution: **B.**

Page 169

WORD SEARCH: Plagues of Egypt

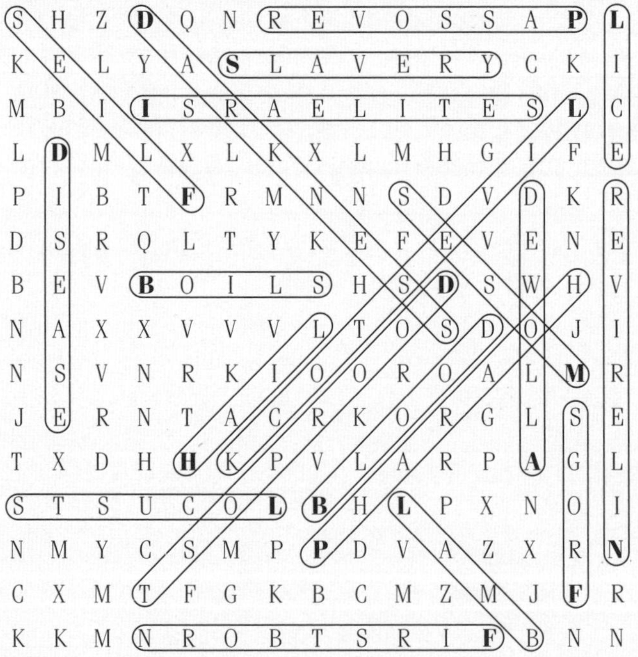

SOLUTIONS

Page 170

WORD SEARCH: Queen Esther

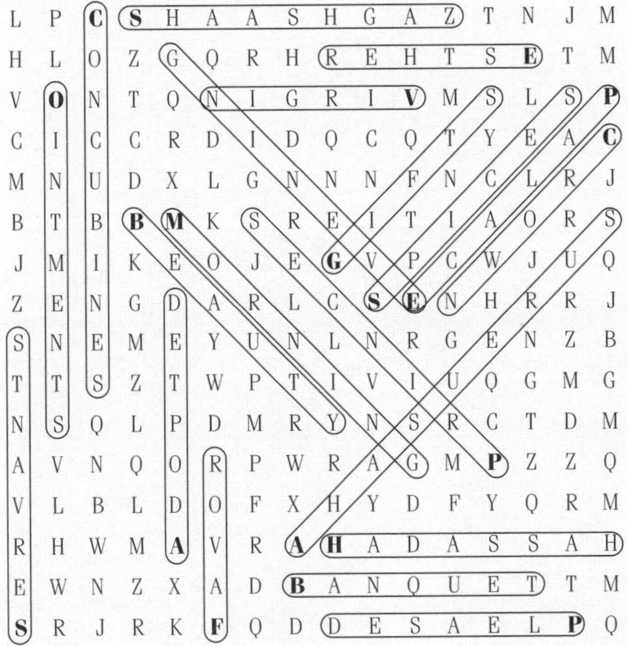

Page 172

MULTIPLE CHOICE: Looking Good, Smelling Good

1 solution: **A**; 2 solution: **D**; 3 solution: **C**;
4 solution: **B**; 5 solution: **C**; 6 solution: **D.**

Page 173

MULTIPLE CHOICE: Looking Good, Smelling Good

1 solution: **C**; 2 solution: **B**; 3 solution: **A**;
4 solution: **C**; 5 solution: **D**; 6 solution: **C.**

Page 171

WORD SEARCH: Rebekah and Isaac

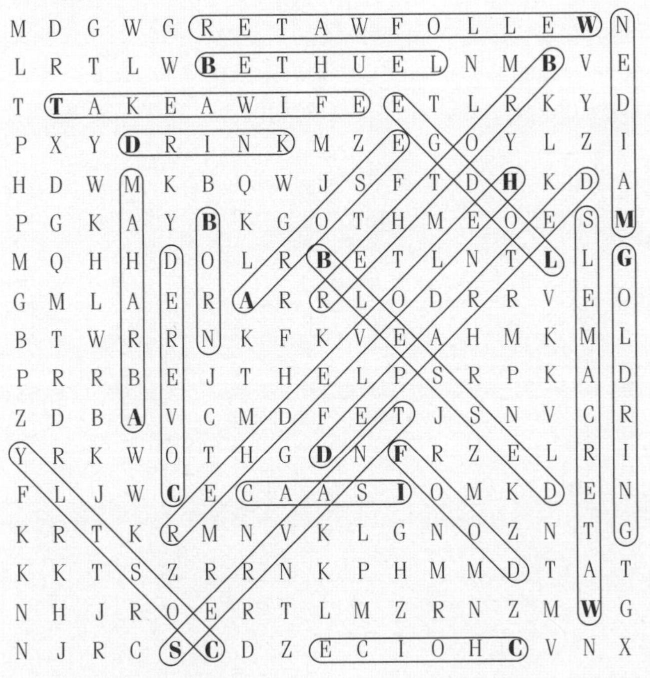

Page 174

WORDSEARCH: The First Couple

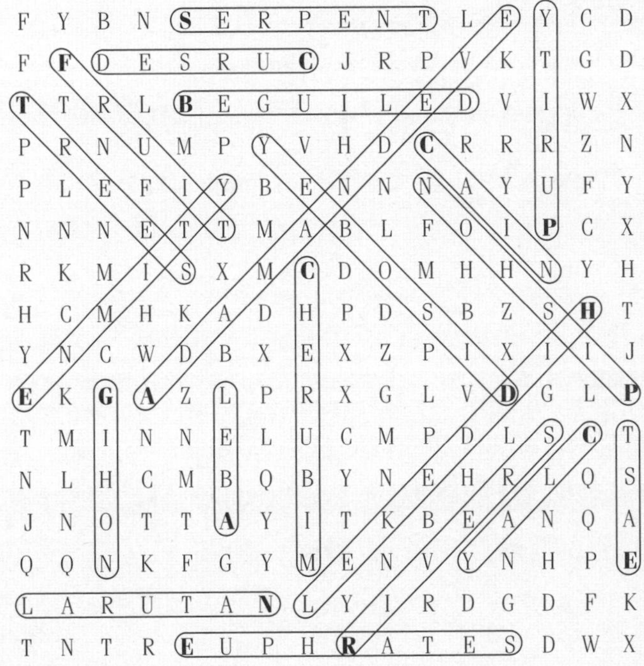

SOLUTIONS

Page 175

WORD SEARCH: The Spirit vs. The Flesh

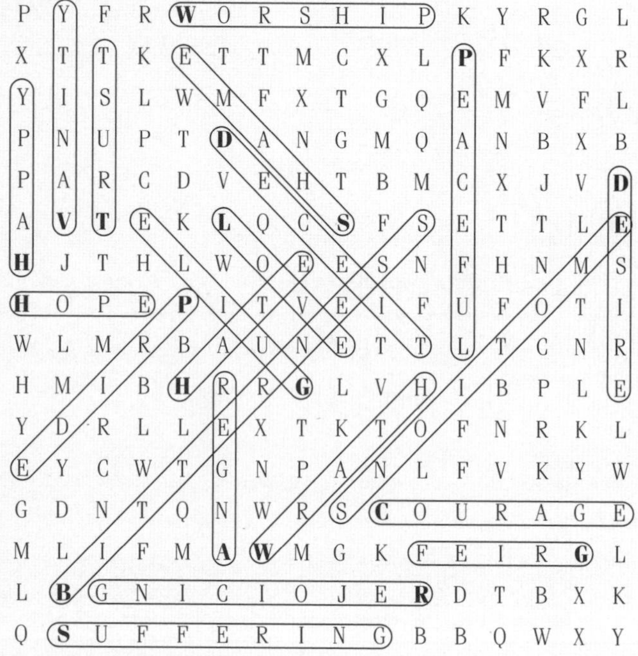

Page 176

MULTIPLE CHOICE: My Name Means "O"

1 solution: **A**; 2 solution: **D**; 3 solution: **B**;

4 solution: **A**; 5 solution: **C**; 6 solution: **A.**

Page 177

MULTIPLE CHOICE: My Name Means "O"

1 solution: **D**; 2 solution: **C**; 3 solution: **B**;

4 solution: **B**; 5 solution: **D**; 6 solution: **C.**

Page 178

WORD SEARCH: Wells and Pools

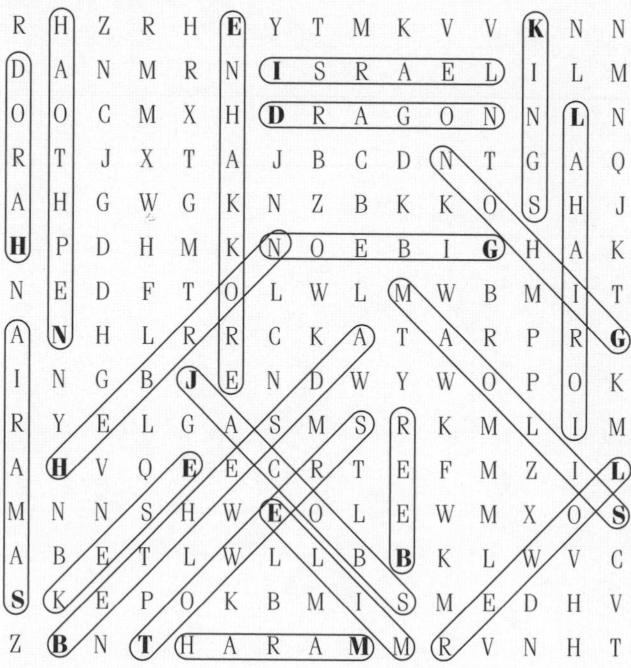

Page 179

WORD SEARCH: Women of the Old Testament

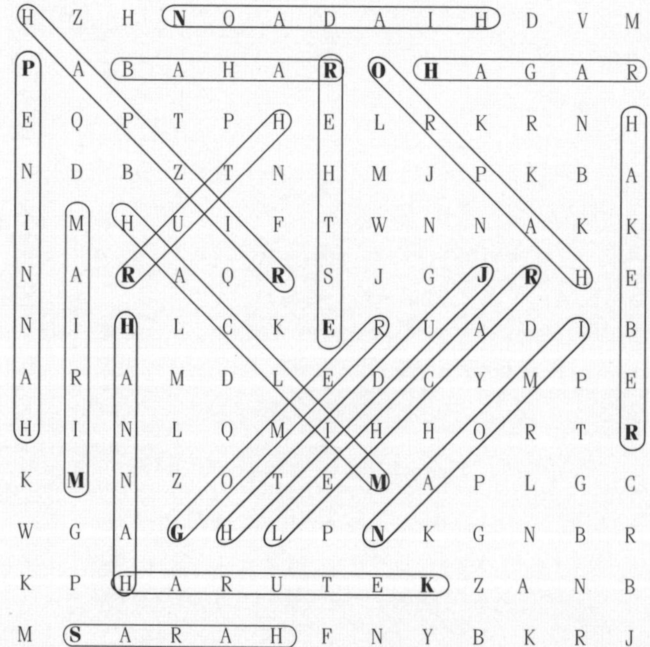

CHAPTER 4

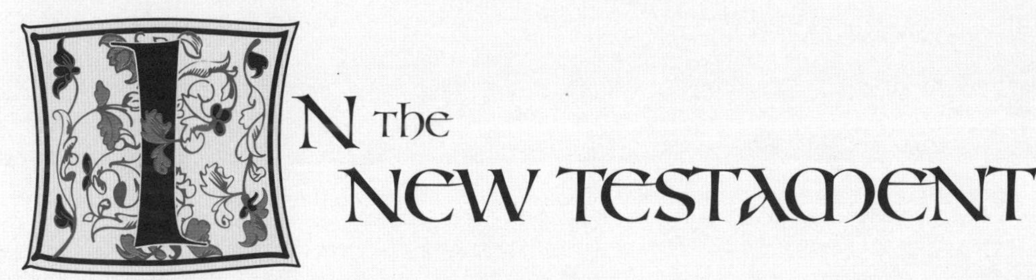

CROSSWORD: **Biblical Towns**

By Rowan Millson

1	2	3	4	■	5	6	7	■	8	9	10	11
12				■	13			■	14			
15				16				■	17			
■	■	■	18				■	19				
20	21	22				■	23				■	■
24				■	25	26					27	28
29			■	30					■	31		
32			33					■	34			
■	■	35				■	36	37				
38	39				■	40				■	■	■
41				■	42					43	44	45
46				■	47			■	48			
49				■	50			■	51			

ACROSS

1 Old Testament book
5 He died "old and full of days"
8 Assist
12 Flood survivor
13 Period of time
14 Like the desert of Sinai
15 City destroyed by God
17 "None is so fierce that dare __ him up" (Job 41:10)
18 Actor Julia
19 "Suzanne" composer Leonard __
20 Sounds from Gideon's trumpet?
23 Ringlet
24 Traditional knowledge
25 Some electrical devices
29 Kimono sash
30 Broadway failures
31 "... and the archers __ him" (1 Sam. 31:3)
32 "And ye are __ in him" (Col. 2:10)
34 Butte kin
35 Grad
36 Wanderer
38 Bandleader Shaw
40 "The __ are a people not strong" (Prov. 30:25)
41 "He saith among the trumpets, __" (Job 39:25)
42 "... Lord Jesus Christ, let him be __ Maranatha" (1 Cor. 16:22)
46 "For __ hereunto were ye called" (1 Pet. 2:21)
47 Wildebeest
48 "Thou shalt not follow a multitude to do __" (Ex. 23:2)
49 Carnivore's diet
50 Son of 12-Across
51 "And Jacob said, __ me this day thy birthright" (Gen. 25:31)

DOWN

1 Chang's twin
2 San Diego tourist mecca
3 Abraham found one caught in a thicket
4 "My kingdom for __!" (2 words)
5 "... children of Judah had fought against __" (Judg. 1:8)
6 Spoken
7 Humbug!
8 Classify
9 "Now when Jesus was born in __ of Judea" (Matt. 2:1)
10 Cleveland's lake
11 Gull relative
16 Betrayer
19 "... as the washing of pots and __" (Mark. 7:8)
20 Alliance
21 Timber wolf
22 Joseph of __
23 Simon Peter's hometown on the Sea of Galilee
26 Decimal point
27 "... and the children shall __ up against their parents" (Matt. 10:21)
28 What the magi followed
30 Chimney part
33 Flexible
34 Prepares potatoes?
37 Mel the Giant baseballer
38 "Pardon me!"
39 Pan's opposite
40 Prophetess mentioned in Luke 2:36
42 Kabul coin (abbr.)
43 Adam's mate
44 Wire measure (abbr.)
45 "Follow peace with __ men" (Heb. 12:14)

MULTIPLE CHOICE: **In the New Testament**

1 A landowner's servants are beaten up in what parable?

A. The lost coin **C.** The tares
B. The hidden treasure **D.** The tenants

2 Which epistle warns against people sent in to "spy on our liberty"?

A. Colossians **C.** Romans
B. Ephesians **D.** Galatians

3 Servants are given money to invest in which parable?

A. The creditor and two debtors **C.** The reaper and the sower
B. The talents **D.** The minas

VERSE DECODER:

1 Revelation 14:3

HINT: In the puzzle below, the letter "X" is actually an "E."

UYS PZXK CJYW UC FP MXNX U YXM CBYW LXGBNX PZX PZNBYX, UYS LXGBNX PZX GBJN LXUCPC, UYS PZX XOSXNC: UYS YB VUY HBJOS OXUNY PZUP CBYW LJP PZX ZJYSNXS UYS GBNPK UYS GBJN PZBJCUYS, MZFHZ MXNX NXSXXVXS GNBV PZX XUNPZ.

LETTER SQUARES:

1 Revelation 1:5

I N S	W A	O D	S O	S ,	U N T	H I	S H E
I M	R S	B L O	O V E	W N	I N	D U	T H A
S F	D U	A N D	R O M	T L	O U	O H	,

LETTER SQUARES: **In the New Testament**

1 Revelation 1:8

N G ,	N D	E G I	G A ,	I A	N D I	N G	E B
T H	M A	A A	N N I	T H	L P H	O M E	E E
A N D							

MULTIPLE CHOICE:

1 What did John the Baptist tell the tax collectors who came to him to be baptized?

A. To stop collecting taxes

B. To collect no more than was legal

C. To come follow him

D. To give 10 percent of their income to the poor

2 Which of these women became the first Christian missionary?

A. Priscilla

B. Salome

C. Anna

D. Drusilla

3 Who wore a tunic made from camel hair?

A. Jesus

B. John the Baptist

C. Daniel

D. Joseph

VERSE DECODER:

1 Revelation 5:5

HINT: In the puzzle below, the letter "P" is actually an "A."

PFW AFG AK USG GDWGEX XPZUS VFUA NG, OGGL FAU: QGSADW USG

DZAF AK USG UEZQG AK HVWPS, USG EAAU AK WPIZW, SPUS LEGIPZDGW

UA ALGF USG QAAB PFW UA DAAXG USG XGIGF XGPDX USGEGAK.

CROSSWORD: **Songs of Faith**

By Thomas W. Schier

ACROSS

1 King of Judah (1 Kings 15:9)
4 Advertiser's target
8 See 45 Across
12 Wrestling site
13 Post-Christmas event
14 Hebrew calendar month
15 Song of faith
18 Ollie's comedic partner
19 New Haven school
20 Song of faith
26 "The voice of __ crying in the wilderness" (Matt. 3:3)
27 Where Adam was born
28 Activate the lights
32 Olympic awards
34 "... blackbirds baked in __"
35 Matchsticks game
36 Song of faith
42 "... gain the whole world, and lose his own __"
43 Hot and iced drinks
45 Line from a classic song of faith, with 8-Across
50 Saintly ring
51 Dove, for one
52 Understood, as a punch line
53 "Beverly Hillbillies" daughter
54 Strong inclinations
55 Part of Q&A

DOWN

1 Book after Joel
2 __ Clara, CA
3 Varsity starters
4 1996 Summer Olympics host
5 "For verily I __ unto you" (Matt. 5:18)
6 Comedienne Boosler
7 Change price labels
8 Like most taxi fares
9 A judge of Israel
10 Bottom-line amount
11 Shout to a matador
16 Gene ID
17 HS math subject
21 Animal park
22 "... there was no room for them in the __" (Luke 2:7)
23 Tooth treaters' org.
24 Piece of animation
25 Anne's pair?
28 Mai __ (rum drink)
29 FedEx rival
30 River inlet
31 Paper hawker
32 .001 inch
33 British record label
35 "Whoa, __!"
37 You, in Paris
38 Wifey's mate
39 Mobile phone co.
40 Hägar the Horrible's wife in comic strips
41 Eagle's grabber
44 High-alt. jets
45 __ Lord's Prayer
46 Prince or Holbrook
47 Golf club shape
48 Fish-eating bird
49 NFL scores

MULTIPLE CHOICE: **In the New Testament**

1 What New Testament word means "teacher"?

A. Savior
B. Apollos
C. Rabbi
D. Rabbith

2 When Jesus said, "God is a Spirit: and they that worship Him must worship Him in spirit and in truth," who was he talking to?

A. The crippled woman
B. Mary Magdalene
C. The Samaritan
D. Martha

3 Who was the son of Zebedee?

A. John the Baptist
B. Peter
C. James
D. Paul

VERSE DECODER:

1 Luke 14:12

HINT: In the puzzle below, the letter "K" is actually an "E."

DAKB LGFH AK GSLI DI AFQ DAGD RGHK AFQ, PAKB DAIY QGMKLD G

HFBBKE IE G LYXXKE, ZGSS BID DAJ CEFKBHL, BIE DAJ REKDAEKB,

BKFDAKE DAJ MFBLQKB, BIE DAJ EFZA BKFWARIYEL; SKLD DAKJ

GSLI RFH DAKK GWGFB, GBH G EKZIQXKBLK RK QGHK DAKK.

LETTER SQUARES:

1 James 3:10

P R	R S I	T H	T H	E S	M O	N G .	O U T
C U	S S I	O C E	U T H	N G	A N D	A M E	B L E
E D E	O F						

MULTIPLE CHOICE: **In the New Testament**

1 Paul's first traveling companion was Barnabas. Who was his second?

A. Peter **C.** Mark
B. Silas **D.** Timothy

2 Who called Mary the "mother of my Lord"?

A. James **C.** Elizabeth
B. John the Baptist **D.** Zacharias

3 Which man was temporarily punished with dumbness because he failed to believe the angel Gabriel?

A. Caiaphas **C.** Zacharias
B. John the Baptist **D.** Annas

LETTER SQUARES:

1 James 3:12

E ,	B R E	B E R	E F	V E	R I E	T R E	T H
E N ,	O L I	C A N	T H R	B E	I G	A R	S ?
M Y							

VERSE DECODER:

1 Luke 6:1

HINT: In the puzzle below, the letter "M" is actually an "I."

DBX MI VDRN IQ FDLL QB ITN LNVQBX LDUUDIT DGINO ITN GMOLI, ITDI TN ANBI ITOQJZT ITN VQOB GMNCXL; DBX TML XMLVMFCNL FCJVENX ITN NDOL QG VQOB, DBX XMX NDI, OJUUMBZ ITNR MB ITNMO TDBXL.

CROSSWORD: **Seasonal Songs**

By Thomas W. Schier

1	2	3	4	5	■	6	7	8	■	9	10	11
12					■	13			14			
15					16							
17			■	18				■	19			
■	■	■	20			■	■	21			■	■
22	23	24		■	25	26	27		■	28	29	30
31				32					33			
34			■	35				■	36			
■	■	37	38		■	■	39	40		■	■	■
41	42			■	43	44			■	45	46	47
48				49					50			
51							■	52				
53			■	54			■	55				

ACROSS

1 Start of 15- and 31-Across
6 Eggs of science
9 Thai tongue
12 __ metabolism
13 Part of KJV
15 Starting with 1-Across, seasonal Christian song
17 Name of 13 popes
18 Aquatic bird
19 ABA member (abbr.)
20 *The Fountainhead* author Rand
21 Letters in some church names
22 Trio in Bethlehem
25 Caroling song
28 __ gratias
31 Starting with 1-Across, seasonal Christian song
34 Siouan Native American
35 Radar screen image
36 Copied
37 Apply lightly
39 Hot temper
41 Mass garments
43 "... also __ herself received strength" (Heb. 11:11)
45 Bonnet invader
48 Seasonal Christian song
51 Rings of color
52 Uneven, as if gnawed away
53 Map abbrs.
54 "With him is an __ of flesh" (2 Chron. 32:8)
55 "... glory of the Lord is __ upon thee" (Isa. 60:1)

DOWN

1 Son of Joktan (Gen. 10:28)
2 Auto racer Yarborough
3 Norwegian capital
4 "... call him, that he __ eat bread" (Ex. 2:20)
5 A song of mourning
6 Racetrack shape
7 "And the __ of the temple ..." (Mark 15:38)
8 "And he said, Who __ thou?" (Ruth 3:9)
9 "And he __ his eyes on his disciples" (Luke 6:20) (2 words)
10 Hot time in Quebec
11 One's partner
14 Pillow cover
16 Tornado part
20 "We __ to please!"
21 Chicken __ King
22 Cow's remark
23 Make a scene?
24 Farewells
26 Gosh preceder?
27 Holy Roman __
29 Ample shoe width
30 Methuselah-like
32 Fall off, as the tide
33 Dundee denial
38 "... __ fill so great a multitude?" (Matt. 15:33) (2 words)
40 Less refined
41 Open just a bit
42 Jesus Christ
43 "... there shall come a __ out of Jacob" (Num. 24:17)
44 "Excuse me!"
45 Cain and Abel, for example (Abbr.)
46 "I am the LORD, and there is none __" (Isa. 45:5)
47 Biblical garden spot
49 Ending for pay or Cray
50 "__ only and Barnabas" (1 Cor. 9:6) (2 words)

VERSE DECODER: **In the New Testament**

1 **Acts 28:17**

HINT: In the puzzle below, the letter "G" is actually an "I."

LVQ GP ULOI PB DLZZ, PKLP LRPIH PKHII QLXZ DLCF ULFFIQ PKI UKGIR BR

PKI TIJZ PBNIPKIH: LVQ JKIV PKIX JIHI UBOI PBNIPKIH, KI ZLGQ CVPB PKIO,

OIV LVQ AHIPKHIV, PKBCNK G KLMI UBOOGPPIQ VBPKGVN LNLGVZP PKI

DIBDFI, BH UCZPBOZ BR BCH RLPKIHZ, XIP JLZ G QIFGMIHIQ DHGZBVIH

RHBO TIHCZLFIO GVPB PKI KLVQZ BR PKI HBOLVZ.

***King James Games* Facts:** NEW TESTAMENT STATISTICS

The number of books in the New Testament is 27.

The middle book of the New Testament is 2 Thessalonians.

The middle chapters of the New Testament are Romans 8, 9.

The middle verse of the New Testament is Acts 27:17.

The shortest book of the New Testament is 3 John.

The shortest verse of the New Testament is John 11:35.

The longest verse of the New Testament is Revelation 20:4.

The longest chapter in the New Testament is Luke 1.

The longest book of the New Testament is Luke.

LETTER SQUARES:

1 **1 John 1:4**

S W	Y M	AND	NTO	T Y	AY	TH	JO
YO	THA	E W	FUL	ING	U,	TH	ESE
RIT	OUR	E U	BE	L.			

MULTIPLE CHOICE: **In the New Testament**

1 What sweet-smelling substance was brought to the infant Jesus?

A. Spikenard **B.** Cinnamon **C.** Frankincense **D.** Hyssop

2 Which friend of Paul was both an apostle and a co-author of 1 Thessalonians?

A. Peter **B.** Timothy **C.** Matthias **D.** John

3 While sleeping, who was visited by an angel of the Lord?

A. Saul **B.** Joseph **C.** Stephen **D.** King Herod

4 Sleep is used as a metaphor for physical death in which epistle?

A. 2 Corinthians 5 **C.** 1 Corinthians 15

B. 2 Thessalonians 2 **D.** 1 Thessalonians 1

5 Which apostle was a tax collector from Capernaum?

A. Paul **B.** Matthew **C.** Bartholomew **D.** John

6 What travel companion of Paul was called an apostle?

A. Peter **B.** John **C.** Barnabas **D.** Titus

VERSE DECODER:

1 Hebrews 1:3

HINT: In the puzzle below, the letter "S" is actually an "I."

HRO ACSBI KRC ANSIRKBCMM OD RSM IWONZ, UBF KRC CQTNCMM SGUIC OD RSM TCNMOB, UBF LTROWFSBI UWW KRSBIM AZ KRC HONF OD RSM TOHCN, HRCB RC RUF AZ RSGMCWD TLNICF OLN MSBM, MUK FOHB OB KRC NSIRK RUBF OD KRC GUYCMKZ OB RSIR:

CROSSWORD: **Rolling Stones**

By Joseph Mantell

1	2	3	4	■	5	6	7	■	8	9	10	11
12				■	13			■	14			
15				16				17				
18					■	19				■	■	■
■	■	■	20		21	■	■	22		23	24	25
26	27	28		■	29	30	31		■	32		
33				34					35			
36			■	37				■	38			
39			40		■	■	41	42		■	■	■
■	■	■	43		44	45	■	46		47	48	49
50	51	52					53					
54				■	55			■	56			
57				■	58			■	59			

ACROSS

1 East European
5 Historical time
8 Disorderly crowds
12 Hägar the Horrible's daughter
13 Toupee, informally
14 "Woe to the __ shepherd that leaveth the flock!" (Zech. 11:17)
15 "... roll a great stone __" (1 Sam 14:33) (4 words)
18 Electronics pioneer Nikola
19 "For Joshua drew not his __ back" (Josh. 8:26)
20 "Do they not __ that devise evil?" (Prov. 14:22)
22 Slogan
26 "And they took Joseph's __" (Gen. 37:31)
29 Emanation
32 Cereal grass
33 "... __ for to keep them" (Josh. 10:18) (5 words)
36 Record label
37 Maple fluids
38 Scandinavian capital
39 "Whosesoever sins ye __" (John 20:23)
41 Result of sun exposure
43 "As an eagle stirreth up her __" (Deut. 32:11)
46 Choir member
50 "... it will __" (Prov. 26:27) (3 words)
54 Declare as true
55 "There is none righteous, no, not __" (Rom. 3:10)
56 Actress Catherine __ Jones
57 Heredity factor
58 "He" is Big in London
59 Revival meeting shout

DOWN

1 "And Miriam was __ out from the camp" (Num. 12:15)
2 Single
3 Aardvark's diet
4 "Roses are red, __ are blue"
5 Formerly before
6 OT book
7 Turkish officer
8 Botch
9 "... wherewith the __ number of them is to be redeemed" (Num. 3:48)
10 Deadly reptile
11 Crafty
16 "... lest I __ mine own inheritance" (Ruth 4:6)
17 "... and it became lice __" (Ex. 8:17) (2 words)
21 Proportionately (with "pro")
23 Some Christmas presents
24 "... and not the __" (Deut. 28:13)
25 Film director Preminger
26 Singer Vikki
27 "... not __ nor twice" (2 Kings 6:10)
28 Father of Seth
30 Baseball official (abbr.)
31 "... and I will give you __" (Matt. 11:28)
34 Organic compound
35 Where Ben fed his Hoss?
40 Harden
42 Blood system
44 Arrogant person
45 Melody
47 Son of Noah
48 Location
49 Muscat locale
50 Discarded cloth
51 "For Adam was first formed, then __" (1 Tim. 2:13)
52 " __ cubits shall be the length of a board" (Ex. 26:16)
53 "... my tongue is the __ of a ready writer" (Ps. 45:1)

MULTIPLE CHOICE: **In the New Testament**

1 In the strange riddle of the Sadducees, how many husbands did the woman have?

A. 5 **C.** 7

B. 2 **D.** 10

2 What Greek scholar taught in the synagogue at Ephesus but was taught himself by Aquila and Priscilla?

A. Gamaliel **C.** Apollos

B. Peter **D.** Paul

3 Whose death caused the persecution of Christians throughout Judea and Samaria?

A. John the Baptist's **C.** Stephen's

B. Judas' **D.** Herod's

LETTER SQUARES:

1 Titus 1:1

AN	CHR	OF	AP	A S	ANT	ERV	AND
JES	OF	L ,	OST	GO	LE	D ,	IST
PAU	US	,					

VERSE DECODER:

1 Hebrews 9:9

HINT: In the puzzle below, the letter "F" is actually an "I."

KDFOD KRQ R YFHPSV YBS JDV JFWV JDVL CSVQVLJ, FL KDFOD KVSV

BYYVSVE TBJD HFYJQ RLE QROSFYFOVQ, JDRJ OBPAE LBJ WRUV DFW

JDRJ EFE JDV QVSNFOV CVSYVOJ, RQ CVSJRFLFLH JB JDV OBLQOFVLOV;

VERSE DECODER: **In the New Testament**

1 Colossians 1:9

HINT: In the puzzle below, the letter "J" is actually an "O."

NJB UKWZ MTCZF YF TSZJ, ZWOMF UKF ATG YF KFTBA WU, AJ OJU

MFTZF UJ HBTG NJB GJC, TOA UJ AFZWBF UKTU GF DWQKU XF

NWSSFA YWUK UKF EOJYSFAQF JN KWZ YWSS WO TSS YWZAJD TOA

ZHWBWUCTS COAFBZUTOAWOQ;

MULTIPLE CHOICE:

1 Paul, Aquila, and Priscilla were in the same trade. What was it?

A. Tentmaking **B.** Farming **C.** Shepherding **D.** Fishing

2 Who was exiled to the island of Patmos?

A. Peter **B.** John **C.** James **D.** Noah

3 Who succeeded Judas Iscariot as an apostle?

A. Barsabas **B.** Matthias **C.** Barabbas **D.** Justus

4 Which apostle addressed the Pentecost crowd in a loud voice?

A. Stephen **B.** Peter **C.** John **D.** Judas

5 Because of a vow, which Christian shaved his head at Cenchrea?

A. Peter **B.** John **C.** Paul **D.** Matthew

6 The Bible mentions a place where shepherds received angels as late visitors. Where is it near?

A. The Jordan River **C.** Bethlehem

B. Nazareth **D.** Jerusalem

CROSSWORD: **Not the First**

By Marjorie Berg

1	2	3	■	4	5	6	■	7	8	9	10	11
12			■	13			■	14				
15			16				■	17				
■	■	■	18				19			■	■	■
20	21	22		■	23			■	24	25	26	27
28				29	■	30		31	■	32		
33					34	■	35		36			
37			■	38		39	■	40				
41			42	■	43		44	■	45			
■	■	■	46	47				48		■	■	■
49	50	51			■	52				53	54	55
56					■	57			■	58		
59					■	60			■	61		

ACROSS

1 "... he warmeth himself, and saith, __, I am warm" (Isa. 44:16)

4 California's Fort __

7 SECOND oldest man (Gen. 5:20)

12 "Absolutely!"

13 Airline watchdog grp.

14 Egg-shaped

15 SECOND son of Joseph (Gen. 41:52)

17 SECOND martyr (Acts 12:2)

18 Et cetera (3 words)

20 Travelers from the east

23 "Moses brought Israel from the Red __" (Ex. 15:22)

24 "... they set a __, they catch men" (Jer. 5:26)

28 Kind of coffee or stew

30 English Inc.

32 Boxing legend

33 SECOND son of Jacob (Gen. 29:33)

35 SECOND day creation (Gen. 1:8)

37 Brother of Japheth

38 Crumpet companion

40 Plain as day

41 "Hold on __!" (2 words)

43 One-time connector (2 words)

45 "And lead us not __ temptation"

46 Gridiron pitchout

49 SECOND traveling companion of Paul (Acts 15:40)

52 Covenant recipient (Gen. 17:9)

56 Practical joke

57 Almost worthless French coin

58 "__ got a secret"

59 SECOND plague (Ex. 8:6)

60 Seabird

61 "I have __ the Lord always before me" (Ps. 16:8)

DOWN

1 "Sure thing, skipper!"

2 With it, '40s-style

3 __ Wednesday

4 "... in the twinkling __ eye" (1 Cor. 15:52) (2 words)

5 Late-night refrigerator visits?

6 "And straightway the __ arose, and walked" (Mark 5:42)

7 Skater Starbuck

8 ___-garde

9 "Thou shalt also take one __" (Ex. 29:15)

10 French summer

11 __ Moines, Iowa

16 Employee's goal

19 "Let there be now an __ betwixt us" (Gen. 26:28)

20 Baryshnikov, to friends

21 Operatic songs

22 Greedy person's demand

25 "And he sent forth a __" (Gen. 8:7)

26 On the ball

27 Spotted pony

29 "And my wrath shall wax __" (Ex. 22:24)

31 In excelsis __

34 Spiffy

36 St. Teresa's birthplace

39 "His soul shall dwell __" (Ps. 25:13) (2 words)

42 Trolley sound

44 Shady retreat

47 Questions

48 Make __ for it (2 words)

49 Coppertone no.

50 Abbr. on sale items

51 Vientiane native

53 "... he gave __ only begotten Son" (John 3:16)

54 Hail, classically

55 2000 World Series participant

VERSE DECODER: **In the New Testament**

1 **1 Corinthians 1:2**

HINT: In the puzzle below, the letter "K" is actually an "O."

ATMK MFJ DFAYDF KS CKP NFEDF EH QM DKYETMF, MK MFJV MFQM QYJ

HQTDMESEJP ET DFYEHM XJHAH, DQIIJP MK GJ HQETMH, NEMF QII MFQM

ET JWJYR BIQDJ DQII ABKT MFJ TQVJ KS XJHAH DFYEHM KAY IKYP, GKMF

MFJEYH QTP KAYH:

***King James Games* Facts:**

There are still more than 5,000 manuscripts in existence
that contain all or part of the New Testament.

MULTIPLE CHOICE:

1 Which one of these men was a carpenter?

A. Jacob **B.** David **C.** Joseph **D.** Cain

2 Who did Paul meet and oppose in Antioch?

A. Peter **B.** John **C.** Jonah **D.** Silas

3 The main subject of one of Paul's epistles was what runaway servant?

A. Philemon **B.** Timothy **C.** Onesimus **D.** Epaphroditus

LETTER SQUARES:

1 **Hebrews 2:13**

LL	AG	UST	PUT	MY	, I	IN	M.
TR	HI	AND	AIN	WI			

VERSE DECODER: **In the New Testament**

1 **2 John 1:6**

HINT: In the puzzle below, the letter "L" is actually a "T."

SVI LEBQ BQ XYHG, LESL PG PSXJ SRLGA EBQ FYWWSVIWGVLQ. LEBQ BQ LEG FYWWSVIWGVL, LESL, SQ ZG ESHG EGSAI RAYW LEG TGKBVVBVK, ZG QEYCXI PSXJ BV BL.

MULTIPLE CHOICE:

1 Luke called which daughter of Phanuel a prophetess?

A. Mary **B.** Eunice **C.** Lois **D.** Anna

2 In what city did Paul cast out demons from a girl?

A. Philippi **B.** Neapolis **C.** Ephesus **D.** Antioch

3 Lazarus, Mary, and Martha came from what hometown?

A. Samaria **B.** Bethany **C.** Jericho **D.** Jerusalem

***King James Games* Facts:**

The New Testament was written from circa A.D. 50 to A.D. 100. The earliest known manuscript fragments date to circa A.D. 120.

VERSE DECODER:

2 **Acts 12:6**

HINT: In the puzzle below, the letter "F" is actually an "A."

FUB SAKU AKXVB SVDJB AFNK GXVDHAQ AYT RVXQA, QAK ZFTK UYHAQ IKQKX SFZ ZJKKIYUH GKQSKKU QSV ZVJBYKXZ, GVDUB SYQA QSV EAFYUZ: FUB QAK WKKIKXZ GKRVXK QAK BVVX WKIQ QAK IXYZVU.

LETTER SQUARES: **In the New Testament**

1 3 John 1:4

J 0 Y	I L D	T O	T H .	R E N	W A	M Y	E A T
N O	H E A	T R U	C H	E R	L K	I H	R T
H A T	T H	I N	A N	A V E	G R		

MULTIPLE CHOICE:

1 Who raised Eutychus, a young man, from the dead?

A. Peter **C.** Paul
B. Jesus **D.** John

2 Who is thought to have been a missionary to Armenia?

A. Thaddaeus **C.** Andrew
B. Bartholomew **D.** Philip

3 Which of these disciples denied Jesus?

A. Philip **C.** Thomas
B. Peter **D.** John

LETTER SQUARES:

2 Hebrews 12:4

H A V	S T	I N G	S I N	B L O	O D ,	Y E T	T O
.	S I S	O T	R I V	R E	E N	S T	A G
T E D	A I N	U N	Y E				

CROSSWORD: **In the Driver's Seat**

Edited by Timothy E. Parker

1	2	3	4		5	6	7	8		9	10	11
12					13					14		
15					16					17		
18				19					20			
			21					22			23	24
25	26	27		28		29	30		31			
32			33					34				
35					36					37		
38				39			40		41			
		42			43	44				45	46	47
48	49			50					51			
52				53					54			
55				56					57			

ACROSS

1 Enlivens, with "up"
5 Startled reaction
9 Adam's donation
12 To be, in ancient Rome
13 Repeat what you heard
14 "... be a wise man ___ fool?" (Ecc. 2:19) (2 words)
15 "... take thine ___, eat, drink, and be merry" (Luke 12:19)
16 PGA mounds
17 "... which hath five barley loaves ..." (John 6:9)
18 Start of a saying (3 words)
21 Matterhorn, e.g.
22 Snacks in shells
25 "... he gave ___ only begotten Son ..." (John 3:16)
28 Tennis great Arthur
31 Whip
32 Second part of the saying (3 words)
35 "... thrust through with a ___ ..." (Heb. 12:20)
36 The ___ of life
37 His wife was a pillar
38 Become hardened to
40 "... the name of the wicked shall ___" (Prov. 10:7)
42 End of the saying (3 words)
48 Type of leaf or type of 36-Across
50 Father of Menahem (2 Kings 15:14)
51 Old-fashioned poems
52 "And the lean and the ___ favoured kine" (Gen. 41:20)
53 Give off, as light
54 Really smell
55 Barely manage (with "out")
56 "... petition of thee, ___ me not" (1 Kings 2:16)
57 Silent assents

DOWN

1 Chick's sound
2 Brother of Jacob
3 "Hey, there!"
4 "Take it easy!" (2 words)
5 Become irritated (2 words)
6 Dell competitor
7 "___ me thy ways, O Lord" (Ps. 25:4)
8 Put forward for study
9 Head count (2 words)
10 "... a chief ruler about David" (2 Sam. 20:26)
11 "... nor change it, a good for a ___" (Lev 27:10)
19 Pearl Buck heroine
20 Chorus syllables
23 ___ buco (Italian dish)
24 "And the archers ___ at King Josiah" (2 Chron. 35:23)
25 Cover up
26 "My foot standeth ___ even place ..." (Ps. 26:12) (2 words)
27 Conflict
29 He supported Moses (Ex. 17:12)
30 "... One that inhabiteth ___, ..." (Isaiah 57:15)
33 Another, south of the border
34 Vintage autos
39 Neatened the outskirts of the lawn
41 " ___ in the flesh, ..." (2 Cor. 12:7)
43 Showed up
44 Babylonian exile returnee (Ezra 2:15)
45 Logical start?
46 "The lips of the righteous ___ many" (Prov 10:21)
47 Head-shakers' syllables
48 Old expression of disgust
49 Same kind

VERSE DECODER: **In the New Testament**

1 Acts 21:5

HINT: In the puzzle below, the letter "L" is actually an "A."

LMT ZYVM ZV YLT LOODEFXANYVT UYDNV TLBN, ZV TVFLCUVT LMT ZVMU

DQC ZLB; LMT UYVB LXX SCDQWYU QN DM DQC ZLB, ZAUY ZAHVN LMT

OYAXTCVM, UAXX ZV ZVCV DQU DK UYV OAUB: LMT ZV

IMVVXVT TDZM DM UYV NYDCV, LMT FCLBVT.

MULTIPLE CHOICE:

1 Which relative of Jesus ate locusts, preached repentance, and baptized sinners in the Jordan River?

A. Peter
B. John
C. John the Baptist
D. Joseph

2 Who is thought to have been a martyr in Ethiopia?

A. Peter
B. Paul
C. Matthias
D. Bartholomew

3 Which apostle was the first to be martyred?

A. John
B. Stephen
C. James
D. Thaddaeus

LETTER SQUARES:

1 1 Peter 5:7

T I N	L L	R C	R Y	YOU	ARE	; F	CAS
ETH	G A	OU.	FO	OR	UP	HE	HIM
ON	CAR						

LETTER SQUARES: **In the New Testament**

1 Jude 1:2

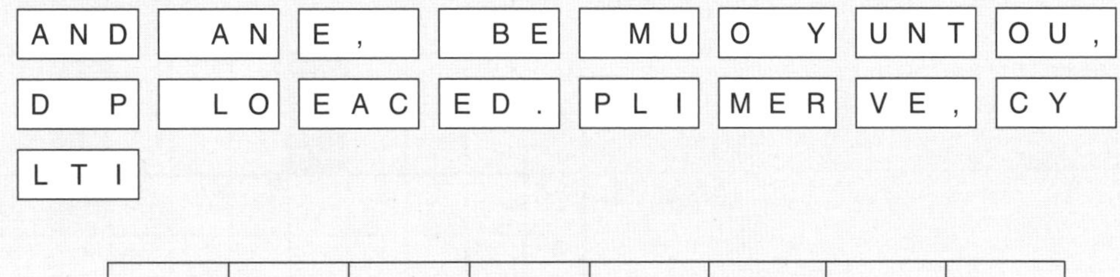

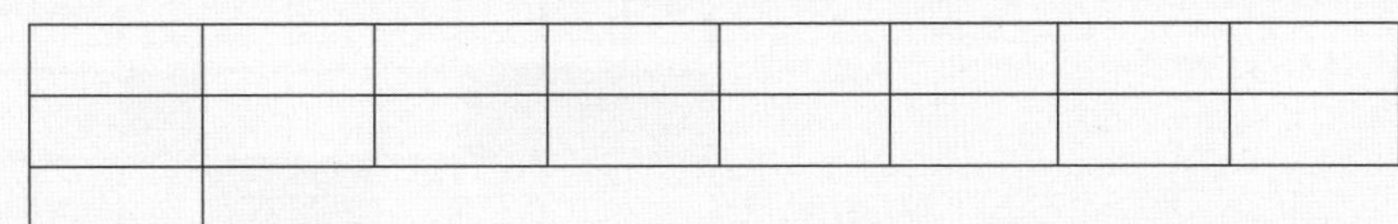

***King James Games* Facts:**

The New Testament was originally composed in the Greek language.

MULTIPLE CHOICE:

1 Who was the main voice for all the apostles at Caesarea Philippi?

A. Mark **B.** Paul **C.** Matthew **D.** Peter

2 Who was bitten by a snake on the island of Melia?

A. Mark **B.** Paul **C.** John **D.** Peter

3 After hearing the teachings of Paul, which woman of Athens became a Christian?

A. Priscilla **B.** Phoebe **C.** Joanna **D.** Damaris

4 Who recognized the voice of Peter after he was miraculously delivered from prison?

A. Rachel **B.** Candace **C.** Rhoda **D.** Jochebed

5 Who is the most mentioned apostle in the Bible after Peter and Paul?

A. Mark **B.** Barnabas **C.** Thomas **D.** John

CROSSWORD: **Go**

By Rowan Millson

1	2	3	4	■	5	6	7	■	8	9	10	11
12				■	13			■	14			
15				16				■	17			
18								19				■
■	■	■	20			■	21			■	■	■
22	23	24		■	■	25			■	26	27	28
29				30	31				32			
33			■	34			■	■	35			
■	■	■	36			■	37	38		■	■	■
■	39	40				41				42	43	44
45				■	46							
47				■	48			■	49			
50				■	51			■	52			

ACROSS

1 While beginning?
5 Partners of "ands" or "buts"
8 "Loose thy __ from off thy foot" (Josh. 5:15)
12 Burrower in Leviticus 11:30
13 Short sleep
14 Loooooong time
15 Jib relative
17 Loll
18 "... go, __" (John 8:11) (4 words)
20 Wrath
21 Expose to UV rays
22 Starchy root
25 Make a scene?
26 Mr. counterpart
29 "Go __: for I have hardened his heart" (Ex. 10:1) (3 words)
33 Mel of baseball
34 Score 100 percent
35 Small whirlpool
36 Sheikdom __ Dhabi
37 "... the __ number of them is to be redeemed" (Num. 3:48)
39 "Go, and do __" (Luke 10:37) (2 words)
45 Fly like an eagle
46 Nacre suppliers
47 Mine entrance
48 Fictional sleeper
49 Pindar's poems
50 Soft drink
51 Star Wars inits.
52 Measure of force

DOWN

1 Jane Austen novel
2 Reddish-brown horse
3 Used a firehouse pole
4 Stress
5 Foolish
6 "... he would __ flee out of his hand" (Job 27:22)
7 Large irregular spot
8 Beauty parlor
9 "The Lord __ thee in the day of trouble" (Ps. 20:1)
10 Seep
11 180 degrees from WSW
16 "__, give me this water" (John 4:15)
19 Spy Hari
22 Spanish uncle
23 "Go to the __, thou sluggard" (Prov. 6:6)
24 Furrow
25 Barbary beast
26 "... much learning doth make thee __" (Acts 26:24)
27 Aaron's staff
28 Not bold
30 Chanel No. 5 alternative
31 Add bin to see far with them
32 California giant
36 Main blood vessel
37 Giraffe relative
38 "Runaway" singer Shannon
39 "God hath shewed Pharaoh what he is about __" (Gen. 41:25) (2 words)
40 "... and the Lord sent thunder and __" (Ex. 9:23)
41 Ref. word
42 500-mile race, for short
43 "For mine eyes have __ thy salvation" (Luke 2:30)
44 To be, to Caesar
45 Pouch

WORD SEARCH: **Bodies of Water**

M	M	J	J	R	G	Q	N	O	H	S	I	P	N	C	V	V
E	Z	Y	M	G	B	P	C	H	K	L	L	H	C	I	N	L
D	G	J	M	M	H	T	R	L	L	J	K	N	E	M	L	D
I	M	K	E	A	S	E	A	O	F	G	A	L	I	L	E	E
T	T	H	R	U	Q	N	L	N	T	Q	K	N	T	Q	U	R
E	N	P	T	C	P	V	I	D	P	R	O	A	T	H	K	H
R	A	T	B	I	L	H	L	A	N	L	B	E	B	A	K	P
R	G	T	T	W	G	B	R	A	L	J	B	S	Q	B	M	V
A	I	F	R	K	H	R	E	A	Z	P	A	D	Z	A	P	K
N	H	J	R	D	T	S	I	C	T	K	J	E	F	R	N	N
E	O	M	T	L	D	N	N	S	J	E	K	R	H	A	A	G
A	N	N	A	A	B	R	F	D	N	D	S	Y	N	D	O	W
N	M	S	E	K	T	V	X	T	K	T	L	L	R	Z	B	L
P	W	D	V	K	Q	R	N	M	T	R	G	O	A	Z	M	W
H	K	J	E	N	R	O	G	E	L	Z	J	N	J	V	G	Q
V	J	Y	L	E	K	E	D	D	I	H	T	M	V	R	V	P
R	R	Y	W	V	D	L	H	T	M	R	K	I	S	H	O	N

ARABAH
DEAD SEA
ENROGEL
EUPHRATES
GIHON
GOZAN
HIDDEKEL
HULEH
JABBOK
JORDAN
KISHON
MEDITERRANEAN
NILE
PHARPAR
PISHON
PLAIN
RED SEA
SALT
SEA OF GALILEE
TIGRIS

WORD SEARCH: **Men Found in the New Testament**

B	N	W	T	T	O	I	R	A	C	S	I	S	A	D	U	J
S	M	M	X	Q	R	N	N	E	T	A	L	I	P	H	C	B
U	N	T	T	Y	P	M	L	J	E	D	E	L	Z	J	N	T
T	N	K	M	S	P	L	M	G	D	K	B	W	A	O	P	K
S	H	X	K	A	I	V	K	V	U	M	M	M	C	H	A	J
U	K	L	L	Z	T	T	B	L	J	H	P	S	H	N	U	N
G	Q	F	K	R	A	T	P	Y	J	R	R	F	A	V	L	V
U	N	F	K	N	J	C	H	A	C	R	W	R	R	L	Q	Z
A	X	J	A	M	E	S	H	E	B	D	N	V	I	K	I	D
R	T	I	M	O	T	H	Y	A	W	E	J	M	A	R	K	S
A	G	V	W	V	D	L	T	L	E	O	H	Y	S	N	C	H
S	K	K	Y	O	F	S	K	L	S	U	J	T	M	Q	K	K
E	R	D	R	Q	A	C	P	E	N	N	S	E	N	T	Q	L
A	N	E	Z	M	C	E	P	D	O	X	D	L	S	H	C	R
C	H	J	O	W	T	H	L	G	M	Y	T	T	V	U	O	P
M	Q	H	L	E	Z	W	Q	Q	I	R	J	V	H	B	S	J
B	T	N	R	L	Q	R	R	X	S	D	J	L	Z	Y	Z	M

CAESAR AUGUSTUS
HEROD
JAMES
JESUS
JOHN
JOHN THE BAPTIST
JOSEPH
JUDAS ISCARIOT
JUDE
LUKE
MARK
MATTHEW
PAUL
PETER
PILATE
SILAS
SIMON
THOMAS
TIMOTHY
ZACHAEUS
ZACHARIAS

WORD SEARCH: **New Testament Books**

M	B	R	K	B	F	T	R	P	Z	X	T	Y	X	R	S	B
M	P	M	T	J	L	K	I	E	W	R	V	G	P	C	W	N
K	X	M	X	V	J	G	Y	M	T	F	N	Z	M	T	E	Z
D	G	L	S	S	L	O	V	B	O	E	L	M	K	Y	R	K
G	Z	Z	N	W	N	F	H	W	D	T	P	T	X	T	B	T
T	P	Y	A	E	Y	A	Q	N	K	X	H	R	T	E	E	I
S	N	A	I	H	T	N	I	R	O	C	O	Y	D	K	H	T
K	Z	H	S	T	M	T	Y	T	S	M	K	U	J	W	G	U
W	W	A	E	T	B	M	K	N	A	R	J	A	G	T	W	S
L	B	C	H	A	J	L	A	N	A	L	M	K	L	U	K	E
K	D	T	P	M	G	I	S	M	J	E	A	F	N	L	P	N
R	Z	S	E	V	S	K	Q	V	S	K	G	G	L	R	M	T
R	P	L	D	S	S	N	A	I	P	P	I	L	I	H	P	G
X	G	N	O	M	E	L	I	H	P	R	F	Q	B	C	R	L
J	N	L	T	H	E	S	S	A	L	O	N	I	A	N	S	N
H	O	V	H	V	N	R	E	V	E	L	A	T	I	O	N	T
C	K	N	M	N	M	D	X	N	N	T	M	K	B	H	R	B

ACTS
COLOSSIANS
CORINTHIANS
EPHESIANS
GALATIANS
HEBREWS
JAMES
JOHN
JUDE
LUKE
MARK
MATTHEWS
PETER
PHILEMON
PHILIPPIANS
REVELATION
ROMANS
THESSALONIANS
TIMOTHY
TITUS

WORD SEARCH: **New Testament Practices**

```
R D R R T J L P N L P X G P E A C E
D K W R Y F U R Q C R R C C K T K C
K N M C K R D T B K A R Z B J B W X
L V R Z I N E R T N Y Y F I T S E T
X E Z T Z P V C Y H E B Z Z M L D Y
M Z Y S T K O V T D R L B L N W T L
R R L F K Z L C O M M U N I O N N B
T B N A C N H V H M F N T F K K P M
R G N I H S A W T O O F E K H M E E
P G R T N J M H L S Y L Q R S R H S
V E M H Y F P P T J L K E I N K T S
R B R T P T N E W O Y R T N J R I A
D E G S H N A T W W T P N R D Z T F
M T L T E D R S M K A R N M T U V D
F K U B F V H K Q B V Z L M W M R N
Y R L A M I E N O I T A V L A S T E
T L S N P U P R F W I T N E S S T Y
J T K X L F H M E R B R G R L K R Q
```

ASSEMBLY
BAPTISM
COMMUNION
ENDURE
FAITH
FELLOWSHIP
FOOT WASHING
HUMBLE
LOVE
MERCY
PEACE
PERSEVERE
PRAYER
PURITY
SALVATION
STEADFAST
TESTIFY
THANKS
TITHE
TRUTH
WITNESS

Page 195

CROSSWORD: Biblical Towns

1 E	2 Z	3 R	4 A	■	5 J	6 O	7 B	■	8 A	9 B	10 E	11 T
12 N	O	A	H	■	13 E	R	A	■	14 S	E	R	E
15 G	O	M	O	16 R	R	A	H	■	17 S	T	I	R
■	■	■	18 R	A	U	L	■	19 C	O	H	E	N
20 B	21 L	22 A	S	T	S	■	23 C	U	R	L	■	■
24 L	O	R	E	■	25 A	26 D	A	P	T	E	27 R	28 S
29 O	B	I	■	30 F	L	O	P	S	■	31 H	I	T
32 C	O	M	33 P	L	E	T	E	■	34 M	E	S	A
■	■	35 A	L	U	M	■	36 R	37 O	A	M	E	R
38 A	39 R	T	I	E	■	40 A	N	T	S	■	■	■
41 H	A	H	A	■	42 A	N	A	T	H	43 E	44 M	45 A
46 E	V	E	N	■	47 G	N	U	■	48 E	V	I	L
49 M	E	A	T	■	50 H	A	M	■	51 S	E	L	L

SOLUTIONS

Page 197

LETTER SQUARES: In the New Testament

1 solution:
I am Alpha and Omega, the beginning and the ending,
Revelation 1:8

MULTIPLE CHOICE:

1 solution: **B**; 2 solution: **C**; 3 solution: **B**.

VERSE DECODER:

1 solution:
And one of the Elders saith unto me, weep not: behold, the lion of the tribe of Judah, the root of David, hath prevailed to open the book and to loose the seven seals thereof.
Revelation 5:5

Page 196

MULTIPLE CHOICE: In the New Testament

1 solution: **D**; 2 solution: **D**; 3 solution: **B**.

VERSE DECODER:

1 solution:
And they sung as it were a new song before the throne, and before the four beasts, and the elders: And no man could learn that song but the hundred and forty and four thousand, which were redeemed from the earth.
Revelation 14:3

LETTER SQUARES:

1 solution:
Unto him that loved us, and washed us from our sins in his own blood,
Revelation 1:5

Page 198

CROSSWORD: Songs of Faith

1 A	2 S	3 A	■	4 U	5 S	6 E	7 R	■	8 M	9 E	10 S	11 O
12 M	A	T	■	13 S	A	L	E	■	14 E	L	U	L
15 O	N	E	16 D	A	Y	A	T	17 A	T	I	M	E
18 S	T	A	N	■	■	19 Y	A	L	E	■	■	■
■	20 A	M	A	21 Z	22 I	N	G	G	R	23 A	24 C	25 E
■	■	■	■	26 O	N	E	■	■	27 E	D	E	N
28 T	29 U	30 R	31 N	O	N	■	32 M	33 E	D	A	L	S
34 A	P	I	E	■	■	35 N	I	M	■	■	■	■
36 I	S	A	W	37 T	38 H	E	L	I	39 G	40 H	41 T	■
■	■	■	42 S	O	U	L	■	■	43 T	E	A	44 S
45 T	46 H	47 E	B	I	B	L	48 E	49 T	E	L	L	S
50 H	A	L	O	■	51 B	I	R	D	■	52 G	O	T
53 E	L	L	Y	■	54 Y	E	N	S	■	55 A	N	S

SOLUTIONS

Page 199

MULTIPLE CHOICE: In the New Testament

1 solution: **C**; 2 solution: **C**; 3 solution: **C**.

VERSE DECODER:

1 solution:

Then said he also to him that bade him, when thou makest a dinner or a supper, call not thy friends, nor thy brethren, neither thy kinsmen, nor thy rich neighbours; lest they also bid thee again, and a recompense be made thee.
Luke 14:12

LETTER SQUARES:

1 solution:

Out of the same mouth proceedeth blessing and cursing.
James 3:10

Page 200

MULTIPLE CHOICE: In the New Testament

1 solution: **B**; 2 solution: **C**; 3 solution: **C**.

LETTER SQUARES:

1 solution:

Can the fig tree, my brethren, bear olive berries?
James 3:12

VERSE DECODER:

1 solution:

And it came to pass on the second sabbath after the first, that he went through the corn fields; And his disciples plucked the ear of corn, and did eat, rubbing them in their hands.
Luke 6:1

Page 201

CROSSWORD: Seasonal Songs

1 O	2 C	3 O	4 M	5 E		6 O	7 V	8 A		9 L	10 A	11 O
12 B	A	S	A	L		13 V	E	R	14 S	I	O	N
15 A	L	L	Y	E	16 F	A	I	T	H	F	U	L
17 L	E	O		18 G	U	L	L		19 A	T	T	Y
			20 A	Y	N			21 A	M	E		
22 M	23 A	24 G	I		25 N	26 O	27 E	L		28 D	29 E	30 O
31 O	C	O	M	32 E	E	M	M	A	33 N	U	E	L
34 O	T	O		35 B	L	I	P		36 A	P	E	D
		37 D	38 A	B			39 I	40 R	E			
41 A	42 L	B	S		43 S	44 A	R	A		45 B	46 E	47 E
48 J	O	Y	T	49 O	T	H	E	W	50 O	R	L	D
51 A	R	E	O	L	A	E		52 E	R	O	S	E
53 R	D	S		54 A	R	M		55 R	I	S	E	N

Page 202

VERSE DECODER: In the New Testament

1 solution:

And it came to pass, that after three days Paul called the chief of the Jews together: he said unto them, men and brethren, though I have committed nothing against the people, or customs of our fathers, yet was I delivered prisoner from Jerusalem into the hands of the Romans.
Acts 28:17

LETTER SQUARES:

1 solution:

And these things write we unto you, that your joy may be full.
1 John 1:4

SOLUTIONS

Page 203

MULTIPLE CHOICE: In the New Testament

1 solution: **C**; 2 solution: **B**; 3 solution: **B**;

4 solution: **C**; 5 solution: **B**; 6 solution: **C**.

VERSE DECODER:

1 solution:

Who being the brightness of his glory, and the express image of his person, and upholding all things by the word of his power, when he had by himself purged our sins, sat down on the right hand of the majesty on high:
Hebrews 1:3

Page 204

CROSSWORD: Rolling Stones

1 S	2 L	3 A	4 V		5 E	6 R	7 A		8 M	9 O	10 B	11 S
12 H	O	N	I		13 R	U	G		14 I	D	O	L
15 U	N	T	O	16 M	E	T	H	17 I	S	D	A	Y
18 T	E	S	L	A		19 H	A	N	D			
			20 E	R	21 R			22 M	O	23 T	24 T	25 O
26 C	27 O	28 A	T		29 A	30 U	31 R	A		32 O	A	T
33 A	N	D	S	34 E	T	M	E	N	35 B	Y	I	T
36 R	C	A		37 S	A	P	S		38 O	S	L	O
39 R	E	M	40 I	T			41 T	42 A	N			
			43 N	E	44 S	45 T		46 B	A	47 S	48 S	49 O
50 R	51 E	52 T	U	R	N	U	53 P	O	N	H	I	M
54 A	V	E	R		55 O	N	E		56 Z	E	T	A
57 G	E	N	E		58 B	E	N		59 A	M	E	N

Page 205

MULTIPLE CHOICE: In the New Testament

1 solution: **C**; 2 solution: **C**; 3 solution: **C**.

LETTER SQUARES:

1 solution:

Paul, a servant of God, and an apostle of Jesus Christ
Titus 1:1

VERSE DECODER:

1 solution:

Which was a figure for the time then present, in which were offered both gifts and sacrifices, that could not make him that did the service perfect, as pertaining to the conscience;
Hebrews 9:9

Page 206

VERSE DECODER: In the New Testament

1 solution:

For this cause we also, since the day we heard it, do not cease to pray for you, and to desire that ye might be filled with the knowledge of his will in all wisdom and spiritual understanding;
Colossians 1:9

MULTIPLE CHOICE:

1 solution: **A**; 2 solution: **B**; 3 solution: **B**;

4 solution: **B**; 5 solution: **C**; 6 solution: **C**.

SOLUTIONS

Page 207

CROSSWORD: Not the First

1 A	2 H	3 A		4 O	5 R	6 D		7 J	8 A	9 R	10 E	11 D
12 Y	E	S		13 F	A	A		14 O	V	A	T	E
15 E	P	H	16 R	A	I	M		17 J	A	M	E	S
			18 A	N	D	S	19 O	O	N			
20 M	21 A	22 G	I		23 S	E	A		24 T	25 R	26 A	27 P
28 I	R	I	S	29 H		30 L	T	31 D		32 A	L	I
33 S	I	M	E	O	34 N		35 H	E	36 A	V	E	N
37 H	A	M		38 T	E	39 A		40 O	V	E	R	T
41 A	S	E	42 C		43 A	T	44 A		45 I	N	T	O
			46 L	47 A	T	E	R	48 A	L			
49 S	50 I	51 L	A	S		52 A	B	R	A	53 H	54 A	55 M
56 P	R	A	N	K		57 S	O	U		58 I	V	E
59 F	R	O	G	S		60 E	R	N		61 S	E	T

Page 208

VERSE DECODER: In the New Testament

Unto the Church of God which is at Corinth, to them that are sanctified in Christ Jesus, called to be saints, with all that in every place call upon the name of Jesus Christ our Lord, both theirs and ours:
1 Corinthians 1:2

MULTIPLE CHOICE:

1 solution: **C**; 2 solution: **A**; 3 solution: **C**.

LETTER SQUARES:

And again, I will put my trust in him.
Hebrews 2:13

Page 209

VERSE DECODER: In the New Testament

1 solution:

And this is love, that we walk after his commandments. This is the commandment, that, as ye have heard from the beginning, ye should walk in it.
2 John 1:6

MULTIPLE CHOICE:

1 solution: **D**; 2 solution: **A**; 3 solution: **B**.

VERSE DECODER:

2 solution:

And when Herod would have brought him forth, the same night Peter was sleeping between two soldiers, bound with two chains: and the keepers before the door kept the prison.
Acts 12:6

Page 210

LETTER SQUARES: In the New Testament

1 solution:

I have no greater joy than to hear that my children walk in truth.
3 John 1:4

MULTIPLE CHOICE:

1 solution: **C**; 2 solution: **B**; 3 solution: **B**.

LETTER SQUARES:

2 solution:

Ye have not yet resisted unto blood, striving against sin.
Hebrews 12:4

SOLUTIONS

Page 211

CROSSWORD: In the Driver's Seat

P	E	P	S	■	G	A	S	P	■	R	I	B
E	S	S	E	■	E	C	H	O	■	O	R	A
E	A	S	E	■	T	E	E	S	■	L	A	D
P	U	T	Y	O	U	R	W	I	L	L	■	■
■	■	■	A	L	P	■	■	T	A	C	O	S
H	I	S	■	A	S	H	E	■	L	A	S	H
I	N	T	O	N	E	U	T	R	A	L	S	O
D	A	R	T	■	T	R	E	E	■	L	O	T
E	N	U	R	E	■	■	R	O	T	■	■	■
■	■	G	O	D	C	A	N	S	H	I	F	T
F	I	G	■	G	A	D	I	■	O	D	E	S
I	L	L	■	E	M	I	T	■	R	E	E	K
E	K	E	■	D	E	N	Y	■	N	O	D	S

Page 212

VERSE DECODER: In the New Testament

1 solution:

And when we had accomplished those days, we departed and went our way; and they all brought us on our way, with wives and children, till we were out of the city: And we kneeled down on the shore, and prayed.
Acts 21:5

MULTIPLE CHOICE:

1 solution: **C**; 2 solution: **C**; 3 solution: **C**.

LETTER SQUARES:

1 solution:

Casting all your care upon him; for he careth for you.
1 Peter 5:7

Page 213

LETTER SQUARES: In the New Testament

1 solution:

Mercy unto you, and peace, and love, be multiplied.
Jude 1:2

MULTIPLE CHOICE:

1 solution: **D**; 2 solution: **B**; 3 solution: **D**;

4 solution: **C**; 5 solution: **D**.

Page 214

CROSSWORD: Go

E	R	S	T	■	I	F	S	■	S	H	O	E
M	O	L	E	■	N	A	P	■	A	E	O	N
M	A	I	N	S	A	I	L	■	L	A	Z	E
A	N	D	S	I	N	N	O	M	O	R	E	■
■	■	■	I	R	E	■	T	A	N	■	■	■
T	A	R	O	■	■	A	C	T	■	M	R	S
I	N	U	N	T	O	P	H	A	R	A	O	H
O	T	T	■	A	C	E	■	■	E	D	D	Y
■	■	■	A	B	U	■	O	D	D	■	■	■
■	T	H	O	U	L	I	K	E	W	I	S	E
S	O	A	R	■	A	B	A	L	O	N	E	S
A	D	I	T	■	R	I	P	■	O	D	E	S
C	O	L	A	■	S	D	I	■	D	Y	N	E

SOLUTIONS

Page 215

WORD SEARCH: Bodies of Water

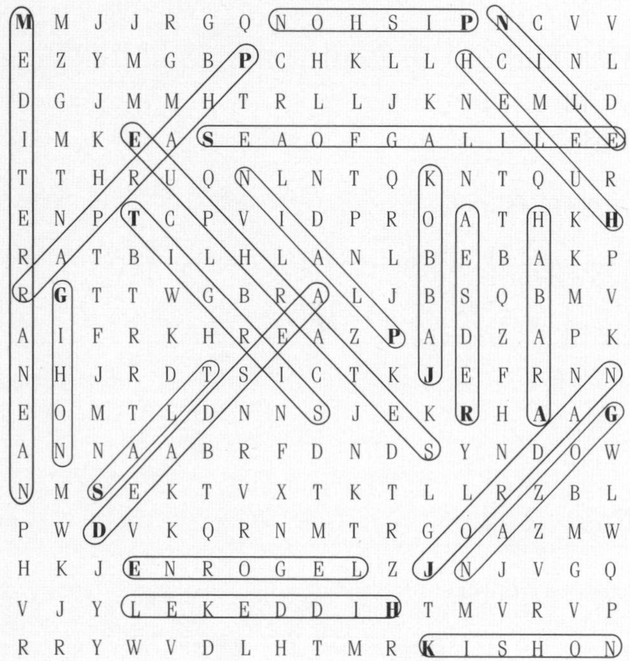

Page 216

WORD SEARCH: Men Found in the New Testament

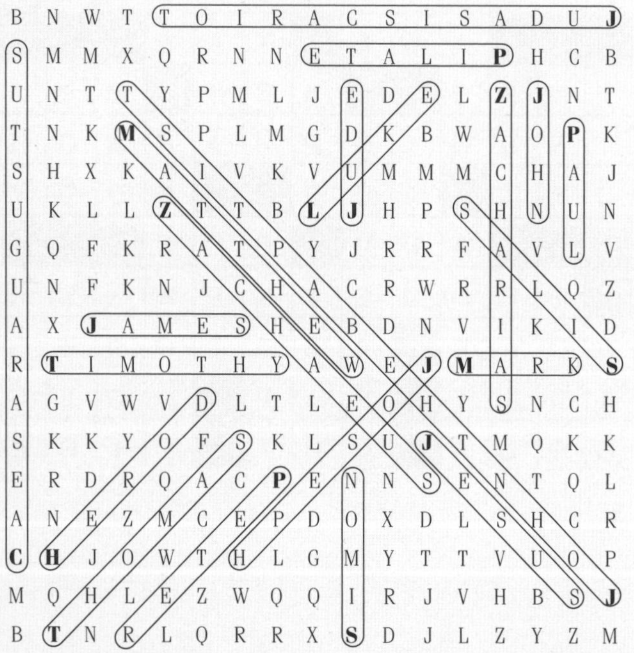

Page 217

WORD SEARCH: New Testament Books

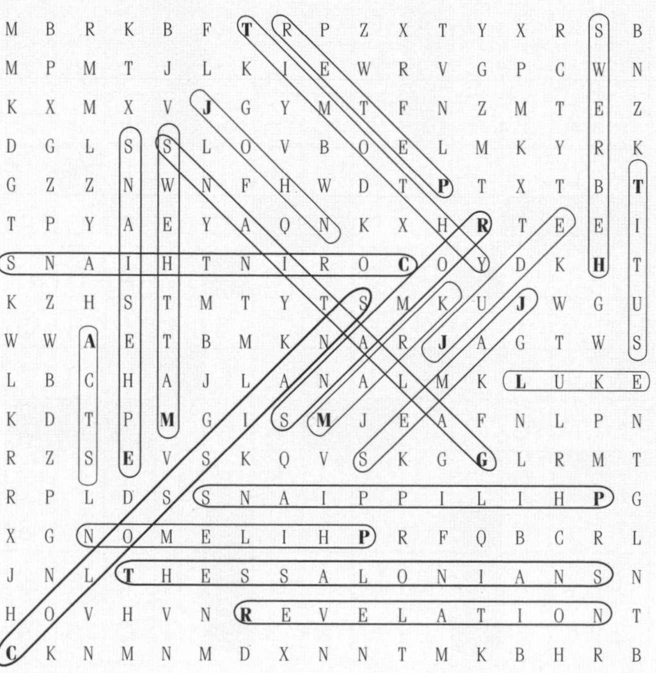

Page 218

WORD SEARCH: New Testament Practices

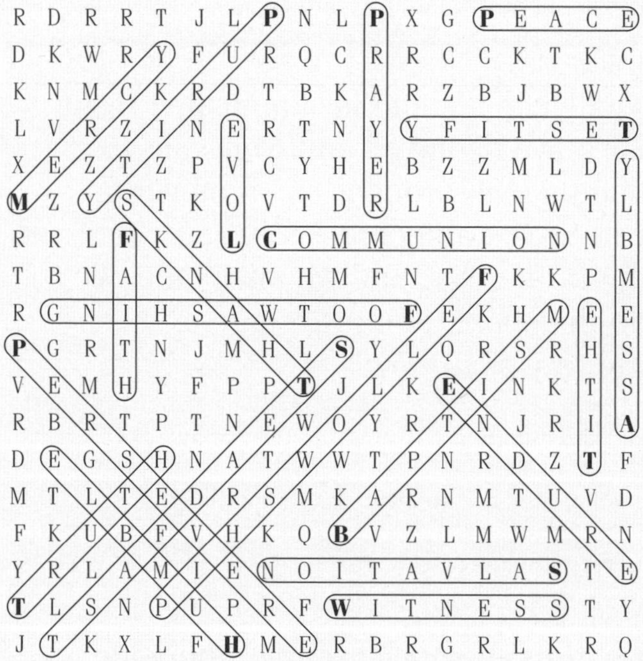

CHAPTER 5

CROSSWORD: **A Test of Faith**

By Vivian O. Collins

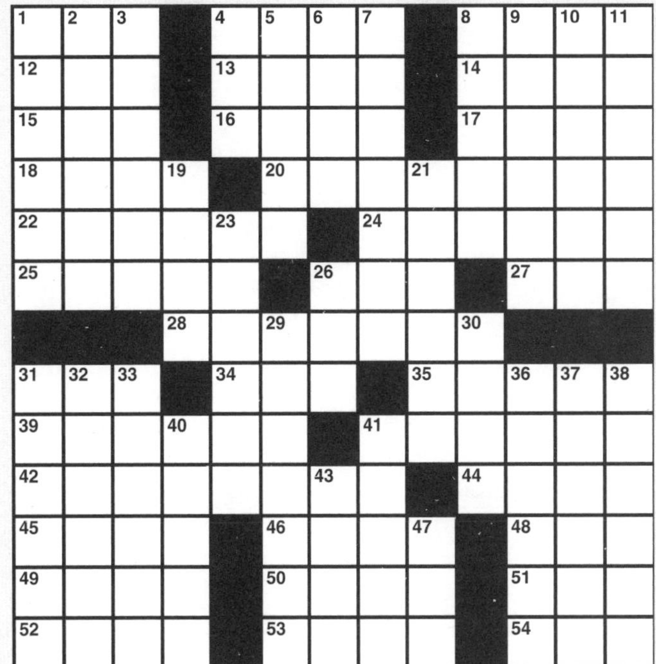

ACROSS

1 "And a third part shall be at the gate of ..." (2 Kings 11:6)

4 "The inhabitants of the land of __ brought water" (Isa. 21:14)

8 Sere

12 Compass dir.

13 Composer Stravinsky

14 Major-__ (chief steward)

15 Some hymns are on these

16 Grand __ (baseball term)

17 Lendl of tennis

18 What David walked upon (2 Sam. 11:2)

20 One of a Biblical three

22 "... thou didst __ the kings of the earth" (Eze. 27:33)

24 "... for now is our salvation __ than we believed" (Rom. 13:11)

25 Aquarium fish

26 Martha, to Mary (abbr.)

27 Sound of a tire losing air

28 One of a biblical three

31 Org. with the motto "Be prepared"

34 Jeanne d'Arc, for one (abbr.)

35 "And they sat down in __" (Mark 6:40)

39 "... lest there be an __ among the people" (Matt. 26:5)

41 "Speak, I pray thee, unto thy servants in the __ language" (Isa. 36:11)

42 One of a Biblical three

44 Taj Mahal site

45 "Behold, __ I am" (Gen. 22:1)

46 "Only the gold, and the silver, the brass, the __, the tin, and the lead" (Num. 31:22)

48 "And the earth opened __ mouth" (Num. 16:32)

49 Part of QED

50 Rent

51 Lead for kwon do

52 Exercise units

53 "Have they not __?" (Judg. 5:30)

54 Calls for quiet

DOWN

1 "The __ things belong unto the Lord our God" (Deut. 29:29)

2 "... these ought ye to have done, and not to leave the other __" (Matt. 23:23)

3 "Be thou my strong habitation, whereunto I may continually __" (Ps. 71:3)

4 Poetic contraction

5 "And the sixth, Ithream, by __ David's wife" (2 Sam. 3:5)

6 "And the first born bore a son, and called his name __"(Gen. 19:37)

7 Where Adrammelech escaped (Isa. 37:38)

8 "__ the son of Shiza the Reubenite" (1 Chron. 11:42)

9 Band that attacked David (1 Chron. 12:21)

10 "... the groves and __ shall not stand up" (Isa. 27:9)

11 Contributors

19 "And the priests that bore the ark of the covenant of the Lord stood __" (Josh. 3:17)

21 "And the house of Joseph sent to __ Bethel" (Judg. 1:23)

23 "Is it lawful to give tribute unto __, or not?" (Matt. 22:17)

26 " __ shall be called Woman" (Gen. 2:23)

29 What man shall be in (Job 20:22)

30 "Halah, and Habor, and __, and to the river Gozan" (1 Chron. 5:26)

31 "Among the __ they betrayed" (Job 30:7)

32 Geometric figure

33 "... call together against her the kingdoms of __, Minni, and Ashchenaz" (Jer. 51:27)

36 "And the rain was upon the earth forty days and forty __" (Gen. 7:12)

37 "then called he Johanan the son of __" (Jer. 42:8)

38 Captures

40 American playwright

41 "... largeness of heart, even as the sand that is on the sea __" (1 Kings 4:29)

43 "And he shall pluck away his __ with his feathers" (Lev. 1:16)

47 Actor Beatty

MULTIPLE CHOICE: **The Life of Jesus**

1 Once possessed by demons, what woman was the first to see the risen Christ?

A. Martha **C.** Joanna

B. Mary **D.** Mary Magdalene

2 Whose voice does Jesus say the sheep know?

A. The wolf's **C.** The hunter's

B. The shepherd's **D.** The lion's

3 What unusual person saw Jesus from a distance and ran to worship him?

A. The paralytic **C.** The Samaritan woman

B. The Gadarene demoniac **D.** The adulteress

VERSE DECODER:

1 Matthew 28:2

HINT: In the puzzle below, the letter "R" is actually an "E."

OXD, CRGWUD, QGRKR EOF O PKROQ ROKQGBYOSR: TWK QGR OXPRU WT

QGR UWKD DRFJRXDRD TKWV GROLRX, OXD JOVR OXD KWUURD

COJS QGR FQWXR TKWV QGR DWWK, OXD FOQ YNWX AQ.

2 John 10:6-7

HINT: In the puzzle below, the letter "Y" is actually an "A."

WOLH EYMYTSP HEYGP IPHXH XZWB WOPJ: TXW WOPU XZCPMHWBBC

ZBW ROYW WOLZFH WOPU RPMP ROLQO OP HEYGP XZWB WOPJ.

WOPZ HYLC IPHXH XZWB WOPJ YFYLZ, DPMLSU, DPMLSU, L HYU XZWB

UBX, L YJ WOP CBBM BN WOP HOPPE.

CROSSWORD: **Jesus is Lord**

By Rowan Millson

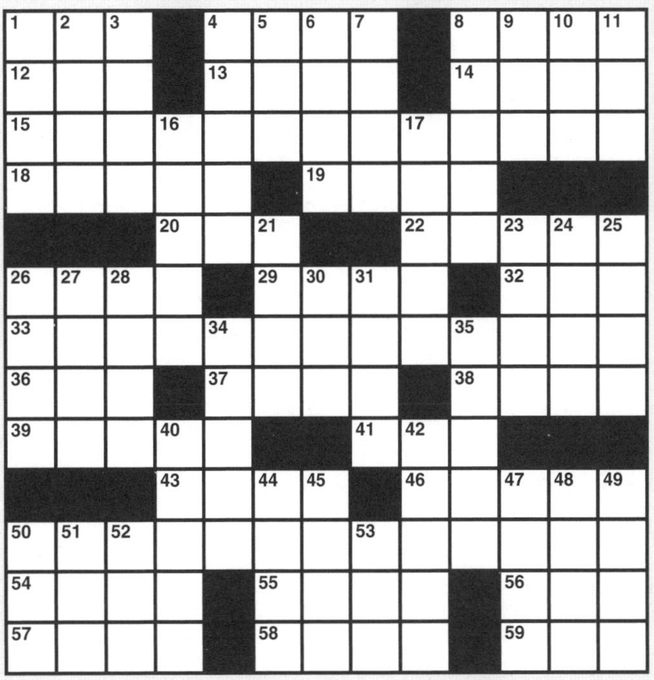

ACROSS

1 Pet for Solomon (1 Kings 10:22)
4 Chromosome part
8 Prepare potatoes, in a way
12 "And they __ down to eat bread" (Gen. 37:25)
13 Actor Baldwin
14 Region
15 Jesus (Matt. 2:2) (4 words)
18 Growl
19 Passable
20 Bit of residue
22 "... but they shall be snares and __ unto you" (Josh. 23:13)
26 Rani's dress?
29 Nabisco cookie
32 Stadium shout
33 Jesus (Isa. 9:6) (3 words)
36 Feel under the weather
37 "Money __ everything!"
38 Still in the sack
39 Chef's or Caesar
41 Sink
43 Meal at boot camp
46 "Go, __ the Lord your God" (Ex. 10:8)
50 Jesus (Micah 5:2) (3 words)
54 Persia, now
55 Whittle
56 "And she answered and said unto him, __" (Mark 7:28)
57 Hit partner
58 "When he had thus spoken, he __ on the ground" (John 9:6)
59 Compass dir.

DOWN

1 Requests
2 "Why is my __ perpetual" (Jer. 15:18)
3 Lab burner
4 Prisons of Penzance
5 Sprite
6 "Let the wicked fall into their own __" (Ps. 141:10)
7 Repeat
8 Military rank
9 Exist
10 "A time to rend, and a time to __" (Ecc. 3:7)
11 Possesses
16 "... heaven is like to a __ of mustard seed" (Matt. 13:31)
17 Prevent legally
21 Digging tools
23 Omani, for one
24 Tempo
25 "And Reuben said unto them, __ no blood" (Gen. 37:22)
26 Watering holes
27 Opera solo
28 Small stream
30 Howard or Reagan
31 Immature newts
34 Apple drink
35 Gung ho
40 Prayer endings
42 Not a liability
44 Tentative tastes
45 Partner of crackle and pop
47 Mantas
48 Some sweater necks
49 "Give me children, or __ I die" (Gen. 30:1)
50 Outer edge of a basketball hoop
51 "... the son of Hur, of the tribe of Judah" (Ex. 31:2)
52 __ Cruces, NM
53 "... the son of Ikkesh the Tekoite" (1 Chron. 27:9)

LETTER SQUARES: **The Life of Jesus**

1 Matthew 10:39

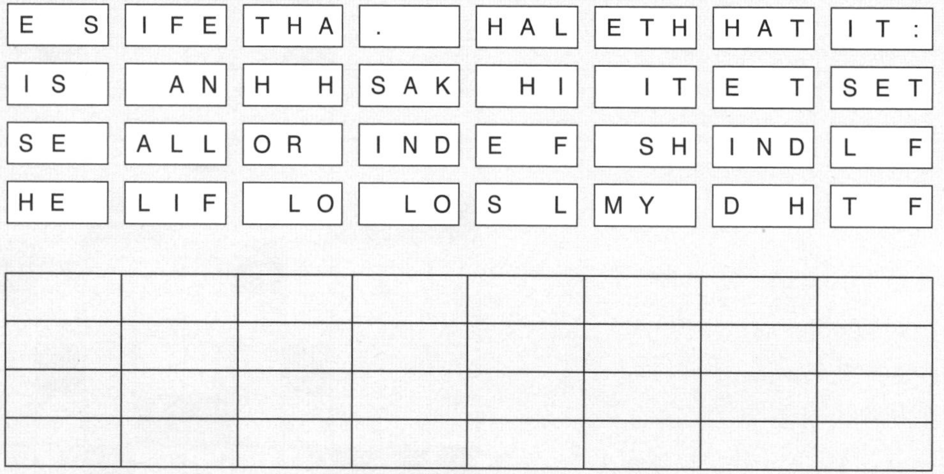

2 Luke 6:37

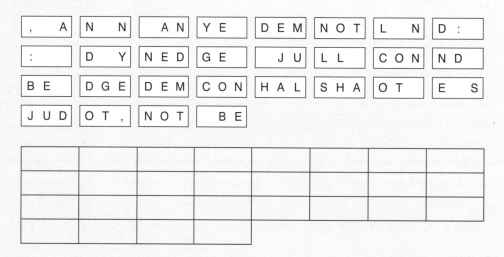

, A	N N	A N	Y E	D E M	N O T	L N	D :
:	D Y	N E D	G E	J U	L L	C O N	N D
B E	D G E	D E M	C O N	H A L	S H A	O T	E S
J U D	O T ,	N O T	B E				

MULTIPLE CHOICE:

1 "This is my beloved Son, in whom I am well pleased," was said at which event?

A. The birth of Jesus
B. Jesus' baptism
C. Jesus' ascension
D. Jesus on the cross

2 The enemies of Jesus met to plot against him in whose home?

A. Ananias
B. Caiaphas
C. Zacharias
D. King Herod

VERSE DECODER: **The Life of Jesus**

1 Acts 1:3

HINT: In the puzzle below, the letter "D" is actually an "O."

LD TCDN YFWD CM WCMTMJ CONWMFH YFOAM YHLMQ COW KYWWODI UR

NYIR OIHYFFOUFM KQDDHW, UMOIV WMMI DH LCMN HDQLR JYRW, YIJ

WKMYEOIV DH LCM LCOIVW KMQLYOIOIV LD LCM EOIVJDN DH VDJ.

LETTER SQUARES:

1 John 1:18

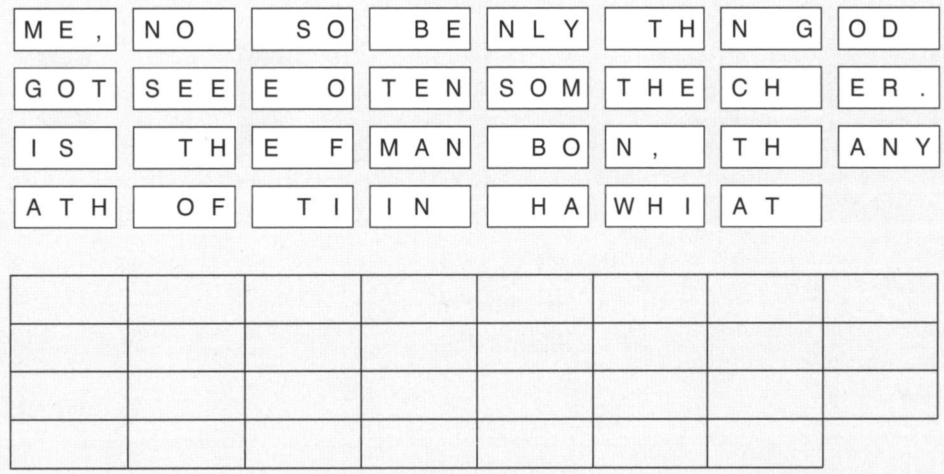

2 John 9:39

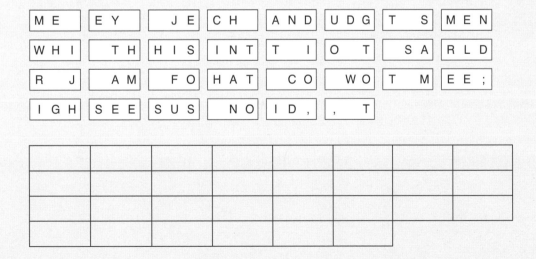

ME	EY	JE	CH	AND	UDG	T S	MEN
WHI	TH	HIS	INT	T I	O T	SA	RLD
R J	AM	FO	HAT	CO	WO	T M	EE ;
IGH	SEE	SUS	NO	ID ,	, T		

CROSSWORD: **Glory of the Lord**

By Joseph Mantell

ACROSS

1 Sonar signal
5 Former U.S. airline
8 Perceptive
12 "... thou dash thy __ against a stone" (Luke 4:11)
13 "... and to every fowl of the __" (Gen. 1:30)
14 Jason's ship
15 "... for the glory of the Lord had filled __" (2 Chron. 5:14) (4 words)
18 More sensitive
19 "__! The Herald Angels Sing"
20 Confederate general
22 Brother of Moses
26 Graven image
29 "... the Holy Ghost is come __ you" (Acts 1:8)
32 In the past
33 "... the Lord was like __" (Ex. 24:17) (2 words)
36 Paris water
37 December song
38 Caesar's fateful day
39 Let in
41 Hankering
43 *The King and I* locale
46 Rope a cow
50 "... earth __ with the glory of the Lord" (Num. 14:21) (3 words)
54 American Revolutionary hero
55 Hawaiian wreath
56 God Almighty
57 Spew
58 __ out a living
59 Affirmatives

DOWN

1 Immature newts
2 Silver salmon
3 Weeder
4 Shakespeare character
5 T-shaped cross
6 Expression of desire
7 Width times length
8 Author Franz __
9 Work unit
10 Freud subject
11 Assent or drowse
16 Mineral-bearing earth
17 Large long-armed ape, for short
21 Continental currency
23 Sneak attack
24 Folklore fiend
25 Opposition votes
26 Notion
27 __ Sea Scrolls
28 Egg cell
30 __ in the sky
31 "So that not __ this our craft is in danger" (Acts 19:27)
34 "__ I make thy foes thy footstool" (Acts 2:35)
35 At long last
40 Ait
42 Priest of Israel who looked after Samuel
44 "And they were not __ to resist the wisdom" (Acts 6:10)
45 They shall inherit the earth
47 Gin type
48 Doris Day song word repeated after "Que"
49 Chances
50 "And __ said, Yea, for so much" (Acts 5:8)
51 Son of Noah
52 "I am the greatest" claimant
53 Exclamation of disgust

LETTER SQUARES: **The Life of Jesus**

1 Matthew 5:10

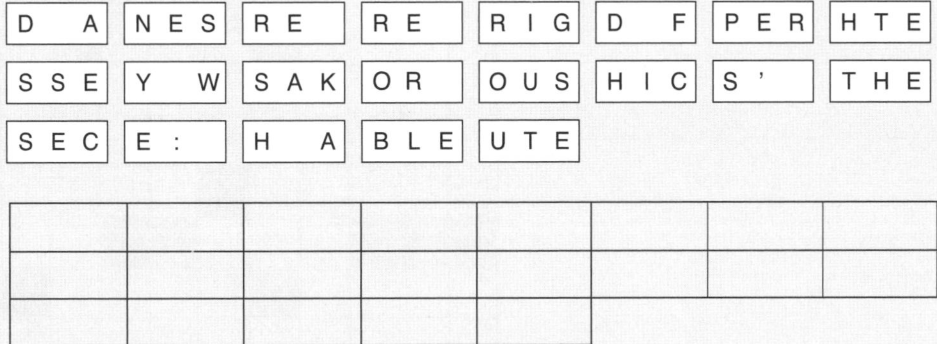

VERSE DECODER:

1 2 Timothy 1:9

HINT: In the puzzle below, the letter “F” is actually an “O.”

HDF DEPD TEJSR VT, EKR AEOOSR VT HGPD EK DFOM AEOOGKN, KFP

EAAFQRGKN PF FVQ HFQCT, YVP EAAFQRGKN PF DGT FHK WVQWFTS EKR

NQEAS, HDGAD HET NGJSK VT GK ADQGTP BSTVT YSLFQS PDS HFQOR YSNEK.

LETTER SQUARES:

2 Matthew 23:9

THE	AND	YO	NO	FAT	EAV	HER	HER
EN.	H I	IS	MAN	UR	ON	RTH	HIC
YO	UR	N H	CA	FAT	: F	EA	OR
LL	S I	, W	UP	ONE			

CROSSWORD: **Heaven Sent**

By Rowan Millson

ACROSS

1 Take aback
5 Weep convulsively
8 Christmas delivery
12 Continental currency
13 "... and wilt give __ to his commandments" (Ex. 15:26)
14 Bridal shower?
15 "... __ along upon the ground" (Ex. 9:23) (4 words)
18 First lady in 2005
19 "I have given you every herb bearing __" (Gen. 1:29)
20 Baseball official
22 Vending-machine buys
26 "And __ gave names to all cattle" (Gen. 2:20)
29 On the sheltered side
32 Basic unit of electric current
33 "... if any man preach any other __" (Gal. 1:9) (3 words)
36 Biblical judge and priest
37 Interlocking plastic toys
38 Russia, once
39 Rod of Moses
41 Pose for an artist
43 "Though ye have __ among the pots" (Ps. 68:13)
46 "And they shall take away the __ from the altar" (Num. 4:13)
50 "For I came down from heaven, not to __" (John 6:38) (4 words)
54 Skin-cream ingredient
55 Mekong dweller
56 "But he said, Ye are __" (Ex. 5:17)
57 Tidings
58 "Reward her even as __ rewarded you" (Rev. 18:6)
59 Hoover Dam's lake

DOWN

1 "And when he had opened the second __" (Rev. 6:3)
2 Albacore or bluefin
3 Official language of Pakistan
4 Bridge-game declaration by Ivana? (2 words)
5 "And, behold, your eyes __" (Gen. 45:12)
6 Stumblebums
7 Soft surface-ripened cheese
8 System of beliefs
9 Broadcast on TV
10 "His Master's Voice" company
11 Daniel survived it
16 Brother of Japheth
17 Readjust
21 "And I looked, and behold a __ horse" (Rev. 6:8)
23 "All his __ of the separation he is holy" (Num. 6:8)
24 Old Testament book
25 Goad
26 Rock of __
27 Blockhead
28 "The churches of __ salute you" (1 Cor. 16:19)
30 Tote
31 Grandson of Adam
34 Small and mischievous
35 Win a butterfly race
40 "He sent diverse sorts of __ among them" (Ps. 78:45)
42 Author Fleming
44 Conger and moray
45 Father of Shem
47 "And the flesh and the __ he burnt with fire" (Lev. 9:11)
48 Jazz singer Fitzgerald
49 Iditarod transport
50 "__ shall judge his people" (Gen. 49:16)
51 Corrida cheer
52 Trim the grass
53 "__ to thee, Moab!" (Num. 21:29)

LETTER SQUARES: **The Life of Jesus**

1 Luke 1:11

.	ON	IGH	LTA	ING	RED	E R	OF
AN	E L	AN	GEL	AND	R O	NCE	ERE
T S	PEA	TH	UN	NSE	ST	TH	TH
IDE	TO	OF	AND	F I	TH	ORD	AP
HIM	E A						

VERSE DECODER:

1 1 Peter 1:3

HINT: In the puzzle below, the letter "V" is actually an "E."

PSVJJVI PV KFV MNI WGI XWKFVY NX NZY SNYI BVJZJ LFYUJK, HFULF

WLLNYIUGM KN FUJ WPZGIWGK TVYLC FWKF PVMNKKVG ZJ WMWUG ZGKN

W SUAVSC FNQV PC KFV YVJZYYVLKUNG NX BVJZJ LFYUJK XYNT KFV IVWI.

MULTIPLE CHOICE:

1 Who anointed Jesus' head with the expensive ointment spikenard?

A. Mary, Lazarus' sister
B. Martha
C. The Samaritan woman
D. Mary Magdalene

2 Who asked that her two sons have high places in Jesus' kingdom?

A. The mother of John and James
B. The mother of Martha
C. The mother of John the Baptist
D. The mother of James and Jude

LETTER SQUARES: **The Life of Jesus**

1 John 16:23

F A	T H E	R Y	W H A	S K	T S O	G I	Y N
L A	Y O U	H A L	E S	A M E	V E	R I	I L L
I T	E V E	T H E	E W	.	N M	, H	

MULTIPLE CHOICE:

1 Who is thought to have labored harder for the gospel than anyone else?

A. Paul **B.** Timothy **C.** Matthew **D.** Matthias

2 Who was reluctant to have Jesus wash his feet?

A. James **B.** John **C.** Paul **D.** Peter

3 At Jesus' crucifixion, a man ran to find what for Jesus?

A. Linen **B.** Sponge **C.** Food **D.** Water

LETTER SQUARES:

2 Luke 9:24

V E	O S O	E V E	R W	H I S	S H	E V E	F E
E S	L O S	L O	S A	F O R	M Y	A M E	L I
R W	O S O	S H A	K E ,	I L L	F O R	V E	L I
T H	I T .	H I S	S A	L L	S A	B U T	W H
T :	I L L	E I	F E	W H	S E	A L L	

CROSSWORD: **Love Thy Neighbor**

By Joseph Mantell

ACROSS

1 Sword handle
5 Santa's helper
8 Phi __ Kappa
12 Middle Eastern title
13 Brewed beverage
14 Roman poet
15 "__ against thy neighbour without cause" (Prov. 24:28) (4 words)
18 Boredom
19 Medicine or narcotic
20 Quilting or spelling
22 Keepsake
26 False god mentioned in Judges
29 Early Scot
32 Number of gods in monotheism
33 "And if a man cause __ neighbour" (Lev, 24:19)
36 Prefix meaning "new"
37 Zenith
38 Antiquated old times
39 Harvest
41 Cloud near the ground
43 "... but Benjamin's __ was five times so much" (Gen. 43:34)
46 "For it came to pass, when the __ went up" (Judg. 13:20)
50 "__ against thy neighbour" (Prov. 3:29) (3 words)
54 "And Aaron said unto Moses, __, my lord" (Num. 12:11)
55 Staff of Moses
56 State of deep unconsciousness
57 Clamors
58 Ram's mate
59 Esau, to Jacob

DOWN

1 Mythical goddess of youth
2 Prayer ender
3 Helsinki native
4 "Now, behold, in my __" (1 Chron. 22:14)
5 O'Hare abbr.
6 Obscene
7 "And the damsel was very __ to look upon" (Gen. 24:16)
8 Hand-played drum
9 First woman
10 "__ the season ..."
11 Promos
16 Suit partner
17 ___-frutti
21 *The Ten Commandments,* for one
23 Ex-chancellor Helmut
24 Geraint's spouse
25 Capone's nemesis, Eliot __
26 Sudden loud noise
27 Biblical victim
28 Lotion ingredient
30 Belief system
31 Expert cook
34 Hair on the necks of animals
35 Fail to fix
40 Out of order
42 Frequently, in verse
44 Withered
45 "Miriam became leprous, white as __" (Num. 12:10)
47 Swear
48 Mrs. Eisenhower
49 Flair
50 Father, informally
51 "Then __ answered and said, Go in peace" (1 Sam. 1:17)
52 Cargo vehicle
53 "__ to a Nightingale"

LETTER SQUARES: **The Life of Jesus**

1 Luke 6:21

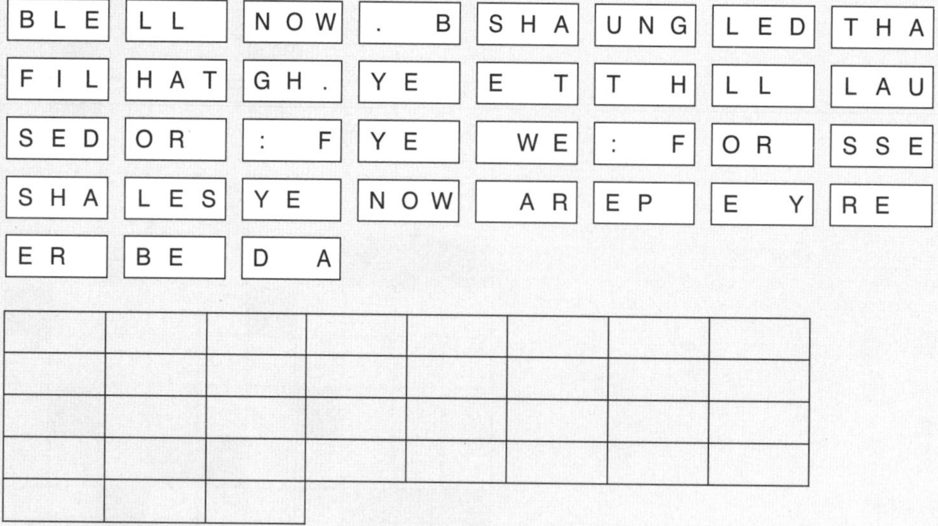

2 Luke 6:20

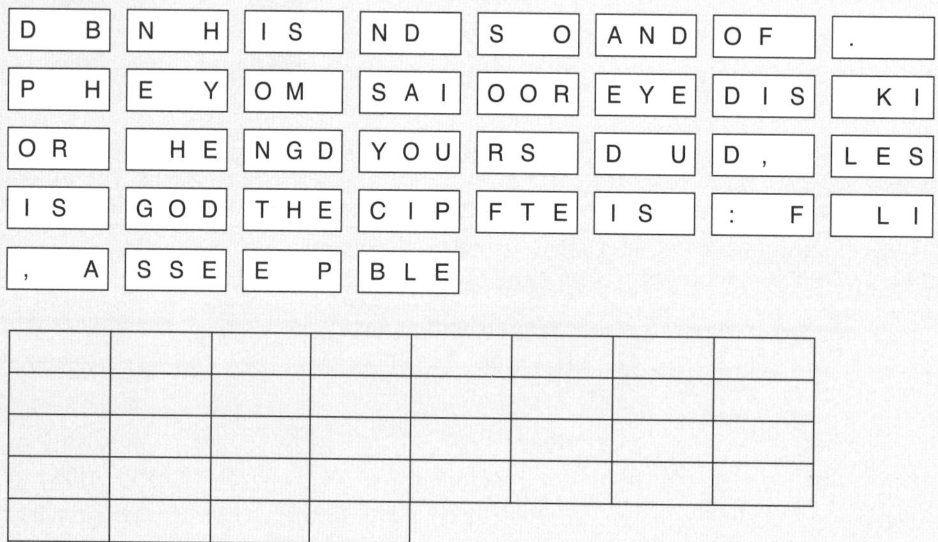

VERSE DECODER:

1 1 Corinthians 15:10

HINT: In the puzzle below, the letter "V" is actually a "T."

ANV AH VZL YDETL WG YWC X EK UZEV X EK: EQC ZXJ YDETL UZXTZ UEJ

ALJVWULC NIWQ KL UEJ QWV XQ PEXQ; ANV X REAWNDLC KWDL

EANQCEQVRH VZEQ VZLH ERR: HLV QWV X, ANV VZL YDETL WG YWC

UZXTZ UEJ UXVZ KL.

CROSSWORD: **Miracles**

By Joseph Mantell

1	2	3	4	■	5	6	7	■	8	9	10	11
12				■	13			■	14			
15				16				17				
18					■	19				■	■	■
■	■	■	20		21	■	■	22		23	24	25
26	27	28		■	29	30	31		■	32		
33				34					35			
36			■	37				■	38			
39			40		■	■	41	42		■	■	■
■	■	■	43		44	45	■	46		47	48	49
50	51	52					53					
54				■	55			■	56			
57				■	58			■	59			

ACROSS

1 Female sheep
5 100 percent
8 Swerve
12 Marshal's minion
13 Grazing land for the flock
14 "Beauty is jealous, and __ bears ..." (T. Jefferson)
15 "But Jesus said, ... that can lightly __" (Mark 9:39) (4 words)
18 Walking on eggshells
19 Short descriptive poem
20 Santa __, CA
22 Metrical units
26 "He maketh the deep to __ like a pot" (Job 41:31)
29 *Buddenbrooks* novelist
32 Wrath
33 "... thine eyes have seen, the signs, __ miracles" (Deut. 29:3)(3 words)
36 Opening day pitcher
37 To be, to Caesar
38 "... in the two __ of the mercy seat" (Ex. 25:18)
39 "It is good for me that I have been afflicted; that I might __ thy statutes" (Ps. 119:71)
41 "... as a __ lappeth, him shalt thou set by himself" (Judg. 7:5)
43 Lunch box cookie
46 Update, as an atlas
50 "... and my miracles, which I did in Egypt and in __" (Num. 14:22) (2 words)
54 Halo effect
55 Drunkard
56 "... and cut off his thumbs and his great __" (Judg. 1:6)
57 Sea bird
58 Notable time period
59 Type of police team

DOWN

1 "... and dwelt in the land of Nod, on the __ of Eden" (Gen. 4:16)
2 "... and the Lord God will __ away tears from off all faces" (Isa. 25:8)
3 Adam's garden
4 It makes the briny briny (2 words)
5 Schooner beverage
6 Tribe of Israel
7 "... and __ him on the altar upon the wood" (Gen. 22:9)
8 Stringed instrument
9 North Pole toy maker
10 Shade tree
11 Deli bread
16 Griffey of baseball
17 Breaking a commandment
21 Hebrew prophet
23 Bearing
24 Actor Pitt
25 Tennis match units
26 "And they forsook the Lord, and served __ and Ashtaroth" (Judg. 2:13)
27 "Now therefore forgive, I pray thee, my sin only this __" (Ex. 10:17)
28 "It seemed like a good __ at the time!"
30 "And Abraham rose up early in the morning, and saddled his __" (Gen. 22:3)
31 "... so that he shall have no __ of spoil" (Prov. 31:11)
34 Artist Rousseau
35 Trustees
40 Mr. Bean portrayer Atkinson
42 Former hockey great
44 "So what __ is new?"
45 Offensive smell
47 Feline remark
48 On the briny
49 Whispered call
50 Make lacework
51 Color property
52 "To __ is human"
53 LAX posting

LETTER SQUARES: **The Life of Jesus**

1 Matthew 10:8

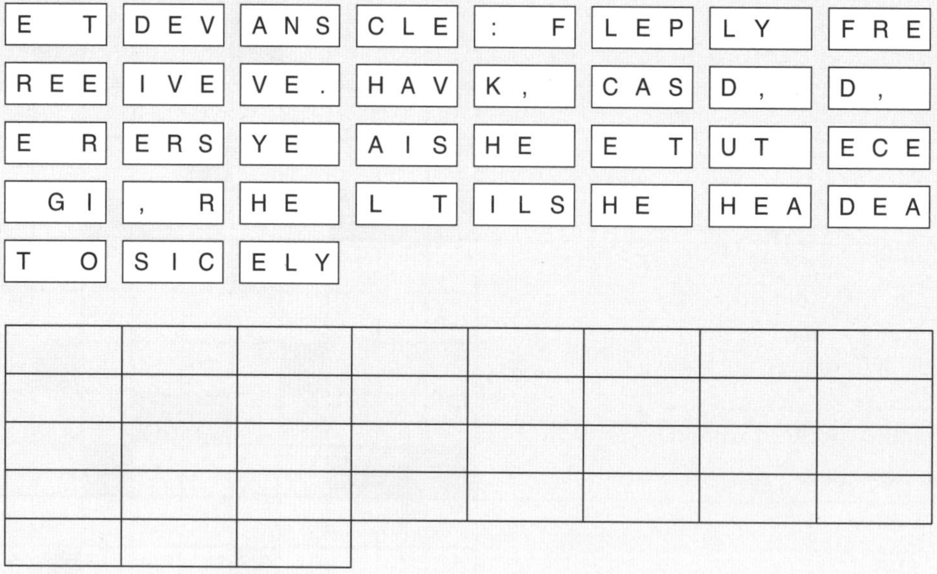

***King James Games* Facts:**

The shortest verse of the Bible is John 11:35, "Jesus wept."

LETTER SQUARES:

2 Mark 11:25

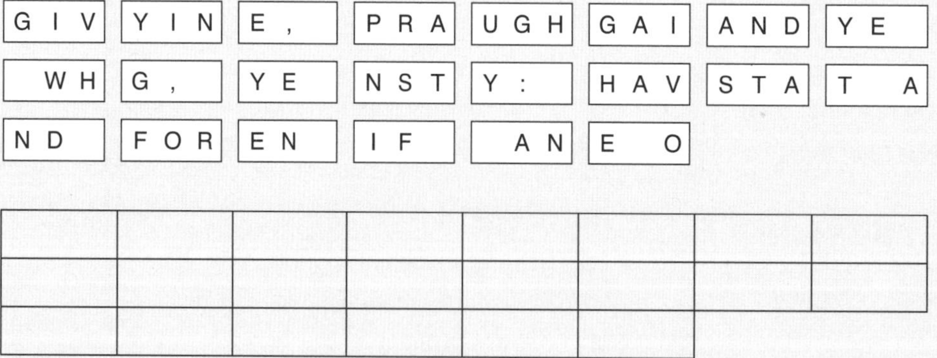

***King James Games* Facts:**

The word Christ means "the anointed one."

VERSE DECODER: **The Life of Jesus**

1 John 19:4

HINT: In the puzzle below, the letter "J" is actually an "E."

DYFQIJ IXJOJZVOJ HJBI ZVOIX QMQYB, QBA KQYIX NBIV IXJR, SJXVFA, Y

SOYBM XYR ZVOIX IV LVN, IXQI LJ RQL EBVH IXQI Y ZYBA BV ZQNFI YB XYR.

LETTER SQUARES:

1 Matthew 6:11-12

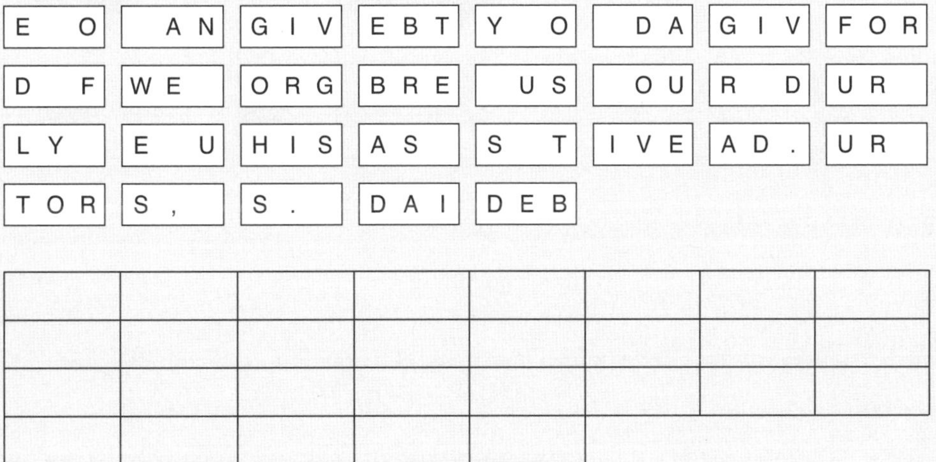

MULTIPLE CHOICE:

1 Who was known as "The man with camel's knees"?

A. John **B.** James **C.** Philip **D.** Andrew

2 Who is the blind man healed by Jesus?

A. Zacchaeus **B.** Bartimaeus **C.** Barsabas **D.** Elymas

3 Who brought Peter to Jesus?

A. Matthew **B.** Andrew **C.** Philip **D.** John

CROSSWORD: **Parables**

By Rowan Millson

1	2	3	4	■	5	6	7	■	8	9	10	11
12				■	13			■	14			
15				16				17				
18					■	19				■	■	■
■	■	■	20		21	■	■	22		23	24	25
26	27	28		■	29	30	31		■	32		
33				34					35			
36			■	37				■	38			
39			40		■	■	41	42		■	■	■
■	■	■	43		44	45	■	46		47	48	49
50	51	52					53					
54				■	55			■	56			
57				■	58			■	59			

ACROSS

1 Old Testament book
5 Prohibit
8 "... name of the __ is called Wormwood" (Rev. 8:11)
12 Agitate
13 Ginger follower
14 Singer __ Falana
15 Parable told in Luke 10:30-37 (Ps. 23:2) (2 words)
18 Prefix meaning "bone"
19 Amaze
20 Pencil stump
22 Polar home
26 "__ She Lovely?"
29 Harness
32 __ de Cologne
33 Parable told in Matthew 25:31-46 (3 words)
36 "He maketh me to __ down in green ..." (Ps. 23:2)
37 Change the decor
38 "You there!"
39 "He setteth an __ darkness" (Job 28:3) (2 words)
41 Necklace of flowers
43 Minor part of the world?
46 Haggard
50 Parable related in Luke 13:6-9 (3 words)
54 Frosted
55 Hockey Hall of Famer Bobby
56 Self-images
57 "... he should __ the armies of the living God?" (1 Sam. 17:26)
58 "My beloved is like a __ or a young hart" (Song of Sol. 2:9)
59 "Also he __ forth a dove from him" (Gen. 8:8)

DOWN

1 Consequently
2 Where leopards get spotted
3 "... having faithful children not accused of __ or unruly" (Titus 1:6)
4 Firm, like pasta (2 words)
5 Sheep shout?
6 "Sell that ye have, and give __" (Luke 12:33)
7 __ as a pin
8 David's weapon
9 Small child
10 Pie __ mode
11 "And the servant __ to meet her" (Gen. 24:17)
16 French coin
17 Feeling remorse
21 Scottish hillside
23 Pastures
24 Food grains
25 Kick out
26 "Be still, ye inhabitants of the __" (Isa. 23:2)
27 Leg part
28 "They that be whole __ not a physician" (Matt. 9:12)
30 "... endureth to the __ shall be saved" (Matt 10:22)
31 Golden calf, e.g.
34 Ordinary writing
35 Narcotics
40 Late
42 "Or if he shall ask an __, will he offer him a scorpion?" (Luke 11:12)
44 "Are you __ out?" (2 words)
45 Early Michael Jackson hairdo
47 Encourage
48 Light gas
49 Pop quiz, for one
50 Make an offer
51 Excellent tennis serve
52 Ump's relative
53 Wrath

LETTER SQUARES: **The Life of Jesus**

1 Matthew 6:33

EOU	GOD	OM	BUT	FIR	HIS	THE	OF
GHT	ST	KI	EK	SS;	NGD	SNE	SE
, A	ND	YE	RI				

***King James Games* Facts:**

Jesus existed before He came to Earth in human form. John 17:5 states:

"And now, O Father, glorify thou me with thine own self

with the glory which I had with thee before the world was."

LETTER SQUARES:

2 John 16:33

ME	UNT	OU,	HAV	YE	E S	E P	EN
MIG	IN	O Y	THI	AT	NGS	POK	E.
THE	I	EAC	HT	TH	SE	HAV	

VERSE DECODER: **The Life of Jesus**

1 James 1:25

HINT: In the puzzle below, the letter "B" is actually an "H."

WAQ FBSGS NSSELQB TXQS QBL RLHYLUQ NZF SY NTWLHQV, ZXP USXQTXALQB QBLHLTX, BL WLTXO XSQ Z YSHOLQYAN BLZHLH, WAQ Z PSLH SY QBL FSHE, QBTG IZX GBZNN WL WNLGGLP TX BTG PLLP.

MULTIPLE CHOICE:

1 What did Jesus put in the eyes of the blind man at the pool of Siloam?

A. Water
B. Mud
C. Copper
D. Silver

2 What crime did the high priest charge Jesus with?

A. Being God
B. Blasphemy
C. Stealing
D. Breaking the king's law

3 When Jesus came into Peter's house, he saw Peter's mother-in-law sick with what?

A. Paralysis
B. Leprosy
C. A fever
D. An issue of blood

LETTER SQUARES:

1 Matthew 5:44

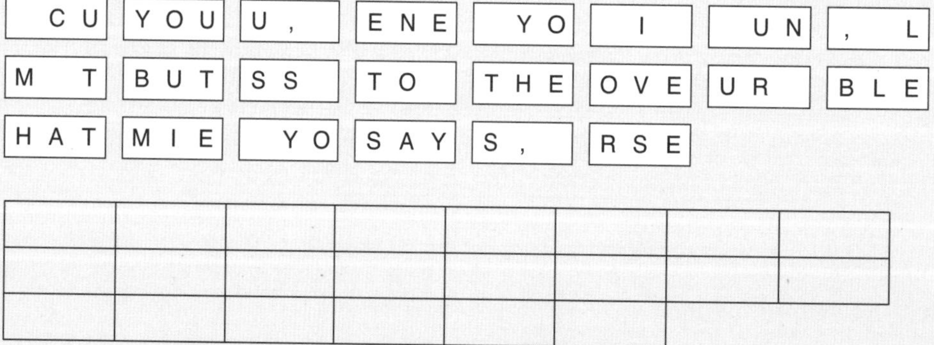

CROSSWORD: **Treasure Trove**

By Rowan Millson

1	2	3	4	■	5	6	7	■	8	9	10	11
12				■	13			■	14			
15				16				■	17			
■	■	■	18			■	■	19			■	■
20	21	22			■	23	24				25	26
27				■	28				■	29		
30			■	31					■	32		
33			■	34				■	35			
36			37				■	38				
■	■	39			■	■	40			■	■	■
41	42			■	43	44				45	46	47
48				■	49			■	50			
51				■	52			■	53			

ACROSS

1 15- and 43-Across
5 "If I be wicked, __ unto me" (Job 10:15)
8 Extraordinary
12 Glasgow hillside
13 Hee follower
14 Dashing style
15 "The first foundation was jasper; the second, __" (Rev. 21:19)
17 Jars of Clay, e.g.
18 Stuff similar to Noah's pitch
19 Kind of site
20 Curved
23 Cutting ironic remark
27 "And it is a rare thing __ the king requireth" (Dan. 2:11)
28 Peace or organ follower
29 Timid
30 "__ the land of the free ..."
31 Standish's friend
32 Rocky hill
33 Well-worn pencil
34 "I have coveted no man's silver, or __" (Acts 20:33)
35 Verb with down or out
36 Strive to equal or match
38 Measurement around the waist
39 "Eat not of it raw, __ sodden" (Ex. 12:9)
40 Negative replies
41 Like doilies
43 12th foundation of Jerusalem's walls in Rev. 21:20
48 Jazz singer Fitzgerald
49 "And the earth __ without form" (Gen. 1:2)
50 Lug
51 Boat's backbone
52 Sodom escapee
53 "There is bdellium and the __ stone" (Gen. 2:12)

DOWN

1 "Saint Joan" writer's initials
2 Big Band or Christian
3 Where X marks the spot
4 Band of seven
5 Blender sound
6 "And all that handle the __" (Eze. 27:29)
7 Ram's mate
8 Three-stringed instrument
9 "... an __ box of very precious ointment" (Matt. 26:7)
10 Sprinted
11 "The __ of all flesh is come before me" (Gen. 6:13)
16 "Yet I __ planted thee a noble vine" (Jer. 2:21)
19 Songbird
20 Turn away from sin
21 Rhubarb
22 "... row was a sardius, a topaz, and a __" (Ex. 39:10)
23 Move like a crab
24 Mimicked
25 Piglet
26 "A bundle of __ is my well-beloved unto me" (Song of Sol 1:13)
28 Secret plan
31 Culture base
35 "I __ be excused" (2 words)
37 Patriotic
38 Acquired
40 It's out on a limb
41 Albanian monetary unit
42 Ginger __ (soda choice)
43 Tool for punching holes
44 Chinese revolutionary leader
45 Hither's partner
46 Pig's place
47 ___-Mex cooking

LETTER SQUARES: **The Life of Jesus**

1 Matthew 5:5

F O	M E	S S E	I N	R E	.	D A	T H E
A L L	H E Y	B L E	R T	E K :	E A	H E R	T H E
I T	S H	R T H					

MULTIPLE CHOICE:

1 By night, Joseph took the young child and Mary to what location?

A. Jerusalem **B.** Egypt **C.** Nazareth **D.** Bethlehem

2 What problem plagued the ten men that called to Jesus in a loud voice and begged him for mercy?

A. Paralysis **B.** Deafness **C.** Leprosy **D.** Blindness

3 Which of Jesus' miracles caused the priests to conspire to have him executed?

A. The healing of a centurion's servant
B. The temple tax found in a fish's mouth
C. The raising of Lazarus
D. Turning water into wine

LETTER SQUARES:

2 Matthew 10:28

B U T	C H	T H	H E	A R	E S	A N D	T H
I L L	L T	O T	N O T	Y ,	E M	K I L	F E
E N	:	A R	W H I	A B L	O U L	O K	E T
B O D							

LETTER SQUARES: **The Life of Jesus**

1 Matthew 5:9

O F	E D	I L D	D A	G O	M A K	T H E	H A L
B L E	P E	C H	A C E	S S E	E R S	T H E	L B
Y S	R E N	T H E	O R	: F	A L L	D .	E C
R E							

MULTIPLE CHOICE:

1 To whom did Jesus say, "It is written again, Thou shalt not tempt the Lord thy God"?

A. Peter **B.** Satan **C.** Judas **D.** Michael

2 Of what woman did Jesus say, "She hath chosen the good part, which shall not be taken away from her?"

A. Mary of Bethany **C.** Mary

B. Martha **D.** The disciples

3 To whom was Jesus speaking when he said, "Whence shall we buy bread, that these may eat?"

A. Peter **C.** Philip

B. John the Baptist **D.** Andrew

VERSE DECODER:

1 Matthew 10:1

HINT: In the puzzle below, the letter "B" is actually an "N."

FBC GMJB MJ MFC TFUUJC DBAW MHX MHE AGJUQJ CHETHIUJE, MJ NFQJ

AMJX IWGJO FNFHBEA DBTUJFB EIHOHAE, AW TFEA AMJX WDA, FBC AW

MJFU FUU XFBBJO WR EHTSBJEE FBC FUU XFBBJO WR CHEJFEJ.

CROSSWORD: **Well Versed**

By Donald L. Blocher

ACROSS

1 "... and __ on the east: and there he builded an altar" (Gen. 12:8)

4 "... Philistines, to sharpen every man his __"

9 "And God said, __ there be light"

12 "... wherewith the __ number of them is to be redeemed"

13 An ancestor of Joshua

14 "... let all the inhabitants of the world stand in __ of him" (Ps. 33:8)

15 "Arise, lift up the __, and hold him" (Gen. 21:18)

16 Chief captain of David's mighty men

17 "He lieth in wait secretly as a lion in his __"

18 "... waters cannot quench love, neither can the floods __"

20 "For all the land which thou __, to thee will I give it"

22 "For length of days, and long life, and peace, shall they __"

24 "... and see this great sight, __ the bush is not burnt"

25 Operates, as machinery

28 "And God said, Let us make man in __ image"

30 Hearing organs

34 "Long __ and far away"

35 Fifth son of Gad (Gen. 46:16)

36 Dad's day gift?

37 Had been

39 Gain a lap?

40 Oldest son of Cush (Gen. 10:7)

41 "Pull me out of the __ that they have laid privily for me"

43 Judge of Israel (1 Sam. 4:18)

45 Fourth son of Midian (Gen. 25:4) (Var.)

48 "Now there __ up a new king over Egypt" (Ex. 1:8)

52 "And David put his hand in his __ and took thence a stone"

53 Son of Bani (Neh. 3:17)

57 Second son of Aram (Gen. 10:23)

58 Son of Ikkesh the Tekoite (2 Sam. 23:26)

59 The ones over there

60 King of Judah (1 Kings 15:9)

61 A Babylonian god (Isa. 46:1)

62 Put on the payroll

63 Poorly lit

DOWN

1 Office telephone button

2 Twelfth month on the Jewish calendar

3 Father of Ahinadab (1 Kings 4:14)

4 "Behold, I __ here by the well of water" (Gen. 24:13)

5 "And God saw every thing that he __ made" (Gen. 1:31)

6 Son of Shamer (1 Chron. 7:34)

7 Took to one's heels

8 A grandson of Adam (Gen. 5:6-11) (Var.)

9 "... my father did __ you with a heavy yoke" (1 Kings 12:11)

10 Farm mothers

11 Canvas shelter

19 "And the earth __ without form" (Gen. 1:2)

21 Hurricane center

23 "If thou __ well, shalt thou not be accepted?" (Gen. 4:7)

24 Compose prose

25 Animal's breadbasket

26 "... for I have born him a son in his old __"

27 "Now therefore be not grieved, __ angry with yourselves"

29 A son of Hur (Ex. 31:2)

31 "I __ no pleasant bread" (Dan. 10:3)

32 Eve's genesis

33 "... and have dominion over the fish of the __" (Gen. 1:28)

38 Finish

40 "Saying, __, we remember that that deceiver said" (Matt.27:63)

42 "In the beginning God created the heaven and the __" (Gen. 1:1)

44 Hobbled

45 First month on the Hebrew calendar (Ex. 12:2)

46 Just sufficient

47 Spy sent by Moses to the land of Canaan (Num. 13:7)

49 A son of Simeon (Gen. 46:10)

50 Father of Gaddi, of the Tribe of Manasseh (Num. 13:11)

51 A son of Shem (Gen. 10:22)

54 A son of Benjamin (Gen. 46:21)

55 Mount where Aaron died and was buried (Num. 20:22-28)

56 Put to good __

LETTER SQUARES: **The Life of Jesus**

1 Matthew 11:25

JE	AVE	HER	THA	, L	AN	AN	ND
ANK	TH	RED	EAR	OF	N A	AID	TH
HE	ORD	, I	EE,	D S	IME	SUS	SWE
AT	O	T T	FAT	TH,			

MULTIPLE CHOICE:

1 What Jewish Christian woman had once lived in Rome, Corinth, and Ephesus?

A. Bernice **B.** Anna **C.** Priscilla **D.** Ruth

2 What leper of Bethany entertained Jesus in his home?

A. Simeon **B.** Nimrod **C.** Nadab **D.** Simon

3 Who healed Aeneas, who suffered from paralysis?

A. John **B.** Stephen **C.** Jesus **D.** Peter

VERSE DECODER:

1 Matthew 11:5

HINT: In the puzzle below, the letter "A" is actually an "E."

LNA PYCQU FAJACDA LNACF WCBNL, ZQU LNA YZVA KZYS, LNA YAOAFW

ZFA JYAZQWAU, ZQU LNA UAZH NAZF, LNA UAZU ZFA FZCWAU MO,

ZQU LNA OIIF NZDA LNA BIWOAY OFAZJNAU LI LNAV.

CROSSWORD: **Trinity**

By Rowan Millson

1	2	3	■	4	5	6	7	■	8	9	10	11
12			■	13				■	14			
15			16					17				
18					■	19				■	■	■
■	■	■	20		21	■	■	22		23	24	25
26	27	28		■	29	30	31		■	32		
33				34					35			
36			■	37				■	38			
39			40		■	■	41	42		■	■	■
■	■	■	43		44	45	■	46		47	48	49
50	51	52					53					
54				■	55				■	56		
57				■	58				■	59		

ACROSS

1 What Adam and Eve did, being naked
4 Cummerbund
8 Practice with George Foreman
12 "... the Holy __ of God" (Mark 1:24)
13 Cleveland's lake
14 Imogene of early TV
15 "O ye __" (Matt. 16:8) (3 words)
18 "I have set the __ of the sword against all their gates" (Eze. 21:15)
19 Smell
20 Hither and __
22 Ablaze
26 Sound rebound
29 Molecular building block
32 "And the priest shall __ his right finger in the oil" (Lev. 14:16) (4 words)
33 "__ in the day of evil" (Jer. 17:17) (4 words)
36 Item to pick up in a restaurant
37 Actor/singer Lovett
38 Peter Fonda role
39 See 19-Across
41 Where many vets went
43 "And he said, __, what seest thou?" (Amos 8:2)
46 Yoga position
50 "Greet ye one another with a __" (1 Pet. 5:14) (3 words)
54 In the past, in the past
55 Number of Gospels
56 "In a __ it shall be made with oil" (Lev. 6:21)
57 "... good __ from a far country" (Prov. 25:25)
58 "... a rod out of the __ of Jesse" (Isa. 11:1)
59 "That's all __ wrote"

DOWN

1 Basketball target
2 Inside stuff, briefly
3 It's full of baloney
4 Free-for-all
5 "Our Father, who __ in Heaven"
6 Storage tower
7 "Take ye __ every one of his neighbour" (Jer. 9:4)
8 Winter neckwear
9 Hawaiian paste
10 Take the stage
11 Word heard at a pep rally
16 "Didn't know you had it __"(2 words)
17 Sudsy
21 Not any, country-style
23 Aaron's calf, for one
24 "Put ye in the sickle, for the harvest is __" (Joel 3:13)
25 Saber relative
26 Miss Kett of comics
27 Burn a bit, as a burger
28 Stereotypical boxcar rider
30 Final amt.
31 Evil sign
34 San Antonio mission
35 Whim
40 "... cedars from Lebanon to make __ for thee" (Eze. 27:5)
42 "When ye blow an __ the second time" (Num. 10:6)
44 Switch positions
45 Man from Dundee
47 Gratuities
48 Beehive state
49 "Auld Lang __"
50 Barbie's boy doll
51 Fury
52 Point opposite NNE
53 Color property

WORD SEARCH: **Biblical Cities**

H T E R A Z A N C E M R C X N
K M A L V B H L F M R M K J I
B C A N T I O C H M I M E B N
N D G W T J T B N A W R P T E
D A N M R I A R R U U B B Q V
F C R F E B P O N S M F R S E
A C U L E H D A A Q R T E A H
P A P L D A E L T J Y I G E T
O S P Z M I E L X R T L O R L
L A I Y Y M B N H I I P M A R
L M N H Q M D O C T T S O S T
O A L E H T E B N V E V R E K
N R N C O R I N T H M B R A W
I I R H D A M A S C U S A C X
A A L P M O D O S K V M H P R

ACCAD
ADORAIM
ANTIOCH
ANTIPATRIS
APOLLONIA
BABEL
BETHEL
BETHLEHEM
CAESAREA
CITIES
CORINTH
DAMASCUS
DIBON
EMMAUS
GOMORRAH
JERUSALEM
NAZARETH
NINEVEH
NIPPUR
SAMARIA
SODOM

WORD SEARCH: **Waters**

T	R	M	O	R	E	M	J	A	L	H	J	Z	Y	Q
A	E	G	E	A	N	Z	I	A	M	T	B	E	M	M
K	C	T	L	B	H	N	T	J	I	I	Y	R	T	F
R	L	R	E	D	R	A	B	O	A	R	Y	E	M	H
L	J	S	K	U	N	N	W	R	H	E	N	D	S	G
M	O	R	N	I	Y	F	I	D	D	H	C	U	H	A
R	V	J	H	A	L	U	S	A	A	C	C	D	E	N
M	R	E	T	T	I	B	M	N	P	S	N	R	K	G
B	Y	T	L	J	N	K	Z	D	A	S	D	M	S	R
R	C	A	A	L	A	M	H	M	M	A	A	W	I	J
J	O	Y	R	Q	X	B	A	P	G	R	C	C	R	V
P	T	H	Q	M	A	D	B	N	Q	N	H	G	G	C
C	Q	V	I	Y	U	B	Q	O	K	O	G	L	I	R
Q	C	M	D	H	L	K	A	B	K	N	P	C	T	K
R	H	K	G	T	S	F	W	A	T	E	R	S	R	N

ADHAIM	**CASPAIN**	**MEROM**
ADREA	**CHERITH**	**SHIHOR**
AEGEAN	**DAMASCUS**	**TIGRIS**
AQABA	**HALUS**	**URNIA**
ARNON	**JABBOK**	**WATERS**
BESOR	**JORDAN**	**YARMUK**
BITTER	**LATANI**	**ZERED**

MULTIPLE CHOICE: **A Friend Loves at All Times**

1 What afflicted the woman who touched the hem of Jesus' robe?

A. Leprosy
B. Blindness
C. An issue of blood
D. Demon-possession

2 Who sent the wise men to Bethlehem in search of the baby Jesus?

A. Pilate
B. Herod
C. Archelaus
D. Caiaphas

3 Who raised a young man named Eutychus from the dead?

A. Jesus
B. Peter
C. Paul
D. John

4 Who acknowledged the innocence of Jesus but still allowed him to be crucified?

A. Herod
B. Pontius Pilate
C. Joseph of Arimathea
D. Archelaus

5 Who was married to Herodias?

A. Pharaoh
B. Archelaus
C. Herod
D. Pilate

6 What book claims that Pilate had the plaque "The King of the Jews" fastened on Jesus' cross?

A. Genesis
B. John
C. Psalms
D. Matthew

WORD SEARCH: **Birds and Reptiles**

D	Z	K	X	L	Q	Y	E	K	A	N	S	K	H	D	C	W
D	L	N	F	V	X	U	Z	M	N	L	V	N	Q	N	Y	X
Q	R	Y	X	D	P	D	A	O	C	Y	H	L	N	K	D	F
Z	R	A	V	M	D	T	E	I	K	E	Z	L	N	M	R	W
Y	D	T	Z	E	T	L	Z	X	L	R	T	X	R	X	A	Y
T	F	M	A	I	E	T	R	L	K	P	J	L	F	L	Z	B
D	T	G	Q	M	L	S	U	H	R	S	R	K	T	K	Z	R
M	L	H	A	V	E	T	C	R	O	O	M	Y	Y	M	U	A
E	F	H	G	A	D	I	B	X	T	H	R	R	V	R	B	V
Z	C	L	G	Q	R	W	R	B	S	L	Q	B	G	B	G	E
L	M	U	R	T	A	M	O	B	V	D	E	T	W	F	D	N
H	L	T	S	D	G	Z	C	R	E	A	T	U	R	E	S	K
L	K	O	R	N	O	K	K	Z	R	F	T	M	N	V	G	V
M	T	K	A	X	N	V	P	Q	Z	A	Y	R	G	D	T	C
V	G	W	R	R	T	M	E	X	M	X	P	C	J	Z	L	C
T	S	G	T	O	R	T	O	I	S	E	K	S	K	W	A	H
Z	C	R	L	T	N	P	N	W	P	I	G	E	O	N	R	H

BUZZARD
CHAMELEON
CREATURES
DOVE
DRAGON
EAGLE
HAWK
LIZARD
OSPREY
OSTRICH
PIGEON
QUAIL
RAVEN
SEAGULL
SNAKE
SPARROW
STORK
SWAN
TORTOISE
TURTLE

WORD SEARCH: **Cities East of Jordan**

D K R T A D R D A R R K L K Y J R M
F Z V T K S R H M M B N Q G W L L H
K M W L C K A D E S U R E A H C A M
C X B R L H K R D J A M K V K R Z L
D F K E E W Z M E D L R F R M P K B
H B V B T V Y A M G I E K I M M I E
Z W G P F H B M P Z B Z N E H R R T
N O X H K E N H F H A A M X N B I H
J F M B T T T I M J O J J N V A A R
M T M O F O L R M B R N F M T M T E
Q R N I R R P M L R L V M M T C H H
N I B A A L G A D O A P D G V R A O
M K T F P N L N D X L H X V G B I B
R A Q G N V A E M K A M O N P Q M T
A R A D A G B H Q Y W K N T L Z V N
R C H T K A L T A B B A T H V M X J
M X K R R F M T T M J F Q H F M R F
N H X N J F H N Q L K M T Y X M X K

ABILA
ATAROTH
BAALGAD
BETHNIMRAH
BETHREHOB
BETONIM
GADARA
GERASA
JAZER
JOGBEHAH
KAMON
KENATH
KIRIATHAIM
LODEBAR
MACHAERUS
MAHANAIM
MEDEMA
NIMRAH
TABBATH
ZAPHON

MULTIPLE CHOICE: **And the Word Was God**

1 By what other name is Luke mentioned in the Bible?

A. Lemuel
B. Lucas
C. Lucius
D. Lecah

2 At the time of Jesus' death, who was the emperor of Rome?

A. Tiberius Caesar
B. Herod
C. Cyrus
D. Demetrius

3 What was the surname of the apostle Thomas?

A. Dishon
B. Deuel
C. Bibri
D. Didymus

4 At whose house did Paul leave his cloak?

A. Carpus
B. Carcas
C. Chuza
D. Cornelius

5 Who was the ruler of the Jewish synagogue at Corinth?

A. Cyrenius
B. Dedan
C. Crispus
D. Birsha

MULTIPLE CHOICE: **And the Word Was God**

1 What prophet mentions a voice crying in the wilderness?

A. Amos
B. Jeremiah
C. Nahum
D. Isaiah

2 What apostle fled the soldiers of king Aretas in Damascus?

A. Thaddaeus
B. Thomas
C. Paul
D. Simon

3 What is the fifth book of the New Testament?

A. Acts
B. Ephesians
C. 1 Timothy
D. Hebrews

4 Who objected to Jesus washing his feet?

A. Philip
B. Matthew
C. Peter
D. John

5 Where did Jesus heal a centurion's servant?

A. Nazareth
B. Bethany
C. Capernaum
D. Bethlehem

6 Which name did Jesus give to Peter?

A. Carpus
B. Clement
C. Cleopas
D. Cephas

WORD SEARCH: **Food and Spices**

J	B	R	R	Z	S	S	Y	L	B	L	Z	P	B	C	R
N	N	R	N	N	G	T	E	B	Y	J	K	M	N	S	R
T	W	M	E	L	I	G	B	V	W	S	W	M	E	P	M
V	K	R	S	A	F	O	Z	F	I	C	A	L	V	I	H
Z	M	T	D	N	D	A	Y	G	I	L	P	L	L	C	R
V	K	D	N	H	G	T	M	N	W	P	O	Z	T	E	R
T	G	H	O	H	D	A	N	X	A	N	R	O	C	S	W
N	X	M	M	L	N	A	R	L	R	A	I	S	I	N	S
V	Q	V	L	N	M	Q	T	L	X	M	L	Z	N	K	Z
R	M	Z	A	O	K	V	M	G	I	I	V	T	A	E	M
D	L	K	N	C	Z	C	K	R	A	C	N	M	R	F	S
F	O	O	D	C	N	A	S	U	B	A	R	L	E	Y	N
R	L	B	K	N	B	K	Q	D	V	K	N	V	H	J	O
X	W	H	Z	J	K	E	T	K	R	M	M	S	J	D	I
Y	W	C	T	M	Y	S	W	J	J	U	I	C	Y	T	N
V	P	V	E	N	I	S	O	N	C	F	C	T	P	C	O

ALMONDS
APPLES
BARLEY
BREAD
CAKES
CINNAMON
CORN
CURDS
FIGS
FISH
FOOD
GARLIC
GOAT
MANNA
MEAT
OLIVES
ONIONS
QUAIL
RAISINS
SALT
SPICES
VENISON

WORD SEARCH: **Gems and Stones**

F	W	M	L	F	T	B	Z	J	K	T	W	V	L	D	Q	N
N	Y	H	M	B	Q	Q	L	C	L	K	V	X	L	K	F	E
Y	N	O	D	E	C	L	A	H	C	D	Q	A	T	K	N	T
W	J	P	B	R	W	R	H	R	Y	R	R	Z	G	Z	C	A
P	N	E	F	D	B	L	E	M	K	E	J	N	P	L	Y	G
M	M	R	T	U	E	T	N	S	M	H	L	F	K	P	R	A
E	L	X	N	I	S	L	E	E	K	P	L	L	Y	W	X	L
C	R	C	W	A	L	N	L	L	V	V	B	A	C	D	N	A
G	L	I	B	N	O	O	L	I	R	R	V	Z	Y	D	J	R
E	L	A	H	T	L	L	S	R	U	T	R	U	X	Y	N	O
L	L	N	S	P	G	A	C	Y	A	M	B	L	K	C	R	C
A	H	W	N	B	P	L	P	K	R	E	F	I	Z	L	B	D
P	K	C	J	W	W	A	L	I	W	H	P	V	I	K	E	H
D	J	R	P	L	C	T	S	L	S	G	C	G	C	W	R	Y
V	N	V	J	A	C	I	N	T	H	B	U	Y	F	C	Y	B
X	A	M	E	T	H	Y	S	T	Y	R	C	Q	W	N	L	U
T	O	P	A	Z	R	G	P	X	E	N	Z	M	G	C	N	R

AGATE
ALABASTER
AMETHYST
BDELLIUM
BERYL
CARBUNCLE
CHALCEDONY
CHRYSOLITE
CORAL
EMERALD
JACINTH
LAPIS
LAZULI
LIGURE
ONYX
PEARL
RUBY
SAPPHIRE
STONES
TOPAZ

MULTIPLE CHOICE: **And the Word Was Made Flesh**

1 Who was the wife of Aquila?

A. Phoebe
B. Priscilla
C. Peninnah
D. Phanuel

2 What famous Moabite woman was married to Chilion of Israel?

A. Esther
B. Merad
C. Keturah
D. Ruth

3 What woman gave up her son to the household of an Egyptian but came to raise him in her own home anyway?

A. Jochebed
B. Rebekah
C. Elizabeth
D. Sarah

4 Other than Luke, what book did Luke write?

A. Acts
B. Colossians
C. Jude
D. Philippians

5 What apostle did Herod execute?

A. Mark
B. James
C. Peter
D. Luke

6 Where was Jesus when he gave his disciples the great commission?

A. Antioch
B. Bethany
C. Nazareth
D. Galilee

WORD SEARCH: **His Birth**

```
M B R L W F S W A R N E D T V
V S H Y J L G U N R N R R K T
G D P D L O G J S L G E M F E
R R E W H C Y R N E G G N R B
O E S D D K C A P N J K M A A
I H O D R R Z Q A C D R G N B
V P J D E A E M R E G F N K P
A E H T R C W A H T K L G I I
S H F E N T I T M T N R G N H
N S T K M G O O M A R Y N C S
K H W N I R K M J B Y I L E R
F M K F T N K L Y E G K J N O
T V T E G N W Q M R R H T S W
R S B D L T H G I N R D R E K
M L B I R T H V P D L H D K P
```

BABE	**GOLD**	**NIGHT**
BETROTHED	**JESUS**	**REJOICED**
BIRTH	**JOSEPH**	**SAVIOR**
DREAM	**MANGER**	**SHEPHERDS**
FLOCK	**MARY**	**VIRGIN**
FRANKINCENSE	**MYRRH**	**WARNED**
GIFTS	**NAZARETH**	**WORSHIP**

WORD SEARCH: **Jesus at the Temple**

G	N	I	R	A	E	H	L	Z	M	Q	K	S	R	M	L	D	N
L	D	M	L	M	C	V	W	F	W	E	T	T	S	R	E	K	N
J	L	Y	W	V	Z	M	A	T	K	A	L	R	K	V	X	P	Z
T	T	D	T	W	L	T	J	M	T	G	E	A	L	X	N	X	T
K	P	O	N	J	H	K	J	U	L	W	D	E	S	T	T	Y	Q
V	L	C	Q	E	Z	C	R	K	S	B	W	L	K	U	X	H	X
S	R	T	R	U	D	E	H	N	H	T	Z	T	D	V	R	P	D
C	R	O	N	L	E	G	A	R	T	C	E	J	B	U	S	E	N
R	K	R	R	M	Z	S	T	M	I	D	J	T	B	T	T	S	J
I	E	S	Z	K	A	N	T	K	K	S	E	C	T	L	W	O	G
P	L	B	K	Z	M	F	M	I	L	H	T	I	R	N	F	J	T
T	P	D	K	J	A	K	F	T	O	V	N	L	R	Y	L	Z	T
U	M	L	X	B	R	W	R	G	R	N	R	W	W	R	W	K	L
R	E	V	L	E	X	K	G	R	Y	Z	S	M	I	T	A	K	G
E	T	Q	H	M	N	A	Z	A	R	E	T	H	K	S	N	T	X
R	N	T	C	W	J	A	S	T	O	N	I	S	H	E	D	K	C
Z	O	G	N	I	D	N	A	T	S	R	E	D	N	U	H	O	C
M	C	X	P	K	G	G	S	Y	A	D	E	E	R	H	T	C	M

AMAZED	**JERUSALEM**	**SUBJECT**
ANSWERS	**JOSEPH**	**TARRIED**
ASTONISHED	**MOTHER**	**TEMPLE**
CHRIST	**NAZARETH**	**THREE DAYS**
DOCTORS	**QUESTIONS**	**TWELVE**
FATHER	**SCRIPTURE**	**UNDERSTANDING**
HEARING	**STATURE**	**WISDOM**

1 Who said, "Thy father and I have sought thee sorrowing"?

A. Bathsheba
B. Mary
C. Herodias
D. Rebekah

2 What king wanted to see miracles when the arrested Jesus was sent to him?

A. Archelaus
B. Pilate
C. Herod
D. Caiaphas

3 What New Testament woman holds the record for widowhood, with eighty-four years?

A. Mary
B. Lois
C. Eunice
D. Anna

4 Who came forth when Jesus called him in a loud voice?

A. Joseph
B. John
C. Peter
D. Lazarus

5 Whose name wasn't mentioned as one of the first women to see Jesus' empty tomb?

A. Joanna
B. Salome
C. Mary Magdalene
D. Martha

6 What Christian woman was noted for helping the poor in the early church?

A. Bernice
B. Dorcas
C. Candace
D. Priscilla

WORD SEARCH: **Jesus in the Wilderness**

N	H	M	Z	B	M	K	E	S	C	C	H	W	K	L
C	T	R	E	B	T	V	Y	L	J	O	H	X	I	L
Y	O	D	T	L	R	Y	D	E	K	M	F	Y	N	D
B	O	X	E	E	C	A	D	G	H	M	D	K	G	L
S	F	X	S	T	E	A	S	N	H	A	F	P	D	P
P	E	F	K	R	S	O	N	A	Y	N	N	L	O	Q
R	V	N	B	X	N	A	Y	N	D	D	O	D	M	J
O	V	T	O	O	N	R	F	A	I	R	T	Y	S	H
C	G	T	F	T	O	N	S	C	D	P	T	C	G	O
E	H	G	K	L	S	H	W	J	G	C	A	S	T	L
E	O	A	G	L	I	V	E	D	X	H	K	W	N	Y
D	F	O	R	T	Y	D	A	Y	S	M	Q	V	A	C
E	L	R	L	G	Z	T	E	M	P	T	E	D	T	I
T	K	D	Z	K	E	R	T	N	L	L	X	Y	A	T
H	F	G	Z	W	N	I	A	T	N	U	O	M	S	Y

ANGELS
BREAD
CAST
CHARGE
COMMAND
DASH
DEVIL
FASTED
FOOT
FORTY DAYS
GLORY
HANDS
HOLY CITY
KINGDOMS
LORD
MOUNTAIN
PINNACLE
PROCEEDETH
SATAN
SERVE
SON OF GOD
STONES
TEMPTED

WORD SEARCH: **Jesus**

T	S	H	N	O	I	X	I	F	I	C	U	R	C	H	C	L
V	E	S	Z	G	L	M	R	K	Z	M	Y	B	L	M	R	R
V	B	S	T	G	V	W	U	K	C	K	T	N	R	Q	I	R
R	I	E	X	L	M	D	Y	L	H	O	W	R	H	M	M	K
D	R	N	K	P	V	T	E	J	T	D	N	P	T	J	E	I
H	C	K	T	Y	N	I	C	N	G	I	E	T	D	Z	X	N
M	S	R	R	B	F	R	N	T	O	S	T	T	E	S	B	G
R	G	A	C	K	O	I	K	E	O	I	Q	U	R	M	M	O
T	R	D	G	S	H	R	C	J	G	M	T	E	D	D	P	F
L	K	X	S	W	Z	M	P	U	M	A	I	S	N	E	L	T
N	M	W	W	D	U	W	P	Y	R	D	R	P	E	S	S	H
W	V	H	J	R	X	B	R	M	L	C	D	R	W	U	W	E
L	G	D	D	L	B	A	K	O	T	O	M	B	J	C	Q	J
T	Q	E	L	B	V	W	S	F	Y	J	F	M	Q	C	N	E
Y	R	R	L	L	M	O	C	K	E	D	M	K	R	A	N	W
T	Z	Y	A	T	M	G	E	T	A	L	I	P	R	R	D	S
K	R	C	C	Q	C	E	N	T	U	R	I	O	N	W	D	K

ACCUSED
CALVARY
CENTURION
CONTEMPT
CRIME
CROSS
CRUCIFIXION

CRUCIFY
DARKNESS
JOSEPH
KING OF THE JEWS
MOCKED
MULTITUDES
MURDER

PILATE
QUESTIONED
SCRIBES
SOLDIERS
TOMB
VINEGAR

WORD SEARCH: **The Lord's Prayer**

G	R	B	R	H	T	R	A	E	Z	P	N	V	L	Y
D	K	W	F	W	E	F	K	F	O	R	G	I	V	E
P	Y	P	E	V	V	X	C	M	R	B	T	X	W	F
L	K	C	E	N	P	M	N	P	E	X	N	W	E	T
F	I	R	D	A	I	L	Y	T	H	M	R	D	H	E
J	O	V	E	N	D	H	T	N	T	T	G	A	T	M
F	M	M	E	O	J	N	T	N	A	N	L	D	T	P
D	A	W	N	R	T	E	G	J	F	L	N	E	A	T
N	E	E	D	P	J	M	T	I	O	M	W	B	M	A
G	L	L	Y	T	F	A	T	W	V	R	F	T	T	T
L	N	F	I	M	T	D	E	C	G	E	D	S	K	I
O	F	Y	L	V	A	D	Q	N	J	M	Y	A	T	O
R	B	L	R	E	E	R	J	K	K	R	D	K	E	N
Y	Z	D	R	L	C	R	N	E	V	A	E	H	M	L
M	Q	B	P	O	W	E	R	M	O	D	G	N	I	K

AMEN
BREAD
DAILY
DEBTS
DELIVER
DONE
EARTH
EVIL
FATHER
FOREVER
FORGIVE
GIVE
GLORY
HALLOWED
HEAVEN
KINGDOM
LEAD
MATTHEW
NAME
POWER
TEMPTATION
THINE

WORD SEARCH: **Miracles**

E	J	P	S	T	O	R	M	K	N	D	H	P	J	T
Q	E	E	D	N	A	H	D	E	R	E	H	T	I	W
I	G	R	T	F	E	V	E	R	M	T	F	F	H	Y
D	N	T	T	U	X	P	N	O	G	I	T	C	L	S
R	I	F	Y	G	M	S	R	H	V	D	I	V	N	R
O	D	N	I	K	I	R	U	E	F	T	T	O	D	Y
P	E	M	B	R	H	F	T	R	P	H	I	P	B	N
S	E	H	X	A	M	H	L	E	A	R	L	A	V	A
Y	F	V	G	Q	O	D	L	N	U	Z	K	R	N	M
H	L	I	E	U	N	I	E	T	N	M	A	A	Z	B
R	N	N	S	R	P	N	N	M	W	Z	Q	L	V	M
G	I	A	K	E	Q	E	B	C	O	P	N	Y	G	U
W	N	N	J	P	C	Y	M	N	G	N	J	T	L	D
D	J	X	T	E	R	D	N	I	L	B	S	I	M	G
Z	Z	P	V	L	E	S	C	A	P	E	Z	C	B	M

BLIND
CENTURIONS
DEMONS
DROPSY
DUMB MAN
EPILEPTIC
ESCAPE
FEEDING
FEVER
FIG TREE
FIVE THOUSAND
HEMORRHAGING
INFIRM
LAZARUS
LEPER
MUTE
PARALYTIC
STORM
WINE
WITHERED HAND

MULTIPLE CHOICE: **Jesus: Our High Priest**

1 What is the 21st book of the New Testament?

A. Titus
B. 1 Peter
C. Colossians
D. 1 John

2 Where was Jesus at the time of his ascension?

A. Galilee
B. Nazareth
C. Bethany
D. Damascus

3 Which of the following was Joseph's hometown?

A. Nazareth
B. Galilee
C. Capernaum
D. Nineveh

4 Who asked Jesus, "How can we know the way?"

A. James
B. Thomas
C. Peter
D. John

5 What is the only gospel that mentions Jesus riding on a donkey?

A. Matthew
B. Mark
C. Luke
D. John

6 What island did Paul and his companions land on after they were shipwrecked?

A. Melita
B. Crete
C. Patmos
D. Malta

MULTIPLE CHOICE: **Jesus: Our High Priest**

1 When Jesus said, "What, could ye not watch with me one hour," whom was he speaking to?

A. Thaddaeus
C. Peter
B. Andrew
D. Judas

2 Which New Testament book ends with: "My love be with you all in Christ Jesus. Amen."?

A. 1 Corinthians
C. Galatians
B. Acts
D. 1 Peter

3 "For to be carnally minded is death; but to be spiritually minded is life and peace." What book of the Bible contains this verse?

A. Galatians
C. Matthew
B. Romans
D. Jude

4 When Paul said, "Are ye so foolish? Having begun in the Spirit, are ye now made perfect by the flesh?" whom was he talking too?

A. The Ephesians
C. The Corinthians
B. The Romans
D. The Galatians

5 Which one of the four gospels contains the genealogy of Christ?

A. Matthew
C. Luke
B. Mark
D. John

6 How many sons of Sceva were there?

A. Nine
C. Seven
B. Eleven
D. Ten

WORD SEARCH: **Names for Jesus**

P	B	J	Z	Y	B	L	M	R	L	M	F	L	D	B	X	N
Y	R	L	M	T	F	R	E	X	L	I	T	R	T	C	K	R
G	E	Z	G	I	N	K	L	U	N	K	E	K	O	R	E	M
N	A	A	F	E	G	P	K	I	N	H	D	M	H	R	M	J
M	D	G	H	D	D	N	S	B	P	A	M	K	E	D	O	V
B	O	E	J	F	L	H	I	E	E	A	M	V	N	T	R	D
X	F	M	L	P	E	A	H	R	N	L	I	M	N	M	N	R
F	L	O	M	R	H	S	W	D	P	L	O	R	I	L	I	E
L	I	K	D	P	Z	H	E	N	E	S	N	V	H	N	N	T
C	F	R	L	O	N	R	N	D	L	D	Y	F	E	V	G	A
P	E	A	H	V	O	A	U	T	H	O	R	A	M	D	S	C
D	I	A	D	E	M	R	L	V	Q	K	R	I	D	J	T	O
C	K	N	R	O	B	T	S	R	I	F	Y	T	J	R	A	V
M	A	D	A	D	N	O	C	E	S	V	L	H	Q	R	R	D
G	J	M	J	Q	Y	F	K	W	W	C	R	F	K	R	M	A
R	Q	J	W	Y	K	R	O	L	E	S	N	U	O	C	T	R
D	M	F	C	D	V	C	Y	X	L	J	N	L	V	W	W	C

ADVOCATE
ALPHA
AUTHOR
BELOVED
BREAD OF LIFE
COMMANDER
COUNSELOR
DAYSPRING
DEITY
DELIVERER
DIADEM
DOOR
FAITHFUL
FINISHER
FIRST BORN
IMMANUEL
MORNING STAR
OMEGA
SECOND ADAM
SHEPHERD

MULTIPLE CHOICE: **Lion of the Tribe of Judah**

1 Where are the Beatitudes?

A. Luke 7
B. Mark 11
C. Matthew 5
D. John 12

2 According to 1 Peter, what person is like a ravenous lion?

A. Satan
B. Judas
C. Herod
D. Elymas

3 What kinsman of Jesus was imprisoned for criticizing King Herod's marriage to Herodias?

A. John
B. John the Baptist
C. Joseph
D. Zacharias

4 Which book has a total of eight chapters?

A. 2 Peter
B. Deuteronomy
C. Acts
D. The Song of Solomon

5 Who spoke for all the apostles at Caesarea Philippi?

A. Paul
B. Jesus
C. Peter
D. John

6 What book speaks of the Lion of the Tribe of Judah?

A. Revelation
B. Genesis
C. Nahum
D. 1 Samuel

D	W	K	L	V	M	P	R	O	D	I	G	A	L	P
R	E	G	K	V	E	R	U	S	A	E	R	T	X	M
H	E	E	U	R	W	L	G	Z	T	S	I	K	H	B
R	T	P	S	E	B	L	R	M	E	U	W	P	Z	Q
O	D	N	P	D	S	N	T	E	R	R	E	W	O	S
O	R	K	F	U	R	T	D	F	X	F	K	T	X	D
D	G	O	O	D	S	A	M	A	R	I	T	A	N	J
W	L	F	N	H	P	G	T	M	Z	L	T	F	K	R
O	A	S	M	B	F	U	W	S	O	W	G	M	E	I
R	M	T	R	L	T	T	B	S	U	N	N	T	E	C
R	P	N	R	K	T	N	T	L	B	M	K	F	R	H
A	T	A	T	S	F	C	L	R	I	R	Q	K	T	F
N	E	N	A	M	O	H	K	Y	B	C	L	H	G	O
P	H	E	R	I	P	R	E	G	A	N	A	M	I	O
T	Y	T	N	V	I	N	E	Y	A	R	D	N	F	L

FIG TREE
FRUIT
GOOD SAMARITAN
GUEST
LAMP
LOST COIN
MANAGER
MUSTARD SEED
NARROW DOOR
PEARL
PRODIGAL
PUBLICAN
RICH FOOL
SEED
SOWER
SUPPER
TENANTS
TREASURE
VINEYARD
YEAST

MULTIPLE CHOICE: **The Knowledge of the Truth**

1 Who heard the divine voice telling him to eat unclean animals?

A. John
B. Thomas
C. Thaddaeus
D. Peter

2 To what earthly woman did Jesus say, "God is a spirit"?

A. The Samaritan woman
B. Mary
C. Anna
D. The daughter of Jairus

3 Which one of the apostles was a Roman citizen?

A. Thaddaeus
B. Philip
C. Paul
D. Simon

4 Who was the angel Gabriel speaking to when he said, "Blessed art thou among women"?

A. Elizabeth
B. Sarah
C. Mary
D. Anna

5 What woman had five husbands and was living with another man?

A. Martha
B. The woman with the issue of blood
C. Mary Magdalene
D. The Samaritan woman

6 What wealthy woman made her living selling purple dye?

A. Priscilla
B. Claudia
C. Lydia
D. Lois

WORD SEARCH: **Teachings of Jesus**

```
N M W S S E I M E N E V W X F R X
R W X J S W N D T I T H E S H R K
P N F U W E F D K B E T R A Y A L
L T R S J Y N T X G Q L K W T E C
V K D T D R B K Q J D R C R H C R
N Q Y I W E P Q R O L O D P Q R E
O N A C B T D Z O A M C J Y C O S
I T W E J L P F C P D N S R H V U
T K W F L U E T A L Z A G R A I R
A J O C D D J S A V T N M H R D R
V N R T N A S B S S H T J D I K E
L T R P V I O J O I D A M L T D C
A Y A G O R F P M N N R R P Y B T
S H N N H L A Q B C R G A V L V I
T X C X T V D R R N Z Y S W E B O
N O I S R E V N O C N L L V E S N
H R T R Y L G I V I N G L R T R T
```

ADULTERY
APOSTASY
BETRAYAL
BLESSINGS
CHARITY
COMPASSION
CONVERSION
DARKNESS
DIVORCE
ENEMIES
FOOD
GIVING
HARVEST
JUSTICE
LABOR
NARROW WAY
RESURRECTION
REWARD
SALVATION
TITHES

WORD SEARCH: **The Last Supper**

D	S	S	T	J	M	F	L	D	T	Z	M	T	M	Y
J	Z	E	E	B	E	S	T	S	E	I	R	P	A	W
O	L	E	L	B	R	S	H	T	A	E	D	R	K	B
H	V	R	Z	P	I	E	U	T	R	V	T	N	M	R
N	E	A	E	P	I	R	A	S	N	E	I	R	C	E
R	C	P	L	P	C	C	C	D	B	R	B	M	O	T
Y	N	E	L	T	P	M	S	S	D	T	K	C	N	E
X	A	R	S	A	G	U	B	I	J	Q	O	V	F	P
Z	R	P	E	B	C	K	S	U	D	V	H	X	E	E
T	B	Y	L	L	L	C	D	T	E	P	V	M	R	D
V	M	H	T	E	K	A	K	N	S	R	R	X	R	I
F	E	A	S	T	S	M	A	Z	V	A	Y	N	E	V
N	M	G	O	M	R	N	V	Z	M	N	L	M	D	I
B	E	Z	P	L	T	N	R	B	L	O	O	D	H	D
T	R	B	A	B	M	A	L	N	H	K	F	Y	M	K

APOSTLES
BETRAY
BLOOD
BREAD
CONFERRED
COVENANT
DEATH
DISCIPLES
DIVIDE
DRINK
FEAST
JESUS
JOHN
JUDAS
LAMB
LAST SUPPER
PETER
PREPARE
PRIESTS
REMEMBRANCE
SCRIBES
TABLE

WORD SEARCH: **The Sermon on the Mount**

D	S	S	E	N	S	U	O	E	T	H	G	I	R	N	R	R
R	C	G	L	P	T	N	Y	N	M	O	D	G	N	I	K	M
A	R	K	P	G	H	R	N	M	M	M	T	T	N	R	M	I
W	L	O	N	C	K	E	Q	B	V	T	P	V	V	J	N	K
E	O	W	R	K	R	J	A	M	O	U	R	N	R	H	B	M
R	M	G	W	D	Y	N	T	V	D	L	I	T	E	N	G	N
T	K	X	L	B	P	Q	M	R	E	A	N	R	P	T	Q	J
V	W	I	K	Q	T	E	R	L	T	N	I	B	E	W	C	R
D	H	K	K	K	K	G	A	N	C	T	K	T	R	M	P	L
C	T	E	A	R	T	H	U	C	M	T	I	E	S	W	H	U
H	B	L	R	S	T	O	E	G	E	R	T	Q	E	C	U	F
M	F	J	N	S	M	R	Q	C	I	M	L	N	C	M	N	I
R	T	T	G	E	V	L	X	P	I	F	A	Y	U	Q	G	C
N	M	N	M	L	K	K	S	Z	D	O	K	K	T	X	E	R
M	T	N	N	B	C	H	B	W	Q	N	J	L	E	J	R	E
B	M	F	Y	T	R	T	H	I	R	S	T	E	D	R	Q	M
K	T	R	A	E	H	N	I	E	R	U	P	H	R	Z	S	D

BLESS
CHILDREN
EARTH
HEAVEN
HUNGER
INHERIT
KINGDOM
MEEK
MERCIFUL
MOUNTAIN
MOURN
PEACE MAKERS
PERSECUTED
POOR
PURE IN HEART
REJOICE
REWARD
RIGHTEOUSNESS
SPIRIT
THIRST

WORD SEARCH: **The Transfiguration**

D	S	S	T	S	E	I	R	P	B	N	L	T	Z	Y
I	T	U	D	E	C	I	F	I	R	C	A	S	R	A
S	N	E	S	T	H	C	W	B	R	E	A	D	D	R
C	X	N	C	E	R	H	M	S	T	W	J	O	L	T
I	M	M	C	N	J	L	L	A	H	G	O	X	T	E
P	L	U	R	O	A	L	W	D	H	L	R	G	M	B
L	O	F	N	Q	V	R	P	U	B	L	F	P	O	R
E	P	F	K	L	M	E	B	J	B	R	E	H	O	C
S	A	J	F	H	E	D	N	M	C	T	N	Y	R	R
E	S	K	W	I	I	A	B	A	E	W	K	L	R	K
B	S	T	J	V	C	M	V	R	N	M	O	N	E	Y
I	O	G	I	T	A	E	X	E	F	T	E	F	P	K
R	V	D	T	L	D	J	R	D	N	T	R	R	P	C
C	E	D	N	V	L	N	R	S	N	E	D	V	U	M
S	R	H	V	W	N	G	K	N	I	R	D	R	H	K

BETRAY	**JESUS**	**PRIESTS**
BLOOD	**JUDAS**	**REMEMBRANCE**
BREAD	**LAMB**	**SACRIFICED**
COVENANT	**MONEY**	**SCRIBES**
DISCIPLE	**OFFICERS**	**UNLEAVENED**
DIVIDE	**PASSOVER**	**UPPER ROOM**
DRINK	**PETER**	

MULTIPLE CHOICE: **Worthy is the Lamb**

1 Who appeared at Jesus' transfiguration?

A. Daniel and Joel

B. Malachi and Zephaniah

C. Moses and Elijah

D. Jeremiah and Isaiah

2 According to the book of Revelation, how many years will Satan be bound in the bottomless pit?

A. 7,000 yrs

B. 7 yrs

C. 100 yrs

D. 1,000 yrs

3 In Jesus' messages to the seven churches, which church did he say was neither cold nor hot?

A. The Church of Laodicea

B. The Church of Ephesus

C. The Church of Sardis

D. The Church of Pergamos

4 What book in the Bible promises that those who hear the words of this prophecy will be blessed?

A. Jude

B. Matthew

C. Hebrews

D. Revelation

5 Which chapter is known as the "faith chapter"?

A. 1 Corinthians 13

B. Hebrews 11

C. Romans 8

D. Ephesians 6

6 Complete this verse: "Finally, my brethren, be strong in the Lord, and in the power of …"

A. His love

B. His glory

C. His hope

D. His might

WORD SEARCH: **Unto Us a Child is Given**

```
C H T S O H G Y L O H E H T B E H O L D N
B W R N E M E S I W E H T S L Z L G Q Z A
L E N P Y N N T M R D V A F H Z E R R T Z
T C T Z J X B V B E G L Y T D X G E R W A
L T Q H F X D C R B V B M P V B N A P T R
K N R H L N M O D A A T J C S M A T N M E
K M Z Q H E V T T B T B K H K N R J G D T
G K C L D A H I Y L O H E Z I H N O Y D H
R O X R F B O E Q T K P K G D L H Y H D T
I K O K M N N P M H H X R A L O L C M E G
G L L D Q M M H W E W I V T L R T L R T N
H J C E T W V A R X V I Z I H L M O H L I
T J V H U I R D R H D R N R T Y J T P A L
E X R J K N D H Q Y Q E G G Y P C H E X D
O K R U R K A I G R S K C R X X B E S E D
U S V H O V M M N S L Z P W M P M S O J A
S T U X J I T N E G R T M R W Y N K J H W
N L X S Y H V B T R S H T E B A S I L E S
E X C R E G G A B R I E L P C M T L V H G
S Q R C M J N M S N K J M A N G E R T K X
S B F H T R A E N O E C A E P G L J D K T
```

ANGEL
BABY
BEHOLD
BETHLEHEM
CLOTHES
DAVID
ELISABETH
EMANUEL
EXALTED
FAVORED

GABRIEL
GOOD TIDINGS
GREAT JOY
HOLINESS
HOLY
JESUS
JOSEPH
LORD
MANGER
MARY

NAZARETH
PEACE ON EARTH
RIGHTEOUSNESS
SALVATION
SAVIOUR
SHEPHERD
SWADDLING
THE HOLY GHOST
THE WISE MEN
VIRGIN

MULTIPLE CHOICE: **You Were Bought at a Price**

1 What man asked the high priest for letters of commendation so he could work in the synagogues of Damascus?

A. Peter
B. Paul
C. Nebuchadnezzar
D. Cornelius

2 In John's gospel, who is the "son of perdition"?

A. The prodigal son
B. Jesus
C. Judas
D. Thomas

3 Who did the Sanhedrin put in jail for disturbing the peace?

A. Paul and Barnabas
B. Timothy and Titus
C. Peter and John
D. Stephen and Silas

4 Who preached to the intellectuals of Athens?

A. Paul
B. Peter
C. Jesus
D. Gamaliel

5 While in Athens, Paul passed by an altar. What was inscribed on it?

A. To the God of Athens
B. To the unknown God
C. To the God of life
D. To the God of men

6 How many pots of water were turned into wine during Jesus' first miracle?

A. Four
B. Five
C. Six
D. Seven

MULTIPLE CHOICE: **You Were Bought at a Price**

1 Who said, "How can a man be born when he is old?"

A. Josaphat
B. Nicodemus
C. Jairus
D. Jared

2 Who cried unto Jesus, "Thou Son of David, have mercy on me?"

A. Timaeus
B. Bartimaeus
C. Cornelius
D. Cleopas

3 Which prophet came from Jerusalem unto Antioch and prophesied through the Holy Spirit that there would be a great dearth throughout the entire world?

A. Agabus
B. Claudius
C. Clement
D. Demas

4 What man so loved the world that he deserted his friend, the apostle Paul?

A. Nicodemus
B. Philip
C. Carpus
D. Demas

5 Which man who liked to take the lead and put himself first refused to acknowledge the authority of the apostle John?

A. Diotrephes
B. Demetrius
C. James
D. Dedan

6 Which of the twelve disciples was the only one who was not a Galilean?

A. John
B. Philip
C. James
D. Judas

SOLUTIONS

Page 227

CROSSWORD: A Test of Faith

1 S	2 U	3 R	■	4 T	5 E	6 M	7 A	■	8 A	9 R	10 I	11 D
12 E	N	E	■	13 I	G	O	R	■	14 D	O	M	O
15 C	D	S	■	16 S	L	A	M	■	17 I	V	A	N
18 R	O	O	19 F	■	20 A	B	E	21 D	N	E	G	O
22 E	N	R	I	23 C	H	■	24 N	E	A	R	E	R
25 T	E	T	R	A	■	26 S	I	S	■	27 S	S	S
■	■	■	28 M	E	29 S	H	A	C	30 H	■	■	■
31 B	32 S	33 A	■	34 S	T	E	■	35 R	A	36 N	37 K	38 S
39 U	P	R	40 O	A	R	■	41 S	Y	R	I	A	N
42 S	H	A	D	R	A	43 C	H	■	44 A	G	R	A
45 H	E	R	E	■	46 I	R	O	47 N	■	48 H	E	R
49 E	R	A	T	■	50 T	O	R	E	■	51 T	A	E
52 S	E	T	S	■	53 S	P	E	D	■	54 S	H	S

Page 228

MULTIPLE CHOICE: The Life of Jesus

1 solution: **D**; 2 solution: **B**; 3 solution: **B**.

VERSE DECODER:

1 solution:

And, behold, there was a great earthquake: For the angel of the LORD descended from heaven, and came and rolled back the stone from the door, and sat upon it.
Matthew 28:2

Page 228, (continued)

VERSE DECODER:

2 solution:

This parable spake Jesus unto them: But they understood not what things they were which he spake unto them. Then said Jesus unto them again, verily, verily, I say unto you, I am the door of the sheep.
John 10:6-7

Page 229

CROSSWORD: Jesus is Lord

1 A	2 P	3 E	■	4 G	5 E	6 N	7 E	■	8 M	9 A	10 S	11 H
12 S	A	T	■	13 A	L	E	C	■	14 A	R	E	A
15 K	I	N	16 G	O	F	T	H	17 E	J	E	W	S
18 S	N	A	R	L	■	19 S	O	S	O	■	■	■
■	■	■	20 A	S	21 H	■	■	22 T	R	23 A	24 P	25 S
26 S	27 A	28 R	I	■	29 O	30 R	31 E	O	■	32 R	A	H
33 P	R	I	N	34 C	E	O	F	P	35 E	A	C	E
36 A	I	L	■	37 I	S	N	T	■	38 A	B	E	D
39 S	A	L	40 A	D	■	■	41 S	42 A	G	■	■	■
■	■	■	43 M	E	44 S	45 S	■	46 S	E	47 R	48 V	49 E
50 R	51 U	52 L	E	R	I	N	53 I	S	R	A	E	L
54 I	R	A	N	■	55 P	A	R	E	■	56 Y	E	S
57 M	I	S	S	■	58 S	P	A	T	■	59 S	S	E

SOLUTIONS

Page 230

LETTER SQUARES: The Life of Jesus

1 solution:

He that findeth his life shall lose it: and he that loseth his life for my sake shall find it.
Matthew 10:39

2 solution:

Judge not, and ye shall not be judged: condemn not, and ye shall not be condemned:
Luke 6:37

MULTIPLE CHOICE:

1 solution: **B**; 2 solution: **B**.

Page 231

VERSE DECODER: The Life of Jesus

1 solution:

To whom also he shewed himself alive after his passion by many infallible proofs, being seen of them forty days, and speaking of the things pertaining to the kingdom of God.
Acts 1:3

LETTER SQUARES:

1 solution:

No man hath seen God at any time, the only begotten Son, which is in the bosom of the Father.
John 1:18

2 solution:

And Jesus said, For judgment I am come into this world, that they which see not might see;
John 9:39

Page 232

CROSSWORD: Glory of the Lord

1 E	2 C	3 H	4 O	■	5 T	6 W	7 A	■	8 K	9 E	10 E	11 N
12 F	O	O	T	■	13 A	I	R	■	14 A	R	G	O
15 T	H	E	H	16 O	U	S	E	17 O	F	G	O	D
18 S	O	R	E	R	■	19 H	A	R	K	■	■	■
■	■	■	20 L	E	21 E	■	■	22 A	A	23 R	24 O	25 N
26 I	27 D	28 O	L	■	29 U	30 P	31 O	N	■	32 A	G	O
33 D	E	V	O	34 U	R	I	N	G	35 F	I	R	E
36 E	A	U	■	37 N	O	E	L	■	38 I	D	E	S
39 A	D	M	40 I	T	■	■	41 Y	42 E	N	■	■	■
■	■	■	43 S	I	44 A	45 M	■	46 L	A	47 S	48 S	49 O
50 S	51 H	52 A	L	L	B	E	53 F	I	L	L	E	D
54 H	A	L	E	■	55 L	E	I	■	56 L	O	R	D
57 E	M	I	T	■	58 E	K	E	■	59 Y	E	A	S

Page 233

LETTER SQUARES: The Life of Jesus

1 solution:

Blessed are they which are persecuted for righteousness' sake: Matthew 5:10

VERSE DECODER:

1 solution:

Who hath saved us, and called us with an Holy calling, not according to our works, but according to his own purpose and grace, which was given us in Christ Jesus before the world began. 2 Timothy 1:9

LETTER SQUARES:

2 solution:

And call no man your father upon the earth: for one is your Father, which is in heaven. Matthew 23:9

SOLUTIONS

Page 234

CROSSWORD: Heaven Sent

S	T	U	N		S	O	B		C	A	R	D
E	U	R	O		E	A	R		R	I	C	E
A	N	D	T	H	E	F	I	R	E	R	A	N
L	A	U	R	A		S	E	E	D			
			U	M	P			S	O	D	A	S
A	D	A	M		A	L	E	E		A	M	P
G	O	S	P	E	L	U	N	T	O	Y	O	U
E	L	I		L	E	G	O		U	S	S	R
S	T	A	F	F			S	I	T			
			L	I	E	N		A	S	H	E	S
D	O	M	I	N	E	O	W	N	W	I	L	L
A	L	O	E		L	A	O		I	D	L	E
N	E	W	S		S	H	E		M	E	A	D

Page 235

LETTER SQUARES: The Life of Jesus

1 solution:

And there appeared unto him an angel of the LORD standing on the right side of the altar of incense.
Luke 1:11

VERSE DECODER:

1 solution:

Blessed be the God and Father of our LORD Jesus Christ, which according to his abundant mercy hath begotten us again unto a lively hope by the resurrection of Jesus Christ from the dead.
1 Peter 1:3

Answers continue next column

Page 235, *continued*

MULTIPLE CHOICE:

1 solution: **A**; 2 solution: **A**.

Page 236

LETTER SQUARES: The Life of Jesus

1 solution:

Whatsoever ye shall ask the Father in my name, he will give it you.
John 16:23

MULTIPLE CHOICE:

1 solution: **A**; 2 solution: **D**; 3 solution: **B**.

LETTER SQUARES:

2 solution:

For whosoever will save his life shall lose it: but whosoever will lose his life for my sake, the same shall save it.
Luke 9:24

Page 237

CROSSWORD: Love Thy Neighbor

H	A	F	T		E	L	F		B	E	T	A
E	M	I	R		T	E	A		O	V	I	D
B	E	N	O	T	A	W	I	T	N	E	S	S
E	N	N	U	I		D	R	U	G			
			B	E	E			T	O	K	E	N
B	A	A	L		P	I	C	T		O	N	E
A	B	L	E	M	I	S	H	I	N	H	I	S
N	E	O		A	C	M	E		E	L	D	S
G	L	E	A	N			F	O	G			
			M	E	S	S		F	L	A	M	E
D	E	V	I	S	E	N	O	T	E	V	I	L
A	L	A	S		R	O	D		C	O	M	A
D	I	N	S		E	W	E		T	W	I	N

SOLUTIONS

Page 238

LETTER SQUARES: The Life of Jesus

1 solution:

Blessed are ye that hunger now: for ye shall be filled. Blessed are ye that weep now: for ye shall laugh.
Luke 6:21

2 solution:

And he lifted up his eyes on his disciples, and said, Blessed be ye poor: for yours is the kingdom of God.
Luke 6:20

VERSE DECODER:

1 solution:

But by the grace of God I am what I am: And his grace which was bestowed upon me was not in vain; But I laboured more abundantly than they all: Yet not I, but the grace of God which was with me.
1 Corinthians 15:10

Page 239

CROSSWORD: Miracles

1 E	2 W	3 E	4 S		5 A	6 L	7 L		8 V	9 E	10 E	11 R
12 A	I	D	E		13 L	E	A		14 I	L	L	Y
15 S	P	E	A	16 K	E	V	I	17 L	O	F	M	E
18 T	E	N	S	E		19 I	D	Y	L			
			20 A	N	21 A			22 I	A	23 M	24 B	25 S
26 B	27 O	28 I	L		29 M	30 A	31 N	N		32 I	R	E
33 A	N	D	T	34 H	O	S	E	G	35 R	E	A	T
36 A	C	E		37 E	S	S	E		38 E	N	D	S
39 L	E	A	40 R	N			41 D	42 O	G			
			43 O	R	44 E	45 O		46 R	E	47 M	48 A	49 P
50 T	51 H	52 E	W	I	L	D	53 E	R	N	E	S	S
54 A	U	R	A		55 S	O	T		56 T	O	E	S
57 T	E	R	N		58 E	R	A		59 S	W	A	T

Page 240

LETTER SQUARES: The Life of Jesus

1 solution:

Heal the sick, cleanse the lepers, raise the dead, cast out devils: freely ye have received, freely give.
Matthew 10:8

2 solution:

And when ye stand praying, forgive, if ye have ought against any:
Mark 11:25

Page 241

VERSE DECODER: The Life of Jesus

1 solution:

Pilate therefore went forth again, and saith unto them, behold, I bring him forth to you, that ye may know that I find no fault in him.
John 19:4

LETTER SQUARES:

1 solution:

Give us this day our daily bread. And forgive us our debts, as we forgive our debtors.
Matthew 6:11-12

MULTIPLE CHOICE:

1 solution: **B**; 2 solution: **B**; 3 solution: **B**.

SOLUTIONS

Page 242

CROSSWORD: Parables

1 E	2 Z	3 R	4 A		5 B	6 A	7 N		8 S	9 T	10 A	11 R
12 R	O	I	L		13 A	L	E		14 L	O	L	A
15 G	O	O	D	16 S	A	M	A	17 R	I	T	A	N
18 O	S	T	E	O		19 S	T	U	N			
			20 N	U	21 B			22 I	G	23 L	24 O	25 O
26 I	27 S	28 N	T		29 R	30 E	31 I	N		32 E	A	U
33 S	H	E	E	34 P	A	N	D	G	35 O	A	T	S
36 L	I	E		37 R	E	D	O		38 P	S	S	T
39 E	N	D	40 T	O			41 L	42 E	I			
			43 A	S	44 I	45 A		46 G	A	47 U	48 N	49 T
50 B	51 A	52 R	R	E	N	F	53 I	G	T	R	E	E
54 I	C	E	D		55 O	R	R		56 E	G	O	S
57 D	E	F	Y		58 R	O	E		59 S	E	N	T

Page 243

LETTER SQUARES: The Life of Jesus

1 solution:

But seek ye first the kingdom of God, and his righteousness;
Matthew 6:33

LETTER SQUARES:

2 solution:

These things I have spoken unto you, that in me ye might have peace.
John 16:33

Page 244

VERSE DECODER: The Life of Jesus

1 solution:

But whoso looketh into the perfect law of liberty, and continueth therin, he being not a forgetful hearer, but a doer of the work, this man shall be blessed in his deed.
James 1:25

MULTIPLE CHOICE:

1 solution: **B**; 2 solution: **B**; 3 solution: **C**.

LETTER SQUARES:

1 solution:

But I say unto you, Love your enemies, bless them that curse you,
Matthew 5:44

Page 245

CROSSWORD: Treasure Trove

1 G	2 E	3 M	4 S		5 W	6 O	7 E		8 R	9 A	10 R	11 E
12 B	R	A	E		13 H	A	W		14 E	L	A	N
15 S	A	P	P	16 H	I	R	E		17 B	A	N	D
			18 T	A	R			19 W	E	B		
20 A	21 R	22 C	E	D		23 S	24 A	R	C	A	25 S	26 M
27 T	H	A	T		28 P	I	P	E		29 S	H	Y
30 O	E	R		31 A	L	D	E	N		32 T	O	R
33 N	U	B		34 G	O	L	D		35 W	E	A	R
36 E	M	U	37 L	A	T	E		38 G	I	R	T	H
		39 N	O	R			40 N	O	S			
41 L	42 A	C	Y		43 A	44 M	E	T	H	45 Y	46 S	47 T
48 E	L	L	A		49 W	A	S		50 T	O	T	E
51 K	E	E	L		52 L	O	T		53 O	N	Y	X

Page 246

LETTER SQUARES: The Life of Jesus

1 solution:

Blessed are the meek: for they shall inherit the earth.
Matthew 5:5

MULTIPLE CHOICE:

1 solution: **B**; 2 solution: **C**; 3 solution: **C**.

LETTER SQUARES:

2 solution:

And fear not them which kill the body, but are not able to kill the soul:
Matthew 10:28

Page 247

LETTER SQUARES: The Life of Jesus

1 solution:

Blessed are the peacemakers: for they shall be called the children of God.
Matthew 5:9

MULTIPLE CHOICE:

1 solution: **B**; 2 solution: **A**; 3 solution: **C**.

VERSE DECODER:

1 solution:

And when he had called unto him his twelve disciples, he gave them power against unclean spirits, to cast them out, and to heal all manner of sickness and all manner of disease.
Matthew 10:1

SOLUTIONS

Page 248

CROSSWORD: Well Versed

1 H	2 A	3 I	■	4 S	5 H	6 A	7 R	8 E	■	9 L	10 E	11 T
12 O	D	D	■	13 T	A	H	A	N	■	14 A	W	E
15 L	A	D	■	16 A	D	I	N	O	■	17 D	E	N
18 D	R	O	19 W	N	■	■	■	20 S	21 E	E	S	T
■	■	■	22 A	D	23 D	■	24 W	H	Y	■	■	■
25 M	26 A	27 N	S	■	28 O	29 U	R	■	30 E	31 A	32 R	33 S
34 A	G	O	■	■	35 E	R	I	■	■	36 T	I	E
37 W	E	R	38 E	■	39 S	I	T	■	40 S	E	B	A
■	■	■	41 N	42 E	T	■	43 E	44 L	I	■	■	■
45 A	46 B	47 I	D	A	■	■	■	48 A	R	49 O	50 S	51 E
52 B	A	G	■	53 R	54 E	55 H	56 U	M	■	57 H	U	L
58 I	R	A	■	59 T	H	O	S	E	■	60 A	S	A
61 B	E	L	■	62 H	I	R	E	D	■	63 D	I	M

Page 249

LETTER SQUARES: The Life of Jesus

1 solution:

At that time Jesus answered and said, I thank thee, O Father, LORD of heaven and earth,
Matthew 11:25

MULTIPLE CHOICE:

1 solution: **C**; 2 solution: **D**; 3 solution: **D**.

VERSE DECODER:

1 solution:

The blind receive their sight, and the lame walk, the lepers are cleansed, and the deaf hear, the dead are raised up, and the poor have the gospel preached to them.
Matthew 11:5

SOLUTIONS

Page 250

CROSSWORD: Trinity

1 H	2 I	3 D	■	4 S	5 A	6 S	7 H	■	8 S	9 P	10 A	11 R
12 O	N	E	■	13 E	R	I	E	■	14 C	O	C	A
15 O	F	L	16 I	T	T	L	E	17 F	A	I	T	H
18 P	O	I	N	T	■	19 O	D	O	R	■	■	■
■	■	■	20 Y	O	21 N	■	■	22 A	F	23 I	24 R	25 E
26 E	27 C	28 H	O	■	29 A	30 T	31 O	M	■	32 D	I	P
33 T	H	O	U	34 A	R	T	M	Y	35 H	O	P	E
36 T	A	B	■	37 L	Y	L	E	■	38 U	L	E	E
39 A	R	O	40 M	A	■	■	41 N	42 A	M	■	■	■
■	■	■	43 A	M	44 O	45 S	■	46 L	O	47 T	48 U	49 S
50 K	51 I	52 S	S	O	F	C	53 H	A	R	I	T	Y
54 E	R	S	T	■	55 F	O	U	R	■	56 P	A	N
57 N	E	W	S	■	58 S	T	E	M	■	59 S	H	E

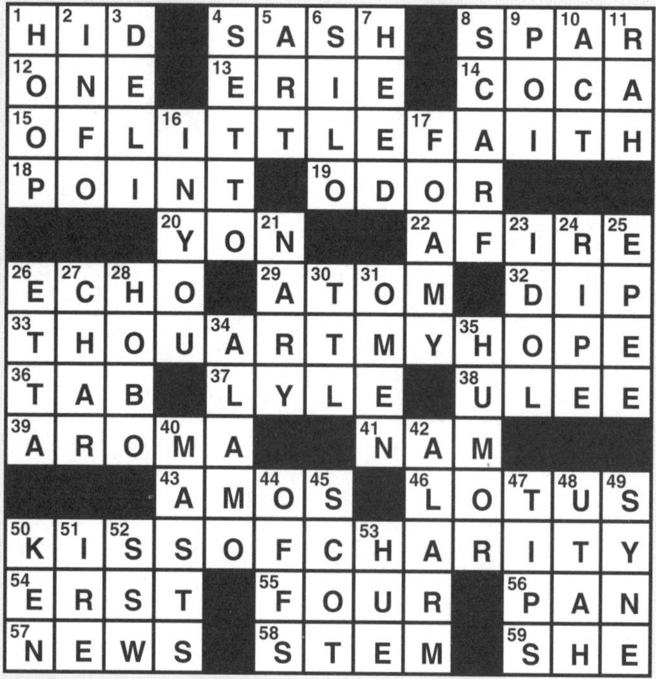

Page 251

WORD SEARCH: Biblical Cities

H	T	E	R	A	Z	A	N	C	E	M	R	C	X	N
K	M	A	L	V	B	H	L	F	M	R	M	K	J	I
B	C	A	N	T	I	O	C	H	M	I	M	E	B	N
N	D	G	W	T	J	T	B	N	A	W	R	P	T	E
D	A	N	M	R	I	A	R	R	U	U	B	B	Q	V
F	C	R	F	E	B	P	O	N	S	M	F	R	S	E
A	C	U	L	E	H	D	A	A	Q	R	T	E	A	H
P	A	P	L	D	A	E	L	T	J	Y	I	G	E	T
O	S	P	Z	M	I	E	L	X	R	T	L	O	R	L
L	A	I	Y	Y	M	B	N	H	I	I	P	M	A	R
L	M	N	H	Q	M	D	O	C	T	T	S	O	S	T
O	A	L	E	H	T	E	B	N	V	E	V	R	E	K
N	R	N	C	O	R	I	N	T	H	M	B	R	A	W
I	I	R	H	D	A	M	A	S	C	U	S	A	C	X
A	A	L	P	M	O	D	O	S	K	V	M	H	P	R

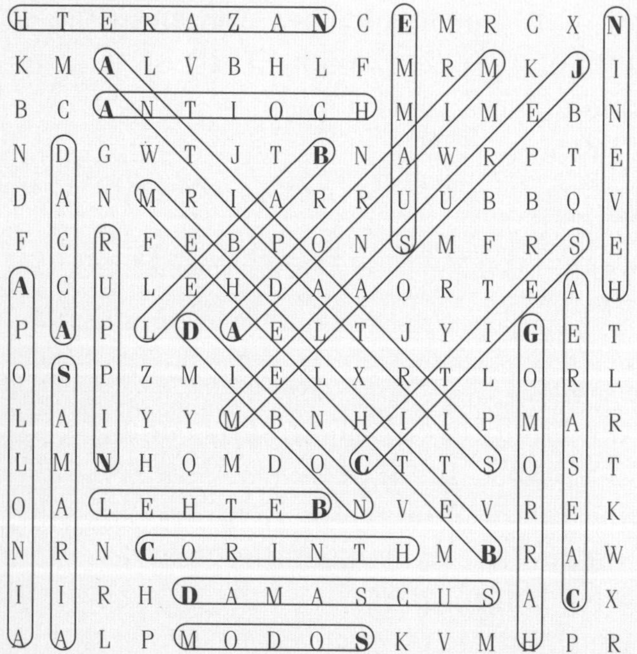

Page 252

WORD SEARCH: Waters

T	R	M	O	R	E	M	J	A	L	H	J	Z	Y	Q
A	E	G	E	A	N	Z	I	A	M	T	B	E	M	M
K	C	T	L	B	H	N	T	J	I	I	Y	R	T	F
R	L	R	E	D	R	A	B	O	A	R	Y	E	M	H
L	J	S	K	U	N	N	W	R	H	E	N	D	S	G
M	O	R	N	I	Y	F	I	D	D	H	C	U	H	A
R	V	J	H	A	L	U	S	A	A	C	C	D	E	N
M	R	E	T	T	I	B	M	N	P	S	N	R	K	G
B	Y	T	L	J	N	K	Z	D	A	S	D	M	S	R
R	C	A	A	L	A	M	H	M	M	A	A	W	I	J
J	O	Y	R	Q	X	B	A	P	G	R	C	C	R	V
P	T	H	Q	M	A	D	B	N	Q	N	H	G	G	C
C	Q	V	I	Y	U	B	Q	O	K	O	G	L	I	R
Q	C	M	D	H	L	K	A	B	K	N	P	C	T	K
R	H	K	G	T	S	F	W	A	T	E	R	S	R	N

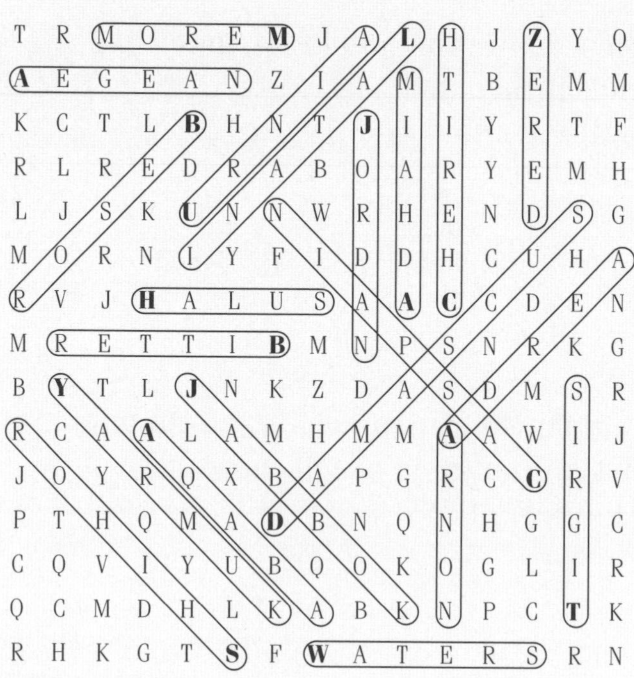

Page 253

MULTIPLE CHOICE: A Friend Loves at All Times

1 solution: **C**; 2 solution: **B**; 3 solution: **D**;

4 solution: **C**; 5 solution: **A**; 6 solution: **D**.

SOLUTIONS

Page 254

WORD SEARCH: Birds and Reptiles

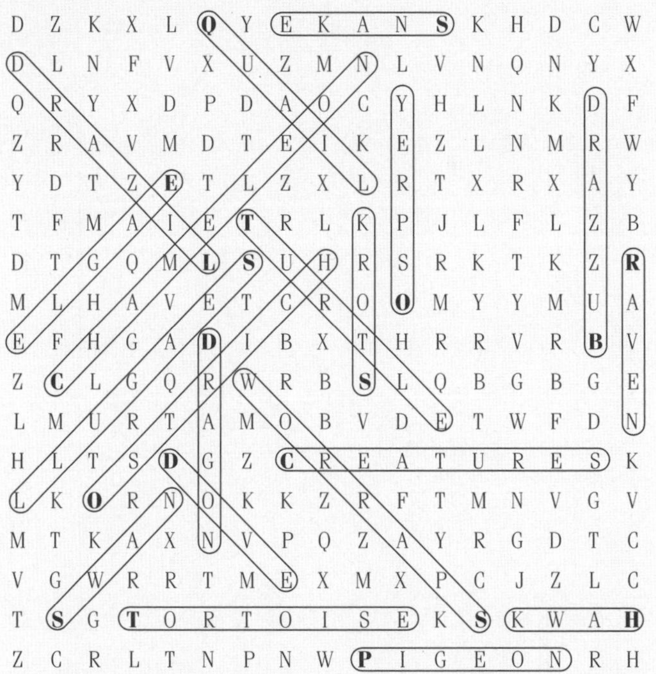

Page 256

MULTIPLE CHOICE: And the Word Was God

1 solution: **B**; 2 solution: **A**; 3 solution: **D**;
4 solution: **A**; 5 solution: **C.**

Page 257

MULTIPLE CHOICE: And the Word Was God

1 solution: **D**; 2 solution: **C**; 3 solution: **A**;
4 solution: **C**; 5 solution: **C**; 6 solution: **D.**

Page 255

WORD SEARCH: Cities East of Jordan

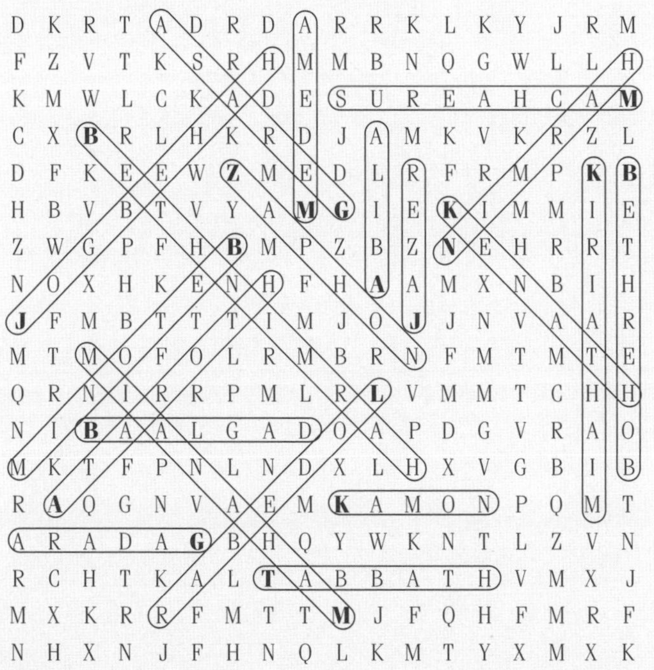

Page 258

WORD SEARCH: Food and Spices

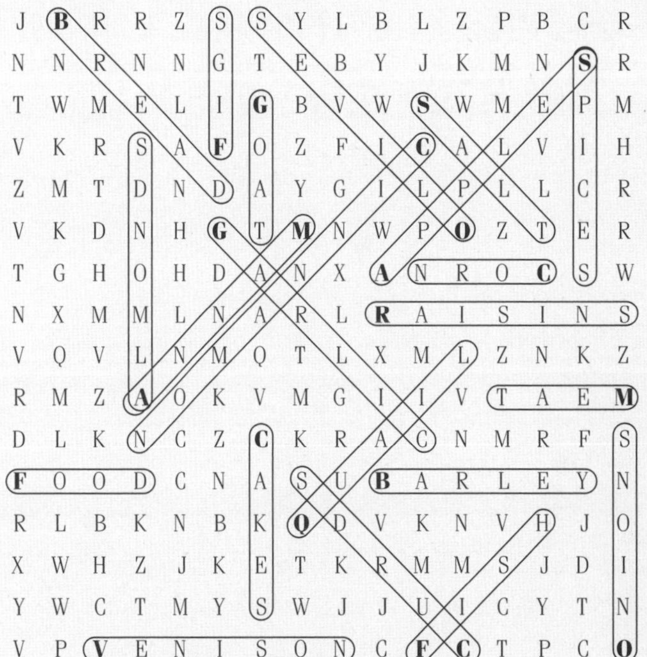

SOLUTIONS

Page 259

WORD SEARCH: Gems and Stones

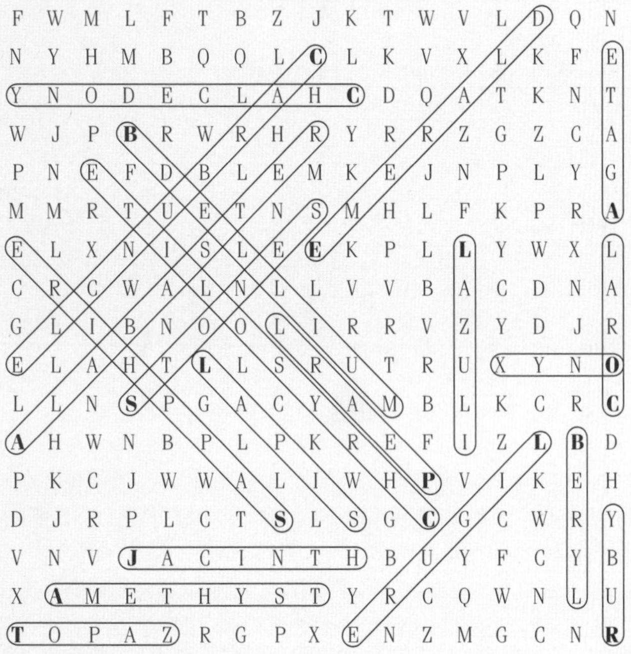

Page 260

MULTIPLE CHOICE: And the Word Was Made Flesh

1 solution: **B**; 2 solution: **D**; 3 solution: **A**; 4 solution: **A**; 5 solution: **B**; 6 solution: **D**.

Page 261

WORD SEARCH: His Birth

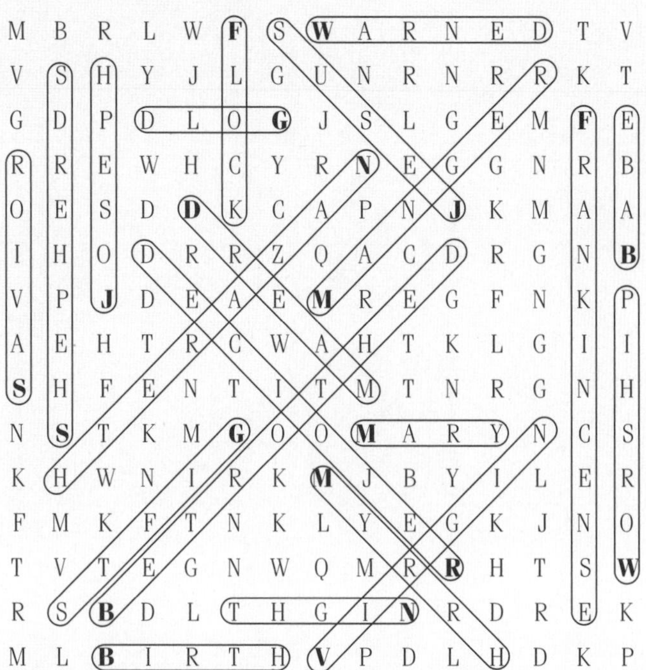

Page 262

WORD SEARCH: Jesus at the Temple

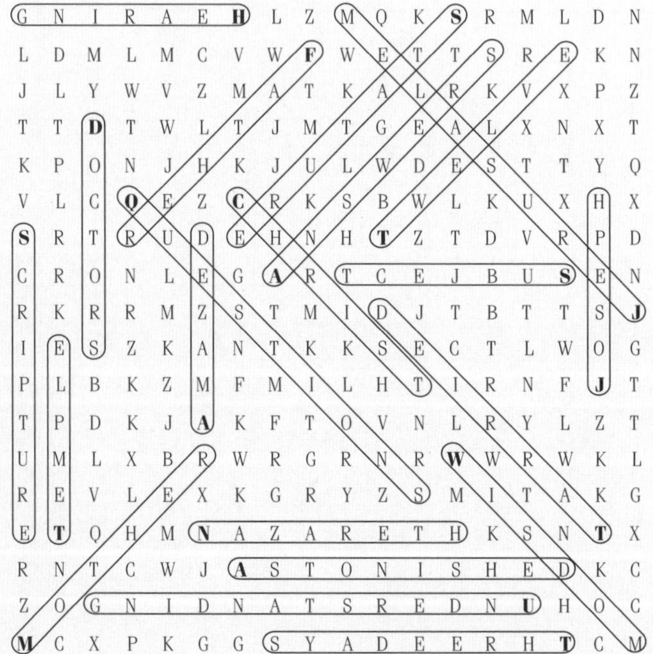

SOLUTIONS

Page 263

MULTIPLE CHOICE: Excel

1 solution: **B**; 2 solution: **C**; 3 solution: **D**;

4 solution: **D**; 5 solution: **D**; 6 solution: **B.**

Page 264

WORD SEARCH: Jesus in the Wilderness

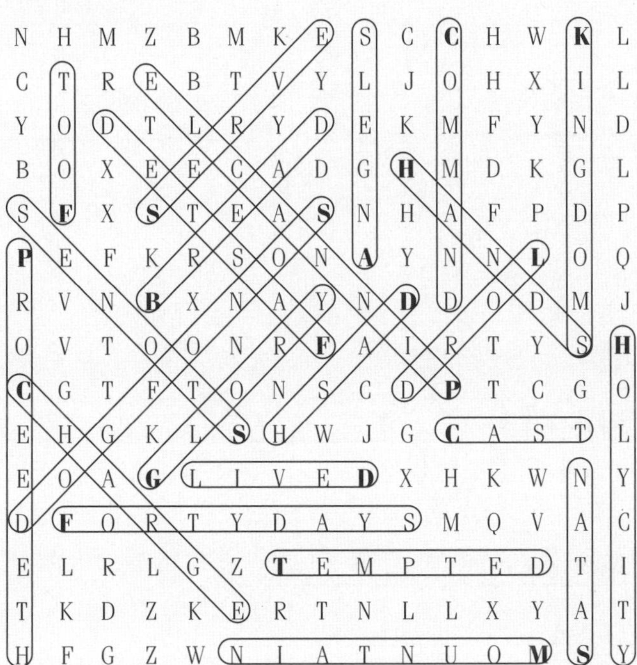

Page 265

WORD SEARCH: Jesus

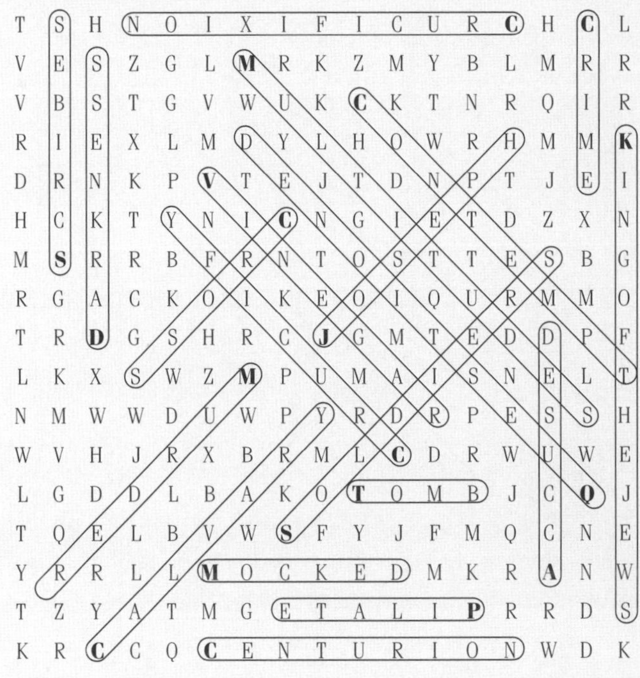

Page 266

WORD SEARCH: The Lord's Prayer

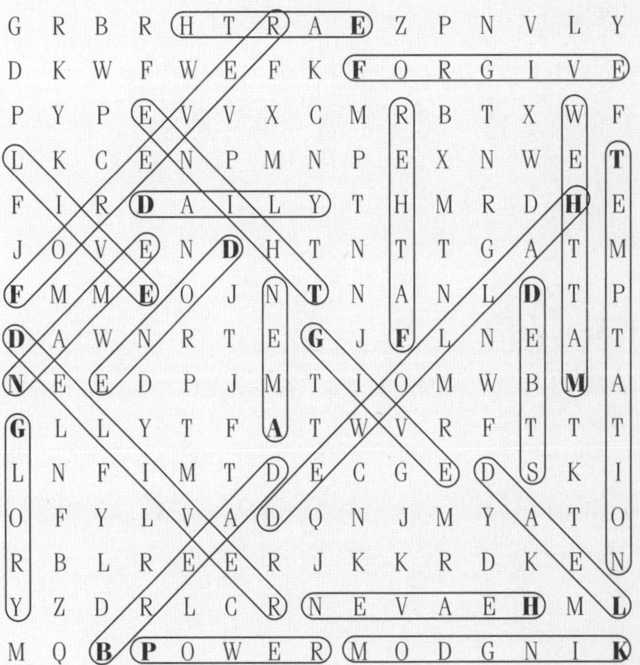

SOLUTIONS

Page 267

WORD SEARCH: Miracles

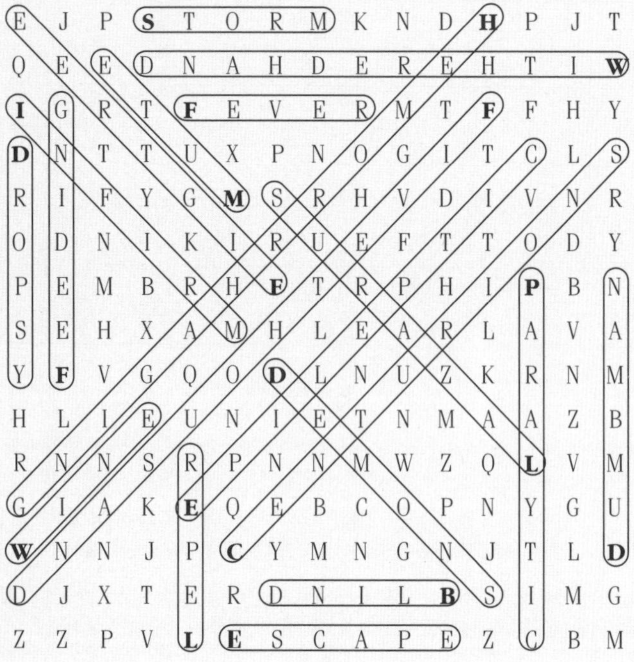

Page 268

MULTIPLE CHOICE: Jesus: Our High Priest

1 solution: **B**; 2 solution: **C**; 3 solution: **A**;

4 solution: **B**; 5 solution: **A**; 6 solution: **A.**

Page 269

MULTIPLE CHOICE: Jesus: Our High Priest

1 solution: **C**; 2 solution: **A**; 3 solution: **B**;

4 solution: **D**; 5 solution: **A**; 6 solution: **C.**

Page 270

WORD SEARCH: Names for Jesus

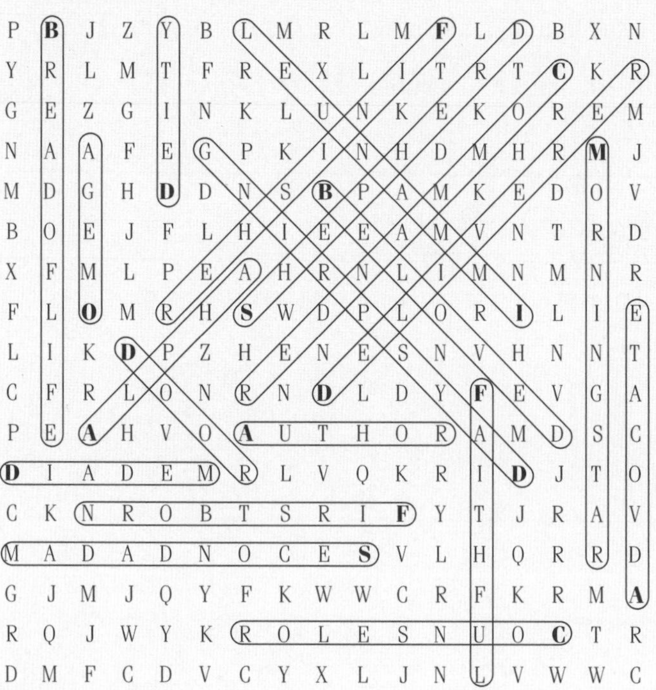

Page 271

ANSWERS NEXT PAGE 293.

Page 272

WORD SEARCH: Parables

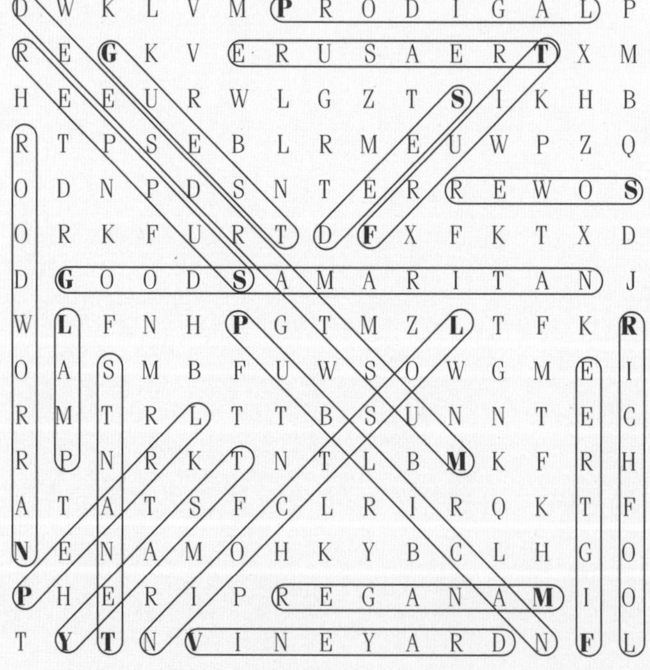

SOLUTIONS

Page 271

FROM PREVIOUS PAGE.

MULTIPLE CHOICE: Lion of the Tribe of Judah

1 solution: **C**; 2 solution: **A**; 3 solution: **B**;

4 solution: **D**; 5 solution: **B**; 6 solution: **A.**

Page 273

MULTIPLE CHOICE: The Knowledge of the Truth

1 solution: **D**; 2 solution: **A**; 3 solution: **C**;

4 solution: **C**; 5 solution: **D**; 6 solution: **C.**

Page 274

WORD SEARCH: Teachings of Jesus

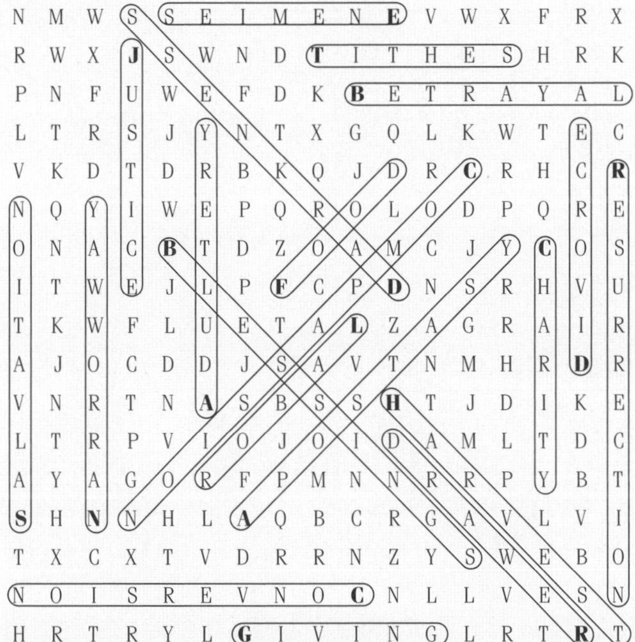

Page 275

WORD SEARCH: The Last Supper

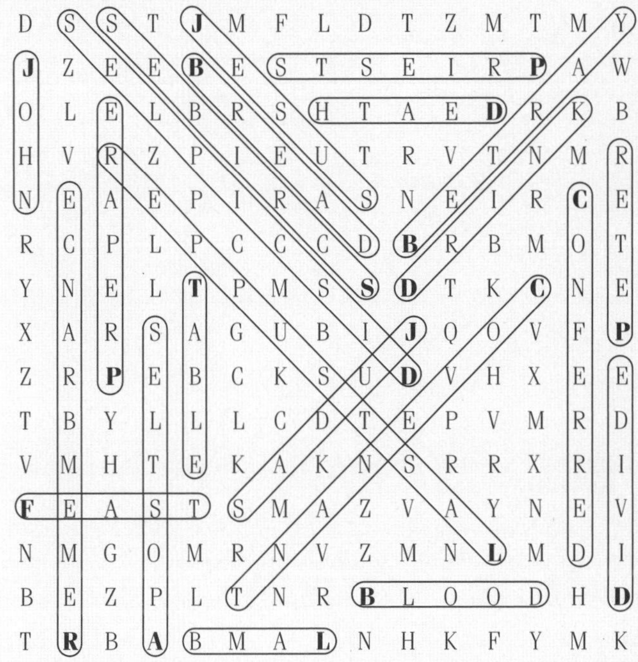

Page 276

WORD SEARCH: The Sermon on the Mount

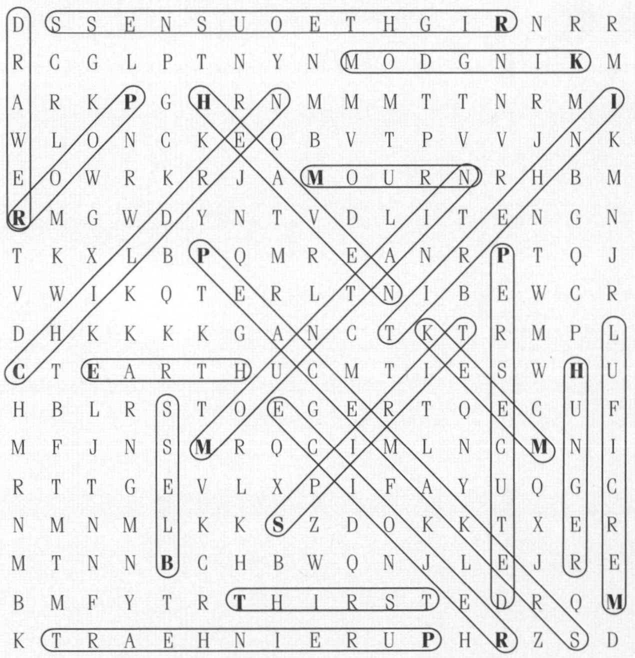

SOLUTIONS

Page 277

WORD SEARCH: The Transfiguration

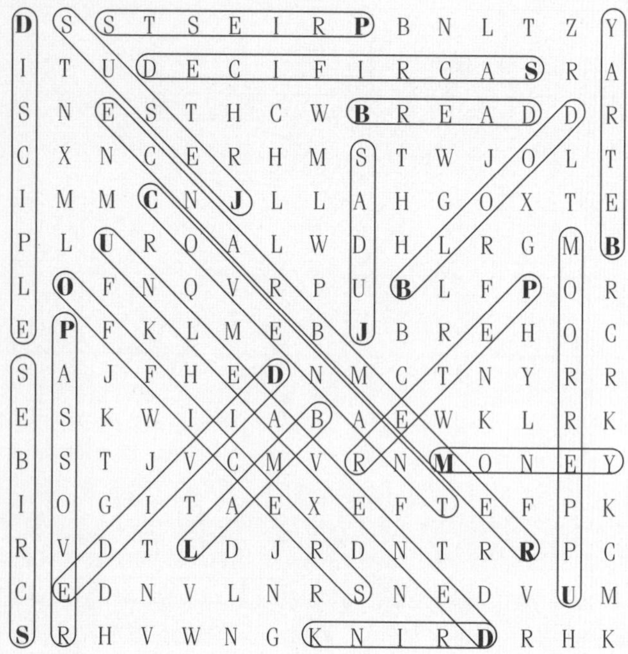

Page 278

MULTIPLE CHOICE: Worthy is the Lamb

1 solution: **C**; 2 solution: **D**; 3 solution: **A**;

4 solution: **D**; 5 solution: **B**; 6 solution: **D.**

Page 279

WORD SEARCH: Unto Us a Child is Given

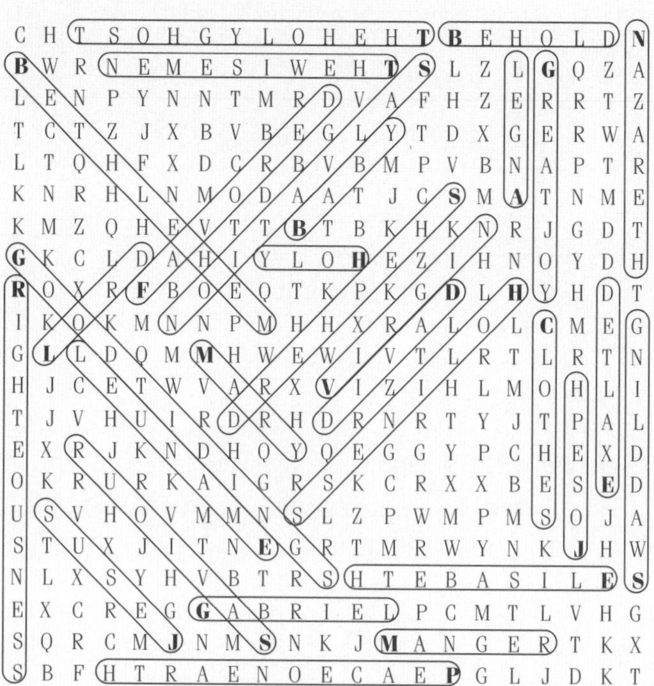

Page 280

MULTIPLE CHOICE: You Were Bought at a Price

1 solution: **B**; 2 solution: **C**; 3 solution: **C**;

4 solution: **A**; 5 solution: **B**; 6 solution: **C.**

Page 281

MULTIPLE CHOICE: You Were Bought at a Price

1 solution: **B**; 2 solution: **B**; 3 solution: **A**;

4 solution: **D**; 5 solution: **A**; 6 solution: **D.**

CHAPTER 6

VERSE DECODER: **God's Promises**

1 Romans 11:22

HINT: In the puzzle below, the letter "X" is actually an "E."

RXOHWP YOXJXNHJX YOX ZHHPSXGG USP GXDXJBYC HN ZHP: HS YOXQ EOBAO NXWW, GXDXJBYC; RKY YHEUJP YOXX, ZHHPSXGG, BN YOHK AHSYBSKX BS OBG ZHHPSXGG: HYOXJEBGX YOHK UWGH GOUWY RX AKY HNN.

COLUMN PHRASE: **Psalms 37:39**

1

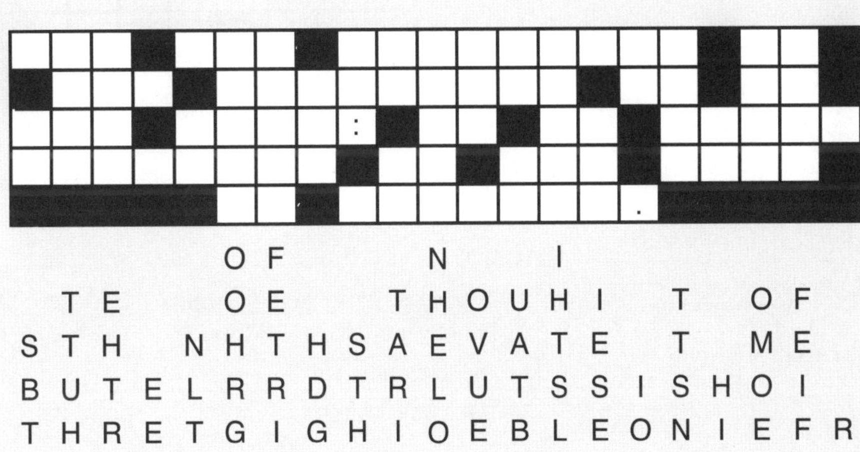

SCRAMBLED VERSE: **Ephesians 1:6**

1 "To the _______ of the glory of his _______, wherein he hath made us _______ in the _______."

parsie
cagre
tccaepde
lvoedbe

CROSSWORD: **The Faithful**

By Gayle Dean

1	2	3	4	■	5	6	7	8	■	9	10	11
12				■	13				■	14		
15				■	16				17			
18				19			■	20				
■	■	■	21				22				■	■
23	24	25	■	26				■	27		28	29
30			31			■	32	33				
34				■	35	36			■	37		
■	■	38		39					40	■	■	■
41	42				■	43				44	45	46
47					48			■	49			
50			■	51				■	52			
53			■	54				■	55			

ACROSS

1 Upside of a recession
5 English novelist Bagnold
9 Poke at Evander
12 Jason's fictional ship
13 Prefix with scope
14 "And the sons of Jether, Jephunneh, and Pispah, and __" (1 Chr. 7:38)
15 Freeway sights
16 "... and made us sit together in __ places in Christ Jesus" (Eph. 2:6)
18 "... he __ upon his knees three times a day" (Dan. 6:10)
20 "So long, amigo"
21 Author W. __ Maugham
23 Swiss peak
26 Venerable saint
27 "And Moses went up from the plains of __" (Deut. 34:1)
30 Certain rodent catcher
32 For the Israelites it was eat manna or __
34 "Then went he inward, and measured the __ of the door" (Eze. 41:3)
35 Hand lotion ingredient
37 "And God __ them in the firmament of the heaven" (Gen. 1:17)
38 Emergency phone links
41 Plant life
43 Conventioneer's pin-on
47 In awe
49 Ore vein
50 Keats creation
51 S-shaped molding
52 Castle's protective feature
53 "They __ my path, they set forward my calamity" (Job 30:13)
54 Little ones
55 "Take heed that ye do not your __ before men" (Matt 6:1)

DOWN

1 "But his wife looked __ from behind him" (Gen. 19:26)
2 Algerian port
3 Fairy tale villain
4 "And __ hid his face" (Ex. 3:6)
5 Transient
6 "And __ not that any should testify of man" (John 2:25)
7 "And __ also the Jairite was a chief ruler about David" (2 Sam. 20:26)
8 Opera stars
9 Their business is picking up?
10 Folk singer Guthrie
11 Chesapeake, Hudson and Green
17 Swelling, particularly in plants
19 Ear part
22 Resounds like a church bell
23 Elec. unit
24 British "water closet"
25 Easy target for a slick salesman
28 "__ Maria"
29 Wager
31 "Laying up in __ for themselves a good foundation" (1 Tim. 6:19)
33 Abound
36 Old World songbird
39 Ominous card
40 King march site in Alabama
41 "And the rib, which the Lord God had taken __ man" (Gen. 2:22)
42 "__ and the Swan" (Yeats)
44 "... thou shalt not lift up any iron __ upon them" (Deut. 27:5)
45 "And the Lord God caused a deep sleep to fall upon __" (Gen. 2:21)
46 Obtains
48 Cause of a swelled head

VERSE DECODER: **God's Promises**

1 **Romans 1:20**

HINT: In the puzzle below, the letter "I" is actually an "O."

RIA UMT ZVBZPZXQT UMZVCP IR MZH RAIH UMT JATLUZIV IR UMT

EIAQK LAT JQTLAQF PTTV, XTZVC DVKTAPUIIK XF UMT UMZVCP UMLU

LAT HLKT, TBTV MZP TUTAVLQ GIETA LVK CIKMTLK; PI UMLU UMTF

LAT EZUMIDU TNJDPT.

COLUMN PHRASE: **Psalms 34:19**

1

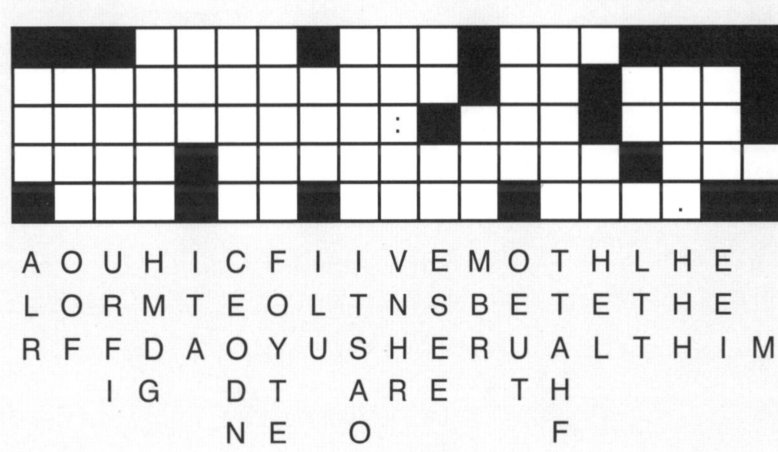

SCRAMBLED VERSE: **John 15:16**

1 "You did not _______ me, but I chose you, and _______ you that you would go and bear _______, and that your fruit would remain, so that _______ you ask of the _______ in My name He may give to you."
John 15:16

coshoe
atippnoed
rufit
weathver
fehatr

CROSSWORD: **The Commandments**

By Thomas W. Schier

1	2	3	4	■	5	6	7	8	■	9	10	11
12				■	13				■	14		
15				16					17			
18					■	■	19			■	■	■
■	■	■	20		21	22	■	23		24	25	26
27	28	29	■	30			31	■	32			
33			34					35				
36				■	37				■	38		
39				40	■	41			42	■	■	■
■	■	■	43		44	■	■	45		46	47	48
49	50	51				52	53					
54			■	55				■	56			
57			■	58				■	59			

ACROSS

1 They wait in church parking lots
5 OT book, for short
9 Fuss
12 "There ought to be __ ..." (2 words)
13 Diamond defect
14 "In __ We Trust"
15 What not to take in vain (4 words)
18 Colorado ski resort
19 "I will __ thy face again no more" (Ex. 10:29)
20 Clobber with rocks
23 Hand-dyeing technique
27 Cash dispenser, for short
30 Saintly emanation
32 Highway hauler
33 See 28-Down (3 words)
36 Top-notch
37 *Cannery Row* character
38 Weekend NBC show (abbr.)
39 Kicks a football
41 "... Sin shall have great __" (Ezek. 30:16)
43 Number one in Paris
45 "... the __ was heard afar off" (Ezra 3:13)
49 Remember to keep it holy (3 words)
54 Start of The Lord's Prayer
55 See 34-Down
56 Ye __ Shoppe
57 By means of
58 "... unless they cause __ to fall" (Prov. 4:16)
59 Unwanted garden growth

DOWN

1 Water-to-wine town
2 Word of regret
3 Access way
4 "... light a candle, and __ the house" (Luke 15:8)
5 "And took __ their chariot wheels" (Ex. 14:25)
6 Sandwich order
7 Checkup sounds
8 Hardly Mr. Cool
9 "Hast thou not heard long __" (2 Kings 19:25)
10 "Le Coq __" (famous opera)
11 Like a TV "Couple"
16 __ a time (individually) (2 words)
17 "... from the __ even to the greatest" (Jer. 42:8)
21 Bergman in *Casablanca*
22 "... were gathered together into a __" (2 Sam. 23:11)
24 Golfers' gadgets
25 Noted fashion model
26 "Thou shalt not __"
27 "Right away!" letters
28 With 33-Across, one of the Commandments (Ex. 20:15)
29 *Buddenbrooks* author
31 Gillette razor brand
34 With 55-Across, priestly invitation (2 words)
35 Sanctified one
40 Ginger __ (cookies)
42 "Absolutely not!" (2 words)
44 River through Aragon
46 "... an __ soul shall suffer hunger" (Prov. 19:15)
47 Pop singer from Nigeria
48 Gave the once-over
49 "... shout from the __ of the mountains" (Isa. 42:11)
50 Colorful Vietnam city?
51 Fall from grace
52 Ka-pow!
53 "Yes, captain!"

VERSE DECODER: **God's Promises**

1 Proverbs 4:20-22

HINT: In the puzzle below, the letter "U" is actually an "O."

GJ CUP, SBBIPZ BU GJ YUQZC; VPHAVPI BMVPI ISQ WPBU GJ CSJVPXC. AIB BMIG PUB ZINSQB LQUG BMVPI IJIC; EIIN BMIG VP BMI GVZCB UL BMVPI MISQB. LUQ BMIJ SQI AVLI WPBU BMUCI BMSB LVPZ BMIG, SPZ MISABM BU SAA BMIVQ LAICM.

COLUMN PHRASE: **Psalms 32:8**

1

												E												
		W	L				H	H	O		R	U		T		T		G	A					
W	E	L	I	L	H		T	E	E	E	Y	S	H	A		T		T	E			I		
I	W	H	I	H	L	T	I	D	S	U	T	N	E	T	L	E	H	E	H		M	N	N	
T	I	A	C	C	G	U	I	N	E	T	I	H	C	E	H	W	I	W	O	Y	A	I	D	E

SCRAMBLED VERSE: **Ephesians 1:4**

1 According as he hath ______ us in him before the foundation of the ______, that we should be ______ and ______ ______ before him in ______:

oscneh
orldw
lyho
tuothiw
melab
veol

CROSSWORD: **Righteous**

By Joseph Mantell

ACROSS

1 Actress Evans
5 __ polloi
8 Top of head
12 Famous redheaded explorer
13 Blood group
14 "... and the earth that is under thee shall be __" (Deut. 28:23)
15 "Wilt thou also destroy the righteous __?" (Gen. 18:23) (3 words)
18 Popular Internet company
19 Pull out, as a tooth
20 __ and outs
22 Miss Jane Pittman portrayer
26 Astronaut Shepard
29 Gardener, at times
32 Commotion
33 "Which is a manifest token of the righteous __" (2 Thes. 1:5) (3 words)
36 __ carte
37 Prayer ending
38 "And it is a __ thing that the king requireth" (Dan. 2:11)
39 Gossiper's tidbit
41 Boxing legend
43 "He shall suck the poison of __" (Job 20:16)
46 Stan's partner in comedy
50 "... for a righteous man, but __ and disobedient" (1 Tim. 1:9) (3 words)
54 Shampoo additive
55 Two or more eras
56 Breastplate
57 Doe or buck
58 "For he is cast into a __ by his own feet" (Job 18:8)
59 Medication unit

DOWN

1 Spangled with morning moisture
2 Opera highlight
3 Suffix meaning "stone"
4 Reverberating
5 "That's a laugh"
6 "Now therefore, my son, __ my voice" (Gen. 27:8)
7 Hawkeye State
8 Fussy
9 Noah's creation
10 "... and upon the great __ of his right foot" (Lev. 14:28)
11 "At the __ of every seven years thou shalt make a release" (Deut. 15:1)
16 Unit of weight
17 Opening remarks
21 Brother of Ham and Japheth
23 It's a long story
24 Offensive smell
25 Lymph gland
26 Slightly open
27 A real humdinger
28 Father of Seth
30 Quarter of four
31 Volcano in Sicily
34 Wetland
35 Ruffled
40 Western movie
42 "Look on every one that is proud, and bring him __" (Job 40:12)
44 Hammer type
45 Blackthorn fruit
47 Brand of toy blocks
48 Mythical fertility goddess
49 In __ (actually)
50 An interest followed with exaggerated zeal
51 Grand __ Opry
52 Fish eggs
53 "Go to the __, thou sluggard" (Prov. 6:6)

VERSE DECODER: **God's Promises**

1 **Matthew 19:9**
HINT: In the puzzle below, the letter "V" is actually an "A."

VJC S NVZ EJIU ZUE, LDUNUXQXA NDVKK TEI VLVZ DSN LSMX,

XGBXTI SI RX MUA MUAJSBVISUJ, VJC NDVKK WVAAZ VJUIDXA,

BUWWSIIXID VCEKIXAZ: VJC LDUNU WVAASXID DXA LDSBD SN TEI VLVZ

CUID BUWWSI VCEKIXAZ.

SCRAMBLED VERSE: **Ephesians 1:11**

1 In whom also we have ______ an inheritance, being predestinated ______ to the purpose of him who worketh all ______ after the ______ of his own ______:

tnaidebo
cagindcor
ngsiht
ouncels
wlil

COLUMN PHRASE: **Proverbs 16:3**

1

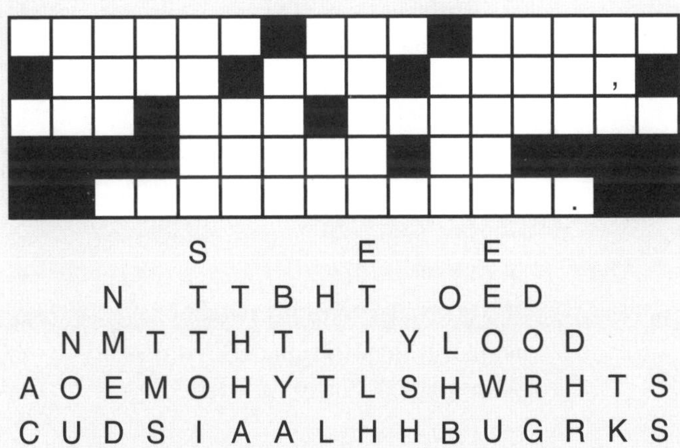

CROSSWORD: **Reading the Bible**

By Barbara A. Marques

1	2	3	4	■	5	6	7	■	8	9	10	11
12				■	13			■	14			
15				■	16			17				
18				19		■	20					
■	■	21			■	22				■	■	■
23	24							■	25	26	27	28
29			■	■	■		■	■	■	30		
31			32	■	33			34	35			
■	■	■	36	37			■	38			■	■
39	40	41				■	42				43	44
45						46		■	47			
48				■	49			■	50			
51				■	52			■	53			

ACROSS

1 Trio that came from the east

5 Neon, e.g.

8 Knotts and Adams

12 Lodgings, such as Joseph and Mary sought

13 "... be gentle unto all men, __ to teach" (2 Tim. 2:24)

14 Fencer's foil

15 "... for we have seen his __ in the east"

16 "For where your __ is, there will your heart be"

18 Herbal tea

20 Paul spent two years here

21 Egg producer

22 "The young lions __ after their prey" (Ps. 104:21)

23 Onesimus' master

25 Geological time periods

29 "For the eyes of the Lord __ to and fro" (2 Chr. 16:9)

30 Sixth sense, for short

31 "And Israel smote him with the __ of the sword"

33 Sabbath (2 words)

36 "And thou shalt bring the __ offering" (Lev. 2:8)

38 "I __ no pleasant bread" (Dan. 10:3)

39 Old Testament city (Num. 32:3)

42 Home of Simon, who carried the cross for Jesus

45 Jesus was one

47 Final word

48 Grandson of Eber

49 Land to which Cain was exiled (Gen. 4:16)

50 "Jesus saith unto him, __ my sheep" (John 21:17)

51 Antiseptic's target

52 Prefix with ode, cycle or pod

53 Blunders

DOWN

1 "But there went up a __ from the earth" (Gen. 2:6)

2 Opposing

3 "... there shall be weeping and __ of teeth" (Matt. 8:12)

4 Promised Land

5 "... and Lot sat in the __ of Sodom"

6 Fools' mo.

7 Trample (2 words)

8 "If any man __ to be first, the same shall be last" (Mark 9:35)

9 *Mr. Holland's* __

10 Roman Emperor during New Testament times

11 "No man hath __ God at any time" (John 1:18)

17 Scorpius' heavenly neighbor

19 Jerusalem-to-Damascus dir.

22 R2-D2 or C-3PO

23 Prefix for fix

24 Fed. housing department

26 "For I know that my __ liveth" (Job 19:25)

27 Third King of Judah

28 "And the five men that went to __ out the land" (Judg. 18:17)

32 Prepare for burial

33 Mourn

34 "And God called the light __" (Gen. 1:5)

35 Fire on from above

37 "He that hath an __, let him hear" (Rev. 2:7)

39 Warm and cozy

40 Fog

41 Descendant of Esau (1 Chr. 1:34-38)

42 Basic monetary unit of Ghana

43 __ do well

44 "... upon whom the __ of the world are come" (1 Cor. 10:11)

46 "He shall not strive, __ cry" (Matt. 12:19)

CROSSWORD: **Proverbs**

By Rowan Millson

ACROSS

1 Pakistani language
5 Shocking swimmer?
8 5th Avenue store
12 Improves one's credit
13 Small cluster of feathers
15 Proverbial advice, Part 1 (4 words)
17 Nabokov novel
18 Away from the house (2 words)
19 The difference between Jan and Joan? (2 "words")
20 Sleep stage
21 "And all the people shall say, __" (Deut. 27:16)
22 Pizzazz
23 "... neither can the floods __ it" (Song of Sol. 8:7)
25 Activity dreaded by QBs
27 "Touch the __ of His Garment" (Sam Cooke song)
29 "I say the truth in Christ, I __ not" (Rom. 9:1)
30 Provided food for a party
34 Singer Youssou __
38 Mine entrance
39 Kind of learning
41 Second Amendment org.?
42 "And __, the city of the priests" (1 Sam. 22:19)
43 Get out of here!
44 Actor's union
45 Proverbial advice, Part 3 (3 words)
48 When February 29 comes around (2 words)
49 Garfield's buddy
50 The sons also of Mushi; Mahli, and __ (1 Chr. 24:30)
51 Like a fox
52 "I am he that liveth, and was __" (Rev. 1:18)

DOWN

1 "Fifteen cubits __ did the waters prevail" (Gen. 7:20)
2 California pro football player
3 Energetic person
4 "__ hospitality one to another without grudging" (1 Pet. 4:9)
5 Downs or salts
6 Makes joyful
7 Phenobarbital
8 Just a __!
9 Acid neutralizer
10 Actor Wynn
11 Proverbial advice, Part 2
14 Sun. follower
16 More foolish?
22 Barely made out
24 "If he turn not, he will __ his sword" (Ps. 7:12)
26 Word at a multiplex
28 "Withhold not thou thy tender __ from me, O Lord" (Ps. 40:11)
30 "The spirit of man is the __ of the Lord" (Prov. 20:27)
31 Worshiped
32 Shinbones
33 Shark's back fin
35 A type of football kick
36 Muse of astronomy
37 Tattered
40 "But the man would not __ that night" (Judg. 19:10)
43 "It will be fair weather: for the __ is red" (Matt. 16:2)
46 *All Things Considered* network
47 "Nearer My __ to Thee"

SCRAMBLED VERSE: **Romans 15:7**

1 Wherefore ______ ye one another, as ______ also received us to the ______ of God.

cieever
hrcsti
yrogl

COLUMN PHRASE: **Psalms 103:12**

1

VERSE DECODER: **God's Promises**

1 **Hosea 1:10**

HINT: In the puzzle below, the letter "O" is actually an "E."

SOH HMO ZIECOJ LT HMO PMWFKJOZ LT WUJVOF UMVFF CO VU HMO UVZK LT HMO UOV, NMWPM PVZZLH CO EOVUIJOK ZLJ ZIECOJOK; VZK WH UMVFF PLEO HL AVUU, HMVH WZ HMO AFVPO NMOJO WH NVU UVWK IZHL HMOE, SO VJO ZLH ES AOLAFO, HMOJO WH UMVFF CO UVWK IZHL HMOE, SO VJO HMO ULZU LT HMO FWXWZY YLK.

CROSSWORD: **Prosperity**

By Joseph Mantell

ACROSS

1 Tater
5 Grazing land
8 Burger and fries go-with
12 Evergreen tree
13 Work unit
14 Runs up an account
15 "__ even as thy soul prospereth" (3 John 1:2) (4 words)
18 Backless seat
19 "... and Lot journeyed __" (Gen. 13:11)
20 Handwoven Scandinavian rug
22 Book before Philemon
26 Operatic melody
29 Blackthorn fruit
32 Epoch
33 "And it shall be our __" (Deut. 6:25)
36 Inflated feeling of pride
37 What mares eat
38 Nursemaid of India
39 Brother of Moses
41 "And the servant took __ camels" (Gen. 24:10)
43 Rice Krispies sound
46 Rental agreement
50 "__ thy walls" (Ps. 122:7) (3 words)
54 Soup vegetable
55 Before, formerly
56 List-heading (2 words)
57 "The hart, and the roebuck, and the fallow __" (Deut. 14:5)
58 Ford model
59 "And the __ of them both were opened" (Gen. 3:7)

DOWN

1 Health resorts
2 Ice-cream unit
3 Reverse an action
4 Hebrew prophetess
5 Hawaiian wreath
6 Sea eagle
7 Turkish officer
8 Raccoon kin
9 "I am like an __ of the desert" (Ps. 102:6)
10 "And God said, __ there be light"
11 "He planteth an __" (Isa. 44:14)
16 1960s TV Tarzan, Ron __
17 Adlai's '56 running mate
21 Between ports
23 Abound
24 Celestial bear
25 Window frame
26 Region
27 Capital of Latvia
28 Stravinsky or Sikorsky
30 Sodom survivor
31 Expel
34 1,000 kilograms (Var.)
35 "No, No, __"
40 Hollywood statue
42 Priest of Israel who looked after Samuel
44 Biblical victim
45 Saucy
47 Nautical attention grabber
48 "Who is on the Lord's __?" (Ex. 32:26)
49 Grandson of Adam
50 Whale group
51 __ out a living
52 "Her ways __ ways of pleasantness" (Prov. 3:17)
53 Tie the knot

CROSSWORD: **To Err is Human**

By Joseph Mantell

ACROSS

1 Cheers' opposites

5 Yes vote

8 "Hold thou me up, and I shall be __" (Ps. 119:117)

12 Unsightly citrus fruit?

13 Demure

14 Astringent substance

15 Crop up again

17 Fish eggs

18 "Then hear thou from the heavens, and forgive the sin of thy ..." (2 Chr. 6:25) (2 words)

20 "__ boom bah"

21 Exclamation of amazement

22 Farm tower

25 PC monitor, often

26 U.S. sprinter Griffith Joyner, familiarly

29 "Blessed is he whose __ is forgiven" (Ps. 32:1)

33 Wood for archery bows

34 Get too nosy

35 Parcel (out)

36 Prospector's find

37 "__ shall be called woman" (Gen. 2:23)

39 "... forgive, __ forgiven" (Luke 6:37) (4 words)

45 __ of roses (2 words)

46 Kitchen appliances

47 "O Lord, __ me; for my bones are vexed" (Ps. 6:2)

48 Sturdy tree

49 Breastplate, (Var.)

50 Friend in war or peace

51 Below-average grade?

52 "And that he was buried, and that he __ again" (1 Cor. 15:4)

DOWN

1 After-dinner faux pas

2 Architectural curve

3 Bread spread

4 Homer or Marge

5 Land units

6 Berra or Bear

7 Graffiti or litter, for example

8 Wife of Abraham

9 Hand lotion ingredient

10 Coal or gas

11 Mommy's threesome?

16 Priest of Israel who cared after Samuel

19 Degenerates

22 Hog haven

23 Wrath

24 Jurisprudence

25 "Because the __ of Sodom and Gomorrah is great" (Gen. 18:20)

26 Old expression of disgust

27 Salty one's spouse

28 "And all went to be taxed, every __ into his own city" (Luke 2:3)

30 Light on one's feet

31 Said "hello" to

32 Ore refinery

36 In a strange manner

37 "... and thou begin with __ to take the lowest room" (Luke 14:9)

38 Possesses

39 Victim in Genesis

40 1963 Oscar® winner Patricia

41 "But the dove found no rest for the __ of her foot" (Gen. 8:9)

42 Interlocking plastic toy brand

43 Jewish rite of circumcision

44 To be, in ancient Rome

45 "So, there you are!"

CROSSWORD: **Love Is All Around**

By Rowan Millson

ACROSS

1 Not quite dry
5 Org. for Marcus Welby, M.D.
8 Actual
12 Helicopter designer Sikorsky
13 Scold
14 Military group
15 "Love Is All Around," Part 1 (Gen. 28:16) (3 words)
18 Japanese swordplay
19 "Woe to them that are at __ in Zion" (Amos 6:1)
20 "He planteth an __" (Isa. 44:14)
22 Charlie Chaplin persona
26 Catty comment
29 Range near contralto
32 Kind of chart
33 "Love Is All Around," Part 2 (4 words)
36 Final amt.
37 Pro __ (proportionate)
38 Panache
39 Inventor Nikola
41 Discarded cloth
43 Caustic
46 Hideaways
50 "Love Is All Around," Part 3 (5 words)
54 Tooth part
55 Boston party drink?
56 Norse verse collection
57 On pins and needles
58 Like 7 or 11
59 Ogler

DOWN

1 Slipped, for one
2 Fever with hot and cold spells
3 Time twixt sunup and noon
4 Like some raids
5 "For if __ be a hearer of the word" (James 1:23)
6 "... every one with her __" (Isa. 34:15)
7 Muslim title of respect
8 "Who made thee a __" (Acts 7:27)
9 Brian of Roxy Music
10 "... that no __ can come between them" (Job 41:16)
11 U.K. business abbr.
16 __ Gatos, CA
17 Bar, legally
21 "He saith among the trumpets, __" (Job 39:25)(2 words)
23 "C'mon, be __" (help me out) (2 words)
24 Isinglass
25 Hammer part
26 Baseball glove
27 Italian princely family
28 Engine and olive
30 Ignited
31 Russian emperor
34 Field's partner
35 Beneficiary
40 Everyone except the clergy
42 He floated "like a butterfly"
44 "For thou hadst cast me __ the deep" (Jonah 2:3)
45 "And whatsoever ye do in word or __" (Col. 3:17)
47 500 for A.J. Foyt
48 "And Ahab __, and went to Jezreel" (1 Kings 18:45)
49 "... there shall come a __ out of Jacob" (Num. 24:17)
50 "... ye __ witnesses this day" (Ruth 4:10)
51 It's east of Eden
52 "... a living __ is better than a dead lion" (Ecc. 9:4)
53 Money roll

CROSSWORD: **Just Rewards**

By Joseph Mantell

1	2	3	4	■	5	6	7	■	8	9	10	11
12				■	13			■	14			
15				16				■	17			
18								19		■	■	■
■	■	■	20			■	■	21		22	23	24
25	26	27		■	28	29	30		■	31		
32				33					34			
35			■	36				■	37			
38			39		■	■	40	41		■	■	■
■	■	■	42		43	44				45	46	47
48	49	50		■	51							
52				■	53			■	54			
55				■	56			■	57			

ACROSS

1 Distinctive doctrines
5 Sound made by a cat
8 Biblical victim
12 "And the archers __ at king Josiah" (2 Chr. 35:23)
13 Spanish article
14 Moses, to Charlton Heston
15 Storyteller
17 Sign seen in a movie theater
18 "For there shall be no reward to __" (Prov. 24:20) (3 words)
20 Years Abram dwelt in Canaan before Ismael was born
21 Food from heaven
25 Commentator Sevareid
28 "... an __ soul shall suffer hunger" (Prov. 19:15)
31 Anointing substance
32 "The Lord rewarded me according to my __" (Ps. 18:20)
35 Sticky substance
36 The same, in footnotes
37 Stew or miscellany
38 Used for sharpening razors
40 Bronx cheer
42 "... the Lord shall reward the doer of evil according to his __"
48 Lounge about
51 Large wiry-coated terrier
52 Biblical herb
53 Short way to go?
54 Like the ark during the flood
55 "And the children of Israel __ for Moses" (Deut. 34:8)
56 Newsman Koppel
57 Trees used for archery bows

DOWN

1 "Money __ everything!"
2 Former monarch of Iran
3 __ or less
4 "And I will __ out my hand, and smite Egypt"
5 Rebelled aboard ship
6 Organic compound
7 Word with toast, often
8 Place for sports action
9 "... the __ of oil, and pour it on his head" (2 Kings 9:3)
10 Priest of Israel who looked after Samuel
11 "And God said, __ there be light" (Gen. 1:3)
16 NYC's Fifth, e.g.
19 Home of Iowa State University
22 "The First __" (seasonal song)
23 Unless, in court
24 Not only that
25 Units of work
26 Public outbreak
27 Prince of Russian opera
29 Unknown Jane
30 Moved clumsily
33 Native American tent, (Var.)
34 "And thine age shall be clearer than the __" (Job 11:17)
39 Young night bird
41 Keats' forte
43 "Now therefore make a new __" (1 Sam. 6:7)
44 Windy-day toy
45 "... when thou wilt __ thyself abroad" (Deut. 23:13)
46 "... Cain rose up against Abel his brother, and __ him" (Gen. 4:8)
47 Red and Black
48 Legislation
49 Bravo for a matador
50 Trim the tree

COLUMN PHRASE: **Isaiah 43:25**

1

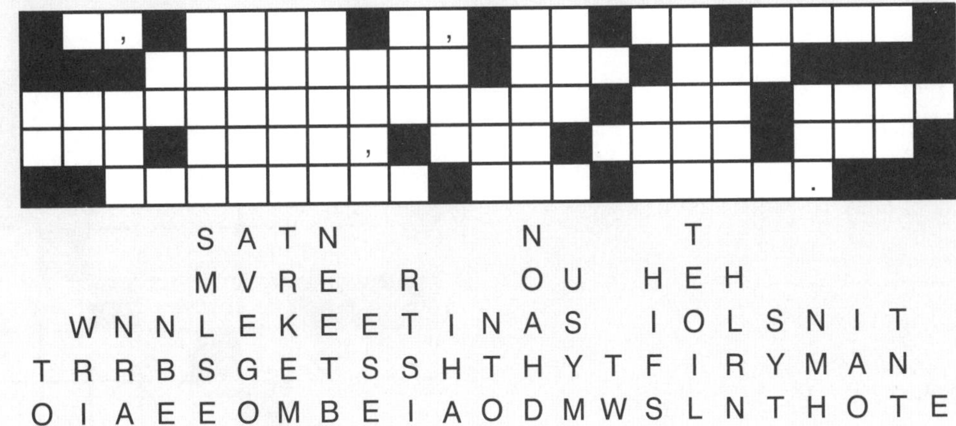

SCRAMBLED VERSE: **1 Corinthians 1:9**

1 "God is ______, by whom ye were ______ unto the fellowship of his Son ______ Christ our ______."

lufthiaf
llaced
susje
drol

***King James Games* Facts:**

The Bible can be read aloud in approximately 70 hours.

VERSE DECODER: **God's Promises**

1 **Jude 1:24-25**

HINT: In the puzzle below, the letter "N" is actually an "A."

LQP WLHQ IUE HINH UM NFSJ HQ BJJG DQW CTQE CNSSULA, NLX HQ

GTJMJLH DQW CNWSHSJMM FJCQTJ HIJ GTJMJLRJ QC IUM ASQTD PUHI

JZRJJXULA YQD, HQ HIJ QLSD PUMJ AQX QWT MNKUQWT, FJ ASQTD

NLX ENYJMHD, XQEULUQL NLX GQPJT, FQHI LQP NLX JKJT. NEJL.

CROSSWORD: **Heavenly Questions**

By Barbara A. Marques

1	2	3	4	■	5	6	7	■	8	9	10	11
12				■	13			■	14			
15				16				■	17			
18							■	19				
■	■	■	20			■	21				■	■
22	23	24		■	25	26					27	28
29			■	30					■	31		
32			33					■	34			
■	■	35				■	36	37		■	■	■
38	39				■	40				41	42	43
44				■	45							
46				■	47			■	48			
49				■	50			■	51			

ACROSS

1 Affirmative votes

5 "Therefore God give thee of the __ of heaven" (Gen. 27:28)

8 Tribe

12 First Gospel (abbr.)

13 Co. stock offer

14 "for she gathered it of the __ of an harlot" (Mic. 1:7)

15 Follower of the law

17 Founder of the Hebrew race

18 "Let the lying lips be put to __ ..." (Ps. 31:18)

19 "... the people cried to Pharaoh for __" (Gen. 41:55)

20 Go downhill fast?

21 He was converted on the road to Damascus

22 "... thine own __ testify against thee" (Job 15:6)

25 Jesus' metaphors

29 Mole's org.

30 Thrash

31 Large shoe width

32 "Behold, O Lord; for I am in __" (Lam. 1:20)

34 "... an __ soul shall suffer hunger" (Prov. 19:15)

35 Litigates

36 "__ a man take fire in his bosom" (Prov. 6:27)

38 "O Come Let Us __ Him"

40 Hamlet

44 Excellent review

45 "Our Father which art in heaven, __ be thy name"

46 "For every __ is known by his own fruit" (Luke 6:44)

47 Feel ill

48 Cast a ballot

49 Knitter's need

50 Certain double helix

51 Flair

DOWN

1 Voice projectors (abbr.)

2 Northern California Indian

3 Abbreviation meaning "and others" (2 words)

4 Emphasize

5 Christ's followers

6 Olympic fencer's foil

7 "__ to thee, Moab!" (Num. 21:29)

8 Member of the second order of angels

9 Defamed (Var.)

10 Region

11 Uncool fellow

16 "... written not with __, but with the Spirit"(2 Cor. 3:3)

19 Canaanite god

21 Aquila's wife

22 Digital, as a watch

23 Caesar's three

24 The feast of unleavened bread

26 Two-year degrees (abbr.)

27 Slippery fish

28 "O taste and __ that the Lord is good" (Ps. 34:8)

30 "... and uphold me with thy __ spirit" (Ps. 51:12)

33 Soup dish

34 Smitten (2 words)

37 "... let thy glory be above __ the earth" (Ps. 57:5)

38 Pretentious

39 A son of Zerah (1 Chron. 2:6)

40 "Thou shalt not take the name of the Lord thy God in __"

41 Military hooky

42 "Can I __ witness?" (2 words)

43 Garden of original sin

45 "But Sarai was barren; she __ no child" (Gen. 11:30)

CROSSWORD: **Good News**

By Diane Epperson

ACROSS

1 It was parted for Moses
4 Burial chamber
8 Effect of auto exhaust
12 Suffix with Method
13 "Zip-___-Doo-Dah" (2 words)
14 Angelic circle?
15 Belonging to one of the disciples of Jesus
17 Angered
18 Moses' mount
19 Plant stem
21 NYC subway manager
23 Inferior
26 "The Lord reigneth; let the earth __" (Ps. 97:1)
30 Where the big fish expelled Jonah
31 From __ Z (2 words)
32 "Give __ to my words, O Lord" (Ps. 5:1)
34 Unnaturally pale
35 "... faith __ name hath made this man strong" (Acts 3:16) (2 words)
38 "I bring you good __ of great joy" (Luke 2:10)
41 What Herodias' daughter did to please Herod (Matt. 14:6)
43 __ Plaines, IL
44 Coup __
46 Abraham's wife's name, at first (Gen. 11:29)
50 "Stop, horse!"
52 Neither hot nor cold
54 "__ to differ!" (2 words)
55 Latin love
56 Soccer star Hamm
57 Winning margin, sometimes
58 "Lord, __ I?" (Last Supper question) (Matt. 26:22) (2 words)
59 "If we __ that we have no sin" (1 John 1:8)

DOWN

1 Jazzman Zoot
2 *La Bamba* actor Morales
3 Envelope abbr.
4 Exotic vacation spot
5 Rhyming tribute
6 Cat calls
7 Outdoes
8 Tabernacle site (Josh. 18:1)
9 Put on sale
10 Bullring bravo
11 "__ is greatly to be feared" (Ps. 89:7)
16 __ shanter
20 Sighs of relief
22 A service winner
24 Strip or bunt intro
25 Longs
26 Surprise attack
27 Sicilian volcano
28 Unknown persons
29 "Take, __ this is my body" (Matt. 26:26)
33 Unburden
36 Historic cold snap
37 Tennis unit
39 Location of 18-Across
40 "__ the Light" (gospel song) (2 words)
42 __ Lama
45 Antacid brand
47 Sacrificial beasts
48 Operatic piece
49 "If __ be so bold ..." (2 words)
50 Pitching credit
51 Cable station
53 Colorful carp

CROSSWORD: **From Start to Finish**

By Marjorie Berg

1	2	3	4	■	5	6	7	8	■	9	10	11
12				■	13				■	14		
15				16					■	17		
18					■	■	19		20			
■	■	■	■	21	22	23				■	■	■
24	25	26	27				■	■	28	29	30	31
32							33	34				
35				■	■	36						
■	■	■	37	38	39				■	■	■	■
40	41	42				■	■	43	44	45	46	47
48			■	49		50	51					
52			■	53				■	54			
55			■	56				■	57			

ACROSS

1 Pillow covering
5 "And Jacob was __ alone" (Gen. 32:24)
9 Word with job, number, or lot
12 "I can't believe __ the whole thing!" (2 words)
13 Father of one of David's mighty men (2 Sam. 23:11)
14 "And Israel said unto Joseph, Now let me __" (Gen. 46:30)
15 "And she brought forth her __ son" (Luke 2:7)
17 Victorian, for one
18 Carry-out item?
19 "And I will fetch a __ of bread" (Gen. 18:5)
21 Sovereign's concern
24 Church official
28 "And __ begat Aminadab" (Matt. 1:4)
32 The beginning and the end (3 words)
35 Exxon predecessor
36 Horticulturist's hangout
37 "... ye have __ from the heart" (Rom. 6:17)
40 Quarterback, at times
43 Upper crust
48 "... but be gentle unto all men, __ to teach" (2 Tim. 2:24)
49 Catholic sacrament (2 words)
52 Coffee alternative
53 Ivan or Nicholas
54 Ooze
55 "Do they not __ that devise evil?" (Prov. 14:22)
56 Highway hauler
57 "And under their hand was an __" (2 Chr. 26:13)

DOWN

1 "... that he may __ you as wheat" (Luke 22:31)
2 Samson's pride
3 Gillette razor brand
4 Big problem
5 Scientist's workplace
6 Swellhead's excess
7 Nobel-winning physicist Enrico
8 Domingo's voice
9 Lyric poems
10 Kind of straits
11 "Come on, let us __ wisely with them" (Ex. 1:10)
16 Letter before iota
20 Paper purchases
22 "Give __ break!" (2 words)
23 "Shew me a __" (Luke 20:24)
24 __ kwon do
25 *Treasure Island* author's monogram
26 __ and downs
27 Chases away, as a fly
29 Mr. __ (old mystery game)
30 Pt. of USDA
31 Starter for flower or hem
33 Word with past or postage
34 Judge's cry
38 Waist circlers
39 Clear, as a disk
40 Top of the head
41 Copycat
42 "And I will give him the morning __" (Rev. 2:28)
44 *Mona* __
45 Roman route
46 Swarm
47 Catch sight of
50 An American uncle
51 Prefix with cycle or angle

CROSSWORD: **Divine Wisdom**

By Joseph Mantell

1	2	3	4	■	5	6	7	■	8	9	10	11
12				■	13			■	14			
15				16				17				
18					■	19				■	■	■
■	■	■	20		21	■	■	22		23	24	25
26	27	28		■	29	30	31		■	32		
33				34					35			
36			■	37				■	38			
39			40		■	■	41	42		■	■	■
■	■	■	43		44	45	■	46		47	48	49
50	51	52					53					
54				■	55			■	56			
57				■	58			■	59			

ACROSS

1 Actor Alda

5 "__ Maria"

8 __ of approval

12 __ *Lisa*

13 Note on the musical scale

14 Small musical group

15 "... hear his wisdom, which God had __" (1 Kgs 10:24) (4 words)

18 Comic actor Martin

19 Distribute cards

20 Always, poetically

22 Blood vessels

26 Italian car

29 Assistant

32 Fur collar

33 "Give therefore thy servant an __ heart" (1 Kings 3:9)

36 VCR brand

37 "... and behold a ladder set __ the earth" (Gen. 28:12)

38 Personal view

39 "And Abraham set seven ewe __ of the flock" (Gen. 21:28)

41 Griffey, Sr. or Jr.

43 "... accompanied him into __ Sopater of Berea" (Acts 20:4)

46 Open-mouthed

50 "... for the price of wisdom __" (Job 28:18) (3 words)

54 Store discount day

55 "Woe unto us! for we __ spoiled" (Jer. 4:13)

56 *Iliad* character

57 Hard work

58 East of Eden

59 Ancient capital of Phoenicia

DOWN

1 Current units

2 Stumblebum

3 Put up

4 Lack of worldliness

5 __ Wednesday

6 Declare invalid

7 Otherwise

8 Inscribed column

9 Notable time

10 "... and to every fowl of the __" (Gen. 1:30)

11 His wife was a pillar

16 Born as

17 "Zebulun shall dwell at the __ of the sea" (Gen. 49:13)

21 Wood file

23 Literally in the same place

24 "... this is __ other but the house of God" (Gen. 28:17)

25 A long story

26 Roll up

27 Machu Picchu dweller

28 He could give a first-person account

30 Japanese statesman

31 Clammy

34 Actress Rene

35 Archie's nickname for Edith

40 Biblical source for the word "babble"?

42 Water in Paris

44 Tennis champ Lendl

45 Prefix for space or nautics

47 Light as a feather

48 Person of equal standing

49 To be, to Caesar

50 Belief system

51 __ Paulo, Brazil

52 "I am the greatest" claimant

53 Sea parted during the exodus

COLUMN PHRASE: **Matthew 21:22**

1

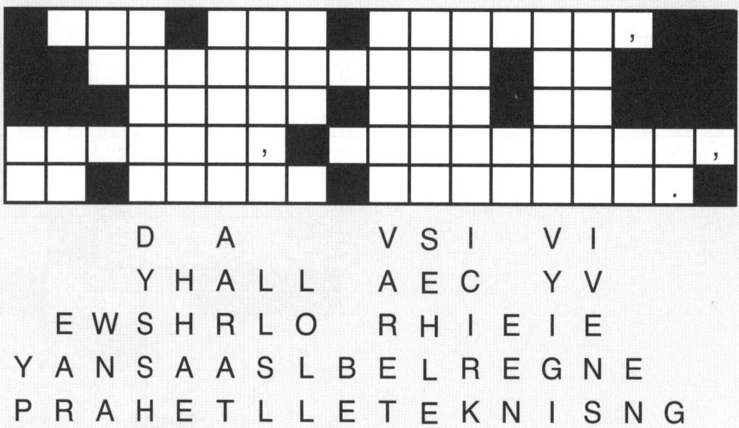

VERSE DECODER: **God's Promises**

1 **1 John 1:3**

HINT: In the puzzle below, the letter "O" is actually an "A."

FSOF MSVNS MY SOQY BYYC OCH SYOLH HYNGOLY MY WCFZ DZW, FSOF DY OGBZ IOD SOQY KYGGZMBSVU MVFS WB: OCH FLWGD ZWL KYGGZMBSVU VB MVFS FSY KOFSYL, OCH MVFS SVB BZC JYBWB NSLVBF.

COLUMN PHRASE: **Jeremiah 29:12**

2

CROSSWORD: **Biblical Pairings**

By Joseph Mantell

1	2	3	4	■	5	6	7	■	8	9	10	11
12				■	13			■	14			
15				16				■	17			
■	18							19				
■	■	■	20			■	21			■	■	■
22	23	24		■	■	25			■	26	27	28
29				30	31				32			
33			■	34			■	■	35			
■	■	■	36			■	37	38		■	■	■
39	40	41				42				43	44	■
45				■	46							47
48				■	49			■	50			
51				■	52			■	53			

ACROSS

1 Lacking in liveliness
5 Fond du __, WI
8 DEA employee
12 Noel
13 Judge Judy's org.
14 Office in the White House
15 Captor
17 Sicilian wine
18 Biblical pairing (2 words)
20 Cards with a photo
21 "For ye shall be as an __" (Isa. 1:30)
22 "... and __ with joy receiveth it" (Matt. 13:20)
25 "... all that were strong and __ for war" (2 Kings 24:16)
26 Paid athlete, in short
29 Biblical pairing (2 words)
33 "... wherewith the __ number of them is to be redeemed" (Num. 3:48)
34 One who takes Capt.'s orders
35 Assistant
36 *Wheel of Fortune* buy
37 Actress Sothern
39 Biblical pairing (2 words)
45 Queen of the Olympian gods, in myth
46 Lifting device
48 Speed skater Heiden
49 Always, poetically
50 Prank
51 Jazz great Thelonious
52 It comes before com or org
53 "__ quam videri" (NC motto)

DOWN

1 Hair coloring
2 Ladder step
3 "__ he sent forth a dove from him" (Gen. 8:8)
4 "Norma" composer
5 Volcano flows
6 Assist in wrongdoing
7 Some waiters at a drive-in
8 Kim of *Vertigo*
9 Tel __
10 Wife of a rajah
11 Lump of earth
16 Help out
19 Input for a computer program
22 "Why make ye this __, and weep?" (Mark 5:39)
23 The Simpsons' neighbor, __ Flanders
24 "... and honour the face of the __ man" (Lev. 19:32)
25 Exclamations of satisfaction
26 Tire pressure unit
27 Staff of Moses
28 "... there remained not __" (Ex. 8:31)
30 Singer Horne
31 Aromatic seed
32 "A certain __ a great supper, and bade many" (Luke 14:16) (2 words)
36 Taken __ (surprised)
37 Warning signal
38 Precedes Dec.
39 "... and Noah begat __, Ham, and Japheth" (Gen. 5:32)
40 Parade recipient
41 __ Moran of *Happy Days*
42 Butter substitute
43 Singer Redding
44 Agrees nonverbally
47 "... and Asahel was as light of foot as a wild __" (2 Sam 2:18)

COLUMN PHRASE: **Isaiah 59:1**

1

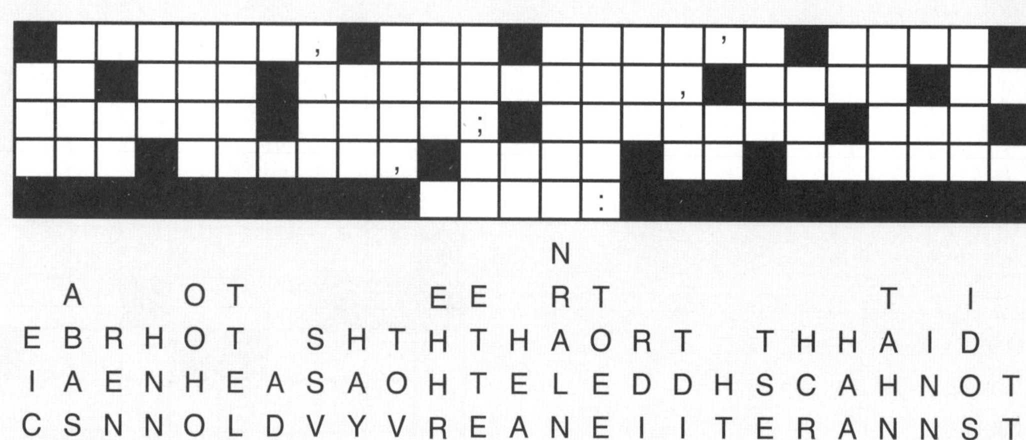

SCRAMBLED VERSE: **Colossians 1:14**

1 In _______ we have redemption _______ his _______, even the forgiveness of _______:

howm
uohgrth
oodbl
inss

VERSE DECODER: **God's Promises**

1 **1 Peter 2:9**

HINT: In the puzzle below, the letter "V" is actually an "E."

HPY BV LIV L OJFCVA WVAVILYXFA, L IFBLE RIXVCYJFFG, LA JFEB ALYXFA,

L RVOPEXLI RVFREV; YJLY BV CJFPEG CJVN QFIYJ YJV RILXCVC FQ JXZ NJF

JLYJ OLEEVG BFP FPY FQ GLIDAVCC XAYF JXC ZLISVEEFPC EXWJY;

CROSSWORD: **The Word**

By Thomas W. Schier

ACROSS

1 Jacob's wife and namesakes
6 Mass robe
9 Waitress in Mel's Diner
12 Chance for a hit (2 words)
13 Bapt. or Episc.
14 He ran from Sodom
15 __ firma
16 "Paul also and Barnabas continued in __" (Acts 15:35)
18 With hands on hips
20 Zap in the microwave
21 __ jongg
23 502, to the Romans
24 Last word of some fairy tales
25 See 49-Across
27 Fall temporarily into sin
29 Prophet who anointed Saul and David as kings
31 Second name of Jacob
35 No longer in
37 He sank with the Scharnhorst
38 Well-suited to the task
41 H in New Testament Greek
43 Methuselah-like
44 Trio in Bethlehem
45 Tracts of wasteland
47 Devotional prayer commemorating the Annunciation
49 With 25-Across, devotional response (2 words)
52 Suffix meaning "resident"
53 __ carte
54 Words before pieces or the good
55 Character actor Beatty
56 Rabbit's foot
57 Wintry precipitation

DOWN

1 Back muscle, briefly
2 Summer, in Paris
3 "And __ rose up early in the morning" (Gen. 21:14)
4 "__! The Herald Angels Sing"
5 Sedate
6 "For this Agar is mount Sinai in __" (Gal. 4:25)
7 Big-jawed TV host
8 Sandwich order
9 Treat with disdain
10 English philosopher John
11 "And he stayed yet __ seven days" (Gen. 8:10)
17 Deduces
19 "... and ground it in __" (Num. 1:8)
21 AWOL pursuers
22 "And the sons of Jether; Jephunneh, and Pispah, and __" (1 Chron. 7:38)
24 "And he found a new jawbone of an __" (Judg. 15:15)
26 BMW driver, maybe
28 Sculpture of the Virgin Mary and Jesus
30 "Thou shalt not __ of it" (Gen. 3:17)
32 Peter, James or John
33 Sushi dish
34 "But God __ the people about" (Ex. 13:18)
36 Playground attraction
38 At full force
39 "The Divine Comedy" poet
40 Urged (with "on")
42 Map book
45 Dance at a luau
46 Satan's abode
48 Once around the track
50 Multipurpose truck
51 Barfly

CROSSWORD: **Thou Art Blessed**

By Donald L. Blocher

ACROSS

1 Biblical month
5 WWII Brit. flyers
8 "Take one young bullock, and two __ with blemish" (Ex. 29:1)
12 "... let us run with patience the __ that is set before us" (Heb. 12:1)
13 Sixth word of the Gettysburg Address
14 Sandwich cookie
15 First man
16 "The words of __ the son of Hilkiah" (Jer. 1:1)
18 "Likewise when the Lord sent you from Kadesh__"(Deut. 9:23)
20 Sings the praises of
21 Settle a bill
22 Related
23 Compensation for a wrong
26 Finder's __
29 "And Miriam was __ out from the camp seven days" (Num. 12:15)
30 "Beloved, let us love __ another: for love is of God" (1 John 4:7)
31 Lively dances
32 Distress signal
33 "... and the tree of __ of good and evil" (Gen. 2:9)
35 Inert gas
36 "Stand in __, and sin not" (Ps. 4:4)
37 Like some heroes
40 "And all the days of Seth were nine hundred and __ years" (Gen. 5:8)
43 "God hath taken away my __" (Gen. 30:23)
45 "... and a __ giveth ear to a naughty tongue" (Prov. 17:4)
46 Pupil locale
47 Sound in a pasture
48 Sicilian volcano
49 "And why beholdest thou the __ that is in thy brother's eye" (Luke 6:41)
50 Not me
51 Changes color

DOWN

1 "__, and Dumah, and Eshean" (Josh. 15:52)
2 Baby's first word?
3 Bearing no fruit
4 "And the __ of the meat offering shall be Aaron's and his sons'" (Lev. 2:3)
5 Hindu prince
6 "Thou shalt be buried in a good old __" (Gen. 15:15)
7 "God hath not cast away his people which he __" (Rom. 11:2)
8 Centurion, e.g.
9 Seed cover
10 Butcher's stock
11 Fifth notes, in music, (Var.)
17 Walk offstage
19 "Thine __ shall not pity him" (Deut. 19:13)
22 "And John also was baptizing in __ near to Salim" (John 3:23)
23 "And Moses took his wife and his sons, and set them upon an __" (Ex. 4:20)
24 Short "although"
25 Requirement of deacons
26 Faithfulness
27 Poultry product
28 Compass point
31 Like royal crowns
33 Lotto relative
34 Legislation
35 Surgeon's assistant
37 __ and Thummim
38 Roman Emperor during New Testament times
39 Barbecue rod
40 Ten Commandments word
41 Wind instrument
42 Epochs
44 Dove's murmur

MULTIPLE CHOICE: **A Divine Appointment**

1 Who slept in the bottom of a ship as it rolled in a storm?

A. Joseph
B. Noah
C. Jonah
D. Timothy

2 When Jesus was brought before the Council, how many false witnesses were brought in to accuse him?

A. One
B. Two
C. Three
D. Four

3 Who was appointed governor of Judah after the people went into exile?

A. Gedaliah
B. Ahikam
C. Shaphan
D. Ishmael

MULTIPLE CHOICE: **Be Doers of The Word**

1 Who told Pilate that a worrisome dream made it clear that Pilate was to have nothing to do with Jesus?

A. His daughter
B. His wife
C. His son
D. Herod

2 What did God change Jacob's name to?

A. Israel
B. Joab
C. Ishmael
D. Jobab

3 Who was told by an angel that his son was to be named John?

A. Zechariah
B. Caiaphas
C. Zacharias
D. Annas

MULTIPLE CHOICE: **A Divine Appointment**

1 What character in a parable wasted his money on prostitutes?

A. David
B. The prodigal son
C. Herod's son
D. The son of perdition

2 Who could not sleep while Daniel was in the lion's den?

A. King Nebuchadnezzar
B. King David
C. King Solomon
D. King Darius

3 Which of David's wives "despised him in her heart"?

A. Bathsheba
B. Abigail
C. Michal
D. Maacah

4 Where was Mary the last time she is mentioned in the New Testament?

A. In Bethlehem
B. In Jerusalem
C. In Nazareth
D. In Judea

5 Who was with David when Bathsheba and Nathan pleaded with him to designate Solomon as his successor?

A. Joab
B. Abiathar
C. Haggith
D. Abishag

WORD SEARCH: **Characteristics of God's People**

K E D Y N T W F V L O V I N G L F
D G R E L B A E C A E P V R K M O
K P K E T O L M G N L N Z K C F L
B R L N C B H E W H W E T E V T L
T F N P M N N H H N A D C K D X O
S J A U M E I R N L N N K M E O W
S G H I R E W S O M A R Z F L B C
E N Q O T T R U Z R T T Z P B E H
L T U L R H S C E Y N L A N A D R
E S P F T Z F P I E N T M T T I I
M A M R N N M U T F I R D G I E S
A F D N X E T N L E U P R Z P N T
L D N X T R O R N Y K L N Z S T M
B A W L T C Y T Q V M B B L O R W
R E J M R C O U R T E O U S H V W
G T C D N I M F O Y T I N U Z X L
R S N K L H Y L D O G B N D J D T

BLAMELESS
CONTENT
COURTEOUS
FAITHFUL
FOLLOW CHRIST
GENEROUS
GODLY
HOLY
HOSPITABLE
HUMBLE
LOVING
MERCIFUL
OBEDIENT
PATIENT
PEACEABLE
SINCERE
STEADFAST
TEMPERANCE
UNITY OF MIND
ZEALOUS

WORD SEARCH: **Christian Virtues**

P	L	Y	K	J	X	V	K	R	O	B	E	D	I	E	N	C	E
L	B	K	R	K	D	S	S	E	N	L	U	F	T	I	U	R	F
N	S	S	E	N	T	S	A	F	D	E	T	S	N	X	B	N	P
B	J	C	O	U	R	A	G	E	S	I	V	T	N	F	Y	P	C
S	S	L	K	S	P	L	Q	R	S	N	L	Y	G	X	Z	T	D
L	S	S	C	S	M	K	B	D	E	R	Q	I	M	W	B	T	S
C	E	E	E	E	T	X	N	E	N	Z	Q	K	G	N	N	S	N
L	N	V	N	N	N	V	V	L	I	K	K	M	F	E	E	K	P
P	D	N	T	I	S	O	X	F	L	P	Z	A	M	N	N	I	J
T	U	O	E	L	L	U	P	L	O	T	I	T	L	T	H	C	P
K	R	I	M	N	N	D	O	Z	H	T	N	U	R	S	L	A	E
H	A	T	P	A	K	K	O	E	H	E	F	T	D	R	T	T	V
P	N	U	E	E	L	V	F	G	T	E	Q	R	R	I	F	F	T
J	C	L	R	L	H	N	J	N	C	H	A	K	E	U	N	R	R
K	E	O	A	C	H	G	O	A	K	W	G	N	K	T	S	R	T
R	Z	S	N	W	R	C	E	D	E	W	C	I	Q	H	Z	T	Y
V	R	E	C	J	V	P	Y	T	M	E	Q	C	R	B	R	L	H
Z	K	R	E	B	Y	P	S	P	Z	E	A	L	N	P	Y	K	K

CLEANLINESS
CONTENTMENT
COURAGE
DILIGENCE
ENDURANCE
FAITH
FRUITFULNESS
GODLINESS
HOLINESS
LOVE
OBEDIENCE
PATIENCE
PEACEFULNESS
RESOLUTION
RIGHTEOUSNESS
STEDFASTNESS
STEWARDSHIP
TEMPERANCE
TRUST
ZEAL

MULTIPLE CHOICE: **A Special Service by God**

1 Who was chosen as queen to save her people from extermination by the Persians?

A. Esther
B. Vashti
C. Deborah
D. Ruth

2 What man of God built the wall around Jerusalem?

A. Obadiah
B. Nehemiah
C. Jeremiah
D. Ezra

3 Who was destined to become God's greatest prophet?

A. Isaiah
B. Ezekiel
C. Daniel
D. Jeremiah

4 Which man of God was called the prophet to the nations?

A. Isaiah
B. Jeremiah
C. Nehemiah
D. Ezra

5 What prophet was Israel's watchman on the wall?

A. Isaiah
B. Jeremiah
C. Ezekiel
D. Daniel

6 Who was called to preach against the sins of the ten tribes?

A. Jeremiah
B. Amos
C. Ezra
D. Jonah

MULTIPLE CHOICE: **A Special Service by God**

1 Who was told to warn Nineveh about coming judgment unless he repented?

A. Ezra
B. Amos
C. Jonah
D. Hosea

2 What young person was told to sell his/her things and follow Christ?

A. The daughter of Jairus
B. The rich young ruler
C. Zacchaeus
D. Rhoda

3 Who was the first king of Israel?

A. Stephen
B. Matthias
C. Nathaniel
D. Saul

4 Who was the first church missionary-evangelist-pastor?

A. Stephen
B. Saul
C. Simon
D. Simeon

5 What man of God was called to help Paul and later pastor a church?

A. Silas
B. Barnabas
C. Timothy
D. Jude

6 Who was called to be an evangelist and pastor?

A. Jude
B. Silas
C. Philip
D. Apollos

WORD SEARCH: **Truth Be Told**

S H S N O I S I C E R P T L V K
C S G S L X T H T P E F E M A P
M E E N E G H H M X G P N K L K
Q I R N M N T G A R S H E X I L
M L N T L P E C K O T C N M D T
J N M F A A T U G U K O I Y I R
R O R T A I U T R M D R U C T L
I I W R L L N T A T L R N A Y E
G T K U X H L X C A V E E R K G
H C W I Y X I I U A D C G U J I
T E K S B M W T B R F T T C W T
N F C M P M C N Q L F N R C K I
E R V E R A C I T Y E E P A D M
S E L M Q M T C A F K S T T K A
S P X T M N R T H R F S R R W C
H O N E S T A U T H E N T I C Y

ACCURACY
ACTUAL
AUTHENTIC
CERTAIN
CORRECTNESS
EXACT
FACT
FACTUALNESS
GENUINE
GOSPEL
HONEST
INFALLIBLE
LEGITIMACY
MAXIM
PERFECTION
PRECISION
RIGHTNESS
TRUENESS
TRUISM
TRUTH
VALIDITY
VERACITY

WORD SEARCH: **False Gods**

N	K	R	G	N	M	M	H	N	P	L	L	F	T	C
U	N	K	O	T	V	A	Z	S	O	M	N	C	D	W
I	M	V	L	M	S	R	N	P	O	M	D	B	L	P
H	V	T	D	N	R	D	T	B	N	M	M	M	R	K
C	Z	W	O	N	E	A	J	A	A	I	E	I	R	T
M	Z	M	D	P	V	V	N	D	D	A	T	H	R	A
R	E	K	T	X	L	A	N	O	H	G	L	N	C	R
D	N	O	O	M	I	V	L	G	H	M	B	Q	V	T
B	G	V	T	T	S	S	A	S	H	E	R	A	H	A
E	T	W	L	Q	D	P	L	A	N	E	T	S	F	K
A	V	Q	L	S	H	R	D	I	A	N	A	K	B	Q
S	Q	Z	T	V	H	B	A	T	X	S	P	E	C	L
T	L	A	V	L	N	G	C	G	U	K	L	D	H	L
L	R	T	X	F	L	L	V	E	O	L	P	T	K	F
S	R	O	T	S	A	C	Z	W	Y	N	F	G	L	G

ADRAM
ANAN
ASHERAH
BAAL
BEAST
BELLY
CASTOR
CHEMOSH
CHIUN
DEMONS
DIANA
DRAGON
GOLD
IDOLS
MOON
PLANETS
RIMMON
SILVER
STARS
TARTAK
ZEUS

MULTIPLE CHOICE: **Be Strong and of Good Service**

1 What king sent an exiled priest back to Samaria to teach the Gentiles how to follow God?

A. The king of Assyria
B. The king of Persia
C. The king of Israel
D. The king of Judah

2 Whose brothers were imprisoned after being falsely accused of being spies in Egypt?

A. Jacob's
B. David's
C. Cain's
D. Joseph's

3 What queen of Israel practiced witchcraft?

A. Bathsheba
B. Jezebel
C. Potiphar's wife
D. Esther

4 Who did Paul oppose when he met him in Antioch?

A. Peter
B. John
C. Silas
D. Elymas

5 What runaway servant was the main subject of one of Paul's epistles?

A. Philemon
B. Epaphroditus
C. Onesimus
D. Timothy

MULTIPLE CHOICE: **Be Strong and of Good Service**

1 What much-married king is considered the author of the Song of Songs?

A. David
B. Solomon
C. Moses
D. Ahaziah

2 Who is the only king in the Bible referred to as "the Mede"?

A. Darius
B. Nebuchadnezzar
C. Arioch
D. Belshazzar

3 Who, according to tradition, preached in Phrygia?

A. John
B. Paul
C. Philip
D. Andrew

4 Who prophesied doom and defeat for King Ahab and was put in prison for his harsh words?

A. Micaiah
B. Daniel
C. Huldah
D. Elisha

5 In Ezekiel, what woman was used as a symbol of wicked Jerusalem?

A. Delilah
B. Aholibah
C. Kezia
D. Athalila

WORD SEARCH: **Gifts and Servants**

```
W D V W R Z E C A E P R G R R Q T N R T M
V I B V K L R W H M K N N T C N J R N B P
B Z S Y K N E C C K B M J R E V I G O R K
W K L D X D P K L L Y R L M H M L L C R N
M N M L O M L M H G N R N M H I Y V A N R
T W K C N M E R E P E R R P Y R L R E L I
Y D N M G Y H N D H E X R B K A W K D P G
W M P N M W T C C C H A E C B C T X M X H
H H E T P L R A S R Y G K B Q L N F W P T
X N Z R E W E I L E D V L N L E K A T N E
J B W N C T D C R E N W L R W S Y I K K O
L M E N Y Y W W L L L C D G Q P J T D B U
W S V Y R H A W T N L Z O M V L H H Y B S
S T L F G R O T J R K L W U F Z C F C R N
R Z L F R N E K V V Q J H X R Y L U E D E
T L Y I K W I S P L O V E T J A M L H N S
L B O M N P L L I T O N G U E S G N P F S
T R G X C F X F A A C L K H F R H E O M D
X C W B R T F L R E R E L D E R G S R D M
K W T V J Y T T T K H P L G R B K S P Z B
N H H N R X N C N H F J N B L T R D F M J
```

DEACON	**HEALING**	**PRAISE**
DISCERNMENT	**HELPER**	**PRAYER WARRIOR**
ELDER	**KNOWLEDGE**	**PROPHECY**
ENCOURAGER	**LOVE**	**RIGHTEOUSNESS**
FAITHFULNESS	**MERCY**	**TEACHER**
GENTLENESS	**MIRACLES**	**TONGUES**
GIVER	**PEACE**	**WISDOM**

WORD SEARCH: **God Is**

R	H	T	U	R	T	P	R	G	C	K	Z	L	R	D	V	N	F
L	F	H	T	C	L	E	A	N	Q	H	U	R	E	B	N	K	R
Q	Q	R	L	U	F	H	T	I	A	F	X	S	P	V	T	L	T
V	L	I	L	N	Y	V	L	W	R	L	S	R	E	F	U	S	E
X	N	G	R	T	J	I	D	E	H	E	U	W	H	O	L	Y	D
R	Z	H	B	Q	G	J	D	E	L	D	M	F	G	V	T	C	B
E	Z	T	Z	H	Y	N	N	B	I	M	H	Z	I	A	Q	T	X
H	S	E	T	Q	O	R	E	Q	Z	F	T	U	E	C	N	J	E
T	U	O	Y	W	H	E	I	M	E	R	I	R	M	R	R	V	Z
A	O	U	R	B	Q	D	R	T	U	N	G	R	T	B	E	E	E
F	I	S	V	L	E	I	F	E	H	N	D	M	O	R	L	C	M
E	C	J	F	P	T	V	A	C	N	E	X	U	L	L	N	E	R
H	A	L	R	L	E	O	N	H	X	C	L	A	R	I	G	R	Q
T	R	J	W	R	R	R	L	Q	B	Q	S	I	R	I	C	H	L
M	G	R	K	J	N	P	M	J	P	T	K	P	G	Z	N	D	C
E	V	O	L	J	A	R	M	G	I	M	I	Y	X	H	M	G	G
T	M	Y	P	X	L	U	H	N	R	W	N	T	F	H	T	V	R
L	P	H	Z	C	T	O	G	P	R	G	G	G	V	Q	R	W	N

A FRIEND
BLESSED
CLEAN
ENDURING
ETERNAL
EVERLASTING
FAITHFUL
GLORIFIED
GRACIOUS
GREAT
HOLY
HUMBLE
KING
LIGHT
LOVE
MERCIFUL
OUR PROVIDER
PRINCE
REFUSE
RIGHTEOUS
THE FATHER
THE LIGHT
TRUE
TRUTH
WONDERFUL

MULTIPLE CHOICE: **Biblical Facts**

1 How many men did Nebuchadnezzar see walking in the fiery furnace?

A. Two
B. Three
C. Four
D. Five

2 What was the sign of the covenant made between God and man?

A. Clouds
B. Stars
C. Moon
D. Rainbow

3 Who was the first to find grace in the eyes of the Lord?

A. Abram
B. Job
C. Noah
D. Jacob

4 What three disciples were on the Mount of Transfiguration with Jesus?

A. Peter, James, and John
B. Paul, Silas, and Timothy
C. Matthew, Mark, and Luke
D. Thomas, Judas, and James

5 What prophet was very hairy and wore a leather belt?

A. Elisha
B. Elijah
C. John the Baptist
D. Jeremiah

6 King David had which man killed so he could have his wife?

A. Saul
B. Jonathan
C. Uriah
D. Samuel

MULTIPLE CHOICE: **Biblical Facts**

1 Which man owned a seamless coat?

A. Jesus
B. Joseph
C. Joshua
D. Jeremiah

2 On which day did God create the grass, herb that yields seed, and fruit-yielding trees?

A. 2nd
B. 3rd
C. 4th
D. 5th

3 How many of Jesus' brothers wrote books of the Bible?

A. One (James)
B. Two (James and Jude)
C. Three (James, Jude, and John)
D. Four (James, Jude, John, and Joel)

4 Who were the first and last judges of Israel?

A. Samson and Samuel
B. Deborah and Barak
C. Othniel and Samuel
D. Samuel and Deborah

5 Which prophet spoke of the killing of children?

A. Isaiah
B. Jonah
C. Jeremiah
D. Elijah

6 Achan was stoned to death in what valley?

A. Valley of lepers
B. Valley of Achor
C. Valley of Forge
D. Valley of horses

WORD SEARCH: **Names of God**

```
T N B Y E V C D L D I V A D F O N O S L P
T B C L Z V F T S I R H C S U S E J G P F
I R N G I X E M K W C M V W X D T R T C J
R F R O J V D R T H Z K T T H L E L M C L
I K W O D A I W L C X H H P H A Z D V O N
P K C D R G H N V A E E Q A T E O K R Z W
S F C S T E L W G V S X N I I G R D W R D
Y L T H S M R M I W L T A O F S O O L H Q
L K H E D O X N P X A M I O Y F S X C M Q
O I E P R D E F K Y F T B N H L T E G K V
H N C H O N N R W T N M E O G R O M M D H
V G H E L A R B L M A K S R V G Q H E L L
Q O R R F A F M Y L Y T J B A T O V F M V
F F I D O H G N C R E A T O R W O D L H F
V K S T D P Y K V K Z N Z M L L E X G C X
K I T L R L D V F V L R L G E K X H F T R
K N Y D O A T Q W R V K Z B J P L W S O B
H G L I L Y O F T H E V A L L E Y B I A Z
K S F K T S E I R P H G I H L N M V K M Y
R H J N G T W Y N V D D P H G H A D P W L
Y V P R I N C E O F P E A C E S H X R N D
```

ALPHA AND OMEGA
BELOVED
CREATOR
EVERLASTING GOD
GOOD SHEPHERD
GREAT I AM
HIGH PRIEST
HOLY ONE
HOLY SPIRIT
JESUS CHRIST
KING OF KINGS
LAMB OF GOD
LILY OF THE VALLEY
LIVING WATER
LORD OF HOST
LORD OF LORDS
MESSIAH
PRINCE OF PEACE
SAVIOR
SON OF DAVID
THE CHRIST
THE ROCK
THE VINE
YASHEWA

WORD SEARCH: **Repent**

D L K V Q N O I L L E B E R X M D
K T W I T C H C R A F T H L J Y R
P M V F P P S T U B B O R N V S U
D J U C J C T F P K F Y D R L I N
P E R R N O I T R O T X E T L R K
L N C E D G H T I M Y M P M E C A
L W Y E D E D R D D T L P F Y O R
W R Q E I N R N E V E E I T C P D
R X N B Y T A N V T L R M M W Y W
Y V D G R J W L A R T R T P L H M
Y B R G E L X E S S P L Z A E Z G
T D A K T N H C R U E L T Y H R V
H R G X L C T V M X J K L M J A Z
I N G L U S T S W Z Z K C T N Y G
E N U V D M I Q K M Z M W I Z H Y
F N L M A N Z X N D B N T A R Z V
M Z S K S L R M L K M Y L R P W N

ADULTERY
CHEAT
CRUELTY
DECEIT
DRUNKARD
ENVY
EXTORTION
HATRED

HYPOCRISY
LAZY
LUST
MURDER
PRIDE
REBELLION
SINS
SLANDER

SLUGGARD
STRIFE
STUBBORN
TEMPER
THIEF
VANITY
WITCHCRAFT

WORD SEARCH: **The Lord is My God**

```
F V N F S U F F I C I E N C Y F L V
M P Z N Y V R M D K W R R O I V A S
D Y V O Q R E H N G V K Y R V M T M
N K K I Q T L E G D U J E W H T K T
F Q N T R K K A R M N R R R P W C H
R V X A E Z C L W E E G F A T H E R
R R H I W Y U E K V T H R F M R P N
P E D T A F B R I T J S N B T F J H
B H C I R M O L N N W D A M Z N E R
D C F P D D E R N D C K S M D L E H
L A L O V D R H T F J A M T P D M T
E E Z R J I T E W R L H L E I G Z N
I T R P X G C G H V E N R V Z K R F
H K X E N M P T A P Q S O D R L R N
S V F E F M X T O B E R S C V J R M
R L R J R U I F N R P H K M M L J H
Y T B H L O S K H M Y N S K M N T R
S Z R X N N M E B G R E D E E M E R
```

BUCKLER | **MASTER** | **SAVIOR**
DELIVERER | **PROPITIATION** | **SHEPHERD**
FATHER | **PROVIDER** | **SHIELD**
FORTRESS | **REDEEMER** | **STRENGTH**
HEALER | **REFUSE** | **SUFFICIENCY**
HELPER | **REWARD** | **TEACHER**
JUDGE | **SALVATION** | **VICTORY**

WORD SEARCH: **The Church**

R D V N O I S S E F N O C S E

E V T V A S S E M B L Y T S C

H N C O M M U N I O N N I T M

C A Z R R N K C H L E A B A C

A I L M E L C C V M R A L U O

E T K L W B R C E P P M P D N

R S T K M U M C G T W I R I G

P I G E H S N E I R H M E T R

M R D C N U U S M S L L T O E

P H P E O D M R W X D E S R G

A C H N A M A O O E R L I I A

S R N Z H C L N R H L S N U T

T A F F M L O K C R C I I M I

O G T Y E Q N N K E D A M W O

R T M F X R N R I O H C J K N

AISLE

ANNOUNCEMENTS

ASSEMBLY

ATTENDANCE

AUDITORIUM

BAPTISM

CHOIR

CHORUS

CHRISTIAN

CHURCH

COMMUNION

CONFESSION

CONGREGATION

DEACON

ELDER

FELLOWSHIP

MEMBER

MINISTER

PASTOR

PRAISE

PREACHER

SOLUTIONS

Page 297

VERSE DECODER: God's Promises

1 solution:

Behold therefore the goodness and severity of God: on them which fell, severity; But toward thee, goodness, if thou continue in his goodness: Otherwise thou also shalt be cut off.
Romans 11:22

COLUMN PHRASE: Psalms 37:39

1 solution:

But the salvation of the righteous is of the Lord: he is their strength in the time of trouble.
Psalms 37:39

SCRAMBLED VERSE: Ephesians 1:6

1 solution:

To the **praise** of the glory of his **grace**, wherein he hath made us **accepted** in the **Beloved**.
Ephesians 1:6

Page 298

CROSSWORD: The Faithful

B	O	O	M		E	N	I	D		J	A	B
A	R	G	O		P	E	R	I		A	R	A
C	A	R	S		H	E	A	V	E	N	L	Y
K	N	E	E	L	E	D		A	D	I	O	S
			S	O	M	E	R	S	E	T		
A	L	P		B	E	D	E		M	O	A	B
M	O	U	S	E	R		S	T	A	R	V	E
P	O	S	T		A	L	O	E		S	E	T
		H	O	T	L	I	N	E	S			
F	L	O	R	A		N	A	M	E	T	A	G
R	E	V	E	R	E	N	T		L	O	D	E
O	D	E		O	G	E	E		M	O	A	T
M	A	R		T	O	T	S		A	L	M	S

Page 299

VERSE DECODER: God's Promise

1 solution:

For the invisible things of him from the creation of the world are clearly seen, being understood by the things that are made, even his eternal power and Godhead; So that they are without excuse. Romans 1:20

COLUMN PHRASE: Psalms 34:19

1 solution:

Many are the afflictions of the righteous: but the Lord delivereth him out of them all.
Psalms 34:19

SCRAMBLED VERSE: John 15:16

1 solution:

You did not **choose** me, but I chose you, and **appointed** you that you would go and bear **fruit**, and that your fruit would remain, so that **whatever** you ask of the **Father** in My name He may give to you. John 15:16

Page 300

CROSSWORD: The Commandments

C	A	R	S		O	B	A	D		A	D	O
A	L	A	W		F	L	A	W		G	O	D
N	A	M	E	O	F	T	H	E	L	O	R	D
A	S	P	E	N			S	E	E			
			P	E	L	T		B	A	T	I	K
A	T	M		A	U	R	A		S	E	M	I
S	H	A	L	T	N	O	T	S	T	E	A	L
A	O	N	E		D	O	R	A		S	N	L
P	U	N	T	S		P	A	I	N			
			U	N	E			N	O	I	S	E
T	H	E	S	A	B	B	A	T	H	D	A	Y
O	U	R		P	R	A	Y		O	L	D	E
P	E	R		S	O	M	E		W	E	E	D

SOLUTIONS

Page 301

VERSE DECODER: God's promises

1 solution:

My son, attend to my words; incline thine ear unto my sayings. Let them not depart from thine eyes; keep them in the midst of thine heart. For they are life unto those that find them, and health to all their flesh.
Proverbs 4:20-22

COLUMN PHRASE: Psalms 32:8

1 solution

I will instruct thee and teach thee in the way which thou shalt go: I will guide thee with mine eye.
Psalms 32:8

SCRAMBLED VERSE: Ephesians 1:4

1 solution

According as he hath **chosen** us in him before the foundation of the **world**, that we should be **holy** and **without blame** before him in **love**:
Ephesians 1:4

Page 302

CROSSWORD: Righteous

1 D	2 A	3 L	4 E	■	5 H	6 O	7 I	■	8 P	9 A	10 T	11 E
12 E	R	I	C	■	13 A	B	O	■	14 I	R	O	N
15 W	I	T	H	16 T	H	E	W	17 I	C	K	E	D
18 Y	A	H	O	O	■	19 Y	A	N	K	■	■	■
■	■	■	20 I	N	21 S	■	■	22 T	Y	23 S	24 O	25 N
26 A	27 L	28 A	N	■	29 H	30 O	31 E	R	■	32 A	D	O
33 J	U	D	G	34 M	E	N	T	O	35 F	G	O	D
36 A	L	A	■	37 A	M	E	N	■	38 R	A	R	E
39 R	U	M	40 O	R	■	■	41 A	42 L	I	■	■	■
■	■	■	43 A	S	44 P	45 S	■	46 O	L	47 L	48 I	49 E
50 F	51 O	52 R	T	H	E	L	53 A	W	L	E	S	S
54 A	L	O	E	■	55 E	O	N	■	56 E	G	I	S
57 D	E	E	R	■	58 N	E	T	■	59 D	O	S	E

Page 303

VERSE DECODER: God's Promises

1 solution:

And I say unto you, whosoever shall put away his wife, except it be for fornication, and shall marry another, committeth adultery: And whoso marrieth her which is put away doth commit adultery.
Matthew 19:9

SCRAMBLED VERSE: Ephesians 1:11

1 solution:

In whom also we have **obtained** an inheritance, being predestinated **according** to the purpose of him who worketh all **things** after the **counsel** of his own **will**:
Ephesians 1:11

COLUMN PHRASE: Proverbs 16:3

1 solution:

Commit thy works unto the LORD, and thy thoughts shall be established.
Proverbs 16:3

SOLUTIONS

Page 304

CROSSWORD: Reading the Bible

1 M	2 A	3 G	4 I		5 G	6 A	7 S		8 D	9 O	10 N	11 S
12 I	N	N	S		13 A	P	T		14 E	P	E	E
15 S	T	A	R		16 T	R	E	17 A	S	U	R	E
18 T	I	S	A	19 N	E		20 P	R	I	S	O	N
		21 H	E	N		22 R	O	A	R			
23 P	24 H	I	L	E	M	O	N		25 E	26 R	27 A	28 S
29 R	U	N				B				30 E	S	P
31 E	D	G	32 E		33 L	O	R	34 D	35 S	D	A	Y
			36 M	37 E	A	T		38 A	T	E		
39 S	40 H	41 E	B	A	M		42 C	Y	R	E	43 N	44 E
45 N	A	Z	A	R	E	46 N	E		47 A	M	E	N
48 U	Z	A	L		49 N	O	D		50 F	E	E	D
51 G	E	R	M		52 T	R	I		53 E	R	R	S

Page 305

CROSSWORD: Proverbs

1 U	2 R	3 D	4 U		5 E	6 E	7 L		8 S	9 A	10 K	11 S
12 P	A	Y	S		13 P	L	U	14 M	E	L	E	T
15 W	I	N	E	16 I	S	A	M	O	C	K	E	R
17 A	D	A		18 N	O	T	I	N		19 A	N	O
20 R	E	M		21 A	M	E	N		22 E	L	A	N
23 D	R	O	24 W	N		25 S	A	26 C	K	I	N	G
			27 H	E	28 M		29 L	I	E			
30 C	31 A	32 T	E	R	E	33 D		34 N	D	35 O	36 U	37 R
38 A	D	I	T		39 R	O	40 T	E		41 N	R	A
42 N	O	B		43 S	C	R	A	M		44 S	A	G
45 D	R	I	46 N	K	I	S	R	A	47 G	I	N	G
48 L	E	A	P	Y	E	A	R		49 O	D	I	E
50 E	D	E	R		51 S	L	Y		52 D	E	A	D

Page 306

SCRAMBLED VERSE: Romans 15:7

1 solution:
Wherefore **receive** ye one another, as **Christ** also received us to the **glory** of God.
Romans 15:7

COLUMN PHRASE: Psalms 103:12

1 solution:
As far as the east is from the west, so far hath he removed our transgressions from us.
Psalms 103:12

VERSE DECODER: God's Promises

1 solution:
Yet the number of the children of Israel shall be as the sand of the sea, which cannot be measured nor numbered; And it shall come to pass, that in the place where it was said unto them, ye are not my people, there it shall be said unto them, ye are the sons of the living God.
Hosea 1:10

SOLUTIONS

Page 307

CROSSWORD: Prosperity

S	P	U	D	■	L	E	A	■	C	O	L	A
P	I	N	E	■	E	R	G	■	O	W	E	S
A	N	D	B	E	I	N	H	E	A	L	T	H
S	T	O	O	L	■	E	A	S	T	■	■	■
■	■	■	R	Y	A	■	■	T	I	T	U	S
A	R	I	A	■	S	L	O	E	■	E	R	A
R	I	G	H	T	E	O	U	S	N	E	S	S
E	G	O	■	O	A	T	S	■	A	M	A	H
A	A	R	O	N	■	■	T	E	N	■	■	■
■	■	■	S	N	A	P	■	L	E	A	S	E
P	E	A	C	E	B	E	W	I	T	H	I	N
O	K	R	A	■	E	R	E	■	T	O	D	O
D	E	E	R	■	L	T	D	■	E	Y	E	S

Page 309

CROSSWORD: Love Is All Around

D	A	M	P	■	A	M	A	■	R	E	A	L
I	G	O	R	■	N	A	G	■	U	N	I	T
S	U	R	E	L	Y	T	H	E	L	O	R	D
K	E	N	D	O	■	E	A	S	E	■	■	■
■	■	■	A	S	H	■	■	T	R	A	M	P
M	E	O	W	■	A	L	T	O	■	P	I	E
I	S	I	N	T	H	I	S	P	L	A	C	E
T	T	L	■	R	A	T	A	■	E	L	A	N
T	E	S	L	A	■	■	R	A	G	■	■	■
■	■	■	A	C	I	D	■	L	A	I	R	S
A	N	D	I	K	N	E	W	I	T	N	O	T
R	O	O	T	■	T	E	A	■	E	D	D	A
E	D	G	Y	■	O	D	D	■	E	Y	E	R

Page 308

CROSSWORD: To Err is Human

B	O	O	S	■	A	Y	E	■	S	A	F	E
U	G	L	I	■	C	O	Y	■	A	L	U	M
R	E	E	M	E	R	G	E	■	R	O	E	S
P	E	O	P	L	E	I	S	R	A	E	L	■
■	■	■	S	I	S	■	O	O	H	■	■	■
S	I	L	O	■	■	C	R	T	■	F	L	O
T	R	A	N	S	G	R	E	S	S	I	O	N
Y	E	W	■	P	R	Y	■	■	M	E	T	E
■	■	■	O	R	E	■	S	H	E	■	■	■
■	A	N	D	Y	E	S	H	A	L	L	B	E
A	B	E	D	■	T	O	A	S	T	E	R	S
H	E	A	L	■	E	L	M	■	E	G	I	S
A	L	L	Y	■	D	E	E	■	R	O	S	E

Page 310

CROSSWORD: Just Rewards

I	S	M	S	■	M	E	W	■	A	B	E	L
S	H	O	T	■	U	N	A	■	R	O	L	E
N	A	R	R	A	T	O	R	■	E	X	I	T
T	H	E	E	V	I	L	M	A	N	■	■	■
■	■	■	T	E	N	■	■	M	A	N	N	A
E	R	I	C	■	I	D	L	E	■	O	I	L
R	I	G	H	T	E	O	U	S	N	E	S	S
G	O	O	■	I	D	E	M	■	O	L	I	O
S	T	R	O	P	■	■	B	O	O	■	■	■
■	■	■	W	I	C	K	E	D	N	E	S	S
L	O	L	L	■	A	I	R	E	D	A	L	E
A	L	O	E	■	R	T	E	■	A	S	E	A
W	E	P	T	■	T	E	D	■	Y	E	W	S

SOLUTIONS

Page 311

COLUMN PHRASE: Isaiah 43:25

1 solution:

I, even I, am he that blotteth out thy transgressions for mine own sake, and will not remember thy sins.
Isaiah 43:25

SCRAMBLED VERSE: 1 Corinthians 1:9

1 solution:

God is **faithful**, by whom ye were **called** unto the fellowship of his Son **Jesus** Christ our **LORD**.
1 Corinthians 1:9

VERSE DECODER: God's Promises

1 solution:

Now unto Him that is able to keep you from falling, and to present you faultless before the presence of his glory with exceeding joy, to the only wise God our Saviour, be glory and majesty, dominion and power, both now and ever. Amen.
Jude 1:24-25

Page 312

CROSSWORD: Heavenly Questions

A	Y	E	S		D	E	W		C	L	A	N
M	A	T	T		I	P	O		H	I	R	E
P	H	A	R	I	S	E	E		E	B	E	R
S	I	L	E	N	C	E		B	R	E	A	D
			S	K	I		P	A	U	L		
L	I	P	S		P	A	R	A	B	L	E	S
C	I	A		F	L	A	I	L		E	E	E
D	I	S	T	R	E	S	S		I	D	L	E
		S	U	E	S		C	A	N			
A	D	O	R	E		V	I	L	L	A	G	E
R	A	V	E		H	A	L	L	O	W	E	D
T	R	E	E		A	I	L		V	O	T	E
Y	A	R	N		D	N	A		E	L	A	N

Page 313

CROSSWORD: Good News

S	E	A		T	O	M	B		S	M	O	G
I	S	T		A	D	E	E		H	A	L	O
M	A	T	T	H	E	W	S		I	R	E	D
S	I	N	A	I		S	T	A	L	K		
			M	T	A		S	H	O	D	D	Y
R	E	J	O	I	C	E		S	H	O	R	E
A	T	O			E	A	R			W	A	N
I	N	H	I	S		T	I	D	I	N	G	S
D	A	N	C	E	D		D	E	S			
		D	E	T	A	T		S	A	R	A	I
W	H	O	A		L	U	K	E	W	A	R	M
I	B	E	G		A	M	O	R		M	I	A
N	O	S	E		I	S	I	T		S	A	Y

Page 314

CROSSWORD: From Start to Finish

S	H	A	M		L	E	F	T		O	D	D
I	A	T	E		A	G	E	E		D	I	E
F	I	R	S	T	B	O	R	N		E	R	A
T	R	A	S	H			M	O	R	S	E	L
				E	M	P	I	R	E			
T	R	U	S	T	E	E			A	R	A	M
A	L	P	H	A	A	N	D	O	M	E	G	A
E	S	S	O			N	U	R	S	E	R	Y
			O	B	E	Y	E	D				
P	A	S	S	E	R			E	L	I	T	E
A	P	T		L	A	S	T	R	I	T	E	S
T	E	A		T	S	A	R		S	E	E	P
E	R	R		S	E	M	I		A	R	M	Y

SOLUTIONS

Page 315

CROSSWORD: Divine Wisdom

1 A	2 L	3 A	4 N	■	5 A	6 V	7 E	■	8 S	9 E	10 A	11 L
12 M	O	N	A	■	13 S	O	L	■	14 T	R	I	O
15 P	U	T	I	16 N	H	I	S	17 H	E	A	R	T
18 S	T	E	V	E	■	19 D	E	A	L	■	■	■
■	■	■	20 E	E	21 R	■	■	22 V	E	23 I	24 N	25 S
26 F	27 I	28 A	T	■	29 A	30 I	31 D	E	■	32 B	O	A
33 U	N	D	E	34 R	S	T	A	N	35 D	I	N	G
36 R	C	A	■	37 U	P	O	N	■	38 I	D	E	A
39 L	A	M	40 B	S	■	■	41 K	42 E	N	■	■	■
■	■	■	43 A	S	44 I	45 A	■	46 A	G	47 A	48 P	49 E
50 I	51 S	52 A	B	O	V	E	53 R	U	B	I	E	S
54 S	A	L	E	■	55 A	R	E	■	56 A	R	E	S
57 M	O	I	L	■	58 N	O	D	■	59 T	Y	R	E

Page 316

COLUMN PHRASE: Matthew 21:22

1 solution:

And all things, whatsoever ye shall ask in prayer, believing, ye shall receive.
Matthew 21:22

VERSE DECODER: God's Promises

1 solution:

That which we have seen and heard declare we unto you, that ye also may have fellowship with us: And truly our fellowship is with the Father, and with his son Jesus Christ.
1 John 1:3

COLUMN PHRASE: Jeremiah 29:12

2 solution:

Then shall ye call upon me, and ye shall go and pray unto me, and I will hearken unto you.
Jeremiah 29:12

Page 317

CROSSWORD: Biblical Pairings

1 D	2 R	3 A	4 B	■	5 L	6 A	7 C	■	8 N	9 A	10 R	11 C
12 Y	U	L	E	■	13 A	B	A	■	14 O	V	A	L
15 E	N	S	L	16 A	V	E	R	■	17 V	I	N	O
■	18 G	O	L	I	A	T	H	19 D	A	V	I	D
■	■	■	20 I	D	S	■	21 O	A	K	■	■	■
22 A	23 N	24 O	N	■	■	25 A	P	T	■	26 P	27 R	28 O
29 D	E	L	I	30 L	31 A	H	S	A	32 M	S	O	N
33 O	D	D	■	34 E	N	S	■	■	35 A	I	D	E
■	■	■	36 A	N	I	■	37 A	38 N	N	■	■	■
39 S	40 H	41 E	B	A	S	42 O	L	O	M	43 O	44 N	■
45 H	E	R	A	■	46 E	L	E	V	A	T	O	47 R
48 E	R	I	C	■	49 E	E	R	■	50 D	I	D	O
51 M	O	N	K	■	52 D	O	T	■	53 E	S	S	E

SOLUTIONS

Page 318

COLUMN PHRASE: Isaiah 59:1

1 solution:

Behold, the LORD's hand is not shortened, that it cannot save; neither his ear heavy, that it cannot hear:
Isaiah 59:1

SCRAMBLED VERSE: Colossians 1:14

1 solution:

In **whom** we have redemption **through** his **blood**, even the forgiveness of **sins**:
Colossians 1:14

VERSE DECODER: God's Promises

1 solution:

But ye are a chosen generation, a royal priesthood, an holy nation, a peculiar people; that ye should shew forth the praises of him who hath called you out of darkness into his marvellous light;
1 Peter 2:9

Page 319

CROSSWORD: The Word

L	E	A	H	S	■	A	L	B	■	F	L	O
A	T	B	A	T	■	R	E	L	■	L	O	T
T	E	R	R	A	■	A	N	T	I	O	C	H
■	■	A	K	I	M	B	O	■	N	U	K	E
M	A	H	■	D	I	I	■	A	F	T	E	R
P	R	A	Y	■	L	A	P	S	E	■	■	■
S	A	M	U	E	L	■	I	S	R	A	E	L
■	■	■	P	A	S	S	E	■	S	P	E	E
A	D	E	P	T	■	E	T	A	■	O	L	D
M	A	G	I	■	H	E	A	T	H	S	■	■
A	N	G	E	L	U	S	■	L	E	T	U	S
I	T	E	■	A	L	A	■	A	L	L	T	O
N	E	D	■	P	A	W	■	S	L	E	E	T

Page 320

CROSSWORD: Thou Art Blessed

A	D	A	R	■	R	A	F	■	R	A	M	S
R	A	C	E	■	A	G	O	■	O	R	E	O
A	D	A	M	■	J	E	R	E	M	I	A	H
B	A	R	N	E	A	■	E	X	A	L	T	S
■	■	P	A	Y	■	A	K	I	N	■	■	■
A	T	O	N	E	M	E	N	T	■	F	E	E
S	H	U	T	■	O	N	E	■	J	I	G	S
S	O	S	■	K	N	O	W	L	E	D	G	E
■	■	■	N	E	O	N	■	A	W	E	■	■
U	N	S	U	N	G	■	T	W	E	L	V	E
R	E	P	R	O	A	C	H	■	L	I	A	R
I	R	I	S	■	M	O	O	■	E	T	N	A
M	O	T	E	■	Y	O	U	■	D	Y	E	S

Page 321

MULTIPLE CHOICE: A Divine Appointment

1 solution: **C**; 2 solution: **B**; 3 solution: **A**.

MULTIPLE CHOICE: Be Doers of The Word

1 solution: **B**; 2 solution: **A**; 3 solution: **C**.

Page 322

MULTIPLE CHOICE: A Divine Appointment

1 solution: **B**; 2 solution: **D**; 3 solution: **C**;
4 solution: **B**; 5 solution: **D**.

SOLUTIONS

Page 323

WORD SEARCH: Characteristics of God's People

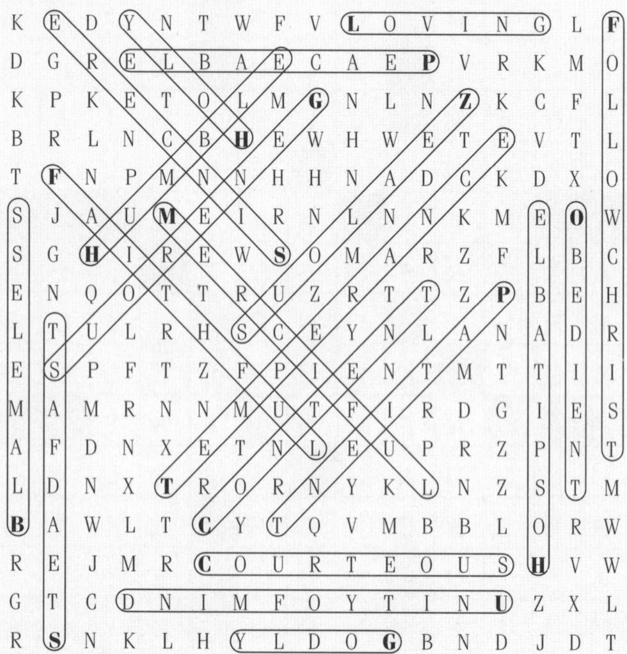

Page 324

WORD SEARCH: Christian Virtues

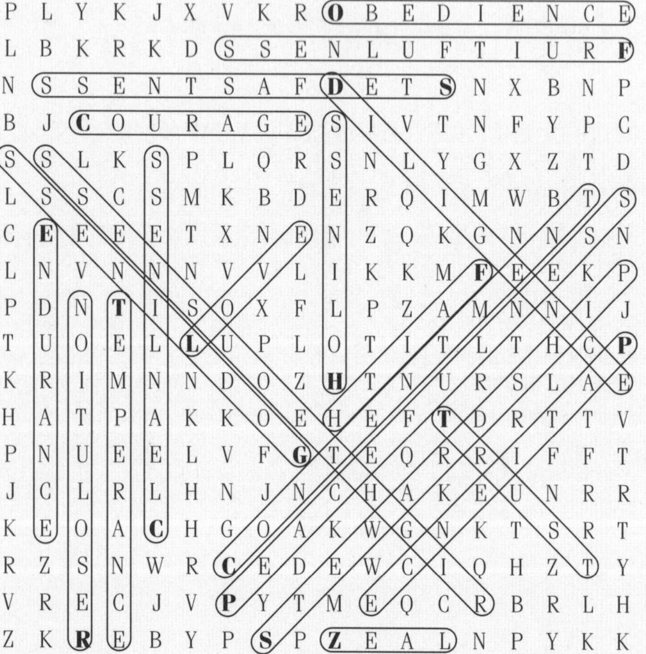

Page 325

MULTIPLE CHOICE: A Special Service by God

1 solution: **A**; 2 solution: **B**; 3 solution: **A**;

4 solution: **B**; 5 solution: **C**; 6 solution: **B.**

Page 326

MULTIPLE CHOICE: A Special Service by God

1 solution: **C**; 2 solution: **B**; 3 solution: **D**;

4 solution: **B**; 5 solution: **C**; 6 solution: **D.**

Page 327

WORD SEARCH: Truth Be Told

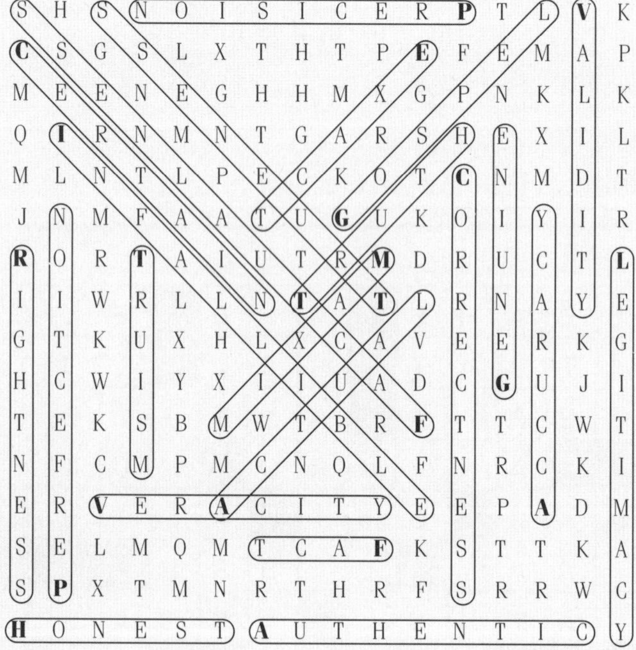

SOLUTIONS

Page 328

WORD SEARCH: False Gods

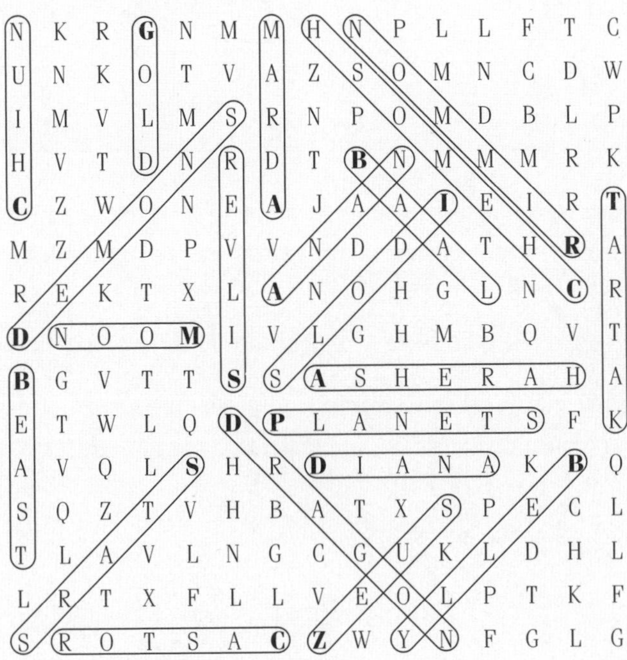

Page 329

MULTIPLE CHOICE: Be Strong and of Good Service

1 solution: **A**; 2 solution: **D**; 3 solution: **B**;

4 solution: **A**; 5 solution: **C.**

Page 330

MULTIPLE CHOICE: Be Strong and of Good Service

1 solution: **B**; 2 solution: **A**; 3 solution: **C**;

4 solution: **A**; 5 solution: **B.**

Page 331

WORD SEARCH: Gifts and Servants

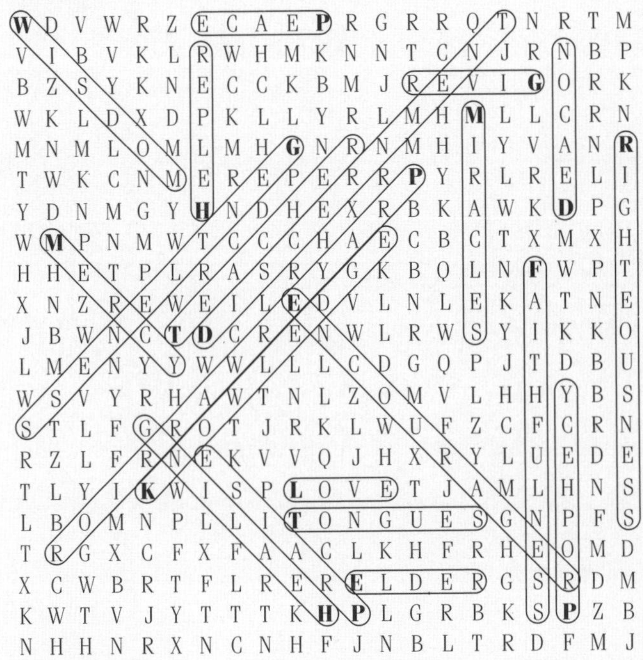

Page 332

WORD SEARCH: God Is

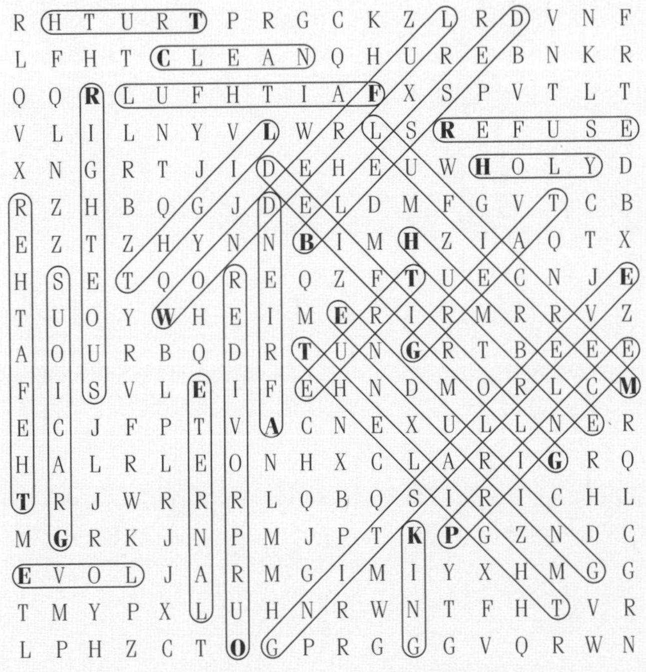

SOLUTIONS

Page 333

MULTIPLE CHOICE: Biblical Facts

1 solution: **C**; 2 solution: **D**; 3 solution: **C**;
4 solution: **A**; 5 solution: **B**; 6 solution: **C.**

Page 334

MULTIPLE CHOICE: Biblical Facts

1 solution: **A**; 2 solution: **C**; 3 solution: **B**;
4 solution: **C**; 5 solution: **C**; 6 solution: **B.**

Page 335

WORD SEARCH: Names of God

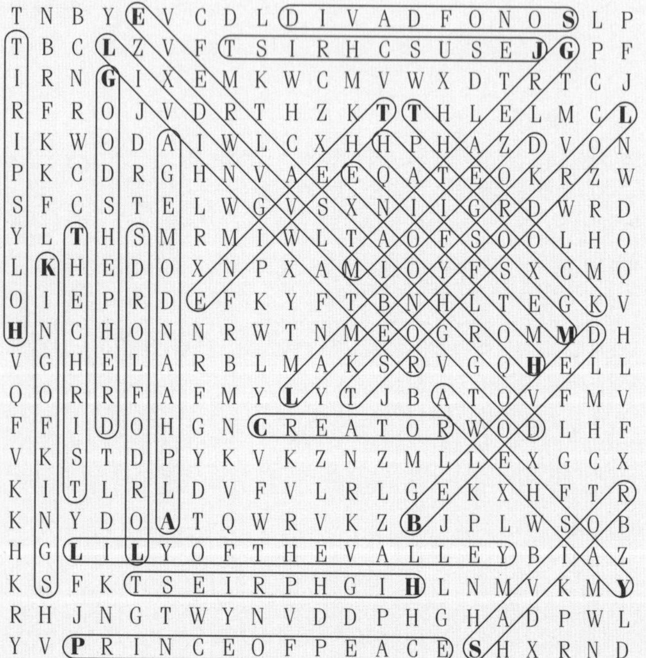

Page 336

WORD SEARCH: Repent

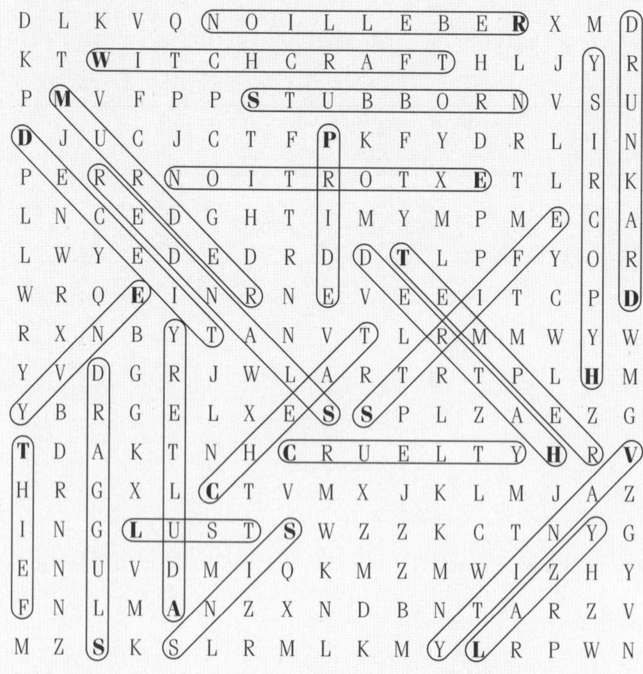

Page 337

WORD SEARCH: The Lord is My God

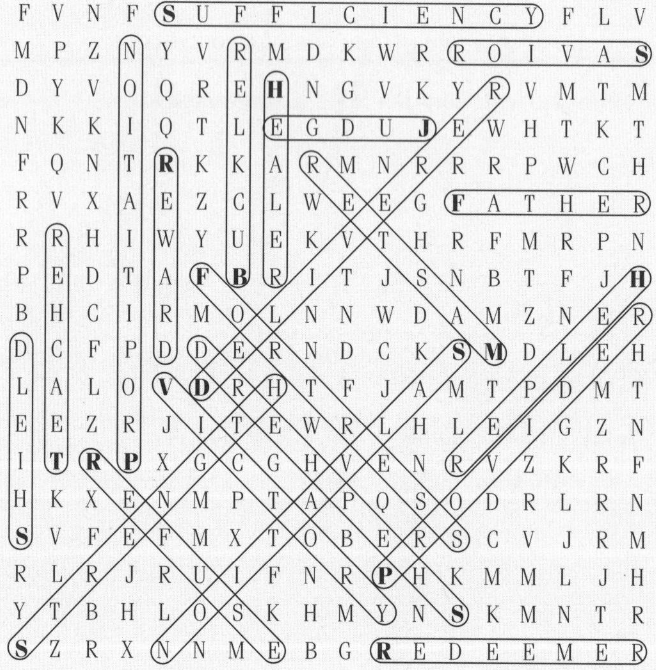

Page 338

SOLUTIONS

WORD SEARCH: The Church

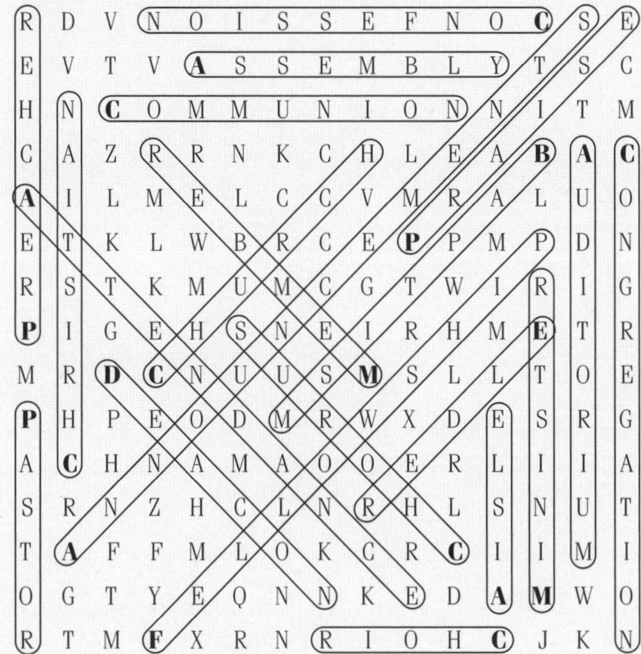